Dear I

Nee Ahh Way

Thank You For
Y-Our For Ever Present
Be-Ing.

AndyCPaintsWords@Gmail.com

07891 169946.

MEMOIRS
of the
Bright Side of the Moon

*"For what profit is it to man,
If he gains the whole world
and loses his own soul?"*

NKJV

MEMOIRS
of the
Bright Side of the Moon

Ginger Gilmour

ANGELSCRIPT.COM

Copyright © 2015 by Ginger Gilmour
Published by Angelscript International LLP.
www.angelscript.com

The moral rights of the author have been asserted.

Page 610 serves as a continuation of this copyright page.

All photographs are courtesy of Ginger Gilmour's personal collection except for the photographs that have specific permission to be used.
All sculptures and paintings are equally Ginger Gilmour's creative expressions as an artist.

All rights reserved. No part of this book may be reproduced by any mechanical, photographic, or electronic process, or in the form of a phonographic recording nor may it be stored in a retrieval system, transmitted, or otherwise be copied for public or private use – other than for "fair use" as brief quotations embodied in articles and reviews – without prior written permission from the author.

For further information, please contact us at:
inquiries@angelscript.com
Cover Design by Ginger Gilmour
Project Manager-Isaac Ian
isaac@angelscript.com
Photographs & Layout Design of artwork by David Graham Photography
www.davidgraham.net
Cover Photograph by Chris Holmes Photography
www.holmesphoto.net
Edited by Cathy Sue Holmes
Co-Edited by Gill Graham

Library of Congress Cataloging in Publication has been applied for.

First Printing
ISBN: 978-0-9933023-0-5

Manufactured in the U.S.A. by Worzalla, Stevens Point, Wisconsin

For my children
    May they know the Love
        From which they were born.

"Angels protect us…
as we protect
the ones we Love."

© 2015 Angelscript

Contents

Foreword		XIII
Author's Note		XV
1	In the Beginning	1
2	Echoes of Love	17
3	Meeting the Parents	23
4	Journey to England	29
5	To Model or Not to Model	37
6	Obscured by Clouds	43
7	Dark Side goes on the Road	47
8	Summer in Lindos 1973	57
9	Today-Spirit of Peace	73
10	The Rose City Marrakech	79
11	Kate Bush	91
12	Knebworth Concert	95
13	Gonna get Married 1975	99
14	Paradise on Young Island	107
15	Baby Alice is Born 1976	115
16	Family Comes to Visit	125
17	Early Childhood	129
18	Animals in Flight	139
19	Pigs on the Road	143
20	The Bright Side is Calling	147
21	Floyd Becomes Cecil DeMille	151
22	Animal Farm Comes State Side	155
23	Saving the Hogs	161
24	Time off in Paradise	165
25	A World Series Rock 'n' Roll Show	171

26	A Reunion of Family	177
27	A Parade of Animals	181
28	Is There Anyone Listening?	189
29	The Building of the Wall	199
30	Ancient History upon the Seas	203
31	Lost in Time at Kaunos	211
32	Tax Exile	215
33	Miracles do Happen	227
34	Another Child is Born-Clare 1979	231
35	The Wall Comes Alive	241
36	New York, New York	247
37	Home Again	253
38	The Clash of the Titans	259
39	Ponji Dies	265
40	Isn't She Lovely	271
41	Sara is Born 1981	275
42	The Land of Smiling People	281
43	"What Was That?"	295
44	Gilmourland at Hook End Manor	301
45	Meeting Mrs. Tweedie	305
46	Searching for Humility	313
47	Flying Again-About Face	319
48	Cecil Collins Classes	323
49	Meeting Elizabeth Collins	327
50	Cecil Exhibition	333
51	Guy Fawkes	337
52	About Face Tour 1984	343
53	Baby Brother Stephen	351
54	Live Aid	359
55	Matthew Gilmour Born 1985	367
56	Affair of the Heart-1st Exhibition London	375
57	Momentary Lapse of Reason	381
58	Harmony out of Chaos	389
59	A Friendly Monster in the House	395
60	Dr. Gerhard Adler	401
61	Working with Lily	409
62	Wembley Concert	413
63	Daddy Too Loud-Japan	417
64	Pip and Emo	425
65	A Magical Tea Party	435

66	Waiting in Greece	441
67	Jill's Accident	447
68	David Leaves the Family	455
69	Sir John Tavener Passes Over	459
70	Talking with Animals	465
71	A Dolphin Experience	473
72	House of Broken Dreams	481
73	Mrs. Hella Adler	487
74	Together We Save the World	495
75	Isle of Dogs Concert 1989	501
76	Christmas Carol Fantasy	505
77	Divorce from a Dream	515
78	Life after David	523
79	Transforming Anger	531
80	Camberley with Lily	537
81	Watts Chapel	541
82	Swimming with Dolphins	547
83	Box of Illusions	555
84	Sanctuary for the Spirit	561
85	Hope	571
86	Visions of Beauty	577
87	Venice-A Night of Wonder	583
88	Doorway to Inner Beauty	589
89	Angel of Might	595
90	Live 8-The Long Walk to Justice	599

Afterword	606
Acknowledgements	608
Photo Credits	610
Collage Directory	614
Notes	616
Curriculum Vitae	619
Further Interests	624
Reviews	633

SEA OF GLASS

As I walk on to this sea of glass,
there is no apprehension
of what has come between
these plays and written in
these lines.

Who am I to question
when the storm will rise
or when the storm has met its match
and when the storm declines.

All I see between us
is this sea of glass,
this pleasant path,
this moment of perception,
and this sparkle through the haze…

© 2015 Angelscript

FOREWORD

"Who"—you might ask, "is Ginger Gilmour?"

The only way to describe her is to offer you an invitation to look inside her heart thru reading her Memoirs.

So many people live their lives and leave no impression other than a single footprint in the sand,...a letter unopened or a passing glimpse of a motorcade of an assemble of mighty Kings and Queens and Movie Stars.

Ginger has seen a place beyond there. So as you read, as you listen, you might find something more. Perhaps, something more of YOU, something more of Life waiting to be discovered.

It might happen on some sunlit day walking the beach with her grand-daughter while looking for shells, for some imaginary art in the sand. Or another story that captivates your heart, awakening some distant memory that unlocks your own doorway to BE What you were born to BE.

Ginger has lived an extraordinary life that she has chosen to share with you. A journey that reaches far into what is special about being Human and Divine. To follow her story, enter thru the doorway that divides the light from the moon, and back from the moon into the Light again.

She calls it,

Memoirs of the Bright Side of the Moon

Isaac Ian

Note from the Author

For you—I have written my memoirs from my heart, being faithful to all of my memories and experiences. Its purpose, I discovered as I placed pen to paper, was to remind us to touch the Sacred essence of Life. Most of all to uplift one's heart beyond the challenges and Remember the Beauty that you are.

I have been guided to share with you my story from above. Some may remember things differently. Some may find it too simple and sweet but in staying true to myself, my Joy, my love, I mean no harm to anyone.

Enter lightly as you walk within my journey of Love.

Bless you,

Ginger

Ginger
1970

CHAPTER 1

IN THE BEGINNING

I begin this story, telling of the events that changed my life forever. As if, a ship sailed by and whisked me in its wake. It was an ordinary day in Ann Arbor, Michigan. The morning sun cast its light washing the trees green. A radio played in the distance as the birds sang and bounced from tree to tree. I was an ordinary girl with dreams and visions of finding adventure, not knowing how big of an adventure I was about to experience.

This is the true story of my life and how I was challenged, survived, and resurrected like the fabled tale of the Phoenix rising out of the ashes on a journey with a band they call Pink Floyd (and beyond). A true story of how a child of adventure became a world traveler, a mother and a seeker on a magnificent path to discover the Living God in a most unusual and unexpected way. I call it "My Journey to the Bright Side of the Moon."

I was on a plane to England, with my head resting upon the shoulder of the man whom I loved. His blue eyes catching the light from the window making them shine like crystal. His long brown hair touching my face as I fell asleep in his arms safe, happy, drifting into the first moment our hearts met. It was Love at First Sight, a dream since childhood that he would come to me, my Prince Charming. And there I was sitting next to him going into my future. I was just twenty-two. He was twenty-five.

IT WAS 28 OCTOBER 1971

I was living with Robert Maxwell, a close friend, in a small mock Tudor house in Ann Arbor, Michigan. At first, we had a traditional relationship, which eventually became one of companionship. He was my best friend. Over the years, Robert took on the ownership and operations of two boutiques, one of which I managed. From our perspective, we were BIG FISH in a little town, interacting with a population that liked the things that we offered in our clothing store. It was profitable and inspired creativity and individuality.

Ann Arbor was waking up after the deluge of the Vietnam War and the 60s movement had left its mark on the souls and taste of our clients. One day a dear friend of ours, Morpheus, returned from London. He had been living with us prior to his adventure across the ocean and had called our home his anchor. In addition to his stories, he brought back with him a taste of Carnaby Street with his snakeskin boots from Gohill's and his leopard skin-tight trousers. He was excited because Pink Floyd was playing that evening in town. Each year the University of Michigan had a festival on the last weekend of October and would invite known and unknown bands to play. This year it was Pink Floyd, Quicksilver and various local bands.

Morpheus had befriended one of the Floyd's roadies, Chris Adamson, who had gifted him with tickets and backstage passes to the show. He asked if we would like to go. I said, "NO, I don't think so!" Both Morpheus & Robert looked at me with disbelief and questionable surprise. Between you and me, I had grown tired of being on show. Often I rebelled by wearing ripped jeans held together at the seams with safety pins. This was just one of the things that I would do to break the image, which often did not meet with others approval. But I continued on this way since I was a sixties child seeking not to be held down by traditional views of how I should dress or be. A new idea of freedom for women was in my heart. The sixties represented an opportunity to dare to break the mold and in my innocence, I did in many ways!

Ann Arbor was a town that in a similar manner, sought to do just that—break the mold. It was the home of SDS-Student Demonstration Headquarters, Alice Cooper, Alternative Hippie Stores, eccentric boutiques and a University full of young students. Our boutique was a franchise across the U.S. at the time and sought to lead the way through fashion. Its ethos was to encourage women to find a way of dressing that would express their individual uniqueness. On the weekends, I used to have models dressed in Carnaby fashions and Twiggy-like makeup, dancing in our windows. Our boutique served as a place that would give advice to women of how to find their own identity beyond keeping up with the JONESES and being carbon copies.

After a while, I had a group of women who shared a similar point of view and together we did fashion shows at gigs and other events. My most memorable was doing a fashion show at the opening of the movie *High Noon*. The New York office had designed the clothes for a promotion and we were encouraged to do something in our local town. The collection had both cowboy and Indian designs so I organized with the cinema to do a fashion show. The cinema had a spiral staircase split in two directions, a bit out of *Gone with the Wind*, which led to the seats in the higher tier. Upon those stairs, we did a pantomime of cowboys and Indians reflecting the theme of the movie. Some of us fell on the stairs pretending to be dead, while the audience had to step over us to get to their seats. Others watched from the foyer as they bought their popcorn. It was novel and fun.

In the end, Robert and Morpheus convinced me to go with them to the concert. I had just returned from NYC buyer's week so I decided to dress up. My head was still swooning from the memory of my first encounter with the World of Ossie Clark, a London fashion designer. I was touched deeply with each dress, the fabric, the colors, the femininity, the dance of the folds as the sales woman twirled them one by one before me. I returned home enchanted and inspired even more by the London Look.

As a young teenager, I was besotted with the Beatles and the Mersey Sound. George Harrison was my favorite who later was to become a good friend. On the weekends, I would often put on an English Accent (I thought) as my friends and I hung out at Arby's and McDonald's in my parent's powder blue Ford. So seeing Ossie Clarke's creations brought me closer to what my silent heart dreamt for my future. Or, perhaps it brought me closer to what my soul journey was to BE?

That night I wore a gold and burgundy tie-dyed velvet maxi dress that I had brought back from my trip. It clung comfortably upon the young sylph-like curves of my body and the frill at the bottom would move in the wind as I walked. I also discovered Biba make-up, Twiggy-like eyelashes and lace up leather boots. My hair was golden blonde with gentle curls to my shoulders. I was ready. We got to the concert early and found our seats in the first few rows. Morpheus and Robert left me sitting there alone while they went backstage to say, "Hello," to Chris Adamson. The last thing I wanted to do was to hang out backstage and be a groupie.

I remember looking up at the stage as the roadies scurried around working the final touches for the concert. They were so attractive with their London haircuts, tight Sterling Cooper black jeans, T-shirts, colored boots and velvet jackets. The sound of their accent touched my heart as they shouted to one another across the stage, "Scot can you get Peter? Can you turn up the sound?" The moment was getting closer as the roadies left the stage. The lights dimmed and the band entered. The audience went silent. The magic began with "Embryo," "Fat Old Sun" and David's guitar. Rick's piano pierced the silence held by the sounds of Roger Waters' bass guitar and Nick's drums. We were spellbound as the notes carried around the audience through the Floyd's *sound-in-the-round.* "Set the Controls" took us deeper, transcending us from what we knew as normal to a World where Peace and Beauty united us all that evening.

After the gig, we all went backstage. I was a rather shy person in those circumstances and continue to be. So I often found myself standing alone in the corner, while Morpheus and Robert ran around in their excitement backstage. Fortunately, one of my customers from the shop was there and we passed the time in idle chatter. Then to my surprise, David came up to me. He had on a black T-shirt that said, "That's All Folks," and was wearing those Sterling Cooper jeans. They all seemed to be wearing them. He was so handsome. He came close and said, "Hello, I am David." I looked up at him, his blue eyes penetrating my heart with the sound of his voice. Time stood still as I stumbled to answer. It was as though my dream of "Love at First Sight" was happening. Was he my "Prince Charming?" The moment held us until Morpheus and Robert broke the spell as they entered our circle. I motioned to them as I introduced myself to David, "Hello, I am Ginger and this is Morpheus, Robert & Susannah," then turned and left them chatting. I was so embarrassed, yet stunned by David's approaching me. I sought refuge in the room where Chris Adamson was loading the equipment into the truck hoping to regain my composure.

As I sat upon one of the road boxes chatting to Chris, Robert appeared and asked if I was open to invite the band and the crew over the next evening for dinner. "Sure Robert, if that is what you would like, Why not?" I then went into the next room where David and the band were standing. He turned towards me and looking him directly in the eyes, I invited HIM and the band over for Roast Beef and Yorkshire Pudding the next evening. Robert and Morpheus were very excited that they accepted.

The following day they spent most of their time canvassing all over town for sight of the band, hoping to confirm that they were coming. I spent most of the day preparing the meal and answering phone calls with their latest report. As the day progressed, it became certain that our evening dinner was going to happen. The band arrived first. Roger Waters, Nick Mason and Rick Wright took their places on our long leather couch. David sat on the floor near the record player his hair falling down over his face as he looked through our albums. He became our DJ for the evening. I was extremely nervous by his presence triggered by his approach the night before. Something stirred in my heart each time as he came near. I was trying hard to resist an ancient calling, which was summoning me.

The next day Quicksilver was playing and David and the band said they would like to go see them. At midnight (that same day) on Halloween, we were having a Roller Skating Party in Detroit. Robert and I invited them to come along if they wanted, schedule permitting. They accepted so we arranged to meet them at the Quicksilver show and then go on to the party.

I was dressed in red satin hot pants and gold hearts with a full body red leotard. I was ready to go Roller Skating. Robert, Morpheus and I arrived at our seats. Soon I was by myself again while they wandered backstage. Steve O'Rourke, the Floyd Manager, Nick and Roger Waters arrived. Their tickets were in the row in front of me. Steve turned around looking like Clark Kent from behind his glasses and said to me, "Ginger, I think you should be with David." My heart nearly stopped. I managed a smile and looked away so as not to show my embarrassment.

A few minutes later, David and Peter Watts, their sound engineer arrived. David sat right next to me with Peter following him. Someone had given them Mescaline that night and David had refused to leave the hotel. He told Peter that he was so attracted to me that he didn't think he could stand being near me tripping, especially as he wasn't sure if I was in a relationship. He felt it would be difficult to resist his feelings. In the end, Peter talked him into coming.

As he sat down David placed his hand onto my leg. The lights dimmed and the music began to play. I could feel his body next to mine in the darkness. Energy surged through my being! My heart opened. I felt we were melting together just in his touch. All my life I dreamt to have a union between a man like this. I became nervous as I tried to resist the feelings that filled my body and heart. What should I do?

Robert and Morpheus reappeared before intermission and rescued me. I asked where they had been. But before they could answer, the band said they had seen enough and wanted to go back to the hotel. We said that we would meet them there. I stood up to follow everyone. David grabbed hold of my hand with Peter behind. At the top of the aisle, I looked at Robert leading his glance down to where David was holding my hand. I said quietly, "He is tripping." He said, "Don't worry. It is ok. Let's walk him back to the hotel."

So, we became guardians of David. We walked hand in hand through the misty fog back to the hotel. David was holding my one hand and Robert holding the other. It felt strange as we each wore the mask of pretend. Ann Arbor was a miniature of Cambridge, England, where David was born and raised. It was so similar even down to the Victorian street lamps and the fog. He made a few comments to that regard as our journey took us through the campus.

When we got to the hotel, we met with the others who were sitting around a table in the bar. There were two seats left. David sat down, pulling me down to sit next to him when Morpheus arrived saying in a panic, "Rick Wright is lost." Robert volunteered to go and find him. I stood. He asked if I would go with him. I shook my head saying, "Perhaps Morpheus and I should take everyone back to our house. I will meet you there." As it turned out, it was just to be Morpheus taking Roger Waters, David, and me. Everyone else would follow.

We went in Morpheus's van. It was empty in the back. Roger sat down on the floor against the back doors and so did David. I quickly sat on the wheel hub. Morpheus closed the door. It was dark. As we drove along David grabbed my hand and pulled me down into his arms. Our passion rose in our embrace. Time stood still. The van stopped with a jerk. We had reached our destination. Morpheus opened the door and I got out first. Walking quickly towards our house, I opened the front door and darted upstairs to my bedroom. I was in tears. I was in a flurry of mixed emotions. I trembled. I felt like I was in a boat in a storm losing control. My Shiatsu, Julie, was sitting on the bed wagging her tail. I picked her up, ran down the stairs, out the door into the fog lit street.

David realized that I had bolted and ran after me, catching me in his arms as I went around the corner. Our lips met. I no longer could hold back my desire to be with him—to be close to him, united in our desire. Suddenly, as though it was a bolt of lightning, a thought shouted in my head, "Oh MY GOD! What am I doing?" I pushed him away saying in the release of our passion "I cannot do this. I don't know you!" David said, "I do not normally do this either". So we walked back to the house. Our silhouettes revealing that we were holding hands as Robert returned having found Rick. David could not let go.

When we got to the house, I went upstairs. Robert followed. I cried and said, "I cannot stand it! David is too attracted to me! I cannot resist. I will stay home!" I pleaded, "PLEASE. Can you take the band?" Robert said, "No you go! I will stay." "This is impossible! We shall both go. We promised. Besides, they are waiting downstairs! I will just have to handle it." Anxiously, I ran out the door and down the stairs, as I implored him to take them. I would go in a different car! In the end, Robert did take the band in his Cadillac and I went with my assistant manager. I cried all the way. My heart racing as we got closer to our destination.

As it was Halloween weekend, our Detroit radio station played the Orson Welles' Dramatization of *War of the Worlds*. It seems that the band had never heard of it and on that evening had not listened to the introduction. By the time they had reached Detroit, enhanced by the fact some were tripping, they thought the Martians had landed. What a psychic adventure that must have been, in addition to then go roller-skating. We played with Reality in those days. Never a worry, that not all would be well. We were explorers daring to enter other dimensions. Casualties did happen. Sid Barrett was one.

Throughout the rest of the evening, I just skated to the music. I twirled, I jumped but I stayed my distance. Robert was looking worried and distant and if I dared stop, David would be there wanting to be close. He couldn't skate very well in his condition so Steve O'Rourke spent most of the time holding him up. Once as I was flying past, I overheard David say to Steve, "That girl is a dream on Wheels!" (Such a sweet and special memory.) All night, we went round and round the skating rink to the theme music from *Shaft*. It seemed to play over and over along with Sly and the Family Stone's *"It's a Family Affair."* Since then they became our theme songs of our first moments of Love.

I have no idea how or when we got home. I was not sure how they made it back to their hotel either. All I remember is waking up in my bed at home. Robert and I slept in, resting from the night before, passing like ships each time we were awake. In one of those silent moments, I remember looking at the cover of *Ummagumma* on which David was sitting in the doorway. I went into a deep review of my life. The last few days had me taking a closer look at my life as if something inside of me had awakened and things had changed.

My greatest dream was coming true. The one I frequently shared with Robert. I was honest and often I tried to leave. We were close friends. He offered a safe harbor. Looking back, I feel, we were playing a part of what we thought we wanted and should do. At least I was, but I was always clear about it. He knew that I felt strongly that my Prince Charming would appear one day. Each time I shared this with him, he called me a dreamer. I was appreciative of his care, his friendship. I often thought maybe over time I would fall in love with him in response to his kindness. However, I had a dream deep in my heart that my *knight in shining armor* would appear.

In the early evening, the phone rang and Roger Waters was on the other end. He wanted to speak to Robert about playing golf the next day, as they had chatted about their mutual love of the game the previous evening. He asked if David could have a word first. I answered "Yes." When David got on the line, he asked if I could speak. I said, "No, not really." He suggested I just say yes or no to his questions. He asked if he could see me the next day. I said, "Yes." He then said that he would call in the morning to arrange where to meet. I then handed the phone to Robert saying that Roger Waters wanted to ask him something about golf. In the end, it was not possible because he was leaving early on a sales trip.

David called me in the morning knowing that I would be alone in order to arrange where we could meet. I chose a Chinese Restaurant. We spoke about the last few days. He still felt the same and if ever I left my relationship, which to me was in a flux, to call him. The owner of the restaurant overheard our conversation and approached us. He asked if we would like our tea-leaves read. We said, "Yes." He said, "There will be a change. There is a house with white birds across the waters." I was to come to know that David's home in England had white doves and of course, it was across the waters.

We went back to the hotel for it was time for David to leave. We hugged in the lobby, as everyone was there ready to leave. We had a farewell kiss goodbye as he handed me a piece of paper with his parents' phone number who lived in NYC. His final words were, "Call me, if things change." I left and walked away feeling that I had left part of my heart behind. He waved from their car as he passed.

It was a warm afternoon. The sunlight felt comforting as I walked through the town back to our boutique. There was a 60s mystical bookshop upstairs and the manager was a close girlfriend. I shared my heart dilemma with her. She knew of all the times I had tried to leave Robert. She knew of all the times he had talked me into staying. She knew my true heart dream. Robert and I were just friends, companions. I asked her as tears ran down my face, "Am I being dishonorable to leave without telling him face to face? I have tried so many times before. Besides, what if David and I are just a flight of fancy?" She said, "Go! It is deeper than that."

At that moment, I realized my decision WAS deeper. I needed to follow what was deep in my heart so that I could finally live its truth. Besides, it was fair for Robert to be set free. David was just a catalyst, putting me onto the path of my Soul. Going was opening the doorway to my next step. That choice was to be the first awakening to trust and act upon the Divine Plan awaiting my future. Of course, I had no idea then that is what it was. God kept it secret.

Over the next few days, I decided to leave for good and dare to go into my next adventure. I wrote out a detailed business plan of what was to come into the shop over the next six months. I paid myself my wages due to me. I called my friends Stephan and Shelley Rubin in NYC and asked if I could stay with them until I got things sorted. We were close and had spent lots of time together over the years. I told them "It was over." They said, "Of course."

I started packing and called the number that David had given me. His mother answered the phone. I shared with her that David had said to call if I were to come to town. I asked if she would tell him that I would be coming into the city on 5 November. He called back. He was in Princeton, New Jersey doing a gig and said he would pick me up.

Just to add to the drama, I had gotten a lead role in a motion picture film. It was a mixture of *Easy Rider* and *West Side Story*. My gentle and innocent nature fit the part perfectly. Because of the unseasonal rain, the directors hadn't needed me on set and no contract had been signed. Throughout the whole evening as I did my packing, they kept calling to convince me to stay. They would give me refuge. I kept saying that I just had to go. Finally, by 4:00 a.m., they said, "Alright, go, but call us when you get there." My childhood dream of being a film actress now surrendered to the meeting of my prince charming, which was closer to my heart.

Morpheus said he would look after Julie, my dog, until Robert returned. He would also drive me in his van to the airport. I kissed my precious Julie goodbye and left our house in Ann Arbor for good. As we went around the corner to the parallel street that led to the freeway, Morpheus suddenly put on the brakes. I looked up through my tears trying to focus.

Two limousines were coming straight for us. One swerved and

stopped in front of us blocking the way, the other went up onto the pavement and blocked us from behind. I panicked trying to figure out what was going on. Flashes of James Bond went through my head as my vision cleared. Two of the directors from the movie emerged from the limos.

To my surprise, they had driven up from Detroit to make one last attempt to keep me from letting go of my role in the movie. As they approached the van, one of them said, "You can't leave!" The softhearted one came to my window. When he saw my tears and flushed expression as I shook my head as if to say, "I can't," he said to the other, "Let her go." Looking around towards the car, he gave the driver the OK to back away and said, "Call us when you get there."

We drove like the wind and I ran, pushing four suitcases, my heart beating from the stress. I am sure passers-by could hear it. I wondered why is it that gates always seem so far away when one needed not to miss one's flight. I made it. I had no idea what my next step would be but something inside was overjoyed, relieved as I stepped on that plane.

"Dream no small dreams for they have no power to move the hearts of men."

Goethe

1749-1832

'ANGEL of MIGHT'

 2003

In his arms in England
1972

CHAPTER 2

ECHOES OF LOVE
ARRIVING IN NYC

5 NOVEMBER 1971

"Excuse me Miss, can you fasten your seatbelt? We will be landing soon." Time had gone by so quickly and I started to get a bit nervous, my heart was racing. Soon, we shall be together…David and I.

I was one of the first to disembark and there he was, standing, waiting for me to arrive. It was like a fairytale. I pinched myself to see if it was really happening. Our eyes met and we fell into each other's arms. His hair smelled of Strawberries as we came close and our hearts melted together in that moment. I couldn't stop smiling as we walked hand in hand into our future.

As it turned out, I didn't go and stay with Stephan and Shelley, only my suitcases. David and I were so in love that we could not leave each other's side. Therefore, I went on tour for his last few weeks in America. Being on the road with a Rock 'n' Roll band was not something I ever thought I would do. But I felt safe in his arms. We went straight to his hotel room. The light filtered through the voile curtains, casting a fine mist like tone into the room.

I walked over to the window and parted them to get a feeling of where we were as David sorted out the suitcases. I was entering the unknown, trusting the adventure. He came up to me from behind and held me in his arms as we looked out the window. Our souls melted, touching our destiny to be together. Unknowingly, we surrendered to God's Plan for our future guided by his Love, his Protection. David had a gig that night though I have no memories. All I remember is the Beauty of our first moments together. Free to love him. Free to be loved.

We left NYC to finish his tour. They had twelve more gigs. We went to Cleveland then Buffalo until we reached Montreal. Every night their music was like a piece of fine silk draping over my heart tenderly. David had one of the roadies, Scot, looking after me while he was on stage. He wanted him to put a chair by their mini-mixer behind the curtain on his side of the stage with a drink for me every night. Each time David was not playing guitar he would come off stage and sit me on his lap. We were constantly in each other's arms, kissing held in a lovers embrace.

I remember Roger's expression, the first time David did this. His head hung low as he was playing his bass guitar. He looked to the right from behind his hair to find David wasn't there. He could see us in the distance hugging. Shrugging his shoulders, he continued playing. David was more known to have his back to the audience when he wasn't singing but always there. I think this behavior was new to the band.

My days were magical as I entered into the World of Pink Floyd. They had hired Arthur Max to be in charge of the lights and special effects. He was so resourceful. Sometimes he went to various schools and rented equipment to enhance the beauty of the show. We got on very well. Once during "Echoes," which had just been released and the blue lights dimmed, I said to him, "Wouldn't it be wonderful to have snowflakes drifting gently down?"

Do you know what he did? He went to a florist and got all of their old flowers, roses and chrysanthemums. During the afternoon, someone must have plucked them apart, put them into bags ready for the show. Later a roadie took them up to his post up on the rafters and let them go slowly during "Echoes." Such Beauty!

I was happy. I kept trying to inspire him to create a rainbow, but it never happened.

I can't remember which gig it was, but during the concert I happened to be at the mixer for the first half. One of the promoters was standing there with me. He began to make advances as if I were an apple he could pluck from the tree. He was drunk. I was shocked! I left and went backstage to our dressing room and waited for David to come. When I told him shaking like a little sparrow, he said in his English accent, "Oh, he was trying to get your knickers down. Ignore him," and he held me in his arms. To me, knickers were a style of trousers, but for the British they were your underpants. Well, that began my education of another aspect of being on the road—that women were for the taking. Not me. I was with my Prince Charming. I was out of bounds, a precious jewel to be treasured.

One night I had an enlightening experience, which to this day has guided me forward silently, unknowingly, through most challenges. We were in Montreal. The gig had been special. The world was a carpet of snow and we were in bliss. Montreal is a wonderful city, old and majestic. I found the Canadians warm and gentle people. The gig was over and David and I went back to our room to catch some rest. During the night, I awoke suddenly. I opened my eyes to find that light filled the room…white light. It was brilliant and through the light looking over at David, I tried to wake him. His face had become the face of Christ. I held my breath, for in that moment, I felt that I had made the right decision to be with him. From then on, in my heart, our Love became boundless, sacred and divine.

I had been raised a Catholic with a belief in God and Christ, but over the years I had become disillusioned. The misuse of his message had soured it. Blocking me from knowing what he really is for us, for the world. It still would take years of being inspired through other teachings before I learned the difference between the institution and the passion of Christ. This night planted a seed. However, I realize now that my inner nature has always been with Christ. Goodness, kindness, compassion, and most of all the loving of all creation, including those, which we do not understand. The basic principles of being a Christian I am. I was not to know this for a long time. Nor would I know that not all Christians live those qualities. I was just a good person. I wouldn't hurt a fly. I always saved stray cats, dogs and people. My heart was big and the Floyd's music opened it further.

.

'LOVERS'

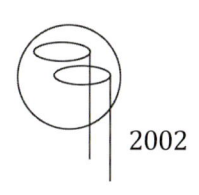

2002

With Love
Doug & Sylvia Gilmour

CHAPTER 3

MEETING THE PARENTS
NYC-CARNEGIE HALL

15 NOVEMBER 1971

I felt like a trouper by the time we came back to New York City. I had made friends with all the road crew as well. Nance Steele was a lovely girl who traveled with the crew and most nights she sat at the mixer. She was a sweetheart. I loved how David would always go out at the end of a gig and say, "Ta Da-Night," waving his hands in the air. He continued to do this over the years. I loved his heart and his Honor toward his team who helped make the show possible. He was gentle and caring, though most of the time held in his silent, quiet English way. The number of times I heard and experienced the truth of those words are innumerable.

This aspect of their culture floats over my life memories. Sometimes it is poetic, sometimes not, especially for an American whose nature was to be free with her joy and her feelings. I have learned a lot being with them. I have become a universal citizen. Experiencing many other ways of being and cultures has opened my mind and heart further to Love Humanity, in all our unique differences. To find Unity, to Love and Appreciate that we are all children of God with a Divine Spark waiting to shine. "Shine On" speaks loudly to us All!

The Floyd was to play Carnegie Hall and Arthur Max had something to show them. So we had to go down near Times Square. There were workmen in a black machine that resembled a Martian

Space Machine from the movie *War of Worlds*, which actually didn't come out until 2005. It was a cherry picker and was used not to pick cherries, but to repair streetlights and things up high on buildings or billboards. It was enormous.

    Arthur arranged a demonstration for the band before they went back for rehearsals and sound check. His vision was to attach lights to them and they would move like beings, lifting from the stage, traveling over their heads. This was a YES and we grew very fond of them as they added a majestic quality to the shows. I can still hear Rick playing as they rose into the night sky. I think the Floyd were the first to use them in this context. As a result, the Lorries got larger as their equipment continued to increase.

    David's parents, Doug and Sylvia, came to the gig and we went out to dinner with them afterwards. I was a bit nervous to meet them, but it turned out to be quite special. Another day, we went to their home. They had an apartment in the village, simple and filled with treasures they loved. Sylvia and I had lots in common. We loved Beauty. She was just like the images in the movies of the gentle *English Rose*, in her flowing dresses. Her quiet demeanor hid another aspect of her nature, which later would be revealed to me. She was intelligent, highly creative and a bundle of Joy. She was a film editor and when I shared my story about leaving the film, she was touched. She was happy her son found the Love of someone who loved so deeply. Over the years we became very good friends, we got along really well.

    David's Dad was quiet, even more so than Sylvia. He was a geneticist and it took a while for me to get used to his eyes that observed. They were very much awake, silently piercing and yet thoughtful. He kept a lot to himself and I never knew what he was thinking half the time except when he was cooking. I loved how close they were with each other. The bond of Love between them helped make me feel comfortable being in their presence. I often found them dancing in the kitchen to a favorite song playing on the radio or in the garden amongst their white roses. They loved life.

Carnegie Hall left an even deeper impression than the magic of the gig. It awakened an interest in me for Architecture and the Art of the Twenties. I was from a coast guard family after my mother remarried and we spent most of our time on the bases or in the shopping mall, barefoot on the weekends. I knew much more about large military boats and the coast guard bases than this aspect of American culture, which I had never known existed. I focused more on my studies and adapting to new schools as my stepfather transferred almost every year. We drank Shirley Temples on the weekends and danced the polka with my sister in the base cantina after catechism.

In Carnegie Hall, even the ladies room reeked of opulence of the Twenties with mirrors and gold everywhere. The stage had a circular part, which could rise from below. Arthur made sure to use it. The music began and the Floyd seemingly appeared from below, it was an awesome moment. Out of the darkness emerged the sound of "Set the Controls for the Heart of the Sun." I can still hear Roger hitting the Gong somewhat quietly. Rick's melodic playing with the repetitive thumping notes of David's guitar held us hypnotized. The lights alternated from red to blue and back again.

The tone of Roger's voice piercing the air merging with David's *"Ah-Ah-Ah"* created a sound, transporting us to being in an Egyptian Tomb. Nick kept it all in a continuous beat eventually building the pace. Red beacons swirled as Roger returns to the Gong madly beating it. The Gong sets alight with the crashing sounds. The audience gasps, holding their breath within the tension, listening. The music drifts and falls upon us, while the only light is the flickering Gong that shaped the band's silhouette. The celestial sounds took us further to the "Heart of the Sun." As the song quietly ends, the next one, "Atom Heart Mother," begins.

***

As I write this from my flat in the UK, overlooking the Arun Valley, I am listening to it once again. Its mastery moves me. Their ability to give us an experience with subtle transitions, creates such Beauty. However, it would take years for the world to understand them, especially the press. Now their music is often likened to classical Rock 'n' Roll, our modern version of Beethoven or Tchaikovsky. On this morning, Clare called from Florida as she does every day before taking our granddaughter to school. Before hanging up they sing in chorus. "One, Two, Three, Nana we love YOU!"

Today she called earlier so I asked if she would like me to read the first few segments of my book. She asked, "What book?" I said, "My life story." As I read it to her, I could tell that she was captivated. As an adult, she has never heard the beginning of the romance of her mother and father. She asked, "Will you share our stories too?" I said, "Of course, for this is my journey of self-discovery and the beauty of life. With every pregnancy, with every child I learned more about Love, which guided me to my next step. Each one was special. Each touched such wonder as you came into the world. It was as though the universe stopped to Honor your entry. Of course, I would share that! And Clare I just wanted to let you know that often I shouted from the top of the world, and said, "God, thank you for giving me the opportunity to birth such wonderful children." My heart rejoices with the Love for them.

After she rang off, I realized that in that conversation I was writing this for my children, for David and for the world. With the hope that we would all dare to trust our hearts, create Beauty and Love one another. For me that has become the best thing to share in Life. Love and Beauty, for they are the bridge to God, but building it has not been easy. It did get a bit rusty and hard to maintain at times. Throughout the years, Life was not without its challenges but it was Love and Beauty that healed our wounds time and time again. Some say it is the crack in the wound that lets the Love return. I often feel the light shining out and love returning.

Ginger
1971

CHAPTER 4

JOURNEY TO ENGLAND

We were somewhere between Cincinnati and Washington DC, driving to the gig. I was sitting on David's lap in the back seat when Steve O'Rourke turned around and said to me, "Well, Ginger are you coming with us back to England?" I turned pink at the suddenness of the question when I looked at David. He said, "Do you want to?" I nodded, "Yes," as I placed my head upon his shoulders. Dreams upon Dreams were coming true. Soon I shall see the house across the waters with the white doves.

The moment came to live another dream …to live in England. It was really happening. We were on the plane. We held hands throughout the journey. Watching a movie to pass the time. Sleeping, occasionally, in each other's arms because the flight was through the night. Morning came with the smell of coffee and bacon. I rubbed my sleepy eyes as I looked out the window at the new country I was about to know. It was like a patchwork of color and extremely green despite the winter. Lines of colorful houses wound round the edges of the streets below with little chimney stacks and grey smoke. Swimming pools were nowhere in sight.

Warwick, a friend of David's, picked us up from Heathrow. He also cared for David's home, doing odd jobs, when he was away on tour. I found out later from Warwick that he had expected a different woman. He almost blew it by saying her name, but David had anticipated this so he quickly introduced me. The story from Warwick went like this, "The Man needed a Maid." Like the song from Neil Young's *Harvest*. Well, Love got there first, I thought.

It seemed as if we drove through the countryside for ages until we finally turned into the drive. David got out and opened the white five bar gate. Before me was the house with the white doves that flew into the sky with the sound of the approaching car. As we went down the drive, we passed a large cluster of Lilac trees and a Mulberry tree with a few outbuildings behind them. David had a small Mock Tudor Home with stables and barns. A duck called Digby, a city cat called Gretel, which he inherited from Toni Howard. A slightly deaf white cat called Naomi and a retired Shire horse from Whitbread,'s called Vim. Vim was really tall, massive and gentle. I had never stood next to a Shire. I had only seen them pulling carts loaded with beer barrels on telly.

My English adventure had begun. The fridge was the size of an American dishwasher. Rather small, I had to stack all the leftovers and shopped very cleverly to fit it all in. Fortunately, there was a cold pantry, which eventually I learned how to use. Warwick and David were little terrors some evenings after I had gone to bed. They would poke holes into the cling film that I had carefully covered the plates of food in order to reduce the risk of food poisoning. Naughty boys! They were stoned.

We were not alone long for Pete Watts, his engineer and road manager, came to stay with his new girlfriend Patricia Gleeson, known as Puddy. Peter had decided to leave his family. He was married to Miv and had two children Naomi and Ben. Naomi has become a famous film actress and Ben a well-known New York photographer. At the time, we only heard unpleasant stories about Miv, which seems to be the way when couples separate, sadly.

Miv actually was to become one of my best friends years later. We have shared friendship, moments of creativity, and stories of the joy and tragedy in life's journey since. She is still a special person dear to me who not only has supported the healing of my heart but also inspired me to discover, *Who I was meant to be creatively*. We laughed. We cried. We shouted often in despair but the giggles won out. She is a treasure of Beauty, a Diamond in my box of memories.

The snow came and then Christmas. Puddy, Warwick and I spent a lot of time in the kitchen playing cards and getting high. David and Peter spent a lot of time in his studio, which was downstairs next to the living room getting high. I was used to having at least $1000 per day modeling, but had no savings or income, as I had not foreseen this adventure to England. Puddy was the same. To have to be dependent on our men in a foreign culture without a work permit was a rather difficult period.

We occupied ourselves by taking cuttings from various houseplants of friends we visited. The kitchen was full of them. Eventually, I asked David if I could start modeling again. He was spending so much time in the studio and on tour that I had very little to do and our passion was a cooler flame. Perhaps returning to England, back into his culture and old patterns of behavior influenced this. I was vulnerable but besotted with my love for him and did my best making Woodley our home.

I was a great cook so that helped. I became very creative and learned to cook Indian curries and Japanese, which I had never had until I came to the UK. Unfortunately, after Puddy and Peter left, I was alone with the BOYS—David's friends from Cambridge. Most evenings I got stuck doing the washing up and keeping them filled with Tea as they smoked their spliffs and watched telly. Not for long though. Eventually, I got them plastic gloves, an apron and had them do their share.

From January through February, the Floyd went on tour in England. I stayed home for many gigs. Television programs did not come on until after 4:00 p.m. by which time it was dark. We didn't have curtains or double-glazing so the winter winds would howl through the lead light windows. I sat shivering with a blanket around me and several jumpers. I was not used to being in the elements indoors. I sat each evening in David's high back leather chair watching whatever was on. There were only three stations: BBC 1, BBC 2 and ITV at the time. It was snowing and a blizzard was happening outside. *Brrr.*

One evening, a man wearing a black coat peered through the living room window where I sat. He was tapping on the pane to get my attention. I absolutely freaked. My mother raised us in an environment, which meant that we were frightened to be alone especially in the country. Every night she would go around to each door and window checking to see if they were locked. Here I was alone in a foreign country with no curtains and no idea who to call…not even the police. He knocked and shouted through the howling wind, "Miss I have brought you your water container." *YIKKEES*!

The local pipes had frozen and we were temporarily having problems with our running water. As a result, I had to bring in buckets of water from outside in the freezing cold constantly. I wondered what planet I had landed upon. *UGH*. Sadly, that was not the only adjustment I had to make. There was no power shower. Just a hand held one, placed upon a Victorian fashioned bracket at the top of the bath. The water pressure was not like America either. I called home crying, seeking her love, "MOM!"

I was discovering that it was a misconception that the English and the USA both spoke the same language, had the same sense of humor, used the same measurements for cooking and on top of which their money was so different. They drove on the other side of the road and we were miles from anywhere. "Mom, they don't even have a large fridge!" I exclaimed. Despite it all—What have I done?—never entered into my mind. Thank God.

The adventure was still special. There were just a few bumps along the road getting used to it. I was getting a new set of tires and a new road map. I was still young, adaptable and in love so it was easy to make it my home. This was never in any of my Sociology books. In fact, the thought of leaving the States didn't enter my mind except in my dreams. In fact, I have found that the manifestation of the dream is still different from the dream.

Every Monday we went over to Jenny and Steve Marriott's (Small Faces and later Humble Pie) cottage to pick up our shared house cleaner, Liezel. We would arrive early, have some tea and a spliff. Jenny was beautiful, a picture of a Classic English Beauty. She worked close with Ossie Clark, which inspired me deeply. David had met her years ago when he drove Ossie's van. Jenny's clothes drifted as she went in and out of the kitchen. She was the first to educate me about Art Nouveaux. Her taste was impeccable. In fact, a year later we had a stall together selling antiques in Antiquarius on Kings Rd when it became necessary that I needed a job. Not being married did create some problems trying to get a visa so that I could work.

Jenny and Steve had an English garden full of Foxgloves, Hollyhocks and Roses straight out of Beatrix Potter. They had lots and I mean LOTS of fluffy cats who all used to come to me to play except one. Eventually our house became the same. We had up to 17 cats at one time, mostly kittens. I was helping a woman who had a cat rescue center, which was always over full. I tried hard to fit in with the quiet nature of Jenny and most of the women I met. It was difficult for it was against my American nature. Fortunately, I was a shy person but a firebird inside. It was a challenge to integrate in itself never mind in a foreign culture.

***

A house full of cats was not dissimilar to my childhood. I was always bringing home stray animals including many rabbits. We kept them under the house because we had a crawl cellar. We lived on a Navy housing estate while my stepfather did a year of isolated duty in Libya. He was a medic. Every morning before school, we had to run around all the houses and gather the ones that had got away. We didn't have much money so our make-shift cage allowed them to burrow under the wire and get out. It was fun.

This period of my childhood required for me to pick up my brother, Stephen, from school and prepare the dinner. Our duties also included cleaning the house. Most days consisted of building tents with all the sheets and blankets with the help of the neighborhood children. When it was time for my mother to return home from work we would stuff everything under the beds and sofas. It must have been a mess but what could a working mother of little means do?

I experimented with different ways of cooking. Some dried out because I put them in the oven on low at lunch and went back to school. I was still learning. I thought my dinners were good. No one ever complained unless I had burned it. My mother was always encouraging me to continue. The most memorable was when I changed the colors of the food as a Biology experiment. The mash potatoes were royal blue; the cheese sauce fuchsia; the chicken bright green and the peas were black. Needless to say, their response was a giggle.

***

One day I had gone around the corner from David's house in Roydon to our little neighborhood shop, Mrs. Little's. She was a wonderful lady. Rose Little was her name and her husband was Stan Little. She became my gran across the waters. We would go there for little things and it was the post office too. This day she said to me holding out this little creature in her hand, "Ginger, look. Isn't it sweet? Someone is going to put it down." It was a Billy Goat.

Well I immediately called David and asked if I could bring it home. "Please, they are going to kill him?" He said rather reluctantly, "Yes, ok." In fact, David was amazing, He got a tiny Johnny Walker bottle he had brought back home from our trip in the states. Found a teat from somewhere, filled it with milk and would sit in his favorite chair feeding Billy who rested upon his chest.

As Billy grew older, we had to move my plants from the floor higher because goats do like to eat them. However, it was not long before he would jump up on the tables, reach up and eat the hanging plants! Eventually we had no choice but to put him outside in the garden. He was so cute. Goats jump with such happiness, sideways sometimes. Watching him was a source of laughter for us. Sadly, he started eating all my tulips we had gotten from Chelsea Flower Show. Jock, our Scottish Gardener and David's mum, Sylvia, and I had the most glorious time picking out tulips the year before at the show but Billy ate them all. Therefore, he just had to go in the field with Vim.

David had let another family, the Robinsons, board their horses in the other stables in return for taking care of Vim. Billy had a great time until his horns grew. As David did not favor having the chap's horns cut off, we kept them. Unfortunately, Billy started chasing the girls who were often seen running for their lives towards the paddock for safety. Billy thought they were playmates and did not mean them any harm. He had grown up with them. They were his friends. Sadly, his horns were rather sharp. Sometimes, he would get them caught in the tails of the horses and last seen being dragged across the field. Eventually, he reached manhood and started to smell. Goats smell from a great distance. So we had no choice other than to find a goat farm that would take him. As far as I know the story ends happily ever after with Billy chasing the female goats and sowing his oats.

lot of famous faces are Leichner

mean
lights go dim,
a sudden hush which ca
the moment has arrived that
She just walks out onto the empty stag
And as soon as this bewitching girl opens her
perfect lips to sing, you stop talking and you listen
go right on listening until nothing else in the world matters.
The atmosphere becomes electric, you can't believe anyone has
the right to look so good, you blink but she's still there,
real, exquisite, alluring, and quite unforgettable.

PRESS. FOR IMMEDIATE RELEASE. C.B., Las Vegas,

Leichner One of the most famous names in the entertainment world.
Lipsticks, tinted foundation, cream powder, eye-shadow, brush-on mascara, nail gloss.

Ginger Modeling
1972

CHAPTER 5

TO MODEL
OR NOT TO MODEL

Time passed and I got used to my new home. David agreed for me to join a modeling agency and it wasn't long before I got a few modeling jobs. One year I was the face of Leichner Cosmetics. I looked like a Hollywood Star from the days of Marilyn Monroe and Jayne Mansfield. It seemed I was being typecast as either Hollywood glamour star or the innocent girl next door. Once a male model pushed me around Hyde Park in a wheelbarrow for a shoot. Then I was taken to the seaside in the blazing sun wearing a fur coat baking. What Fun. Keep smiling. LOL.

On the day of the *Leichner* shoot, my journey home on the train was interesting with all that makeup and false eyelashes. My piano lessons were with a local elder piano teacher that day, so I was rushing home. I had gotten back just in time. My lesson turned out literally rather touchy! All had been going good until this day. David had the famous poster of Marilyn Monroe where her skirt is blowing up showing her legs. The piano teacher was obviously unfamiliar with the picture because he approached me with the question, "Is that you?"

During the lesson he stood behind me and tried to make advances as he reached over to turn the music score. I was shocked as his hand touched my breast. I turned around glaring. Standing up, I demanded for him to leave. He never came back. I always found it difficult when men projected their desire upon me. It was as though they entered into my being and took something with them without my permission.

Storm Thorgerson, of *Hipgnosis,* asked me to be on the cover of one of Al Stewart albums, *Modern Times*. I knew Storm well since he did the Floyd's album covers and was an early Cambridge friend of David's. The photo shoot was in the garden of an English Manor House early in the morning. Al Stewart was sitting in a Cord Automobile owned by Jimmy Page from Led Zeppelin. I was wearing a sequined maxi slinky dress in the likeness of a 20s Hollywood Star with a lynx fur coat. I was running away from him after the night before, pretending it was warm but it was not. Early morning shots were always my least favorite. The lighting was great, but it was cold!

One of the most illogical castings was for a job at the London Playboy Club. When we first arrived, they led us into the Playgirl dressing room. Buxom bunnies surrounded us. The stylist came in with the clothes we were to wear. We had to pretend that we were gambling at the roulette table. It was ridiculous. I just did not understand why they chose me, as the stylist insisted that I should stuff my bra with tissues to give me more cleavage. While the other female model who was rather well endowed, received tape to strap her down. Then they put her in a motorcycle jacket. What was that agency or client thinking?

It was the same in America. I grew tired of being in the line-up, a number being spoke about and judged: her breasts are too small; hers are too large, the legs are not quite right. Turn your head this way. Look up. Waiting for hours. Getting cold. Good pay, but in England the stardust finally wore off. I gave it up. I had to do something to get a visa in order to stay in the country so I went into the antique trade with Jenny Marriott. We got a stall in Antiquarius on Kings Rd selling Art Nouveaux antiques and other objects of Beauty.

From then on, early mornings often found me driving down the A10 to Bermondsey Market in Greater London, off the Old Kent Rd. Especially, when David was away on tour. He bought me a little Morris Minor Estate that enabled me to get around on my own and transport our findings at the markets. My American independence was returning. I loved driving in the early morning as the sun rose over the countryside painting the sky in crimson and pink. The sheep and horses grazing in the countryside added to the majesty of the morning.

The Beauty of England was entering into my soul bringing love. I would get up around 4:00 a.m. so I would reach there as the market opened. In the winter, it was dark when I arrived. I joined in the crowds of people scurrying about with flashlights from vans to stalls desperately trying to find the treasure first. Pearly King and Queens would sometimes be there too. Jellied eels and hot tea stands kept us warm and fed. Though I must confess, I have never been able to try them because I am allergic. However, a hot cuppa was a treat. Besides warming me from the inside, it also helped to warm my fingers, which protruded from my cut-off gloves.

There were rows and rows of little precious things and other antiques from eras gone by. Once I saw two ceramic white pots with handles in one of the stalls. I asked the chap selling them, how much were they and if I could bake with them in the oven. Well, he laughed nudging his mate and in a strong cockney accent he said, "Hey, Stan, this lady's a wonderin' if these pots ere' could be used for bakin'?" They both broke out into uproarious laughter. I did not get the joke and just smiled repeating my question, "Well? Can I?" "Lady are ya sur' you wantin' to bakin' in dem?" "Sure why not?" "Well love, these ere' pots are chamber pots from days of old. Folks use to pee in dem in da' night." My mouth dropped at the thought. Thank God, it was dark for my face turned scarlet. "Oh dear, really?" They simply nodded their heads with a cheeky smile. I decided not to buy them and walked away humbled. Oh well, yet another day in the life of an American in England.

'AWAKENING'

2002

David backstage

CHAPTER 6

OBSCURED BY CLOUDS

1972

The Floyd accepted a request to write the music for a soundtrack for a French film, *La Vallee,* by Barbet Schroeder. It was the first time that I had ever visited a foreign speaking country. The album was recorded at Strawberry Studios at Chateau d' Herouville, just outside of Paris. All of the crew stayed with us at the Chateau including Puddy, Pete Watts' girlfriend. I loved French cuisine. It was my favorite food to cook in America, but the amount of garlic this French chef put in the carrot salad was overwhelming. I have come to love it along with the lemon juice and olive oil dressing that saturated the salad. I have made variations on the theme since, with orange juice, cranberries and garlic! *YUMMM*.

The schedule for the Floyd was very intense, watching the film repeatedly. They did not have time to make long dreamy songs like Echoes. In the end, the album was created in just two weeks. We ate, slept and recorded there in the Chateau. A large table worked perfect to serve Dinner and in the evening doubled for the road crew's contests. I remember once Chris Adamson won because he ate the most amount of raw potatoes and Little Mick won for eating the most amount of fried eggs. I don't remember how they felt the next day. The event was hard enough for me to watch never mind digest. I still remember the laughter.

Puddy and I spent a lot of time riding the Metro to French

markets. Getting lost and seeking help from many that passed by. Neither of us spoke French…None whatsoever. Well, that is not entirely true. We had some help with the basics. David spoke fluent French and wrote down a few words for us on tiny pieces of paper. We got lost once on the metro trying to get to the flea market so we decided to take a taxi. As we were getting out a bicyclist ran into the open door. He crashed onto the pavement severely damaging his bike. To my relief he was all right. A terrible French flurry built between our taxi driver and him. Arms were waving and insults were flying. In the end, I gave him what little money I could towards a new bicycle.

After one outing, upon returning to the Chateau wearing our new fluffy imitation furry platform boots, Nick Mason commented, "You girls should get in a bit of Culture." It was the first time that I had ever heard that word. "Culture…what is that Nick?" We both asked, getting a bit flush with embarrassment because of the innuendo in the tone of his voice. "You know a few museums and galleries and monuments. Perfect place for it," he said. Admittedly and perhaps indignantly, we didn't do it that time. Since then, I have become a serious Culture buff. I have become a messenger for the need of Culture and Beauty and its importance for maintaining World Peace.

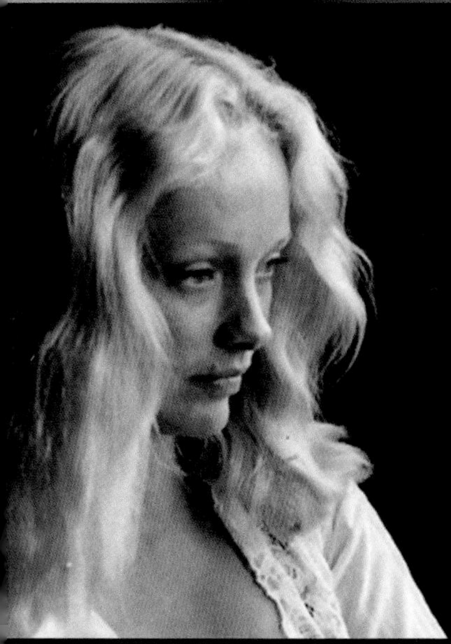
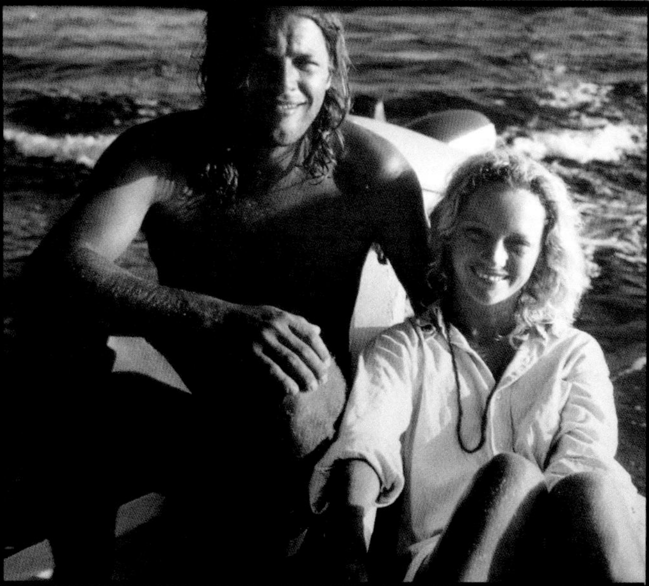
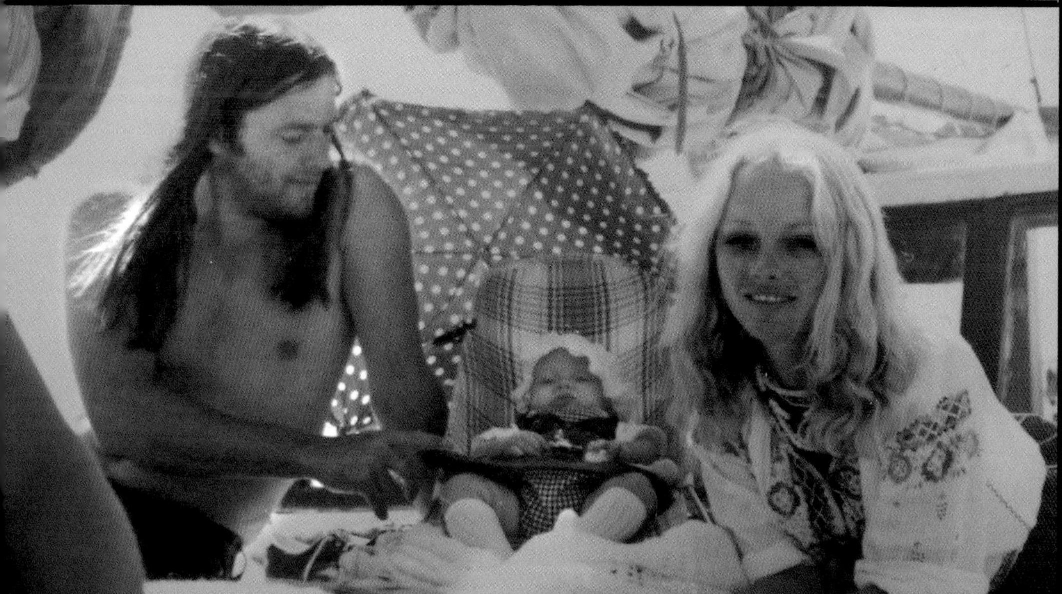
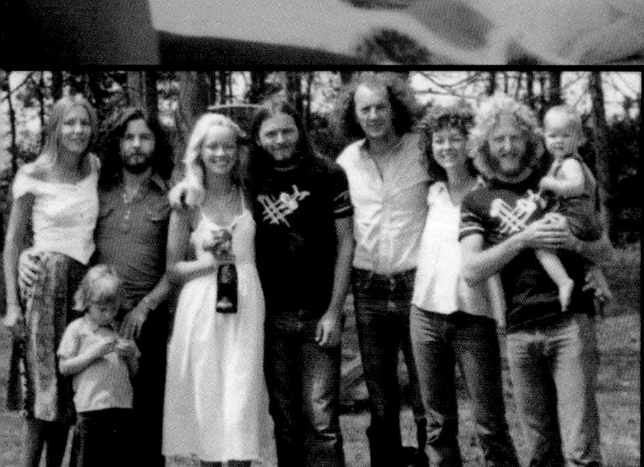
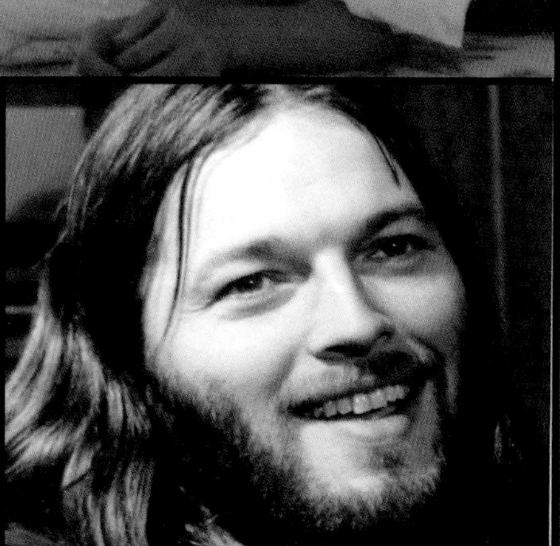

Japan Tour 1972
David & Ted

CHAPTER 7

DARK SIDE
GOES ON THE ROAD

JAPAN TOUR 1972

Between the two weeks it took to record the album, the Floyd did gigs in Japan. It was a long, long, flight. Most of us took some Mandies (Mandrake), a form of happy sleeping pill, which always made me giggle until I fell asleep. Japan was different from France. Some might call it a culture shock for this American at the time, and perhaps it was for them as well? However, this was their second trip. I often felt we were living a modern day *Shogun* walking down the streets with our long hair and different accents.

When we first arrived at the airport, there was a banner hanging over the door at the terminal saying, Welcome *PINK FROYD*. The Japanese had difficulty in pronouncing our L's and it seems even writing it. We had to take a large bus to our hotel and David was sitting next to the window. There was a surge of people towards the bus, flashing cameras everywhere.

David noticed that one of the girls had forgot to take off her lens cap so he was pointing to her through the window that separated them, trying to tell her. She got so excited that he acknowledged her that she did not notice until the bus drove away. She slumped in a pile of tears at the lost opportunity. No photos but she did have a memory that David Gilmour had acknowledged her.

One morning I was ordering room service for David and me. "Please Sir, may we have two orders of eggs." "YES Ma'am." "With two orange juices, bacon, toast and tea with milk?" "YES Ma'am." It never came. I had to order it again. Again, it never came. We decided to go down to the restaurant hungry and confused. The day was getting on and the Floyd had things to do. The queue was long and when we finally got to the front, the maître d' acted as though we did not exist. He kept taking the people behind us to their table. Finally, I stood in front of him and caught his eye, "Hello. May we have a table, Sir?" It worked; he took us to a table.

Later, when I related the story to our promoter, I came to understand. That "YES Ma'am" means I hear you, but I do not necessarily understand. When they ignore you, it usually means they do not approve of who you are. In their world, if they do not acknowledge that you exist, they do not have to serve you. We must have been an unusual sight looking back compared to the usual tourist they serve. Platforms, blue jeans, long hair, T-shirts, and perhaps a cologne that did not agree. Even our different mannerisms were a bit loud in comparison to their inherent quietude. Even their rush hour seemed to breathe of stillness compared to London.

The tour started in Tokyo. A bustling city mixed with many cultures and large billboards with flashing lights. The culture shock really began as we went deeper into the countryside. Finding Mc Donald's in Tokyo amazed me. I gave it a try and everything tasted like fish. Not at all the taste I was accustomed to. One evening our promoter took us out for a special Japanese dinner. Women in beautiful Kimonos served us as we sat on the floor. Thank God, we had to remove our knee-high platform boots before sitting down because I fear that it would have been impossible to do, as I was also wearing very tight jeans. They were so tight in those days that I had to lie down on the bed to zip them up.

The evening began as we sat on the floor atop of fine pillows made from Japanese silk. Warm saké, green and brown teas alternating between each course to cleanse our palates. I had never eaten raw fish before never mind Octopus tails. Over the years, I have come to love raw fish, but not the Octopus tails. Through this experience a seed was planted that would become my future way of eating—Simple, Beautiful and Sacred. Our trip also inspired an interest in the Art of Bonsai, which further led me to appreciate and admire their philosophy in the *Art of Living*.

We all bought cameras, it seemed to be the new jewelry for the tour. Puddy and I went off to visit the food market. The colors of all the vegetables and spices were so vibrant. I took picture after picture not knowing what I was doing with a Nikon. As we went deeper into the market, I noticed a monk wearing black buying some vegetables. His head was shaven and he walked onto the next stall as though he was floating. The calm of his presence held my attention. I so wanted to take his photo.

I hurried up to him and in my form of sign language asked if I could take his picture. Fumbling with the settings being a novice, I panicked because it was not going smoothly. He stood for a moment and turned to walk away. I think he thought I had succeeded but I had not. I once again hurried up to him and asked again. He was very patient with me. He waited again in his silence. I was not sure if this was appropriate in their culture, however, he allowed me to enter his presence. I can still feel the moment. It was like a doorway for me to enter one day, for there is no time where the soul lives.

Puddy and I both wore tall platforms, which was the fashion at the time. We looked like amazons compared to the young students we would pass in the street when we went on our adventures. Going shopping was a challenge despite being a slender size 10. It seemed the Japanese shops had all the sizes below which I never knew existed until that trip. They are a tiny but an elegant people. Their creativity in all aspects, inspired me as I became aware of how its intent was to reveal the Sacred in all of life. I was beginning to understand why Nick suggested for us to seek out the Culture of a place. It wasn't just the Museums and Buildings. It was the people also.

On this tour, the Floyd were testing out *Darkside of the Moon* in preparation to record it when they got home. On the first night, the audience did nothing after each song. We didn't understand because the gig was super. One thing we had to adjust to was that Japanese audiences showed no emotion during the concert. Puddy and I were a bit perplexed for we were used to the American audiences who freely expressed their feelings. Stadiums lit by the little flames of their lighters, I always loved it. Thousands of them adding to the beauty they had just heard.

During intermission, we were going downstairs when a group of fans approached us for autographs. I said, "*No Pink Floyd!*" They nodded and spoke something in Japanese while opening the long rectangular program holding their pens. They kept nodding as they pointed to David's picture. I shook my head saying, "Sorry, *NO Pink Floyd!*" as our pace picked up to escape. I was looking over my shoulder and did not notice that we had reached the stairs. I started to fall and could not catch my balance because of my 4-inch platforms. The pictures that went through my mind were ghastly as I saw my fate below. I tensed preparing myself to hit the bottom when a savior from the crowd behind me grabbed my arm that was waving in the air. Suddenly, my body released the tension and fear with the realization that the nightmare was over. My forward motion stopped and for a fraction of a second so had time. I went into suspended animation until I came back to reality. It was like a rewind of the experience as he pulled me back up onto the lobby floor safe.

We went back to our seats at the mixer for the second half. Our sanctuary we thought. Once the gig was finished and the last note played, the audience went berserk! Their behavior was like chalk and cheese. Wild frantic clapping accompanied with screams and tears of rapture filled the air. Like ants that fled their broken nest, they descended towards the mixer. The roadies and sound engineer, Peter Watts, surrounded us and got us to safety backstage. Phew, but it was not over.

As we left the back of the hall where our limos were waiting, they descended, trying to get to their stars in a mad fervor. I pushed David into the car before me, blocking their grasping hands trying to grab his T-shirt. I became his protector. My lioness arose from the depth of my heart to enable me to have the strength to stop them until he reached the safety of the limo. The drivers had the engines ready to go once we were all safe inside. The limos slowly pierced the desperate waiting crowd in convoy. Their hands wiping against the windows as we left them behind making our way back to the hotel. I began to understand a bit about what the Beatles had experienced every day from the mania stirred from their idolatry as my adrenaline calmed.

The next gig was in Kyoto. The Floyd made a mad dash to the reception because they had discovered that there were some traditional Japanese rooms in each hotel. They were like little boys. Every time we checked into a new hotel, it became a game. David got one for us this time. It was a special experience. The hotel had been a Traditional Shogun Mansion, which was converted. As we entered our room, silent tranquility started to touch my soul with its Beauty. There was a traditional garden with glass sliding doors with a miniature water feature. A sunken square bath you had to sit in instead of lying down. We slept on a futon on the bamboo-matted floor that rolled up in the morning after we went out for the day.

We decided not to have a European breakfast this time and tried a traditional Japanese one instead. Overlooking the garden was a low table and bamboo mat. We ate tofu, a bowl of rice accompanied with pickles, pieces of fish, and miso soup. The sound of the running water in the garden soothed our minds. It was a new and special way to start the day with the *Art of Eating* in stillness.

On their day off, we went to visit the old city of Kyoto, where the main temples and the Nijo Castle were. My most memorable was the Ninomaru Palace, which was inside the Nijo Castle where one of their famous Shoguns lived. Rumor was, the appointed head gardener sat outside for a whole year before designing and planting the garden. He wanted to know the movements of the light and shadow throughout every season. Every aspect of Japanese Architecture also carries this focus and intent to be one with nature and created in Beauty.

The squeaking floorboards made the sound of nightingales as we walked throughout the building, captivating us en masse with the other tourists. Apparently, this was intentional. It was their burglar alarm forewarning the Shogun of night attacks and assassins. Here again, they were inspired to honor the sacredness of our human natures ensuring peace. They valued this, which made a legacy of sound and how to use it to protect. Not to create sounds that destroyed. I often wish our burglar alarms could do the same. I just do not understand why we choose to live in such noise.

We meandered through the village feeling very much at home when we came upon a unique store that sold knives. David was in heaven and bought a few to bring home. I am not sure if he could do that now with all the new laws about transporting knives between countries. We stopped for lunch in another home of a Shogun. Each section of Japan that we visited specialized in a local commodity from their area.

In this palace, their specialty was umeboshi plum. We sat on low platforms amongst an orchard of pink and white flowering umeboshi trees. Everything was flavored with umeboshi from the rice to the tea. To this day, the fragrance and the taste of umeboshi is one of my favorite Japanese delights. My children often give me the powder of umeboshi for the occasional birthdays or when I run out. It has become a staple condiment in our kitchen.

During our time in Japan, David and I went to visit a dear friend Ted and his wife. He used to be a roadie for Brian Ferry who we met through Rick Wills, (Brian's bass guitarist). Rick and Linnie were some of our closest friends. Originally, Rick was in David's first band, Jokers Wild in Cambridge. Ted also toured with Paul McCartney and while on tour, he met a lovely Japanese woman. They fell in love and married, and then moved to Japan to live with her family. He needed a new profession to earn a living so he became a builder at first. I believe, if my memory serves me right, his father-in-law hired him. This allowed him to stay in one place at home in Japan and eventually build their marital home.

He went on to study the art of making ceramics and over time, his career as a potter started to flourish. He built his own kiln in the backyard so he could be close to his creations. As a potter in the traditional Japanese firing technique-Raku, he is a legend. A tall westerner in a foreign land submerged into a new culture for the sake of Love. Their story is so inspiring and familiar.

Ted invited us to stay over for the night with them. As we had a day off, we accepted. When we arrived, they offered for us to take a bath. This apparently is a normal custom when visiting people at home in Japan. They had a similar sit up bath as the hotel with bamboo pots to throw water over us. It was warm and ready for us when we got there. The surplus water ran over the bath onto the floor and out a hole in the wall as we took turns to bath. This ceremony meant we were relaxed and ready to honor our meal. In the middle of the room, our dinner cooked over an open fire. Large stones were warming beside the edge, which were later placed under our covers to keep our feet warm while we slept.

The next gig was in Sapporo and we had to take one of their high-speed trains. It was early morning rush hour. The platform was crowded and as we were boarding the Japanese men, in a rush, shoved me and the other woman aside. In their culture, the men had precedence over woman. In fact, I doubt if they even saw us. The trains were very modern and very comfortable. Several times along our journey, it was their custom to offer warm face towels to all passengers. Not just at home and in the restaurants, but even on the trains! I did miss this ritual of washing hands and bathing ceremonies when we got home. The *taking-off of shoes* when entering private or sacred environments was part of respecting and honoring Life, intrinsic to their culture. Today the *taking-off of shoes* is part of my life at home. I love walking quietly from room to room.

Sapporo hosted the 1972 Winter Olympics. Therefore, the band decided that they would love to have a go skiing down the slope. David wasn't much of a skier then, but was obviously fearless or perhaps stupid since he decided to have a go. I stayed at the bottom and watched him inch his way as he traversed the Olympic slope while keeping fingers crossed. Their long hair was blowing in the wind and snow, resembling the Beatles from afar. Luckily, they all made it down without injury. I do not believe their insurance company would have favored the lark. But, it was a good boyish laugh.

When we got back to the UK, they still had to finish *Obscured by Clouds,* but continued working on *Darkside of the Moon.* Once the final recording was on vinyl, they took it on tour again.

'BROTHERHOOD'

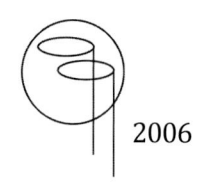

2006

Ginger modeling for
Looms of Lindos
Lindos, Rhodes
1972

CHAPTER 8

SUMMER IN LINDOS

1973

Every morning I awake with such inspiration to continue writing my memoirs. My heart is opening as the moments of Beauty and Love return to me. On this morning I was pondering the time we, most of the band, all went to Lindos, Rhodos, and Greece. David rented a pea green E-type and we set off from London driving across Europe. We stopped to visit his parents first who were having their summer holiday in Ramantuelle, a French village just outside of St. Tropez. I still remember the sounds of the swallows as they flew in between the stone buildings above me. "They never land on the ground," David told me.

    We slept on a very narrow day bed in each other's arms in their living room. I had to dry my hair in the last of the winds of the mistral from the balcony. Its wind blew away the clouds and dust brought from England. As I sat on the porch, the day held in stillness by the blazing sun upon the countryside, forcing me to close my eyes from its brightness. In that moment, the sounds of civilization were far away, melting into the distance as the song of the cicadas called forth the evening, purging all the inner tensions, leaving room for Beauty and Peace to return. The day became the night allowing Provence to fulfill one's calling to dream within the fragrance of Lavender.

    It was hot and we went to the beach on our first day. We had arrived later than his parents who had saved us a couple of beds and an umbrella. I followed David, with my head hung low under the safety of my hat. I was nervous, as everything was so new to me, the language, the culture, the food, even nature. Then it happened, a very embarrassing moment that clutched at my throat as we walked on to the sand. There on the entire long, long beach almost everyone was naked in one form or another, i.e., topless or even totally without clothes both men and women. I didn't know where to put my eyes.

My American upbringing about nudity was quite different to this. My mother never even slept without her nightie and I am not sure if my stepfather ever saw her naked either in the light of day. She was Catholic and had very strong views about the sacredness of the body and intimacy. They were so in love, but very private. Fortunately, David kept his swimsuit on, which made it easier to adapt. Europe was beginning to be quite different. Well, at least Saint Tropez was.

We traveled towards our destination through the mountains of Switzerland. The car was a convertible and with the wind in our hair, we laughed in the sunshine as we drove along. I loved looking at David, his hair, his eyes. Was this really happening? It was as though we had been in Love before, through Life times of togetherness. The landscape was so majestic. It took my breath away. We stopped for little bites of cheese and bread and a glass of wine along the way. I had never had such wonderful wine in my life as I did on this journey.

We drove onto Brindisi, Italy, where we took a boat to Patras, Greece. I felt a little seasick in our room below from the fumes and the loud churning sound of the engine. Consequently, I had to spend most of the journey up on deck. We left the car in Patras and flew to Rhodes. We arrived in the early evening. The Sun was setting as we walked down the stairs of the airplane. The air was full of the scent of orange blossom mixed with sage, rosemary and thyme traveling on the warmth of the Mediterranean breeze as it tousled our hair.

    I stopped for a moment upon the stairs to allow it to enter and refresh my soul. That night was to be the first journey of many that we were to take down the island of Rhodes to Lindos for we eventually bought a house, actually two. One is in Lindos and the other was further down the island in Pefkas, Lindos, which became home away from home for many years. It was a place where we could relax and safely raise our children on holiday. We taught them how to swim and be free. Now, after nearly forty years, we have become part of the community growing old together.

    That evening we took a taxi from the airport. There was no air conditioning in the cars then, so we opened the windows to feel the breeze. There always seems to be a light orange dust that comes in the windows on our way across the island. The earth is rich in Iron oxide that creates that color. The dust blew across the fields in between the Orange and Lemon Trees, their trunks painted white to keep the bugs at bay.

    It takes just about an hour going through little villages with their taverns. One after another full of lights and bouzouki music with lilos and various printed beach towels hanging from the entrances. Cement houses unfinished with steel rods protruding on the roof tops line the road beckoning the day that the architectural rules change allowing another floor.

    Many tourists come to Rhodes and we did not have an inkling that our holiday would be spent walking through crowds on the way to the beach or to the shops. Lindos is quite a historical village and much of their income is dependent on the tourists now. The village gives over to the tourists after Easter until October. There is a knight's castle and an acropolis on the top of the mountain, an amphitheater and the village is around its perimeter at the bottom.

Years later, we would often count the number of tour buses as we were driving to Rhodes to buy what we could not get in the village. Once we counted 45 tour buses coming into Lindos just in the first half hour of the morning.

We had no idea what adventure lay before us on our first holiday there. Food was scarce and there were very few luxury items. Butter was often rancid and the baker would withhold the bread from the tourists. This primarily was because after World War II there were shortages. The village had not gotten back on their feet so the baker was the guardian of the bread for the locals. In fact, I never knew there was even a butcher until one early morning many years later.

***

I was walking and bouncing one of our babies in my arms at 6:00 a.m. so as not to wake everyone in the house. She just wouldn't settle. As I walked into the center of the village, near what now is Yanni's bar, there was a queue of Greek women in black with scarves on their heads. They were waiting at a little doorway in the corner near the church gate. When I approached, they closed their lines blocking my view. It was a butcher selling meat just inside the doorway, which until now remained closed. Finally, one woman motioned for me to get into the queue. I said, "Thank you, but I have not brought any money with me today."

Fresh fish was scarce, as well, but for a different reason. Just after the war the fishermen had taken the easy way out to catch fish, they thought. They decided to use the left over hand grenades. Unfortunately, hand grenades do not discern between young or old. They just kill everything and as a result, when we snorkeled there was not much about worth catching. It took years to restore the ecological balance. So if we wanted fish we had to go to the market in Rhodes, along with the restaurant owners. The same was for any meat, fresh vegetables and fruit except for locally grown produce such as tomatoes, cucumber and lemons. There certainly was not any lettuce for years. Things have gradually changed as they have refrigeration in the grocers and restaurants. Even Coca-Cola and ice cubes have made it.

As one rounds the last corner just before you get to Lindos from Rhodes, the view still takes my breath away especially at night. The village twinkles with the streetlights through the orange trees and the boats in the bay light up the harbor like Christmas. In the distance, you can hear the cicadas and the rustling of the leaves. Night flowering Jasmine, Orange and Lemon trees create a floating fragrance. The stillness takes one into another reality of time. Storybooks are written upon such magical beauty, set off by the stars in the sky. The Knights Castle's silhouette is revealed each night by the light of the rising orange moon. And there we were in Love, holding hands, held captive in a timeless moment.

***

A villager and his trusty wheelbarrow sat waiting when we arrived in the square. He was there to take our bags to the house. He was short. His back hunched over from carrying too many heavy loads. His body wrinkled with age, but he still smiled, revealing the loss of his front teeth. "Ela, Ela," waving his arms, he motioned for us to follow him into the village through the cobbled walkways.

Greetings in this personal fashion have long gone. A Zundap, a little Greek open back van does the fetching of bags. Lindos had developed such a lucrative tourist business that they just had to find another way. A fleet of zundaps took over. As a result, the streets are no longer cobblestones and are replaced by slabs of stone in places, concrete in others. Walking down the street or making deliveries throughout the village one now has to dodge them.

During the day there is also serious donkey traffic taking

tourists up the mountain to the Knights Castle and the Acropolis. We had to have a strategy to miss the crowds, the zundaps and the donkeys when we entered the village. You use the unworn pathways. You go in and get out. What I do love is greeting the shop owners sitting by their doorways with "Yasso. Kalimera," as you pass by. Their eyes glisten with friendship and happiness that we have returned.

Our first summer, we stayed with the Floyd Manager and his Family, (Steve and Linda O'Rourke and their two children Kate and Shanna). They had rented one of my favorite knight houses owned and restored by Sandro and Patrizia Somare. Sandro was an Italian painter from Milan, who worked closely with an Italian architect. Together they restored it from being a derelict donkey stable to its former glory as a knight's residence with an Italian flavor. Many of the older houses built centuries ago were for the knights. Sandro's was one of them. He had created such Beauty especially in his garden.

To this day, I treasure sitting amongst his orange trees and seeing the powder blue Lobelia catching the last sunrays underneath. Sandro and Patrizia often invited us to dinner over the years. Sandro would sit in the courtyard smoking his pipe as he played his Yukelei. He did not speak English, but we became dear friends beyond language. David often played backgammon there with Christian Mouzon, who took care of Sandro's boat. We, too, became close friends united by the love of the sea, Lindos and Backgammon.

Sandro's house had a traditional two story stonewall, which surrounded the property and gardens. We entered in through a huge wooden door in the middle to find a wooden dinner table in the courtyard all aglow with candles and a feast. Everyone was there that had arrived in town from England. Gosh, it was out of a fairytale. My only difficulty that night were my platforms. All the roads were narrow walkways on mini-inclines. Our escort with our bags was walking a fair pace. I stumbled on the cobblestones holding onto the walls fearing that I may twist my ankle. I had to find an alternative.

The next day I bought a pair of the local sandals. With this decision a new self-image was forming. I had to face a model's fear of being too short. Instead of being 5ft 10, I had to live with being only 5ft 6in which was my true height. Back home, I needed the shoes to keep up the illusion that I was taller. This was not all I had to adjust to that was to compound the inner experience. I had no rollers with me either. My world was silently spinning with inner questions of "Who Am I? Will you love me? Will I love me?"

Besides letting go of some of my glamour and facing *Who I truly was born to be*, my London Model agency had asked me not to get a suntan. I needed to stay lily white like a piece of china. Many still remember me in Victorian Lace sitting on the boat under a lace umbrella or in the shade of the trees. This was probably one of the first experiences when I had to accept my true self. David seemed patient with me. He had a silent warmth of understanding as he often held me softly in his embrace. He knew what it was to leave one's culture and enter another. And it wasn't just one. It was many FAST. Between the beauty of the newness and the unknown—my heart and mind were held. Nothing was familiar. Our love carried me. My soul knew the way.

We had no luxuries like we had in our hotels or at home. Our little bedroom was in the back of the courtyard next to the kitchen. It was hot and stuffy. But it didn't seem to be a problem. Even the hardness of the straw mattress and pillows seemed not to matter, as I recall. In fact, I have stayed there on other occasions since then. I have grown to love the simplicity of Sandro's villa and the cold showers at the end of a day whatever the weather. Their dinky Italian kitchen was just big enough to cook pasta and a cup of espresso for we ate most nights in the square at Mavrikos.

Some of their other friends had joined us during our holiday. Germaine Greer, David Hockney, Tony Howard and his wife, Nancy, but they stayed with Melissa North-Tchassey in number 24 down the road from us. Melissa had worked with Tony Howard and Steve for many years and is probably the person who inspired them to come there. Another friend, Tony Gorvitch, stayed with us for some of the time in Sandro's villa. He was another Rock 'n' Roll manager. I entered that summer, an entirely different world than Middle America. I listened. I observed. I went with the adventure. I smiled, I laughed, I cried. I trusted my life. I felt inside, the experiences were destined to be.

Numbers identified most of the village houses then. We spent a lot of time with Melissa at number 24. She became one of my closest and dearest friends along with her sister Mary and Tchaik, her husband. We shared our pregnancies and early motherhood as we often would meet at their London flat in Paddington when we got home. Their parties opened another world of the English culture for me. When we got pregnant, I was first. So by the time Melissa was carrying, I could share my new found knowledge regarding childbearing. Our children grew up together. We were like family. Alice and Dixie were like cousins. Then there came more. As they grew older, taking them all to Lindos was like *rent a crowd*.

That summer was just full of new things to adapt to. On my first visit to number 24, I was caught again by surprise for everyone was sunbathing topless. What was even more difficult as I said before was when some of the lads were starkers. David seemed to be used to this and never participated. Nevertheless, it took me some years to feel comfortable. I must admit it was a good way to lose the white sunbathing lines.

Lindos had many artists staying there either renting or owned houses they were restoring. In the early days before tourism took over the village women were known for throwing rocks from on top of the cliff onto nude sunbathers below in Saint Paul's bay. I didn't realize how disrespectful and difficult that must have been for them at the time. I was in my own process of adjusting to this behavior and my sensitivity for another culture did not develop for a while.

What was interesting was many of the local Greek women were frightened to enter the water. This was considered a bad omen. But things have changed now because on Sunday the Greek families go down to the beach, picnic and all. Our western habits have taken over. All the beaches covered with umbrellas and topless women are no longer felt sacrilegious. Water skiing, banana rides and horns announcing the boat trips break the silence of the mountains reflection upon the water shimmering in the sun. Tourism has become their principle livelihood.

Many other Italian families besides the Somares came before us Brits. They have such grace in the way they restored the homes they bought. Honoring the past, the villagers brought in the wonderful beauty for creating gardens that their culture is renowned. Their plants, their choice of local crockery and fabrics, using the community craftsmen, melting two cultures in harmony is a noticeable quality. One from which I drew inspiration when we were restoring our homes. Most of all, it was their simplicity that awakened a passion that would later lead me to discover the deeper purpose of life and the role that Beauty plays.

During our first visit to Lindos, we went water skiing in Saint Paul's bay with Toralis who was the first to have a speedboat and gave skiing lessons. I will never forget my first lesson. David and Steve instructed me how to sit in the water, arms straight and let the boat pull you up. OMG! I got up but as we went around the Bay, I lost it. In fact, I almost lost my bathing suit. I had bought my first bikini from Biba's in London. It was chocolate brown cotton, skimpy and easy to lose it seems. I held on tight bouncing on the waves.

    Toralis drove the boat faster and faster around the edge of the bay. He loved to show off for the girls in his speedboat, but, unfortunately, I fell. I held onto the rope for dear life, not realizing that I should let go for I was concentrating more somewhere else. I could feel my bikini bottom coming down my legs. I was so shy and panicked, especially as there were lots of men in the boat watching. I kept widening my legs for fear of losing them. I looked up barely seeing through my wet hair that kept splashing into my eyes to notice that all eyes were on me. I could barely understand why they were waving their arms when I finally heard them. David and Steve were shouting, "Let go of the rope! Let go of the rope!" So I let go of the rope. *Ahh*, that helped. The drama was nearly over. There I was treading water in the middle of the bay trying to regain my composure holding onto my bikini bottom. My rescuers arrived smiling. Really, I think they had quite a chuckle. Climbing up the ladder was quite a challenge. How does one get up the ladder holding onto my rather stretched bikini as the elastic had stretched, swish one's hair into an acceptable model's image, while the boat was bobbing up and down? PHEW! I did it with modesty and pride intact. What a day upon the water.

    Most of the time we ate at Mavrikos, our favorite restaurant in the square. Demetri and Michaelis ran the restaurant more and more as their dad, Basili, entered his eldership, who held the helm in the corner. They had fresh fish and other traditional Greek delights. The local wine has improved, but drinking it then gave us horrible headaches. Primarily because it was made from chemicals and not aged like a good French wine. Champagne was the only thing we could tolerate to drink. Some preferred drinking the Retzina or the Ouzo but for me it was like drinking petrol.

Every day we sought to be with the Majestic Beauty of Greece. We had lovely picnics or sought out traditional cafes down the coast at more desolate beaches. Sometimes we came by boat. Other times we drove. One night we were coming back after dark and Tony Howard was driving rather fast! The roads were dusty and full of potholes waiting for the day they would be tarmacked. David and I were thrown around the back seat as he took the corners. I think we all were a bit tipsy from the wine. I was frightened and kept asking him to slow down. He didn't. He just laughed. We held on and I prayed. And yes, we made it back in one piece to the safety of the village. Thank God!

Juliette and Rick Wright had rented a separate house in the village that year. They had no idea that Steve had rented one at the same time. I think they had expected and hoped to have time away from the other members of the band. After the last group holiday in France, they wanted to be alone, but it was not to be. I spent a lot of time with them. Their family had become mine because while in London I was getting close to Juliette, and their two children, Gala and Jamie.

Being in Lindos together brought us closer. I spent a lot of time in the water with the children looking for tiny abalone shells, especially with Gala. I was teaching her how to be a dolphin. This seems to be something I do with younger children. I have come to love giving dolphin lessons. It came naturally for me, for David and I loved the water. We are dolphins in many ways, I believe, and we have inspired other children, especially ours, to love the water.

***

I am jumping time, but I do not know if the memory will come again. So I would like to share this one story. One of the Italian families, the Corvos, had a large Greek Caique with deep wine/terracotta sails, Be-el-za-bub. Often we would go on adventures out to sea to find sanctuary from the tourists on either their boat or Carla Pelegrini's. Sometimes we would go in convoy. Little boats and larger Caiques meeting somewhere down the coast for lunch or sharing our picnic.

Very often, we came back into the bay just before sunset. I would sit at the bow of the boat bathed in the golden reflections upon the water. We surfed with the wind, (sails out) or cruised if the water was calm like glass. There is such a peace at that time of the day. And in those moments, I felt fulfilled with the day's adventure. I was at one with creation and if one listens, one can hear the angels calling forth the night as it enters the day. Often David would be sitting at the back holding the tiller. His body bronzed from the sun and the olive oil we used each day to moisturize our skin. With his long hair and this deep color, he looked like a Native American to me. He too was one with nature and the sea.

As we entered the bay, the sun would be setting behind the mountain. The air would cool in its shade. The beaches were quiet, as the tourists had left to prepare for the evening activities. The sound of sails coming down and clink clink of the ropes on the masts filled the early evening. Often I would jump off at the mouth of the bay and swim in to shore. This day Alice and Dixie, Melissa's daughter, were both there, saw me jump and jumped as well following me. Fortunately, they were wearing their water wings.

Everyone on the boat began shouting to me, "Ginger, Ginger look, the girls!" I looked back and saw these two blonde bobbing heads flipping and stroking the water as hard as they could to catch up. I waited amazed at their courage. That's my girls, fearless and dolphins in the making. We made it back to the shore and climbed the hill back home. They were tired and ready for dinner and bed.

***

During that first summer in Lindos, we often saw David Hockney, pad and pencil in his hand, walking on the promenade of the top balcony in Sandro's house. Years later, the memory would spark a desire to draw when I was on holiday. Each summer I watched other artists at the local cafés capturing the villagers while they fearlessly sat amongst the villagers, like Toulouse Lautrec. I would come to know his and Hockney's work later. I pondered, how do they do that? Sit and draw people in front of them without a worry.

In some of my first attempts, I found it was easier to draw a person's back. I discovered more about the heart of an individual when drawing the back. It seems we put on a mask, a false image, a barrier when facing one another. I wanted to capture the essence not the role. In drawing their backs, all their tenderness, vulnerability, kindness was revealed. Gradually, I grew more daring to draw in public. Now most of us use cameras with telephoto lenses.

During my first few years across the pond, I was so green and innocent but ready to discover my destiny full of Joy. I was impressionable and easily inspired by those that were creating Beauty. And the world I had entered stimulated my own innate creativity. I was so in love that being in the unknown was ok. There was so much to learn and to experience. Life was taking me on a fast track into my future path of Beauty unbeknownst to me. I was just a child touching my dreams, loving the adventure, overjoyed with the feeling of God's grace.

Melissa and her sister, Mary, had set up a business called the Looms of Lindos. Mary and her husband (now deceased) did a lot to help the village to get back on its feet after the war. They set up the looms to give jobs to the local women making fabric and created a local industry to help the economy of the village. They organized a preservation order upon Lindos to hold the encroaching hotel madness at bay and to protect their ancient culture. Their task was not complete until they brought water to village homes.

    Marco Rocca, whose family owned one of the knights houses, related stories of this period when he was just a boy while having dinner recently at Broccolino. His family had water delivered by donkey twice a day. There were metal containers above the kitchen sink and showers, which needed filling. From each house, a small water channel allowed the water from the sinks and bath to run away down through the village to the sea below. Each house was responsible for white washing it regularly, which had become his job as a boy. I could tell that he did so with great pride as his hands mimicked holding the brush.

    Previously, most of the villagers had to go to the square and fetch water in urns carried by their donkeys. Unless, you could afford to have it delivered. Water eventually came into their homes. There are many wonderful stories of how the villagers went wild for a time with their hoses. Giggling voices heard within their courtyards as they got each other wet. Having water directly into their homes enabled the village to have flowers, which the Greeks are so fond of growing. Over time Bougainvilleas, Frangipani, Geraniums, Poinsettias, Oleanders and Lemon trees began to peek out above the walls of the villas. The village became a feast of colors against the background of their traditional white walls.

    Since those days, many have helped to establish a sustainable future for Lindos besides Mary and her husband. It would take years to establish a proper sanitation plant, and the stopping of plastic waste burning on the distant mountainside overlooking our bay. Until then, even the village waste pumped out into the St Nicholas bay. In addition, Keith, a marine biologist, helped to set up regulations preventing incoming boats from dropping their waste into the bay where we swam. All these changes began a new era of health and prosperity for Lindos and the sea.

    St. Nicholas bay is now restored to its original wonder of

Mediterranean Blue and Aqua colors. In 1960, its majestic mountain cliffs provided one of the locations for the movie *Guns of Navarone* in which starred such actors as Gregory Peck, David Niven, and Anthony Quinn. In fact, Anthony Quinn was so taken with the area that he bought land on Rhodes in an area still called Anthony Quinn Bay. Mary helped during the filming.

Mary is now called Auntie Mary. It is a name given to her by our children who adored her stories about Lindos and other lands far away. For our family she became the storyteller, the holder of the history and legends of the Greeks Myths. We loved sitting in the winter room by the fire while the wind blew outside listening as our imagination felt the Gods speaking to us. Jason and the Argonauts came alive each evening, bringing a deeper experience of Greek history and their culture. Those stories made Lindos our home.

'Contemplation Spirit of Peace'
Sculpture by Ginger Gilmour

CHAPTER 9

TODAY
SPIRIT OF PEACE

18 SEPTEMBER 2013

As I go deeper into my memories, my quest for Beauty and Love reveals itself before me. My journey has led me to discover what lies innate in my heart. What seems years ago, a dear friend said to me, "Ginger, try to find what you were before you met David." I was in my fifties then. Throughout the years, after David and I divorced, many have planted seeds of encouragement, inspiring my next step on my quest to discover "What I was truly born to BE." I spent hours studying the philosophy of other teachers in the *ART of LIVING* while sitting under the oak tree at Brockhurst. Little by little, I came to discover a deeper side of life, which had been calling me since a child. It still calls me to go deeper and deeper to touch the feet of God and be of service.

At present, I am sixty-four and I am still discovering new dimensions of *Who I AM*. My journey has awakened me to the realization that I was born with the *Soul of an Artist*. A purpose manifested to uplift the hearts of each of us through creating images and forms of Beauty. Images which seek to reveal the Spark of God Within each of us. The process still beckons me to go further. Humanity has so much more to live, so much more to give. We have not even touched our greatest potential.

Today, Dorothy Maver, President of the National Peace Academy, asked me to participate in a Global Webinar called the

"Spirit of Peace." It is to initiate the opening of the Global Peace Summit in Geneva. I was to be one of seven principal inlets from the major energetic centers around the globe. Its purpose was to establish a link around the world to awaken the Spirit of Peace. They were New York, Geneva, Tokyo, Darjeeling, London, Sydney & Africa. Its intention was to invoke the Spirit of Peace and the Spirit of Goodwill, which is increasing in the hearts of men more so than any other time in History.

Many people invited were ready to participate. Many had worked years within the UN or other organizations creating infrastructures for maintaining and supporting Peace. Such as Nancy Roof who now is the editor for the magazine *Kosmos*.[1] Steve Nation spoke from New York City. He shared a photo of the United Nations Assembly standing all in prayer, heads bowed. He brought to our attention a speech, President Franklin D. Roosevelt gave called the *Four Freedoms* in 1941, which I would like to share with you:

> "In the future days, which we seek to make secure, we look forward to a world founded upon four essential human freedoms.
>
> 1. The first is freedom of speech and expression—everywhere in the world.
>
> 2. The second is freedom of every person to worship God in his own way—everywhere in the world.
>
> 3. The third is freedom from want—which, translated into world terms, means economic understandings, which will secure to every nation a healthy peacetime life for its inhabitants—everywhere in the world.
>
> 4. The fourth is freedom from fear—which, translated into world terms, means a world-wide reduction of armaments to such a

point and in such a thorough fashion that no nation will be in a position to commit an act of physical aggression against any neighbor—anywhere in the world.

"That is not a vision of a distant millennium. It is a definite basis for a kind of world attainable in our own time and generation. That kind of world is the very antithesis of the so-called new order of tyranny which the dictators seek to create with the crash of a bomb." —Franklin D. Roosevelt, excerpted from the State of the Union Address to the Congress, January 6, 1941 [2]

For me, it still applies today, but with my understanding and experiences, this vision has widened. I realized that Peace based upon those freedoms alone is not enough. We are born with the divine spark of Love, of Beauty, and of Goodness, but we have forgotten. Some do not even know and are lost in the wilderness.

Last night after the "Spirit of Peace" Webinar, it became evident to me that Peace lives! That it is our right because it is in us. It is a gift from God. We just have to awaken it! During our conference, someone said, "There is nothing more powerful than when an idea's time has come to be." People, the time is here! Throughout the World, the desire for Peace begs for more Demonstrations. If we just open our eyes to see, if we just open our ears to hear, if we just open our hearts to feel and our minds to know that mankind is on the verge of a Breakthrough Not a Breakdown. Peace can be on Earth.

Last night a memory emerged of when in High School I went to the United Nations with my school debate club. I remembered the feeling of peace and unity as I gazed upon the Gold Emblem before me and the majesty of the room. I was inspired to be a member of a group who had a vision that felt strongly about these principles globally. It came to me that all the times I had rescued those lost animals; all the times I cheered at the Pink Floyd concerts and joined the chorus as the Wall tore down had a purpose. But really, it was a vision, a vision of a future full of Beauty and Peace. One, which would include all of mankind.

Avon Mattison, from Tokyo, has quoted a saying by Nicholas Roerich, *"Where there is Peace, there is Culture. Where there is Culture, there is Peace. Positive Creativity is the fundamental quality of the human spirit. Let us welcome all those who, surmounting personal difficulties,...propel their spirits to the task of Peace-building, thus ensuring a radiant future."*[3] This saying re-activated the *soul of the artist.* I went to bed looking forward to the next day when I took up my paint brush and painted the *Spirit of Peace.* It appeared as a waterfall of fine crystal sparks of lights bathing the earth and humanity with the pure white dove that overshadowed all above the Christ.

Nick Mason had encouraged me to seek out culture. But I had no understanding then of how important that is for us all. Now Culture has become my quest. My vision is becoming more and more aligned with the "Spirit of Peace" through the creating of artwork that reveals our Inner Beauty, our Divine Spark. But first before going to my studio, I needed to return to paper and pen. I wanted to capture the essence of last night before I had forgotten its message. I wanted to capture its moment for it is for us all and for our children's future. It is through Culture that we can stand upon the mountain top and be one with our Creator. I look forward to seeing you there!—Let the story continue...

'DOVE of PEACE'

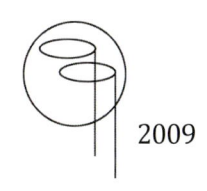

2009

Gini Tour
On to Marrakech

CHAPTER 10

THE ROSE CITY MARRAKECH
GINI PHOTO SHOOT

FRENCH TOUR 1974

A French soft drink company who produced a bitter lemon drink called Gini approached the Floyd to do some advertising for them. It was to be the first of its kind for the Floyd to allow the use of their image in a publicity campaign. It would prove to be an embarrassment later, but it seemed at the time a lucrative adventure. But hey, we would get to go to Morocco and be in the magical rose city of Marrakech. David and a few friends had gone before and spoke of it highly. The only bad memory was the food poisoning from something they had eaten.

Gini booked us into the famous La Mamounia Hotel, which previously had been a historical palace of the Rose City, and then converted into a luxurious hotel. As we entered the lobby of mosaics and carved plaster work, a man was walking away down one of the corridors. He had long hair and was wearing a Hawaiian Shirt. I commented to David that he looked a bit like Mick Jagger. David said whimsically, "That may be because it is Mick Jagger!" Being in the presence of all these rock legends was very new to me. I only ever saw them on telly, in a magazine or at a concert. And everything any of us, the normal public, knew about them was from the music papers and gossip. Here I was within their world. Mick was on holiday with his baby Jade and his nanny. Bianca had just left. Later, we were to meet up with him for dinner and a night out.

Our rooms led out to a private balcony overlooking the gardens and decorated in the Moroccan tradition. The sound of water filled the air from all the fountains. David and I fell in love with the intricacy of the mosaic work, which was on not only the floor, but also half way up the walls. From that point, there were white carved plaster panels to the ceiling and above. We came away thinking perhaps one day we might want to bring one of their craftsmen home to do this in our home. A great idea, but it never materialized.

We had the afternoon to explore amongst all the alleyways and bazaars. Everywhere was lined with tradesmen who tried to lure us to buy their carpets or wares. It was a bustle of tourists and a mixture of many cultures, Arabian, African and European. One could only enter its mystery by walking deeper and deeper amongst the pink-terracotta walls. Each corner spoke of its history reminiscent of a bygone era nestled at the base of the Atlas Mountains. Didn't I tell you I had become a Culture Buff?

By the time we had returned to the hotel there was word that Mick Jagger wanted to be our tour guide and would take us to a very exotic but hidden restaurant in the center of Marrakech. It was his favorite and not many would find it without help. He had a car and a driver. We all took taxis there. There was a copper triple tiered water fountain at the entrance. The sound of water seems to be part of the culture of Morocco. Perhaps, a symbol representing its precious value and importance to life while in the desert. Every drop as it cascades down to the bottom pool refreshes to then return and start again. The circle of life in its presence sings its song.

As we entered the main dining room, the décor was the same as the Mamounia with mosaics and carved plasterwork. We sat upon long seats covered with traditional Moroccan fabric. Hot and cold salads began our meal. Lamb and chicken dishes then arrived in earthenware dishes with pointed tops. Then followed the traditional Tagines of various kinds served with Couscous, which is a Moroccan delicacy. Mint tea followed that cooled and supported our digestion. It was the first time I ever had Moroccan food and I must say it was delicious.

After dinner, Mick suggested that we should go to one of his favorite discotheques. He said that David and I should come with him in his car and arranged another taxi for the rest of our party. He suggested that they should follow. Well, his driver drove like he was in Milan and the other car could not keep up. Their taxi disappeared as we drove through the ancient streets. I often wondered if that was intentional and Mick just wanted us.

Once we entered the club, Jagger danced most of the evening in the center of the crowd, pawed repeatedly. We watched from our table in the corner. He with raised arms swirled with the music. The rhythmic beat carrying all to a fervor upon their heightened adulation. It was like a scene out of *Suddenly Last Summer* where Katherine Hepburn's son was walking up the white streets into the sun with all these men admirers pawing him lustfully to his demise. The local fans devoured Mick and he loved it! When we returned to the hotel, some of the band was in the lobby. They wondered what had happened to us. David just shrugged his shoulders and did a David sheepish smile as we walked away holding hands returning to our room.

The next morning we had to drive out of the city and into the desert. For miles and miles, the vast colors of earth surrounded us. It was hot and dusty as we drove along the dirt roads further away from civilization. At one point we came upon a billboard in the middle of the nowhere saying Timbuktu 52 miles by camel. It was a T-junction in the sand. Our driver turned left. We were in convoy followed by the film crew. Finally, we reached our next hotel where we were to stay until the photo shoot was finished. I think it was for two-three days.

We had to get up early before the sun rose so we set our alarm on our watch. When it rang, David went to get out of bed and started to panic, "I can't see!" The room was darker than any room I had ever been in but I did remember that there was a box of matches and a candle on the desk. I felt my way across the room, found them and struck a match. Phew! David was not blind! It seems that the hotel turns off the electricity at night and being so far away from a city there was no ambient light.

We had breakfast and resumed our journey further into the desert. What was amazing to me was that even though we seemed alone in this vast desolate space in the middle of nowhere came walking three African boys? They were curious as to what was going on. I suppose they saw our dust trails and followed them.

One of the evenings, the promoters arranged a special dinner and a traditional Moroccan concert. We sat outside on pillows covered in traditional tapestries before low wooden tables. A feast awaited us. Terracotta plate after plate kept coming full of traditional delicacies. I was so worried that we might have to eat raw eyeballs from some local animal. I felt this way for earlier Steve had told me that it was a delicacy and if we turned it down, our host would take it as an insult. I am not sure whether Steve was winding me up, but fortunately, this did not happen.

The evening started to cool and a fresh gentle breeze came over from the desert. The night was silent and we could see the stars above. From behind the building, entered a long line of very tall men dressed in white robes. They were majestic as the Masai, with skin the color deep and rich like the earth. As the music played, they sang in high voices the songs of the desert. At the same time, their clapping alternated in a repetitive melodic rhythm as each bent over one by one like a wave upon the ocean. It was beautiful and hypnotic.

We all returned to the Mamounia for a couple days. The band left for the UK, but David and I decided to stay and go on an adventure around Morocco. Before we were to leave, I got the infamous tummy bug. Mick had invited David and me to spend time together in his suite. I rested on the bed in the dim light as the two of them played guitar on the terrace. Jade was asleep in the room next door while the afternoon sun went behind the palm trees.

The next day we rented a car and set off into the blazing sun towards Casablanca. As we walked through the market place, the city reminded me of another movie with Dirk Bogart and Ingrid Bergman, *Casablanca*. I find it interesting how movies have become our modern myths. They tell stories of far off places, we may never come to know, but we are there just the same. They return from our memories either in an image or as a fragrance.

With my blonde hair, hot pants, and platforms I don't know how I survived without being kidnapped. Angels were certainly protecting me in my naiveté and no sense of the differences of Arabian attitudes towards women. Stories of western women kidnapped in Arabian countries and sold to the highest bidder have surfaced. But I did not hear about that until after we got back to the UK. Since then I have a higher regard and respect for other cultures.

As we turned one of the corners, a man approached us from out of the dark shadows with a little bag of weed. David bought it. He trusted this as the way to get marijuana in that country because he has been there before. We returned to our hotel room where we tried to smoke it. It was a weed, but of the desert variety and not marijuana at all. David was irritated because he felt like a fool, but we had to let it go. All we got from it was a headache and bruised pride.

We drove on to Rabat, which was further up the coast. All the ancient towns in Morocco had what they called a *Medina*, which was a very large wall of the pink terracotta earthen bricks like Marrakech. They surrounded the town and were protection from marauders of the past centuries. They served the same purpose similar to the castles in Europe, but without the drawbridges. They were sanctuaries for the villagers and livestock.

David had visited Rabat before, and befriended some of the villagers. The city specialized in making round wooden in-laid tables and other objects made of wood. As we walked further down the streets, the smell of pine and lemonwood grew stronger and filled the air. Boys were carving table legs with lathes between their feet sitting on the earth in their doorways.

We meandered for some time through the little streets and alleyways. Sounds of children, called by their mothers mixed between other sounds of the city drifted between the walls. It was like a maze and I was not sure if we were going back on ourselves. They all looked the same. Finally, David found the house where he had bought a traditional round in-laid coffee table on his last trip. It has survived many moves from house to house, and is still with us.

I forget his name but he was overjoyed to see David again. He took us upstairs to his front room above his workshop. There was a very large colorful painting of Jimi Hendrix on one of the walls straight out of the sixties *Purple Haze*. He motioned for us to sit down on the cushions on the floor. Other men came to join us. His wife brought us mint tea in a silver pot and little glasses.

One of the men lit a pipe, which overflowed with hashish. They passed it to one another and passed it over me to David. The partner of the woman must be the one who passes the pipe to his woman; it was the custom. Therefore, he did. The hashish was very clean and strong. The high had us laughing all day. Everything seemed to be wondrous and psychedelic. Every color, every taste, every smell was more intense in its reality than before.

Rabat was a fishing port where large and small boats came and sold their fish. On the port where they docked, were little metal bucket fires with grates and fisherman cooking the fresh sardines sold to all who came by for lunch. They were sprinkled with sea salt and served with a hunk of fresh bread. I loved it! I had not been a big fish eater in the States and realized that most of the fish wasn't as fresh as these sardines. There is such a difference. First, they do not smell of fish but of the sea. Second, eating as soon as they have come fresh off the boat is beyond description.

***

The closest I ever got to eating fresh fish was when I was a child. My cousins and I, Tommy and Sharon would go crabbing with my family where the Mystic River met the ocean. Blue crabs hid amongst the seaweed just on the edge. Their blue claws always held my attention as I caught them in my net. I still feel the cool clear water between my toes as I walked through the moving green seaweed.

My mother, my sister, Donna and Aunt Dot along with my little brother, Stephen, would spend the morning walking along the sand just as the waves retreated. They were looking for little holes that would appear and then start digging for steamer clams who had given away where they were hiding. It was a delight for the younger children. Something easy for them to do. Homeward bound, our buckets of treasures dumped on to the lawn, washed of sand with the hose and cooked. It was always a special family occasion, especially for us kids.

Sadly, I could not eat any of it without getting sick. Catching the crabs and seeing the blue of their claws was my pleasure. That color to this day is my favorite when placed amongst the green of the seaweed on my canvases. Another pleasure I got was because I did it for my Mom. I loved watching the smile of her delight upon her face as she ate them.

***

Therefore, when I was able to eat sardines in Rabat and not get sick was a revelation. Where previously I thought I was allergic to fish, I was no longer. I was happy for it could have been disastrous, but it wasn't.

The French tour was in 1974 and the photographic session was in 1972. Two years after the Gini shoot, the Floyd did five gigs in France, which turned out to be diabolical. They had forgotten that in their contract with the French company it entitled them to advertise and sell the drink at each gig. The idea of what the promotion would be from the ad agency was beyond what fit within the image of the Floyd. Needless to say, it did not sit easily with their fans either.

They coveted the image of the Floyd as being an underground group. Consequently, Steve O'Rourke, their manager worked at bridging the growing gap between the band and Gini. Thus, the oversight did not go over well with the Floyd. So many times, I felt sorry for him being the punching bag, the go-between. But that was to be only the beginning. The party was just beginning.

At each gig, a circus of trendy groovy people sporting leather jackets and dark glasses carrying Gini bitter lemon signs bombarded the show. There were painted vans, banners and Easy Rider Bikers. The road crews were thrilled for there was a collection of Page Three Models baring their breasts who kept them company in the evenings. Steve O'Rourke was constantly negotiating how to keep them away or at least at a safe distance. Besides a distraught Floyd, the fans were also very bothered by the whole bravado. This was not their Pink Floyd.

This was my first time on tour in France with David and I was extremely happy to have a few American women singing with the band. It was the Blackberries comprsing of Venetta Fields and Carlena Williams. I used to hang out with them and we always had a giggle. It was great to hear their American accents and share in our common sense of humor. Venetta was always telling the band to calm down. "You white boys!" she commented as she stepped out of the dressing room with a laugh. This was nothing compared to Ike and Tina's tour they often told me.

One morning I woke early needing to know the time. David was still asleep so I braved the call to the receptionist, "Tout a l'heure s'il vous plait?" I said confidently. She did not respond, so I tried it again, but louder, "Tout a l'heurer s'il vous plait?" David peeked out from under the blankets and said try, "Quelle heure, s'il vous plait?" It worked! David said that I was asking to meet her later. *Oh Well*, Happy tales that keep me smiling.

Later I went to meet the girls in their room and told them the story. We had a good old giggle. Sadly, it did not stay in the room. That night when the show finished and everyone was waving good night and saying Thank You, the girls said, "Tout a l'heurer s'il vous plait." Thank God, it was our joke. We hugged after. Them wearing a snicker because of their girlie prank, I will always remember their laughter. Naughty but nice.

One day the local press was photographing the Blackberries outside of the hotel. I was standing inside at the door in blue jean hot pants and angel blouse with my platforms. I did not notice that he had taken a photograph of me until the next morning. All the wives were traveling with their respective husbands. We were booked on a rather small plane, as I recall either Nick or Rick was a bit nervous about flying in it. We were in our seats buckling up when the stewardess was handing out the morning newspaper. "Bonjour Monsieur et Madame," And there on the front page was a photo of my long legs and blonde hair with the headline something like, Mrs. David Gilmour, guitarist of Pink Floyd, etc. etc. etc. I turned a few shades of pink, as David and I were not married yet.

So we went from gig after gig with our Gini entourage, the Floyd embarrassed and feeling guilty for they thought they had taken easy money. They decided to give what they had earned away to charity. Was this easy absolution? No idea. For the fans, some of the glitter wore off around their idols, which I don't think was so bad. It was a reality check for them all, including the Floyd. I know the band looked at it deeply. Are we creating or being inspired by music that transcends or is it the glamour of being a star or an audience taken by idol worship. Who knows. Good stuff really. The affair served to challenge everyone to question what is it all about?

'ROSE in the DESERT'

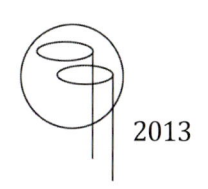

2013

A Man
with a child in his arms

CHAPTER 11

KATE BUSH
MAN WITH THE CHILD IN HIS EYES

1973-1975

Living with a musician and loving a musician was such an adventure. Creativity surrounded me on many levels, which encouraged my own artistic development. I was a witness to David's music as it was given birth plus his support for other musicians. Music was all around me some days twenty-four seven. It wasn't just listening to a record or the radio. It was in the air I breathed. My dreams were escalating from the dreams of a young girl to the life of a woman. It no longer was I existing, yearning for love and creativity. It was my life. I started to create sculptures. They were tiny at first. Little pink resin roses for Christmas presents. Watercolors and clay forms fired in Judy Waters' kiln in London.

Between touring and working with Roland Petite, David had converted one of the out-buildings into his studio. This enabled him to do more work, as he no longer was inside the house with less equipment. The band was having some time off and both Nick Mason and David were open to taking on various projects. One day David met up with Rick Hopper and brought home a cassette of songs from a young singer-songwriter, Kate Bush. She was just fifteen and still in school. Her music inspired him to do a demo initially recorded at Woodley in his new studio. He was helping Unicorn to get kick started and enlisted two of the musicians to help. David had such heart and a drive to not only develop his career, but also to use his talent for others.

Kate would arrive, still in her school uniform, and they would record her songs. She and I grew to be great friends. Woodley had a little fish pond in the front garden with a large Willow tree where often we would sit and chat. I felt like her big sister. As time passed, the little schoolgirl grew into a woman. Some still say that the "Man with the Child in his eyes" carried love for David. He helped her so greatly. I was not surprised that her admiration and gratefulness would hold an element of Love. He seemed to take her under his wing as an Uncle would do insuring her safety. We all did.

Just before we were to marry as I reflect upon our life events, David helped Kate further. While the Floyd were recording *Wish You Were Here* in 1975 he presented a more finished demo of Kate's to Bob Mercer, managing director of EMI, who then signed her to EMI Records. Her passion and talent was born and time passed as we watched it create a star.

It was to be many years later that Kate and I were to meet again, but under different circumstances. In the early 90s I was working with Lily Cornford in a healing clinic. Lily was like everyone's ideal fairy godmother with a heart of gold. After one of our sessions, I walked into the waiting room and there was Kate. It was like our lives had come full circle. I had no idea that they were good friends, though, fairy godmothers do get around. Kate wrote a song for her that is featured on her album *Red Shoes*. Each day we could hear it drifting from Lily's private room upstairs as she had her cup of tea and cucumber sandwiches. A haunting voice of Tragedy and Love.

'BREATH'

1998

Ginger at Knebworth
July 5 1976
"Just met a girl"

CHAPTER 12

KNEBWORTH CONCERT
I'VE JUST MET A GIRL

5 JULY 1975

It was a sunny afternoon. We all sat on blankets on the grass back stage listening to the music as each band played. Stevie Miller, Captain Beefheart, Roy Harper, Linda Lewis, Monty Python. The Floyd were to play in the evening. They had just flown back from the second half of their *Dark Side of the Moon* tour in the States so there was a bit to organize for the jet-lagged roadies.

Backstage was very civilized with Marquees and caravans. The English weather did accommodate and helped the ambience of the day. As the music held us in the palm of its hand, the umbrellas stayed closed. Some brought picnics, others ate at the concession stands. The sunshine was bliss and its warmth relaxed our bodies, we were grateful there was no rain. We laid on blankets on the lawn enjoying the moment together.

At one moment when David had gone to the gents, Terry Doran presented me with a photo he had taken of me standing in a bluebell forest. It had a tiny orange sticker on the lower right hand side, which had written in pen *"I've just met a girl."* In Terry's Liverpudlian accent he said, "George, wanted me to give this to you. He would like to take you out." Goodness, I thought to myself. Here it was a dream coming to me from afar within my secret dreams when I was a teenager in Connecticut. I so fancied George more than John, Paul or Ringo. I created so many ideas of how to reach him, as I am sure many thousands did during Beatlemania. Their life must have been crazy!

I took the photo from him with gratitude while staring into my dream world. I looked up and said, *"Terry, please tell George Thank You, but I am so in love with David."* Having said that I continued, *"George has no idea what this means to me. I hope one day we shall meet and be friends."* An inner smile filled my heart with pink and placed an extra sparkle in my eyes that day. Two dreams had come true. David and I were to be married in a few days was the first. The other was a dream, a memory kept tenderly in my heart. In fact, George and subsequently Olivia did become friends and neighbors many years later.

Finally, the moment arrived when the circular screen was up and the sound system was ready. The audience deserved a merit badge for patience. It took ages to set all the gear up. It wasn't as straightforward because the equipment was wounded after an explosion of fireworks at the last American gig. They had no idea if it would be ok. Plus, all the other bands were using their PA and it was knackered along with their inspiration especially when Rick's Hammond died.

The road crew were still struggling when the scheduled fly pass of two Second World War Spitfires buzzed the unsuspecting audience and the band. They were a bit unprepared and rushed in to starting. Timing was out but it still served to stun the audience into quiet attention as it always did. Unfortunately, the performance was not up to their normal standard. It dragged probably because of their jet-lag, equipment failure and Roger sang out of tune. The fans were sad. The press was relentless.

The UK press knocked them again as they always seemed to do over the years. They complained that they let down their country for appearing infrequently. They were getting boring as they played the same songs again. However, despite the press, the

KNEBWORTH CONCERT

American tour sold out to the surprise of many and so did this one. It was a mystery to them that this underground group was selling out faster than the Stones.

At Knebworth, a sea of heads again sat before us. Many more than allowed for by the promoter's license. The perimeter fences came down to care for the large numbers, over 100,000 turned out instead of the 40,000 expected. Their profile had expanded since "Money" and forced them out of need to do larger venues. On top of which they and the management needed the money. Large concerts were more lucrative and they had the Norton Warburg affair looming to resolve.

There was a growing feeling of agitation after the American tour. The growing numbers and the noise from their American fans' jubilation was changing the intimacy of what went before. It was becoming more a Rave party and not a concert whose intention was to take you on a journey. No longer could the subtleties of "Echoes" be heard. The cheering drowned the spaces between the notes. The alienation and the questioning of why are we doing this began to enter their conscious minds especially Roger's. The screaming could be deafening. The frustration of the waste of it all was loud in our hearts. Where had the Beauty gone? No longer to be heard.

Roger is quoted as saying, *"I cast myself back into how F***ing dreadful I felt on the last American tour with all those thousands and thousands and thousands of drunken kids smashing each other to pieces. I felt dreadful because it had nothing to do with us. I didn't think there was any contact between us and them."*[1] In a peculiar way, this experience would later inspire the albums *Animals* and *The Wall*. However, for now, the return to an English audience was refreshing except that the gig did not turn out quite what they had wished to share.

Day we got married
7 July 1975

CHAPTER 13

GONNA GET MARRIED

7 JULY 1975

As soon as we returned, it was back to the studio. The USA tour and Knebworth were behind us. Our life began to melt together in a more established home life mixed with the Floyd's growing fame as time passed. When I had said "Yes," to come to live with David, I had no idea that "Yes" really had to do with something else. It had to do with saying "Yes" to something growing inside of me that would take many years to awaken, i.e., my own innate calling to be an artist.

I was instinctively inspired by the creative power of the band, especially David's guitar playing and his voice. Most of all our love triggered an internal desire to create a child. So many times, I whispered softly in his ear that when he was ready I was ready to make a baby. I could not have dreamt of doing anything else but that at the time. My body screamed to have our child.

But it seemed that we were drifting apart. A fear crept into my being. The fire was dimming a bit. It worried me. Living with a musician in a band was new to me. One day he was there. The next he was on tour or recording. I was not always aware of the tensions growing in the band. Moreover, just how much of that tension subtly influenced our relationship. David held most of these matters to himself.

It is only now reading some of the stories that I realize more of what went on behind the scenes of our life. But the instinctive impulse to bear a child from our love remained the same, as something seemed to grow quiet between us. Or was it just the process of time, merging the hearts of two individuals and the blending of two cultures? I loved him that was for sure. Does one ever know about the cycles of Love for the first time? We were young learning about life.

During their second leg of the American tour in 1974, I stayed behind. David asked if I would drive him to the airport. I said that I would, but that it most probably would be the last time. Getting to Heathrow from Essex around the North Circular can be painful when your heart is aching. I really missed him when he went off without me. We hugged goodbye and I went home. A week later, I decided to go to Lindos with two girlfriends, Cyndy Shirley, Jerry Shirley's wife, drummer of Humble Pie, and her girlfriend, Sharon, who had just come over from the States. We would stay in Melissa's house with another one of their friends Tony, a roadie for Humble Pie, who would join us.

I was sick with Bronchitis most of the time and observed the girls from my window in the sala in their tight silk Chinese dresses and high-heels dancing in the courtyard. Ghetto-blaster blaring, a bit drunk with a few Greek soldiers, they were. The courtyards in Lindos are made of pebbles upright called *Kuklaki*. I could not figure out how they could dance without catching their heels between the stones. Maybe they floated? Anyway, they did, that is, dance in high heels without injury.

The Greek Soldiers coming into the house was a concern to me because this was something not advised by Melissa or the Villagers. I didn't have the strength to deal with it, especially as I didn't want to throw cold water on their fun. They had no idea of the social customs of the village. Nor were they aware of the fragile inter-relationship we had as foreigners. During my time getting better, I drifted in and out of thoughts and feelings about maybe leaving David. So when I got home this was very much on my mind. What had started out as a *dream come true* was now changing. It seemed. A broken heart loomed in the corner.

David called from the States and asked if I would pick him up the next day. I reminded him of my last statement about doing that. He said, "Please." And I did. I waited at the arrival point for him to come out full of alternating emotions. I was excited but nervous. Happy yet Hurt. Most of the band were first. They smiled as they passed by, anxious to get home, disappearing in the crowd.

When David appeared, he walked straight up to me gently pushing me up against the nearby wall in a passionate embrace. With the return of his passion, I was stunned. Apparently, rumor has it he had had a fair amount to drink on the plane and had flirted with one of the royals. But here it was an embrace so big that it opened my heart once again. He was good at sending Love just whenever I was having a turn away. His timing was always perfect. And it worked for many years. It certainly worked that day.

Warwick McCreddie had become their personal road manager for the tours. As he was a dear friend and neighbor, we gave him a lift home. He drove and stopped for petrol on the North Circular. When Warwick went in to pay, David asked me to marry him. I could not believe my ears. The day was warm and sunny so we laid in the garden sharing stories. We were so happy to be together, close, at home when again he asked me to marry him. I hadn't responded earlier with Warwick returning to the car. Truely, I was a bit in shock. I couldn't believe it. Did David actually propose? I questioned myself years later why I had said, "Yes," for my heart had been so let down. But there I was nestled in his arms and I said, "Yes." I really wanted the dream to be real and continue, and it did. Another cycle began for us.

The Floyd were recording *Wish You were Here* at Abbey Road

Studios, in the afternoon, so David arranged the paperwork needed to get married in the UK in the morning. The Floyd had a gig at Knebworth on the 5 July, so our wedding plans were for the 7 July 1975. Willie Wilson, Ricki and Linnie Wills were staying over for that weekend because of the gig. Both had been in one of David's first bands in Cambridge, Jokers Wild. Willie was doing the washing up, while Rick and Linnie were loading baby gear in their car for the return to London.

David approached Willie and Rick in the kitchen to ask if they could stay another day because we were getting married in the morning. Both went into a bit of shock to the surprise. Willie said, "OMG then I will be the last one not married!" Rick went into the living room, meeting Linnie coming down the stairs and said to her that they had to stay. She asked, "Why?" He said, "David and Ginger are getting married tomorrow." Her face lit up with a smile and said, "Of course."

David had previously scheduled a game of Squash with Jerry Shirley, drummer for Humble Pie. He called him in the morning to ask if he and Cyndy could meet us earlier. Just when Jerry was about to say that it might be a problem, David told him that we were going to get married in the Epping Registry Office. Well, he and Cyndy drove like the wind to get there. We waited in the long room lined with chairs against the wall for the moment to begin.

I wore a simple white cotton summer dress and espadrilles and David wore his trusty blue jeans and "Welcome to the Machine" black T-shirt. There was a rectangular wooden table in the middle with a little red velvet cushion on the top. Finally, the registrar who was to perform the wedding walked in wearing a tan colored suit with a sky blue shirt and matching tie. He looked at us with anticipation. Everyone was quiet, sitting against the wall in a row except for David and I who had walked up to the table. Time stood still waiting for the ceremony to begin.

While clearing his throat, the registrar leaned over towards David and said, "Excuse me, Sir, the ring?" We both looked at each other with a look of...OH NO. I had waited all my life for this moment and we had forgotten to get a ring! Linnie came up to us from behind and offered for us to use a ring she had gotten from a box of Crackerjacks. An American sweet popcorn, which always had a surprise gift inside and she had just happened to eat on the way. God was on our side, even if we didn't realize it. David eventually had a ring designed in white gold with two interlocking hearts by a friend who was a designer of jewelry.

The registrar did turn a few shades of red at the thought but proceeded. When the words, *"You may put the ring on her finger"* was said, neither of us knew which finger or which hand David should put it on. Once my embarrassment settled, I remembered that it was the fourth finger but not which hand. Boy, were we well rehearsed. I had both fourth fingers up. We both teetered between them as we tried to get it right and hold our pride intack. Linnie said in a low whisper trying to say it just low enough for us to hear, "The right one, the right one." David looked relieved and chose the right. Phew, at last we heard the words, *"You may kiss the bride."* We all went on to celebrate at our local pub with a giggle and good cheer. What a tale, it has made a sweet story ever since and brought smiles to my kids' faces many years later.

David had to go to Abbey Road to continue recording *Wish You Were Here*. I went with him so that we could share the day together. The band had no idea until we walked in. There always seem to be stories within stories in our life. You will see why as you read further. Just to add to the day's event, when we arrived, Roger walked up to David pulling him aside and whispered to him, "Look who is sitting on the sofa." They both went slowly over to the place Roger was referring, Nick and Rick following discreetly.

There is a huge sofa in front of the mixing desk in that EMI recording room. I don't think any of them were completely certain who was sitting there until David confirmed it. David looked and his face clouded over with the reality of what he saw. Under his breath, he said, "It's Sid." The atmosphere in the room went silent as they digested the moment. Roger, especially, who is quoted to have had many mixed emotions for the past came flooding back.

There was Sid pear shape, hairless and overweight. They stood silently in disbelief. Old memories rushed into their hearts. What happened? His timing was uncanny! Their lost love and the tragedy of Sid inspired the creation of "Shine On". And there they were in the middle of recording it when Sid appeared weather worn and without hair. They stumbled to have a conversation, inviting him to listen to a track. Sid just sat there lost, on the sofa, wondering why? What a day to ponder. What a day to Remember.

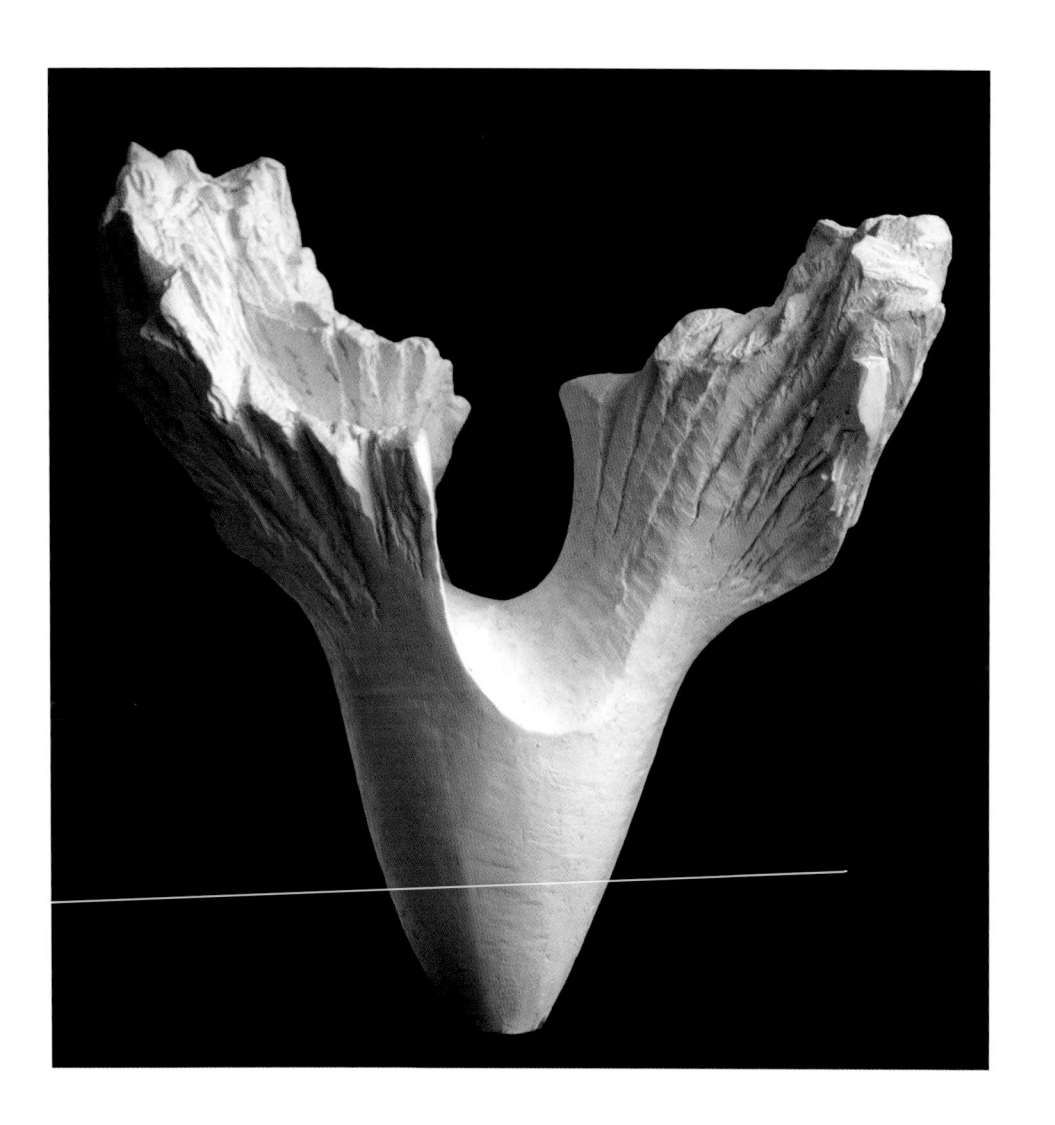

'WINGS of JOY'

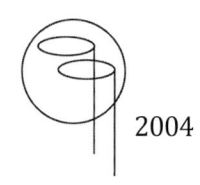

2004

Paradise & Papaya
Young Island, Caribbean

CHAPTER 14

PARADISE ON YOUNG ISLAND

1976

The band was building and designing Britannia Row, which would be their own private studio where they could work in seclusion. Therefore, David and I decided to go away to St. Vincent in the West Indies. I was six months pregnant and still ok to fly. We were to stay on a private island near St Vincent called Young Island. All the rooms were little self-contained huts. Our showers were out doors in a private garden similar to Lindos, Rhodos, and Greece. We ate in the open restaurant amongst the sweet songbirds and the fragrance of the flowers.

    I had my first papaya with fresh lime juice and a pineapple-coconut smoothie each morning for breakfast. The westward winds kept us cool as we baked in the sun. Steel bands played in the night from across the waterway, which separated us from the main island. We could hear voices singing their country anthem, *St Vincent, Land so Beautiful*, drifting across the gentle winds, along with the melodies of Reggae.

    Often we would go across to the mainland in a little covered motor boat provided for people who stayed at Young Island. We took a local taxi and went on adventures into their forests to various gardens and sites. The island of Saint Vincent is volcanic and includes little level ground. The windward side of the island is very rocky and steep, while the leeward side has more sandy beaches. In 1902–1903, devastating volcanic eruptions from Soufriere of St Vincent hindered their agricultural abundance, and over time, the volcanic lava formed black sand. Our first trip was to the black sand beach.

The road wound up and down through the forest, abundant with Banana trees and their phallic purple seed-pods extending down over the road. They reminded me of the 1962 movie *Day of the Triffids,* which scared the lights out of me as a teenager. David and I always seemed to be comfortable in sharing our adventures in silence. We spoke when necessary, allowing us to savor the moments of every experience. This was not out of conscious intent. It seemed to be where our natures met in unison.

After a long drive, we came around a corner where before us, lay the volcanic black sand beach sparkling in the sunlight. We walked barefoot among its crystalline form. I played with it between my toes and fingers watching the sunlight twinkle in my hands. It was hotter than normal sand. The black color absorbed the heat so we could not stay barefoot for long. Its unique beauty remains in my memories like black crystal.

As we both loved to snorkel and be one with the water, we decided to purchase the needed gear to do so. Just beneath the twinkling satin surface of the Caribbean water is a world of wonder. Schools of fish of a thousand different shapes and colors lie below its surface. One would never know unless you entered. The rays of sunlight that filtered into this underground world played upon all the colors as we swam amongst the fish and the coral. Little puffer-fish with their puckered-lips would come up to us hovering seemingly wondering who we were. Gentle beings who, when frightened, blow up to double their size. We swam so as not to disturb. Angelfish and seahorses carried by the current would pass by amongst the splendor.

Growing up I always had a tropical aquarium. To see these fish in large numbers and swim with them was special. Everywhere I swam there would be another familiar fish. I especially loved to see the Lionfish fluttering in between the coral; their wing like fins moving like fluid chiffon. The most beautiful for me, for it is my favorite color, was to see schools of Blue Tangs feeding on the plant life.

Lots of them moving together, not just one in an aquarium that I had in the past. I was in a state of bliss as I saw groups of Blue Tangs moving slowly over the reef snacking on bits of algae. Apparently, this helps keep the reef clean and healthy. In case you are not aware of what they look like, go see the Disney movie *Finding Nemo*. A Blue Tang was *Dory* who has become a star amongst children and divers.

We were lost in this wonderland for hours when it was time for us to return. We had stayed around the water between Young Island and the mainland thinking it was safe. We didn't notice that the current was getting stronger as the afternoon tide was changing. We were strong swimmers with our flippers but on this occasion, I wasn't. I was pregnant and the flow was too strong for me to make it back. I was losing strength and about to pass out when the fear gripped me, imagining myself, swept out to sea. Terrified, I shouted to David for help. I do not know to this day, where he got his strength. He held on to me and we swam and swam against the tide as the waves splashed in our faces. We were exhausted by the time we returned but alive. Our baby was safe!

One day we visited the *oldest* Botanical Garden in the Western hemisphere; The Botanical Garden of St. Vincent founded in 1765. It originated by transplanting a variety of flora and trees from around the World, primarily from the Caribbean. In the early days, the gardens planted many Mango trees, Cinnamon and Nutmeg trees. I was captivated to finally see a breadfruit tree and hear about its historical story.

The establishment of breadfruit on St Vincent was actually delivered by Captain William Bligh, formerly of the HMS Bounty, which was a ship designed for botanical missions.[1] Marlon Brando appeared in my mind as we looked at the trees. *Mutiny on the Bounty* came alive, though it took place in Tahiti. Obviously, Bligh initially came to St Vincent. Amazing how we think in terms of movies these days. I seem to be repeating myself with that realization. Dr. Bronowski once said, *"Documentary movies are becoming our new Myths."* I think he was right.

I had no idea how Cinnamon grew or how it was harvested. I loved it in apple pie and in my morning porridge. The tour guide explained the process. Cinnamon is an evergreen shrub or small tree with dark, leathery, aromatic leaves. In cultivation, young trees are cut back twice a year and sucker shoots grow from the roots. They are laid out in the sun after the bark is removed. The shoots naturally curl as they dry to form the coils that sell in the shops. The flavor of cinnamon freshly harvested is wonderful to chew and I am told builds the immune system and is a natural antibiotic.

I was fascinated, as well, with the Nutmeg seed. Similar to a chestnut, it was shiny and was wonderful to touch and cracking the shell revealed a reddish lacy covering. The trees were tall, most were over twenty years old and the first harvest is normally between seven and nine years of age. This is the only tropical fruit, which bears two different spices, nutmeg and mace, which have similar sensory qualities. Nutmeg has a slightly sweeter flavor and mace a more delicate one. I never knew that they were from the same seed. I have used both in my cooking. To know more about these spices empowered my food as I grated my nutmeg onto my yoghurt. I see the tree. I feel the seed. I feel the sun.

The Gardens shared paths of over 150 different Hibiscus flowering shrubs. Some opened in evening while others closed as the day became the night. I had to include these in our garden back in the UK; sadly, most had difficulty in our damp climate. As we walked amongst the different colors of the Gardens, between the Hibiscus and Bougainvillea Swallowtail butterflies would set flight. Walking in Paradise was wonderful; my imagination loved it.

St Vincent also has over 1500 types of butterflies and moths, hiding in their habitat. All I knew was that the sky filled at times with many different varieties; most were unfamiliar to me. Each day my heart filled with Beauty, with nature expressing itself around every corner. I felt my baby moving gently and stroked my tummy with Love. I experienced calmness within, inspired by all this beauty, together with the Love of the man who helped in its creation.

During our time on Young Island, we met an elder couple who had rented a sailboat and planned to go for a sail to one of the closer islands. I believe it was St Lucia but I am not certain. They exuded the American Friendly Attitude that I was familiar with and I found them easy to talk to while we were there. One day they invited us to come along. The water was a little choppy and the movement was not good for me being pregnant, I got seasick. David advised me to sit on deck and focus upon the horizon to keep from vomiting and it was a challenge.

Eventually, "Thank God," we got to calmer waters so I could enjoy our sail. The sound of the water as we passed through the waves always soothed my body and spirit; both of us loved sailing. They told us that we were heading for a bay where many retired hippies had set up home in houseboats. We entered a time warp for it looked a lot like Sausalito, California in days gone by with hippy decorated converted houseboats. It was a very surreal sight to come upon in the Caribbean. They also told us a story about a woman who lived up on the hill hidden amongst the vegetation who raised peacocks, lots of peacocks, she had become one of the myths of the Caribbean.

Our time at Young Island was ending and it was time to fly home for the Floyd was about to start recording again. Britannia Row should be ready, leaving behind the times of recording at Abbey Rd. The blue skies and colors of the islands faded into the horizon as our plane flew into the clouds above. I loved being pregnant and flying seemed easy. I slept as David watched some of the movies during our journey home. From time to time, turning and holding his hand.

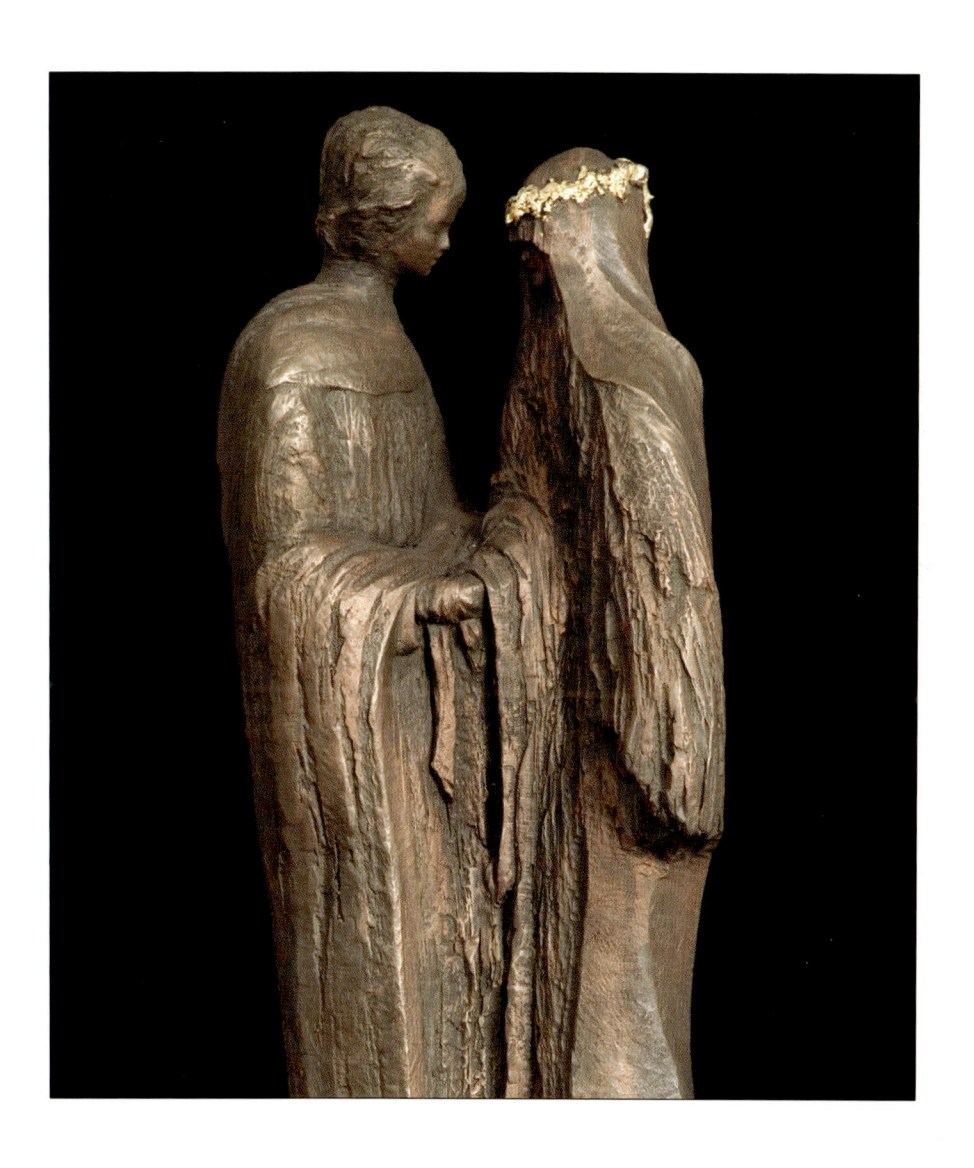

'SACRED VOW'

2003

David asleep with baby Alice
May 1976

CHAPTER 15

BABY ALICE IS BORN

MAY 1976

In the beginning before our trip to Young Island, it came to pass one summer when one of my deepest wishes was to come true. Earlier I shared moments with you of me held in David's arms. Moments when I whispered to him, *"David, when you are ready I would love to have your children."* I had such a calling for our love to bring a wonderful soul into being. My body ached with the desire. We were in Lindos for the summer staying in one of the knight's houses of old. We returned there for many summers as its majestic beauty went deeper into our being.

This summer was our second return to Lindos and became part of many Greek adventures. Melissa was giving a party that evening and we all had to wear white. During the daytime, we went out on Carla's boat until the sunset. The water was crystal with golden reflections of the setting sun. I loved those moments. I would always sit at the front of the boat feeling the brightness of the gold upon my face.

Ossie Clark was staying with Melissa and was giving everyone LSD. We decided to join in. I remember sitting on the wall overlooking the bay. The moon sparkled on the water creating new patterns with the ripples. Melissa had placed many mattresses for us to lie on in the courtyard. There was a grapevine across part of it that dripped light green shapes onto me as I gazed into the starlit sky above. Being a person with an artistic imagination, I always had acid trips that were visual. They were always full of Beauty. Only the best I would see.

The evening flowed by to the sound of "One of these Nights," by the Eagles, playing from the Sala when a panicked Charles Littledale came running in to the party of guests. Desperate, searching for someone to help, his eyes were wide open as though he had seen a monster. He ran over to us, his hands clutching his curls, finding it hard to catch his breath, stumbling over his words, *"I can't light the oven!"* He was tripping and had been down the road in Mary's number 16 in the kitchen since 6:00, trying to light the oven. He had promised to bring us a shepherd's pie and it was now around 11:00 at night. It was way after midnight when it finally showed up.

Many of us went down to the beach for a swim carrying long candles lighting the way. The water felt like silk as we dove beneath its folds. The music drifted on the night air as we laid upon the cushions telling stories and laughing. David and I strolled home hand in hand as the sun rose. The village was still asleep except for the song of the cockerel and the cats dashing behind the garbage bins. Random clinking of bottles could be heard in the distance as the deliverymen removed the crates from their vans.

The nights were so hot we were sleeping on mattresses in the courtyard. It was under the orange blossom our first child became a reality. During this pregnancy, in fact, all four, I felt so fulfilled. A warmth nurtured my heart as the feeling of our child grew inside.

Back home in England, David would make me Cod and Spinach Crespaline, which I craved a lot. Each day in the spring, I felt the flower's beauty when I walked in the garden and gathered the mulberries for making preserves. Thank goodness, while I was breast-feeding I had a daily craving for mulberries and custard with a *Mackeson* (stout beer rich in "B" vitamins). Note: *I did not drink during my pregnancies.*

One evening there was a documentary about Leboyer, a French doctor and his method of childbirth. It held my attention so much that I had to find out more. It was way before Google so it was a challenge to get more information. It certainly was not in my encyclopedias. In addition, the idea of giving birth in water was rather revolutionary. This led to finding a doctor who would allow us to do it in a hospital. English health care in those days insisted that for your first delivery you MUST have it in the hospital! So doing it at home was out.

Even having a thought of having my first baby at home was revolutionary for an average American girl from a working middle class family. Eventually, we did find a doctor at the West London Hospital, who was practicing the method. I regret that I have forgotten his name. He also told us about classes at the hospital called Lamaze. It is a form of breathing and relaxation for Labor. David and I went to the classes to prepare for the day that Alice would enter the world. We were partners all the way.

The Floyd were finishing the recording of the *Animals* album at Britannia Row, so I was home a lot in the evenings. Emo, a childhood friend of David's from Cambridge, was staying with us and was going through a rather unstable phase of his life. I had gone to bed early and could hear him crashing about downstairs. The telly was blaring and so was he, with rather vile swearing. His moods were unpredictable at the time. I was extremely worried so I called David and asked if he could come home, which he did. I was in my later part of my pregnancy and I was very sensitive. I did not feel strong enough to confront Emo and tell him to shut-up for fear of his reaction. I must add that Emo eventually found his Spiritual Master, Charan Singh, started to meditate and became the best friend one could ever have.

As it seems with most women, the day I was to go into labor, I took to washing all our sheets and blankets including our clothes. We had a washing line outside and I loved hanging my wash there. I loved the smell of the outdoors on our clothes and sheets. I had tons of energy, so I cleaned and washed the kitchen. We also went to the pub for dinner. I should have known *my baby was coming*, the classes advised us to look out for this behavior.

We had decided to let life give us the surprise of whether it would be a boy or a girl. David and I had a list of names that we both agreed would be our choice. Therefore, we waited on our decision when we felt the soul of our baby and knew its gender as we held it in our arms. Though soul was not a term we were using then, I am sure our hearts worked that way.

On The evening of 7 May 1976, I went to bed, leaving David watching telly downstairs with another friend, Willie Wilson, who was the drummer in David's first band Joker's Wild. Around 10:00 p.m. after my bath, I started to have weird sensations of energy rising and falling. They were not painful, but I decided to time them. They were coming quite regular and frequent, so I leaned my head out of our bedroom door and asked David to come upstairs. We decided that we should make a move.

David grabbed my suitcase and his little bag with all the helpful essentials, as he was to be my labor partner. We drove into the night towards London. The streetlights were blinding, as the energy was getting stronger. With each corner, I found it more difficult to do my breathing techniques; I twisted, I turned and whimpered. David held my hand gently as we drove through the street lit night. It seemed like we were in suspended animation.

As we entered the hospital and up the stairs, the experience became more intense, I felt like I was on LSD. I held my tummy as David guided me down the corridor. The lights were a surreal color of green. Women and their husbands were walking slowly down the corridors moaning. It was like a Fellini movie. Finally, we reached the area where I needed prepping.

The staff separated David and me, as they assured us that it wouldn't be for long. Two wonderful Philippino women met me in a room that seemed like an operating room. They asked if I had had a bowel moment, which I had. They started to shave me as I kept asking if they had called my doctor. I pleaded, "*Where is my husband?*" I told them that we were to have a "Leboyer" birth in water and my husband was to be by my side. "*Please,*" I cried, as thoughts of it all drifting away as the possibility entered my mind.

The women giggled. They did not see the importance. It was all happening so quickly I had thoughts that I may just have my baby there with them. The energy waves seemed painful but I was panicking. I was tense, as how we had intended the way our baby was to be born might not happen. Finally, the nurse took me to another room where David, thankfully was waiting. The sight of his long hair and loving attention calmed me down for a moment.

They laid me flat, which was not helpful. Gravity works against one in this position, so they lifted the back of the bed as I requested. I wish now I had known more about what helps labor to be easier, i.e., to be on all fours. David was setting out his things to help the contractions to ease. I remember he was betwixt doing that and holding my hand and trying to get someone to call our doctor.

The contractions were very strong and the pace increased. I kept asking for my doctor. David kept trying to get him and at the same time stay by my side. There were noises coming from everywhere as the staff came in and out with metal tools and bowls. The tensions grew, upon reflection; it was becoming evident that our idea of our baby being born in the water was disappearing. I had to adapt, I had to accept with grace what was to come.

The nurses kept asking, *"How are your pains dear."* This so is not the way to help someone to be relaxed and do Lamaze. It was obvious that they had no idea. David and I were adrift in the normal obstetrics' philosophy. I started to analyze the pains and was just about to give in to have an epidural when my doctor arrived and said, "*The baby is coming! Breathe! Push!*"

It was sunrise. The birds were silent. It felt like all the world had stopped to listen to our baby being born. A rush of the most orgasmic feeling ran through my being when someone said, "*It's a girl!*" We laughed with our tears of Joy. Silence captured the Beauty of that moment until she let out her first sound. David leaned over and stroked my face. Looking deep into my heart he said, "*Shall we call her Alice?*" I agreed. She was born on 8 May 1976, as the daylight filtered into the room. She was a sunrise baby full of Light.

A bed in the main ward awaited us, clear bassinets next to each mother. Most mothers were breast-feeding at the time, so I took Alice into my arms and to my breast. After she fed, David took her for a while tenderly in his arms. We were so happy. I thought my heart would burst from our Joy! He went home for a while to phone our parents while we slept.

England was having a hot spell and Alice came over with a rash. The nurses said that we had to stay longer to make sure all was well. Most of the women let their babies be taken away in the night and were given sleeping pills. *I refused*. I wanted to sleep with her next to me. The nurses said she was ill because I held her all the time. I said, *"Nonsense, it was the heat and the blankets!"* I continued and we eventually went home. Moreover, after getting home David and I had Alice sleeping between us for over six months.

During our pregnancy, I had read a book called the *Continuum Concept*, by Jean Liedloff. She was an American writer who had spent two and a half years deep in the South American jungle with Stone Age Indians. The experience demolished her Western preconceptions of how we should live. While reading it, I had the same reaction. This tribe related to each other and did not seem to have any of the psychoses that we have in our culture, and that inspired me. *They carried their babies until they could crawl.*

I bought one of those baby carriers, which enabled us to hold her against our chest hearing our heartbeat. When I wasn't carrying her, David did. The only time she was let down was when she was sleeping next to us. I sang her sounds of Love, and instinctive sounds of the heart. Later in life, I trained in healing harmonics, which are so similar. Sounds can so influence peace.

We had a dear friend and nurse, Rose Renwick, cooking and caring for us so that we could focus on bonding together as a family. She was a great cook! Rose was the wife of Tim Renwick, a fantastic guitarist, who has continued to work with David over the years. He too was from Cambridge and having Rose cook for us brought us even closer as friends. I will always be grateful for her care, because having one's first baby is such a learning curve, I didn't feel alone.

We were riding high on Bliss until one day Alice came down with gastroenteritis, she cried and cried. We had a door that connected our bedroom to the next. We walked around from one room to the hallway and back again, sharing, trying to calm her down. Suddenly, the safety net of being in a hospital was not there and Rose was gone. *The reality hit. What do we do*? This was our first experience of being responsible for a wee one.

She was so precious and our hearts were hurting. We were exhausted and seemed alone; however, we had to get through the night. We were so concerned about our precious child. Honestly, I must admit there was a moment as I was holding her in my arms, looking out into the night sky exhausted, forlorn and desperate for the screaming to stop, that I understood baby abusers. Though I never would have given in to that impulse, the insight was there.

The next morning, we took her bundled up in her blanket to the doctor, he said, *"She's dehydrated and getting gastroenteritis."* If it did not change, we would have to go back into the hospital. Life took a turn in that moment; the fear of losing our precious Alice seized our hearts. As it turned out the liquid antibiotics and extra saline water from the chemist saved us.

The experience tarnished the height of Joy we were having for me, but I cannot speak for David. I took a turn, depression set in coupled with exhaustion. During that time, I never thought I could have another child. They called it post-natal depression and it certainly was a shock. Fortunately, Alice and David were the love of my life and I made it through to find bliss again. Watching the beauty of their love grow was my medicine.

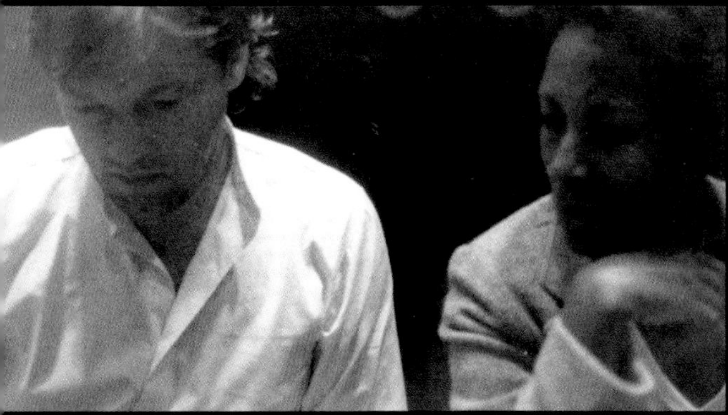

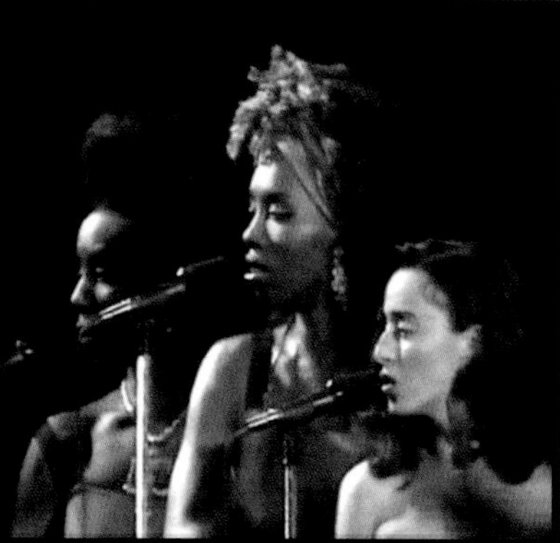

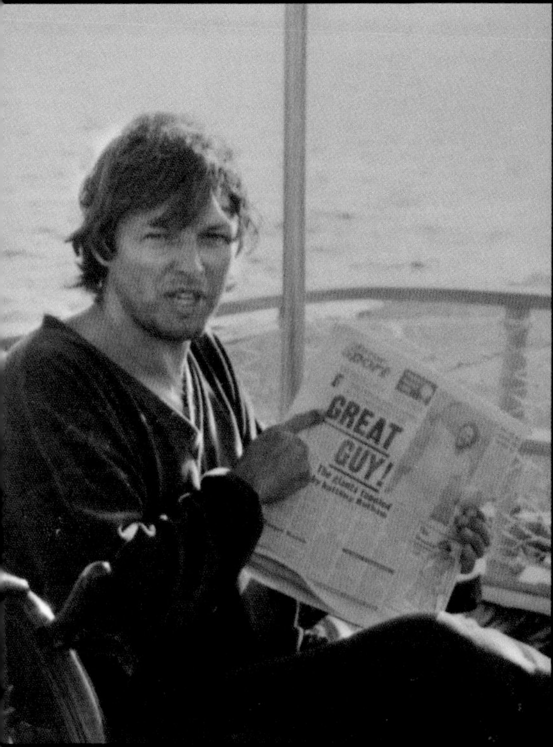
GREAT
GUY!

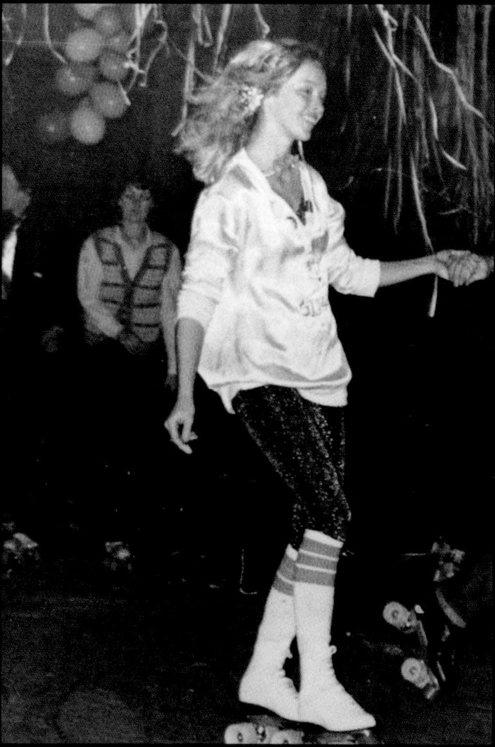

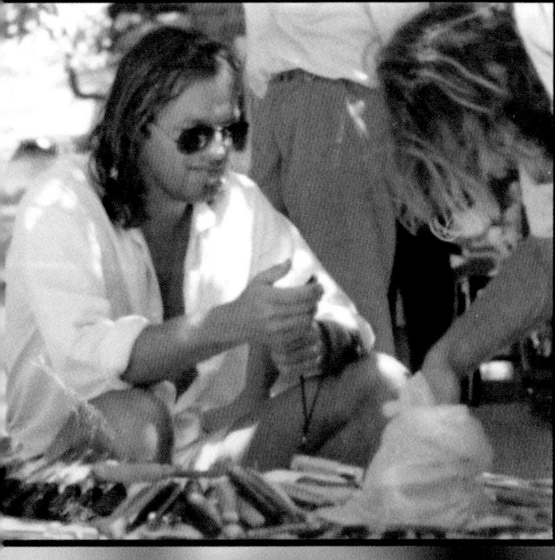

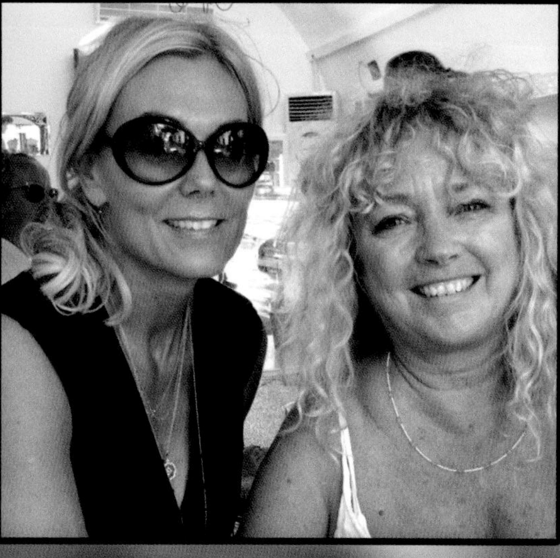

Family comes to visit
Mom & Ron
Toni & Marcus

CHAPTER 16

FAMILY COMES TO VISIT

In the early summer, after Alice was born, my Mom, Ron (stepfather), my sister Toni, and my brother Marcus, came to visit us in our home, where the white doves first led me further along my journey. Our home, Woodley, was in Roydon, Essex. Alice was the first grandchild in our extended family and we so wanted to share this with them. David organized tickets for them making it possible. I was amazed that my Mom especially would dare to come to a foreign country, as she was a very home-orientated person. She had no idea of how different England would be, despite my previous calls home. The reality is always different. However, she came.

Her first shock was the nudity on the telly and the Page 3 Girls, in the morning paper, the *Daily Mirror*. Mom would try to keep my sister and brother from seeing. Watching television often found her telling the kids to turn away from the telly, or even leave the room when she thought there might be some inappropriate images. At the same time, she and Ron just kept watching the program. A bit of hypocrisy passed through my thoughts. I just wonder if this only created curiosity in the kids.

Her second shock was that I was breast-feeding. I would go upstairs so as not to embarrass them. One day Mom came upstairs to talk with me. She asked, *"Why don't you feed your baby naturally?"* I was perplexed by the question and inquired, *"Mom, what is natural to you?"* She replied, *"Why feeding her with a bottle."* Her reply left me astonished. She later said that she had tried with one of her children of five but couldn't get on with it. Modestly, she said, "I was too shy to breastfeed in public or amongst guests, and it was not custom in the States in my day." She found the whole process of hiding away in some room difficult, but equally she could not do what we did either.

There was yet another aspect of how we chose to raise our baby which she found challenging. We slept together in our bed with Alice for the first six months. It was quite bonding to have her close safely resting between us. After which, she slept in the room next door on a mattress upon the floor. My Mom exclaimed, *"WHAT YOU DON'T USE A COT?"* *"No, Mom, many cultures do not use them."*

Mom was not the only one concerned about this. It seemed too extreme in others minds. I never quite understood why. Actually, Alice never crawled out of the room or fell down the stairs. Nor did she become overly demanding about coming back into our bed in the adjoining room. In fact, she often asked to go to bed most nights. *"Mommy can you take me to bed now?"* Brought many a raised eyebrow.

David kindly suggested we take them to Cambridge and show them where he was born and raised. We took them boating amongst the historic buildings of his childhood. Emo came with us and did a lot of the punting in the traditional way, adding a bit of Emo humor as a flavor that had them laughing. I loved sharing this time with Toni and Marcus, for I had missed most of their early childhood. I left for college when they were just little. I think I became a storybook character our parents often spoke about during dinner. I was real and loved them. As years went by, we have become closer and closer, which I treasure.

'MOTHER & CHILD'

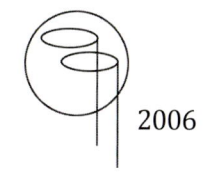

2006

Ginger & sister Donna
Philadelphia, USA

CHAPTER 17

EARLY CHILDHOOD
DAD HIDES US AWAY

I sat looking out from the lead light windows of Woodley, holding little baby Alice close to my breast, feeding her. I pondered my own beginning. Memories of those early years in Philadelphia returned with the reality of now being a Mom. As children, we would often play in the streets playing tag with other children. In the summer, the city fire department would open the fire hydrants on the holiday weekends so that we could cool down and frolic in the water.

One particular morning, I had my toys out on the sidewalk and was pretending to cook dinner for my girlfriend, who lived next door. I didn't hear my mother calling me from inside despite the fact we always left our doors open in those days. *"Charlie, Charlie come here!"* Charlie was my name at home.

My father's name was Charles Hasenbein. He was part of a large German family that migrated to the US several generations ago. My mother's maiden name was Virginia Collins. Both my mother's mother and my father's mother name was Virginia. Both his father and grandfather's name was Charles. Names passed down the Family tree, from one generation to the next. However, my parents had different ideas.

They made an agreement that this would not be the case for their children. But, when it came time to name their first grandchild, my father's parents *demanded that I should be called Virginia*. If not, they would not allow my Catholic baptism to take place. My grandparents were Protestant and the power of their word was so strong that my father gave in to them. Consequently, my mother took a stand later for her priority was first for me to be under the protection of Christ as a Catholic. After the baptism, she proceeded to call me *Charlie Ann* in which my family on both sides continue to use.

On that morning, she came out from the house looking rather tense. *"Charlie, did you not hear me?"* she shouted. *"Pick up your toys and get in here! Now! We are going to visit your Aunt Dot and DO NOT tell anyone!"* My girlfriend had returned outside when she asked what I was doing. I tried not to answer for I was an extremely obedient child down to the letter. I bit my lip, but I could not keep the secret as her demands increased. I was only five years old.

The next thing I remember was my mother hustling my younger sister, Donna and I out the door. Like little ducklings, we rushed down the street behind our Mom trying to catch a cab to the train station, bags and all. Mom then bought the tickets and hurried us to the platform so as not to miss the train. It seemed exciting and yet unexpected. I loved Aunt Dot as we had visited her before. Daddy often drove us up to her house in Connecticut for the odd holiday.

It was a sunny day and I sat next to the window of the train feeling its warmth, daydreaming. Donna was sitting on Mom's lap. We had stopped at another station when I heard my father's voice. *"Where are you going?"* Thereupon, he picked up Donna yanking me with his other hand from where I sat. My mother was so caught off guard. Everything happened so quickly; he was supposed to be at work. She grabbed my other hand as he dragged me across her lap.

I became the *center* of a tug of war, all the other passengers gawked in suspended animation wondering what was going on. All were shocked into silence and non-action. My mother lost her grip as he took us down the coach. I still can hear her feeble cry pleading to him, *"Please don't take them. Please don't take them."* We left the train just as the doors closed; it was over. Daddy hid us in the New Jersey countryside with his parents in their newly built house. *And I forgot that I had a Mother.*

Baking Apple pie, Rival cake and making jam filled the time with our grandparents. Nannan's kitchen was large with a pine table in the center. She was like the perfect image of a fairy godmother, bonnie, gray haired and a smile that warmed your heart. Her apron always covered with flour or some sauce she had been making for dinner. Her pantry was a child's delight full of preserves, chutneys and jams. Herbs hung from the ceiling and filled the room with drifting fragrances, which held me spellbound each time I entered to fetch something for her.

PopPop, my grandfather, was a welder and worked from home in his garage. His white T-shirts always covered with little holes from the sparks. He never shaved, and with his prickly beard, he chased and teased us without mercy. When he finally caught us, he would rub his whiskers across our faces as he held us in his arms. We squealed with glee as he continued to tickle us. It was such a fun game, which we played often in the gravel driveway.

My father's sister, Aunt Dolly, had two children, both were boys, Tommy (Butchy) and Billy, who came to live with us. Story has it that their father wanted girls and my father had wanted boys so we all wound up placed with our grandparents. It really didn't matter, because our grandparents showed us so much love.

My grandparents' house was like a fairyland haven for me. Nannan collected salt n' pepper shakers that adorned her living room windowsill. She would often sit and crochet another doily or tablecloth in her big armchair by the window. She taught me how to do the same, and knit. A grandfather clock hung on the wall; a family heirloom from the old country that had a cuckoo that cuckooed on the hour. PopPop would rewind it each evening by pulling the metal pinecones on the chains that dangled from the main part of the clock. Tick Tock, Tick Tock echoed throughout the house.

Each morning Butchy, Billy and I would go out into the pinewoods and collect blueberries for our morning cornflakes. Donna was too young to go with us so she sat by the window with her head in her hands, grumpy until we returned. Donna and I wore the exact same crinoline dresses that I found out years later were from our mother. She must have sent them to our old address in Philly for she did not know where we were. Dad must have passed them on to our grandparents secretly. They were so pretty.

My grandparents' home was deep in the woods away from any town, down a long dirt drive. I remember often a fog would come permeating everywhere with a terrible smell. I came to know that this was actually DDT to kill the mosquitos and ticks. They even did this at the Drive-in Movies as we played on the swings before the film started. I am not sure when this was finally stopped. However, I hope the chemical used caused no damage to our health.

My grandparents had a large vegetable garden surrounded by a tall fence to keep out the deer and other critters. They raised chickens and turkeys, and we delighted in chasing them. At the end of every summer, there would be a barbecue when all of our uncles and aunts plus their children would come. The men would till the soil and prepare for the next harvest, while the women would help in the kitchen.

Those barbecues were tasty. PopPop would cover the coals with seaweed and place the corn on the cob within it. We also had grilled beef, chicken and fresh fish cooked on another part of the barbecue. Food was plenty: potato salad, barbecue baked beans, goulash and corn muffins fresh from the oven. We played games with all of our cousins until the food was ready. If the weather permitted, a long table would be set up in the garden covered with a white tablecloth.

Christmas too was exceptional. It was like a page out of Peter Pan, our favorite book that Nannan would read to us. There was a large Christmas tree decked with colored lights and baubles in the corner. Weeks before, we had all strung cranberries and popcorn as garlands with white thread. On Christmas morning, wiping the dust from our eyes, we entered the living room. We could not believe what we saw as smiles grew upon our faces. Colorful wrapped presents lined the 10 ft walls on two sides to the ceiling. Mary and her little lamb stood in the middle with large cars, bicycles, scooters, play table and chairs.

My grandparents were not wealthy, but what a memory they created for us. Apparently, each season they took out a loan to pay for the extravaganza. The Hasenbein family was large and they all came with their growing families for lunch. Daddy came with a friend named Agnes, who seemed nice. Nannan would cook the largest turkey that PopPop could find from their pen. Looking back, I know a lot of what I do in my home is inspired by those very impressionable times from making jams, cooking pies and stews, to decorating.

One afternoon, as we were playing in the dust near the main house, a little powder blue car drove up the driveway. A man came out saying he was a *"Fuller Brush man."* Fuller Brush men were door-to-door salesmen in America selling merchandise for the home. My grandmother stood listening as we all gathered behind her skirt like little ducklings. PopPop was out on an errand and we were the only ones home. We were curious who this stranger was and listened from behind Nannan's skirts, peeking out occasionally.

When suddenly a woman with dark hair and eyes sat up from

where she had been secretly lying on the back seat out of sight. In almost the same motion, she opened the door and got out. My gran tensed as I ran out up to her. She was beautiful. I asked, *"Who are YOU?"* She replied, *"Why Charlie I am your mother."* *"OH, REALLY? Would you like to come in and see my toys?"* I asked as I grabbed her hand.

At that moment, my grandmother grabbed my other hand, shouting at my mother to go away while at the same time demanding that we all go inside. The Fuller Brush man called out to my mother, *"Ginny, come on. We know where they are now."* She let go of my hand reluctantly with tears in her eyes as she got back into the little blue car. Gran held me close, wrapping me safely in her arms also with tears in her eyes. I was confused, but returned to play with the others as I watched the car disappear down the drive leaving a trail of dust.

I have no idea how much time had passed before my Dad's summons brought us to court. Daddy, Donna and I all went together. The building was amazing. It was huge with marble floors and round pillars. There were rows and rows of wooden benches with people sitting on them. Daddy led us to one and asked us to sit down. As we waited, we could hear other names called in the distance echoing around the room. We felt very tiny in such a place. I held Donna's hand tightly, hoping this would keep us safe from harm.

Before we arrived from the station, Daddy had said that we must not mention his friend Agnes. I think I was too young to understand or know if they were living together since we spent most of our time in the country. But, that is what he asked.

Daddy stayed, while a nice lady escorted Donna and me out of the room. She held our hands and assured us that we would return soon. We walked across the white marble floors, our shoes clicking as we shuffled along until we came to a rather large door.

She knocked and waited for a voice to speak. *"Come in,"* we heard from the other side. We felt even smaller as we entered the room as the ceiling was so high. All the walls covered in wood with large shelves of books with gold letters. There were carpets in bright colors with a huge desk and large leather chairs. We both sat on one together with our feet dangling over the side. The kind lady left once she knew we were comfortable.

Across the room was a man who was wearing a black type robe and a white collar. I suppose he was our judge, but I am sure we had no idea. What was a judge? He was just a man who had a pleasant voice and gentle eyes. We were there for a while and he asked us many questions. The only one that I can remember was *"Does your Dad have a girlfriend?"* I froze, but Donna shook her head, her blonde bob moving with her gesture, as she said, *"Yes, Agnes."* Later, I was mad and kicked her, I said, *"Daddy said we shouldn't tell anyone."*

Accompanied back to the courtroom, we found Daddy sitting on the bench looking rather forlornly. Three women with dark hair and eyes sat a few rows in front of us smiling and waving their hands. I recognized the one, who said she was our mother. One of the other ladies was her sister, Dorothy (Aunt Dot) and a close Friend of theirs. (I remember her face, but not her name...?) Beside them was the Fuller Brush Man. In fact, he was mom's lawyer and private investigator, Mr. Miller.

Mom had spent years trying to raise enough money so that she could hire one to find us. She worked in factories saving money and sadly was ripped-off by the first investigator she hired. She was living with her sister Dot in Connecticut and her two children, Sharon and Tommy. Finally, she found someone she could trust who also worked in Philadelphia. It was Mr. Miller.

My dad must have had a lawyer but this was such a traumatic time for us. I do not remember nor can I ask him for my dad has passed over 10 years ago. Since writing this chapter my mother also has passed over in October 2014 but she has often shared the story of how she had lost her girls and then got them back. But it was her story. My dad very rarely spoke of it though he was noticeably angry towards my mom by his comments.

When we returned my dad stood up and the three women approached us. We stood at the end of the bench looking up at him with our blonde hair and innocent blue eyes. Wondering what was going on. His voice cracked as he said, *"Girls the judge has decided that you both must go and live with your mother."* We cried as we fell into his legs clutching them, me peeking to the side at those women. He continued to speak to our hearts as his fingers stroked our heads, *"Please, girls don't cry, for we shall be together every summer and I shall come to see you every holiday where you live."* *"NO! NO! Daddy,"* we pleaded.

The women got closer, as I looked at them again through my tears and the safety of my father's legs. *I did not want to leave my Daddy and I had forgotten that I had a mother's love.* These women were strangers. They pulled us away, holding our hands gently, to a path unknown. Trying to comfort us my mother said, *"Come girls."* I kept looking back as my father's waving image, faded amongst the crowd. He went home to an empty house. We were gone.

We had to take a train to Connecticut, where my mother had a small little house near my Aunt Dot. All the way, I sat alone behind them. They kept looking at me and smiling. Donna sat on their lap giggling. I was angry, sad, frightened and alone not knowing that there was another surprise of a little brother, Stephen, waiting at home with my other Nan. We fell asleep in the taxi until they would carry us into our new home.

'BALL of WONDER'

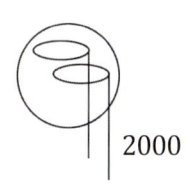

2000

At home
Woodley, Roydon

CHAPTER 18

ANIMALS IN FLIGHT

DECEMBER 1976

It was early December, and the scheduled photography for the *Animals* album cover was to take place at the Battersea Power Station in London. The idea was to suspend a large inflatable pig called Algie, between the four chimney stacks. Algie was 30 ft. long, full of helium and the plan was to tether her within the middle of the antiquated building. For extra safety, there was a trained marksman on standby in the event she broke loose.

Apparently, Roger's daily drive to Britannia Row in Islington inspired the idea. He lived across the river just off Clapham Common and the station was a daily vision along the way. The image of the pig was born from the book *Animal Farm,* by George Orwell, as was the concept for the whole album. Storm Thorgerson, from Hipgnosis, worked together with Roger to design and execute his vision, which the rest of the band accepted.

The day arrived and we all gathered at the station to observe the photographing of the cover. However, the weather proved to be a bit inclement so postponement of the shoot became evident. In addition, the cables were also not secure enough to make it viable. Again, the next day we arrived and despite the weather being a bit calmer, disaster happened. Algie broke loose.

The cable snapped and there was no marksman in sight. She shot up in the air, last reported heading for the English Channel. It made the news with wonderful *caricatures* in the morning papers of two airline pilots looking out of the plane window freaked to see a pig flying next to them. Was it a hallucination? They hadn't been drinking. Oh dear, it is a flying pig!

There was great concern that Algie would cause an accident in the air, but fortunately, she descended on her own accord. Thank God for the winds had diverted her flight plan. The farmer whose field she came to rest in remained perplexed. There amongst the trees she hovered, bouncing gently before his eyes. He went back inside and made the phone call to the local police. "Hello, has anyone reported missing a 30 ft. long pig, have ya?" And the reply, "Are ya' sure ya' ain't had a pint, have ya? Ya sure it ain't a figment of yer' imagination?" "NO, there really is a giant inflatable pig bouncin' around me field. I ain't jokin! Has no one reported a missin' pig?"

Word got back to the Floyd, who then sent Robbie William and few of the stage crew to the rescue. Their mission was to retrieve Algie safely. The famed mishap is amongst many fables in the Pink Floyd History books. Thenceforth, she and a few cousins became a regular feature in the *Animal* "In the Flesh" tours. I even remember that during the *Animals* tour in the States one could find an isolated roadie backstage painting little baby ones. The idea would be to release them from Algie's behind over the audience. However, that never happened or at least not to my knowledge.

When we returned home to Woodley, word had reached our neighbors. And what turned out to be a potential disaster turned out to be the local comical story of the week or perhaps forever. To them it just added to all the animal adventures we had had over the years in their eyes. It brought back memories of how Blu, our peacock, got away and the whole village was on alert trying to capture him, darting from tree to tree, field to field. Steve and Linda O'Rourke had given him to us for our wedding present with a message CLIP HIS WINGS. David didn't want to and unknown to us peacocks could fly. Therefore, he didn't and the adventure began. He just flew out of our fenced chicken run into the sunset.

The Algie adventure brought back another animal memory of the time our neighbor's cow got into our garden. Puddy and I had just returned from shopping, greeted in the dark by a rather large cow. We tried to chase it back into the next-door field flashing our coats, our metallic wellies we had just bought from Biba, glittering in the moonlight. Poor cow, we must have been such a frightful sight. We were hooting and hollering like two crazy Halloween figures down the drive.

We were relieved the cow did make it home, but only after it jumped our five-bar gate like something out of a storybook. Stopping on a dime, its large body just missed the moving rush hour traffic, silhouetted by their lights in the dark. Puddy and I just stood there gasping, as she casually turned right, wandered down the road a bit, then turned into the field from whence it came. Phew, did we need a cup of tea after that one. We giggled at the thought *Ahhh,* another Animal adventure. Many more were to come.

Piglet in Warwick's Room
'Animals' Tour, Frankfurt
1977

CHAPTER 19

PIGS ON THE ROAD
EUROPEAN TOUR

26–27 JANUARY 1977

The Pink Floyd story was out. Capital Radio Nicky Horne had broadcast an epic documentary over the course of six weeks. Each program was 45 minutes long and was the most all-embracing expose of their vision and history to date. John Peel at the BBC jumped in and played the whole album breaking the exclusive arrangements given to Nicky. Even still *Animals* set the stage to awaken their slumbering public, but often it just brought criticism and conflict instead of enlightenment. Acceptance was not yet to come. It seems to be the way with all visions that challenge the status quo.

So the *Animals* tour began, first stop was Germany. The gigs were getting bigger and louder. In addition, as our families grew, our entourage became bigger also. Once again, our personal assistant Warwick McCreddie looked after us. We had Alice and our Nanny, Jeannie with us. We were getting to be a dab hand at moving into hotels with a little one. Bed ready, bottles warmed and dinner was on its way.

After the first concert with Alice safe in bed, David and I joined the others at a nightclub party, which the promoters had set-up. When we arrived there in a box was a live baby pig shivering as the loud music surrounded him and the strobe lights revealed his form to us. The promoters thought that it would be funny. I freaked! The band told Warwick to take it back to the hotel and arrange for the farmer to pick it up as soon as possible, which meant taking him to his room at the hotel until it was resolved.

The next morning, Alice, Jeannie and I went down for breakfast and gathered as much lettuce, other vegetables, and bits of fruit knowing that Warwick for sure had not thought of that. We waited until we thought it was a reasonable hour to visit and see how the baby pig had fared. We were probably a bit early, but it was around 10:00 a.m. Poor Warwick was extremely hung over and moaned as he opened the door. Suddenly he gasped and shouted, "OH MY GOD!" as he looked back into his room.

All the mirrors on the sliding wardrobe doors were cracked. The pig had been snorting at all the other pigs he could see and must have been kissing himself or had an argument to have created such damage. There was excrement everywhere. His room was literally a pigsty! As we looked around, we noticed that our little pink friend had dragged most of his straw out of the box on to the carpet, which Warwick had laid on its side. As he started to put back the straw, he came upon his underpants. The piglet obviously had slept with Warwick's underpants all night.

We didn't know whether to cry or to laugh as the pig was running after Warwick as he tried to rescue his knickers. Alice loved the pig and wanted to feed him. We stayed for a little while when Jeannie shrieked and ran out of the door back to our room. She had forgotten that she was washing the nappies in the bidet and feared she had left the water running. I was against paper nappies then and we used cloth ones instead. It was a small attempt to save the trees. So we washed them in the Hotel bidet while on tour. When she got there, the water was running throughout the room and into the room downstairs as well.

We all left Steve O'Rourke to settle the situation. Between the pigs mess and ours, the hotel was not too happy. Another Rock band destroys a hotel. Actually, the Floyd and their crew really had a good reputation. It was the pyrotechnics that caused a few problems and of course the airplane. But I am foretelling a bit of the future.

On the Road with Alice

CHAPTER 20

THE BRIGHT SIDE IS CALLING
PARIS, FRANCE

In Frankfurt, the audience had been very violent. They were throwing beer cans and other paraphernalia on stage. Some of the flavor of the Beauty I found in the shows was wearing thin. I was getting a bit battle worn. Life on the road with a child, nanny, and struggling with my diet was proving difficult. We traveled to city after city, from hotel to hotel. The Floyd were used to touring; yet, does one ever get used to it? There is a buzz mixed with hardship being away from home. I hear David's voice singing how he liked to be home.

After five more gigs, we reached Paris, where the Floyd were to play at the Pavillon de Paris. Roger, David, and I were in one of the cars, which was taking us to the gig. There was a drive to the back entrance that was about a block long, with a brick wall on the left and a high fence on the right, with only room for a car never mind a limo. When we turned into the drive, there were fans waiting, lots of them up to the gate. The driver went slowly into the crowd. There was nowhere for them to go, except on top of the car and squashed against each other, against the wall.

I started to laugh and laughed hysterically. Roger looked over to David and asked, "Why is she laughing?" David said, "That is what she does when she is extremely panicked." First, I laughed, because I could not believe what I seeing, as the driver kept moving forward. Then, as it worsened, I laughed hysterically because my heart hurt at what I was seeing. They were screaming and banging on the car. Their faces pressed against the windows. Their anxiety was a mixture of excitement that their stars were so close and OH MY GOD I am being crushed. I wanted to get out, but there was no way to do so. I had to close my eyes and hold David's hand tightly. I found refuge against his shoulder until the nightmare was over.

 This was just one of many experiences, which the *Animals* tours seem to attract. The album and the gigs portrayed this very aspect of our supposed modern culture and our inhumanity. The tour was a reflection of the sorrowful state of what was happening in the world. In addition, the topic played on the stage was also becoming backstage. It was filtering into our home life. However, we continued, concert after concert baby in tow. I often wondered what kept us going, but until the pus festers, a wound cannot heal, I suppose.

 For me, the Beauty of those moments were when the audience and the music was ONE, which overshadowed the pain. But more rough seas were to come. I only wish that I could have helped David more, besides being by his side and raising our children. Reading some of their history now, has opened my eyes more to understand what had gone on with the band, often behind closed doors.

 They were a gestalt in many ways bonded together over the years. The band's inner relationships torn, yet lives entangled. This realization, time and time again appeared only after a crack started to emerge. What once was unity was now becoming shattered. Often the family was a refuge for each of them from the storm, but I wonder if it did not cause a schism in both camps. I believe it did. Our lives had become so big and surreal or maybe perhaps unreal? For sure, it was beyond being a normal existence.

Things started to change. Roger's unending pain and anger placed a dark shadow over everything expressed in his lyrics. I have witnessed many times how the music had made his anguish palatable. I saw how David's heart struggled to be heard and Rick retreated into silence, as if they were carrying a heavy stone. And somewhere amongst this turmoil of life, a creative force rose above the storm, touching our hearts out there, on the other side of the wall. Their music brought an archetypal message that one could rise above the challenges of Life to find Beauty waiting.

Sometimes I wish I could go back in time and convey that message to them, not as a lovesick girl, but me as a woman, who has found the value of Beauty. It wasn't the size of the shows. It was the mastery of being human through transforming ugliness into Wonder and the Beauty of Life. That is what their concerts created for us in the audience. That is what brought people back time and time again. Somehow, in revealing the shadows and the light we found balance, even if it was in the subconscious held in our memories.

They say that life only gives you what you can handle. Well, this was a big one. Much given, but with it came the burden we carried. Some days I just wonder, could it have been different? Maybe the path was laid before us that we were destined to walk. The tide was turning. The program set. The Bright Side was calling us to go forward.

Returning Home

CHAPTER 21

FLOYD BECOMES CECIL DEMILLE
WEMBLEY EMPIRE POOL

1977

We had returned from Europe, with a few days at home, before the Floyd's five gigs in the UK at the Wembley Empire Pool. We had bought a property on Mc Gregor Rd., near Portobello Rd. in London, which there were three flats. We kept the top floor flat as a London bolt-hole. In the middle flat we had an elder sitting tenant, Mrs. Hammond. We were obliged to allow her to stay, until she had passed over or was too ill to live by herself. We had no problem with that. She was such a dear. When we were updating the flats, she wanted to stay on her electric coin fed meter. So we waited to do her portion of the building as not to disturb her.

David had contracted Tonsillitis upon our return. Different to America, British children do not have their Tonsil or Adenoids removed. David would often have infections, but this time I presumed it started because of the previous gigs in Germany. They had to substitute the dry ice with smoke and as a result, it entirely covered the stage, the band and the audience below. It was hard to breathe and dried out their throats. And who knows what else it affected.

When we got home, we took David to a specialist who works with opera stars. His treatment was very effective, required a few visits and allowed David to sing. A special lozenge was the remedy, which was an essential in our home medicine cabinet for years. I remember even sending some to Paul McCartney for which he was extremely grateful. He was struggling for his Wembley gigs at the time as well.

We left Alice at home with Warwick's sister, Winsome and Peter Mount with whom we considered our second family. David and I stayed at McGregor Rd., a sweet one bedroom modest flat arranged over three floors with a kitchen on the top floor. It was petite but very serviceable for weekends away. Emo was living on the first floor, and, of course, invited to all five shows. It turned out to be Party Time every night.

It was a relief to be back home with an English audience for they were much more held, absorbing the music. It always seemed they allowed the notes to enter and dance around their being. Or were they stoned? More than 10,000 came each night and more hopefuls lingered outside wishing they were there too. The *Financial Times* called the Floyd the modern day Cecil DeMille as *Animals* was more theatrical than ever before. The music floated from behind the inflatables as the show went on.

By the fourth night, I was feeling rather frail around the edges. I said to David, "I really can't do another late night." He agreed, but when we got home, Emo had invited everyone over and the party was in full swing. After a while I gave in and asked David if we had any "Coke?" He said "No," but he knew someone who did. He took me down to our bathroom where there were two ladies laying down lines. David asked if they would give me some for he had already had some a few moments before.

He left me there and went back to the party. I had a few and started back up the stairs to find him. As I passed our bedroom, I noticed he was lying there in the half-lit room with the door open. An energy of Love took over, but as I came close, I felt I had to vomit. I ran to the window, which was half-open. Leaning out I vomited into the night. I felt like my guts were being yanked out. My head was exploding. Finally, it stopped and I lay down next to him.

I felt shaken but a type of euphoria was taking over. I asked David in a more intimate moment what was that they had given me. He didn't know but it felt good. He hugged me and I fell asleep in his arms. Later I found out it was heroin! That was the last thing I would have EVER taken if I had known. It was a violation of my freedom of choice. Maybe they were unaware that I didn't know. And I didn't know that London was moving away from cocaine to snorting heroin.

From then on, I learned to ask more questions about what I was taking. That experience served to lay down the foundations to quit taking drugs. One good seed planted for the future and one bad seed put away and forgotten. For whenever something was too great of an emotional shock to face, I went into a form of Amnesia. Just like I did when my father took us away from my mother. Mother? What mother. Heroin? What heroin? Life went on.

Fortunately, life was to provide the tools needed to release that subconscious pattern many years later. When I was to meet and have the good fortune to be analyzed first by Werner Engle in NYC, then Gerhard Adler in London until he passed away. Mrs. Adler, his wife, took me under her wing after his death. They were highly respected in their field of Jungian analysis and I am grateful to have known them. This is a story that I shall share with you later.

Rick Wright

CHAPTER 22

ANIMAL FARM COMES STATE SIDE IN THE FLESH TOUR, U.S.A

The tour started in Miami. The warmth of the balmy air was refreshing, as back home, April showers were preparing for spring .We had some time to swim in the ocean with Alice, as she loved the water. There were a few technical problems getting the Pig to be present and it was suspended from a pole as a last minute solution. The highlight of the show was when the pig was set on fire, which was not quite what the crew intended. Fortunately, they were on the case and no one was injured. However, it did set alight a few other fires, namely Roger's and Steve O'Rourke.

We flew everywhere in our private airplane, a 737 Jet. Long gone were the times when we had to walk through airports, wait in lines, check in, and airplane food. Nope, not any more. Our cars would drive up to a small terminal and our personal road manager organized our bags as we made ourselves comfortable inside. Life on the road had become a very complicated affair; families traveling with children and nannies, more equipment, friends, movie stars, fans surrounding us whenever they could find out where we were. We checked into hotels with aliases to insure our privacy that worked sometimes.

The gigs were becoming a blur as we traveled from state to state. The size of the lorries increased and so did the number of road crew. In the past I knew all their names. Now some were familiar while others were hired "Humpers." The stadiums were so big that they needed strong Herculean men to get all their speakers up there. Nick referred to them as the "quad squad," the SAS of humpers. The organization of the whole tour was a feat of great proportions.

As our journey took us through the south, I remember being amazed at what Americans thought was their architectural heritage. I say that, because of what we saw when we went to see some of them, where their history supposedly happened. We visited one that was just a small pile of stones in the middle of the prairie. There was though a parking lot full of tourist buses, a gift shop and, by the way, they didn't fail to charge an entry fee. We left a bit cynical remarking under our breath, "Perhaps we should tell them to go to Europe to know more of their heritage." But I do know as an American, what we dream is as much a reality as a building.

Phoenix, Arizona was our favorite city to enjoy. We played in the desert with land rovers, went surfing in the artificial waves and the Floyd had the best time driving madly on the circuit. There was time to frolic and sit in the motel jacuzzi. One of the most unforgettable memories was the morning when David drove a motorbike through the dining room on a bet. We were all having breakfast when Evil Knievel Gilmour came riding in from the outside terrace, passed our table, out the main door, through the lobby and out of the motel. He parked the bike and returned for breakfast. Nobody said a word. The waiters and all the diners just went on with their day. Business as usual seemed to be their motto.

We traveled like a pack struggling sometimes to keep a smile covering our exhaustion and late nights and frivolity. The constant reminder of the growing conflict within the band took energy from us all. Maintaining anger takes a lot of energy, you know. We put on masks to hide the pain. We were becoming alienated, not only from the audience with the band behind the headphones, but also from each other. Food on the road left us empty with its non-dairy creamers and dried up sandwiches in the dressing room. Tour catering was in its infancy, so for the crew it was burgers delivered. Bottles of Evian began to appear, but I am sure we were all dehydrated.

Finally, we reached California, where it was less like a conveyor belt of Joneses. Friends and family were appearing amongst the waves of the audience. At the time, the band was finding it a challenge to adjust to the large stadiums of nameless faces. Security and safety became more of an issue as the number reached beyond 80,000. I spent most of the concerts in the middle of them at the mixer. Often what the band felt was a bad gig, I discovered that I had a different impression, as I bounced into the dressing room full of Joy. A cloud fell upon me as I went into the changed atmosphere. I recovered my composure and silently poured myself a drink.

On the first night at Anaheim Stadium, the start of the show began with a plane flying over the stadium with computerized lights, on its belly blinking WELCOME PINK FLOYD. *Animals* had become more theatrical. The Floyd were mere puppets it seemed, on the stage and in the distance. I admired this, for it gave an opportunity to listen instead of adulating upon our stars. Taken on a journey, because that was the Floyd they loved. Admittedly, I wished that there was less tragedy, less angst. It was as if Beauty had become a whisper. The music was just about audible amongst the props and the click track.

It was Alice's first birthday on the 8 May and we gave her a party the day before because we had to get to the next gig on her real birthday. Many friends came to celebrate the day she was born in our hotel room. Cyndy Shirley and Aaron, her son, were a delight to share time together as always. Over the years, we often took care of him at Woodley when Cyndy was away. We felt he was our son in a way, so we were close. We have watched him grow up to be a fine man and now we are watching his children grow up. For me, they are still one of our extended families across the ocean.

I always marvel how backstage in California, especially in Los Angeles, it is like a film set of faces one thinks you know, but don't. People you see in movies or on telly become like friends, but you really don't know them. Madonna came one evening and received a rather curt comment from Roger which shook her a bit. He was like that, i.e., he wasn't playing the Hollywood game.

Fame is a weird paradox for me. On one hand, the artist loves what they are doing, wanting to be adored, wanting to be heard but when it gets too large of numbers wanting you, it becomes a challenge. So many people needing, feeding, depending, idolizing can make it difficult to know who your friends are. And perhaps, even to know who you are amongst all the screaming voices in your head?

'HUMANITARIAN HEROES'

2008

Ginger & sister, Donna

CHAPTER 23

SAVING THE HOGS
OAKLAND, CALIFORNIA

My sister Donna had flown in from Wyoming to see the show, but really, she came to see Alice and me. It had been a long time between visits. We went in our limousine to the gig. Both Dick Perry, saxophone player, and Snowy White, guitarist came with us. It was special to share this aspect of my life with my sister. It felt like Star Trek as we went up the ramp and the metal gates lifted allowing us to enter. My sister was casually dressed. I was wearing all white lace, but not for long. As we got out of the limo, I was appalled at what I saw.

Oakland Coliseum was a huge American venue with a large passageway that went completely around the building under the seats above. These passageways were wide enough for several cars and lorries to be there. We had entered just behind the stage, which made us feel very small in front of its majesty. However, to my surprise, there in that area was a pen filled with lots of hogs. Tied below their bellies, were white canvas labels with each band members name inscribed.

Along either side of the pen were ramps leading up on both sides with a thick long rope over the top reaching the floor. There were several very large men standing there as security guards. I approached them and asked, "What is this all about?" They laughed, placing their hands on their hips and said, "Well, we are gonna Whup the Floyd in a tug of war before the show!" The "We" was Billy Graham's team who was the promoter, a very powerful promoter in the San Francisco Bay Area. They were big dudes and the thought of anyone falling onto these animals set me on fire. No way would this happen!

I asked Dick and Snowy if they had a pocket knife, which they did. I took it and in a swirl of white lace, I took flight. I jumped into the pen and started to remove the labels with the Floyd's names on them shouting, "I'll be damned if you will!" My sister stood there in awe of what was happening. Her angelic sister had become a tigress. I said to Snowy and Dick, "Go get Steve!" when one of Graham's roadies jumped into the pen and lifted me out kicking. I then stood there addressing them rather forcefully, "How could you even think of doing such a thing! It's CRUEL!"

Steve eventually arrived and sorted it out with some of the Floyd following. Fortunately, the farmer and his lorry were still there. I think he was hoping for a publicity shot because he wasn't too happy being sent away. I have no idea what or if he was even paid. All I cared about was that it didn't happen. Later, someone told me that hogs could be very aggressive. I never felt that was the case. I think they knew that I was there to save them. I was their friend.

Ever since, I definitely knew, I had an affinity with animals. I had become a vegetarian and with it an awareness of the plight of the animal kingdom. In fact, it has expanded to include the human kingdom and Mother Earth. In fact, before children, I had a strong desire to have a wildlife park in the UK. I spent time looking for property and getting the information necessary to put it in place. I fell in love with white peacocks and other exotic animals. But with my deeper dream to have children with David blossoming, the dear animals had to wait.

'ANGELIC WHISPER'

2005

Time off in Paradise
Kauai, Hawaii
May-June 1977

CHAPTER 24

TIME OFF IN PARADISE
KAUAI, HAWAII

MAY–JUNE 1977

The "In the Flesh" tour came with a much needed and welcomed break. A month off between the middle of May and the middle of June was scheduled. Therefore, David, Alice and I went to Kauai in the Hawaiian Islands. As we landed in Lihue Airport and walked into the terminal, the Hawaiian women greeted us and placed their traditional Pikake Lei around our necks. The air filled with the scent of Tropical Flowers mixed with a warm touch of humidity. Immediately, my body relaxed and a simple smile warmed my heart with joy. This was my first experience of Aloha as the land spoke to me with a deep feeling of coming home.

We had rented a condominium on the north shore in Hanalei Bay, approximately an hour taxi journey away. As we drove down the island, we passed waterfalls and green jungle to find beaches, hidden underneath trees sculpted by the winds. Alice and I looked out the window in wonder as the soft breeze blew her golden curls around her face. I held her hand as she pressed her face against the half opened window jumping up and down on my lap giggling.

The song "Puff the Magic Dragon," by Peter, Paul & Mary, played in my head as we drove along the coast towards Hanalei Bay. It definitely was a time of magic. I felt so at one within each moment and rejoiced each day as Alice played in the sand next to David with triple rainbows overhead.

We often met up with Graham and Susan Nash of Crosby, Stills & Nash who had a house there. I felt very at home with them for they had such heart. They collected shells from different beaches, which inspired me to begin my own collection. In fact, the children to this day bring me some as a present from their journeys around the world. During our stay, I remember getting up early to go to the beach, combing for shells with Billy, one of their friends, so that I could have a necklace made in the Hawaiian tradition. As it turned out, he made me a pair of large hair combs with shells and turquoise. I still have them safe in my jewelry box and every once in a while I take them out to feel the sun and the ocean breeze of Kauai.

We fell so in Love with the island that we nearly didn't return. There is a myth that the Goddess Pele, known for her creative power, passion, purpose, and profound love will wrap you in the magic of Aloha if your hearts are pure. And if not, she spits you out, they say. Upon reflection, I am sure she was with us making our stay a blessed one. She had us in the palm of her hand.

One day Graham told us of a special house that might be for sale. He hooked us up with the agent and at first sight, we were sold. It was a pyramidal shape on stilts, in the middle of a valley with a stream running along the side. Although still under construction, we knew its potential. Paradise filled our being as we gazed out from the platform and listened to the sound of the clear crystal water rippling by.

There were Avocado trees the size of Oaks with Plumeria and Orchids in the underbrush. The unexpected sight of a Red-crested Cardinal totally took my breath away, for as a child this was a bird I loved. It turned out the homeowner was currently in jail, arrested on marijuana charges. We waited many years wondering if he would ever sell. Unfortunately, that day never came.

Nancy was the house cleaner in our condo. She was born and

raised on Kauai and told us stories of her life. She shared with us how she had lost her whole family in the Tsunami of 1964. It is amazing how each country we visit has its own trial with nature. She pointed out the posts that had markings telling you how high you needed to reach to be safe when and if it came again.

The indigenous Hawaiians lived in this fear of its return. Her eyes teared up as she told us how the first wave came catching her, her children and husband. But it was the second one that returned and dragged them all away. She had one child in her arms and her husband had the other. He lost his balance as the force of the wave withdrawing took them. She reached out grabbing his shirt trying to hold on to the ones she loved. She fell, losing her grip on her family and the child she was holding. As she rolled in the mud on the ocean floor, her family swept out. She struggled in her heartache to get to her feet. Somehow, she had survived. She thanks God for saving her life, but still mourns her husband and two children. She did go on to have another family, but ensured me that they live in a safer zone, safe from the storm.

During our month stay, we heard of an old Hawaiian trail that linked the North and the South shore. Many people went on walks and camping trips into the jungle along that trail. There was nothing but nature: No restaurants, No electricity, No smoothie bars. David and I decided to go. He carried Alice in our baby sling on the front of his chest and I carried our minimal supplies for the day. We set off early so we could get back in time for sunset, as we did not plan to stay the night on the beach with a wee one unprepared. We walked and walked in the rising sun. There were flowers everywhere and running streams that we had to traverse. It was Beauty at our finger tips. The growing friction of the Floyd left far behind.

Graham told us that we should try washing with the ginger shampoo, which we would find along the way. They resembled red pine cones at the end of a stick of green leaves. Their cones are full of water and if you squeeze them, a clear, slimy-sudsy, ginger-scented fluid comes out. The indigenous people still use the plant to wash, and to condition their hair and the skin. So we had a go. It was slimy for sure.

Along the way there were walkers going back in the opposite direction. They asked how long we had been in. "A few hours," we replied. LOL. It seems that many stay there for months. Eventually we got to a beach and it was time for Alice to eat. We have the best photo of the moment when she dropped her carrot stick in the sand and proceeded to eat it. She spit and spluttered passing it to me as I rescued her from her dilemma. We played on the edge of the waves for there was an undertow, which made it difficult to swim especially with a toddler.

The trail was full of colorful people seeking time out from the spinning world they left behind. Each finding their own refuge within the Beauty of the tropical jungle. And we too, found our refuge in the tropical jungle–quite opposite from the jungle of Rock 'n' Roll. We were able to relax and laugh again.

Just before we left, we went to a kiddie birthday party. We found the house hidden away off the main road under the trees. There were many children dressed in floating outfits of different colors, barefoot and tan. What was most remarkable was the stillness in their sounds of laughter and joyful play. It touched me very deeply. I saw that life could be different and wanted this for our family.

While on the island, it was easy to eat healthy and organic. There were fresh fruit smoothie huts on almost every corner. In addition, the essence of Kauai empowered the vision that life was sacred and beautiful. The Oneness of Life was there. We felt the unity amongst men and nature–Paradise on Earth. Even the fresh pineapples were divine.

This holiday planted another seed, which later would bring an inner change for me. When we returned to the road, I had decided to stop participating in Mood Enhancers, including alcohol. This put me in a different camp. I was an outsider (at least that is how I felt). No longer did I go to the ladies room for a smoke or a line. No longer did I mingle with the same high or take part in the same conversations. Another aspect of alienation crept into my life on the road.

The tension was growing backstage as Roger grew more unsettled. He was finding it more and more difficult to bridge the growing gap between him and the audience below. He was finding it more and more difficult to continue to work creatively with the band as before. As the days passed, it became more obvious.

As I relive those moments writing, I feel, Roger had a deep inner vision trying to get out. Perhaps it was his soul calling him. Perhaps it was his paradisiacal heart. Everything seemed a conflict, a confrontation. It was evident that he had to make a choice, which was challenging him down to his bones. Anger and frustration were often his way to deal with it. And it would continue that way until he resolved his inner turmoil. Again, quiet desperation was the English way, comes to mind as we were unconsciously drawn into the entanglement.

World Series Rock Show
Nick Mason on Cherry Picker

CHAPTER 25

A WORLD SERIES ROCK 'N' ROLL SHOW CLEVELAND, OHIO

25 JUNE 1977

The band was playing to bigger and bigger audiences. Their *"Animals* in the Flesh" Gig, in Cleveland, has gone down in the Guinness Book of Records as one of the largest Rock 'n' Roll concerts in history. It certainly is One that has stayed in my memory as a testimony of how Beauty can arise out of Chaos. That from the mire of sweat and tears something special can become.

The day was hot and sunny. We took our little Alice with us during the sound check. She had just turned one in May and was learning to walk. We took many photos of her toddling in the middle of the field in her little red and white polka-dot summer dress with matching pantaloons, her nappy peeking out the side. Occasionally she would teeter and fall over with a giggle. She was such a happy little thing.

As she grew older, she was like David's shadow following along after him. Whenever I think of this time, the song lyrics from *Me and my Shadow*, come to mind. I just loved the bond she had with him even when she was a baby. My favorite photo was when she was bending over touching her toes with the inflatables behind floating above the stage. The contrast between her dinky innocence standing in the middle of this enormous patch of green and the majesty of the stage was special and yet surreal.

Crowds were building up outside the stadium. We could hear them getting a bit impatient in the sweltering heat, exposed to the blazing sun, squashed up against each other. Some had waited for seven hours. Some had stayed overnight. I heard later that it had been one confrontation after another between the cops and the punters. (Ohio had passed a decriminalization law the previous year, so they couldn't bust anybody). Instead, they walked amongst them, harassing one person after another who was smoking weed, grabbing the bag of marijuana and dumping it on the ground. How appropriate the theme of the concert was in addressing this situation.

I had decided to sit at the mixer in the middle of the crowd that evening. Normally, the mixer area sat at ground level, but tonight it was raised up high. David suggested that I had better make my way out there before the audience arrived. Mark Brickman showed me the way, as he had to be there at lighting control. We went early and I waited for the show to begin with all the engineers and the setting sun.

Unfortunately, when the gates opened, the tension came into the stadium. Apart from the seats on the side of the stadium, the gig was what they called GENERAL ADMISSION, which meant that it was all for one and one for all, to get a spot on the grass. As the audience came in it was evident that a lot of them had had a grueling day, waiting for hours in the sun to see the concert. Reports vary. Somewhere between 83,000–93,000 people came to this show. They came to see a "World Series of Rock show," described by a fan. They scrambled in desperation to get a spot pushing each other aside. The smell of beer and reefer was in the air. The anticipation mixed with frustration became very noticeable as we were beginning to be surrounded close up and personal with them at the mixer. At one point, I was concerned that they might just push the platform over in their stupor, as they were getting a bit aggressive.

Someone let go of a smoke bomb into the crowd. I really couldn't understand how anyone could do that at a concert meant to feel Beauty and Wisdom. It might have hurt someone. Where had all the Love and Peace gone? My own fears started to build, as I could not escape. Everyone was counting the minutes until dusk when the concert would start at 8:30 p.m.

At the back of the stage were large signs of advertisements for Marlboro, Coco Cola and Winston. The sun was setting and from a distance came flashing lights towards us. It was our Tour Plane. This was even a surprise for me. The pilot broke the federal air safety regulations and flew right over the stadium at 500 ft. The sound and the unexpected rush that occurred when it flew over us shocked the audience into silence. Thank God.

The colors of the day faded into the night and became subtle hues of lilac blue as "Sheep" began to gently fill the stadium. The sounds of "Grand Chester Meadows" and the ringing of church bells took us on a Sunday walk in the English Countryside at dusk. Then from the stage came puffs of smoke, adding to the ambience of the early morning mist, which carried out into the night twilight on the evening breeze. The crowd settled and were held in its wonder. One after another, what seemed to be puffs of smoke filled the air to open like miniature parachutes in the form of sheep.

For me this has to be my favorite concert ever! It exemplified how the Floyd could transform chaos into Beauty and in that moment, it united us all. The album *Animals* theme was mainly "Sheep" (people) followed into "Dogs" (police) and then into "Pigs" (masters/politicians) inspired by George Orwell's book *Animal Farm*. I read the book during college and it was one that got me thinking deeply when I first read it. It was interesting to see how the Floyd interpreted it.

The evening faithfully followed through the story created. It was dark by now and the stillness of the evening took over as we were all further carried into the drama of *Animals*. I could relax for a moment and sat down, allowing myself to take in the music and the sound of David's guitar. During "Dogs," large inflatables began to appear above the band in their shapes of the great American Nuclear Family. Mother, Father and 2.5 children and all our toys: Telly, a Cadillac, a Fridge with phallic sausages hanging out. They deflated right on cue as all sang the lyrics we knew so well.

This tour of *Animals* required a huge amount of precision and timing. Roger was particularly demanding about getting the cues right and actually made a comment in his terse way that night over the PA, which got the crew scurrying around in a panic. A large inflatable Pig appeared and went across the whole stadium. For me, he was one of the most menacing ones that they had created. At one moment the Pig became stuck. An announcer came on and asked, "If anyone has hold of the line on the pig, please let go. It is very dangerous. We are trying to bring it back in from over the audience. Please, please let go of the line."

Despite it all, it was a "World Series of Rock show!" But it was not so for the band. When I finally got backstage, there were just arguments and tension. Roger was just not happy. He even treated the band as though they were hired hands. The Tick, Tick of the click track and the cues took over. Many times, I have felt that they had no idea how special, magical and full of Beauty the gigs were they had created. Even in the mistakes, Beauty can transcend. I suppose it got lost in the details of their own isolated experience. I am glad I had the memory of what they had achieved along with many others.

'HEART 2 HEART'

2008

Hasenbein Family Reunion
Top: Agnes & Daddy
Bottom: Nannan & Poppop

CHAPTER 26

A REUNION OF FAMILY
PHILADELPHIA

JUNE 1977

We stayed in New York and traveled down for the Gigs at the Spectrum in Philadelphia. My dad and step-mum, Agnes, lived in Philly on the north side of town so we took our limousine to pay a visit. They hadn't seen Alice or even a Floyd show so it made their day when we arrived in our limo. Agnes recently told me that over the years Daddy never knew who the DJ Gilmour was that he was always posting my pressies and letters to in England. Until one day, I had sent him a signed album from the entire band. "Pink Floyd, what in the devil is that?" he exclaimed. "What is she getting into now?" That was in the beginning. He eventually showed the album to some of the neighborhood kids who exclaimed, "He's FAMOUS, Chuck!"

Agnes said that my father's chest grew bigger and bigger with pride as the realization dawned. He was ever so popular with all the local children and even more so once they knew who his daughter was married to. So on the day we arrived they all appeared as our stretch limo came up in front of their house on Kirby Drive. Albums and pens in hand, hoping to meet their idol. However, they had to wait, as David would come the next day. Apparently, Daddy had no idea what was happening, but Agnes said he loved it.

There was also a family gathering in the custom of the

"Hasenbeins." Uncle Tom, Aunt Marie and Aunt Anna arrived including Agnes's Mom, Elsie. Nannan and Poppop were still alive and made a special trip from New Jersey to see us as well. It was the last time that I saw them all for they passed over in the following years. It was a great and a lovely reunion with that side of my family from childhood.

***

Many summers as a child were spent walking the boardwalk in Wildwood, New Jersey with them. Uncle Tom especially used to spoil us with lots of cotton candy and funny jokes. The summer evenings were balmy with the sound of children squealing as they twirled on the rides above the crashing waves below. Aunt Anna and Aunt Marie and Elsie loved all the games, which there were lots of to place a few pennies on. The ding ding still plays in my ears.

In our recent phone conversation, Agnes told me that Wildwood was always a place they came during the Great Depression of her childhood. Their home was just on The Frankford Junction, which had a direct line to Wildwood. Her family often would hop on the train for a day out to walk on the boardwalk. Later, when the family could afford it, they went by car. Listening to her brought back so many memories for her and for me.

David came the next day, but had to leave early for sound check and we were to meet him at the gig later. Agnes recalls that David was extremely warm and gracious to them. In fact, she says that all her Pink Floyd memories were joyful and everyone they met were warm and gracious. She chuckled last night as she remembered their first concert. She said, "It was really exciting!" A rock concert was never something either of them would have ever dreamt to experience. She was surprised how much she enjoyed it. I could see the sparkle in her eyes from her voice. Gee, I am so glad to have asked her now. She said, "It was loud!" with a chuckle. In addition, she was amazed how much everyone enjoyed the music. "AND they knew all the lyrics!" she exclaimed. Their attention fascinated her. And my Dad was chuffed how popular he was with the people he sat next to, once they knew he was family.

As Daddy and Agnes got ready, I had the limo driver take Elsie, Uncle Tom and my two Aunts home. Agnes will never forget the look on their faces as they drove away, which was their first limo ride. They felt royal. And I shall never forget the smiles upon my Dad's and Agnes's faces when they saw the neighborhood children standing on the sidewalk saluting as we left the drive.

I don't recall much about the concert as they were beginning to be one of the same. The daily *having a child on the road* took more precedence, which at least added a flavor of humanity within the blur. Insuring that we didn't lose complete reality with daily life. Having said that, it was still special (though taxing), as the hours were long. Early mornings, even with a nanny, traveling with a private plane, unpacking, packing, hotel after hotel, food on the road, the gig and the late nights was not quite, what I thought the path of Love and motherhood would be.

However, as I have often said, there was something that made all of that ok—between the traveling, the gigs, the groupies, the alcohol, the sleeping pills, the uppers, and sometimes cocaine. We were a mule train linked together by a common experience. Somewhere amidst the chaos there was beauty and hope, which kept us, going. Perhaps it was the music or the beauty uniting us all. We just kept *Those Doggies Rollin!*

Animals Gig-NYC
Carriage ride to Madison Garden
Juliette, Jamie, Jennie & I

CHAPTER 27

A PARADE OF ANIMALS
NEW YORK CITY

1–4 JULY 1977

Next stop was New York, New York and it was over the Fourth of July weekend at Madison Square Garden. This would be the first time for the Floyd to perform at MSG and we heard that Columbia Records had staged a publicity stunt to promote the album. Apparently, they paraded live animals up 6th Avenue to Central Park behind a flatbed truck bearing a video camera and loudspeakers blaring the album. A few of Columbia's personnel walked behind with a pig, a sheep, a dog, along with a hundred or more fans. Quite, a stunt. Poor animals, but who are the animals really, I wonder? I am glad I was not there to see it. I might have thrown up a fuss.

***

As we entered MSG for rehearsals, I could feel its history within its walls. This place was where Marilyn Monroe sang "Happy Birthday, Mr. President." It was JFK's 45th birthday celebration on 19 May 1962, and I was thirteen. It was a special day for America to celebrate, the day the president was born. He was a president we loved. I remember just how much it meant to me as I watched it on the telly with my family. It is so powerful when a nation is held in honor together. It reaches beyond the telly. It touched my childhood heart that night with Love.

More memories emerged as I sat in the empty hall listening to

David warming up. Roger walked back and forth across the stage giving directions to the road crew. Things must be right. It was here that John Lennon made his final live performance. It was 28 November 1974. Elton John was in concert, when Lennon walked onto the stage. The audience was silent as the surprise took hold. They had made a bet while recording "What ever gets you through the night." If it made it to number one, Lennon would join Elton in his Thanksgiving Concert, and it did.

It was the only single of John's solo career to hit number one. Therefore, he lived up to the deal and rocked out together with Elton. They also sang "Lucy in the Sky with Diamonds," which further filled the hearts of the audience with Joy and the feeling of Miracles. With arms swaying in the air, the magic of the song came alive once again. Now it was our turn and it was another national celebration, 4th of July, Independence Day.

Juliette Wright and her children, Gala and Jamie, were to fly in from London for the shows. I was looking forward to spending time with them for we had become good friends ever since I arrived in the UK. I had spent a lot of time with Rick and Juliette in their London home watching their children grow up. Juliette was highly cosmopolitan and I met many creative and eccentric people who I found very inspiring. We always had a laugh and I can still hear the sound of Juliette's mirth, as we often sat together at the mixer.

During our time together, Rick and Juliette shared many stories about the early Pink Floyd, especially about Sid. It was all new to me. I had been carried like a feather on the wind into their history. I wanted to know more. Rick had been very close to Sid, trying hard to help him find balance towards the end of his time with the band. One of Sid's girlfriends would often be there at their dinner parties or just over for a cup of tea with the girls for a chat. She was so beautiful and reminded me a bit of Jayne Mansfield.

We spent time together often walking down the Kings Rd.

window shopping, appreciating all the London fashions. We had stopped in a café for a light lunch when she shared with me that Sid was a real challenge, as he was prone to being jealous. Their relationship was during the most difficult period when Sid was becoming rather unstable. He was possessive, controlling and prone to explosions.

I can see why he was that way due to his insecure and drug induced perspective. It seems he had reccurring concerns of the loss of his relationship with her. His insecurity stirred by the fact that she was extremely glamorous and men were very attracted to her. His concern was unfounded, but was real to him. As he was not of sound mind at the time, this characteristic rather dominated their relationship, which had to end sadly to safeguard her own sanity.

***

I hadn't been in the States during the 4th of July celebrations for many years, *let alone,* to be in New York for a Floyd gig at Madison Square Garden. There was such a buzz in the air as the essence of independence marked the moment. American flags came out of the closets and were waving in the breeze, hanging from the apartment buildings and windows. Huge flags were on metal poles everywhere. People were wearing red, white and blue everything. It was a party in the streets. My heart filled with such happiness being home once again in America in the atmosphere of jubilation.

I loved Europe, but 4th of July weekend awakened something archetypal as I looked out of my taxi window. It was my national spirit. On that day, Juliette, Jenny McCreddie and I were going shopping, which was our custom. We always looked for something that was special and not found in London to take home. Jenny was Warwick's wife who was one of the first of David's friends that I had met way back when my journey began. They were part of my family across the waters. Now Warwick was our PA on tour and his sister, Winsome, and her husband, Peter, took care of our home and animals. Later they became surrogate Aunt and Uncle for our children.

The Floyd were always punctual. The gigs started at 8:00 p.m. sharp and the audiences were hyped up and ready. Tickets were hard to get, as they had to be purchased by mail order, so it was a precious evening for most. When the lights dimmed, the crowd went crazy with whistles and shouts of excitement. It was deafening, but you could still hear the music. It was during "Dogs" that the audience were taken to greater heights. David's guitar leads proved the best in the first half while the inflatables floated to the ceiling. The second half was oldies but goodies with "Us and Them" holding the audience silently spellbound. But "Money" as the encore got them to their feet again.

On the 3rd of July, the audience were more restless. It was getting closer to the 4th of July and the city, perhaps the country, was getting rather over-stimulated. Consequently, they set off fireworks in the hall several times during the show. This did alarm the band, the promoter and the NYPD. So much so, that on the 4th there would be stronger precautions and searches at the door.

Fireworks were not to be the only challenge in MSG during our time in NYC. It was the local union's insistence to do our lighting. *UGH*! The show was so dependent on its precision. There were so many elements to coordinate that only the band's trained team could do it. This was not the first time there was an issue with the unions. Steve O'Rourke was on call trying to find a compromise. Roger swore at them at the end of the show for their incompetence and inability to work together. Fortunately, the fans did not seem to notice. They loved the gig. The show went on despite the pops and the bangs.

In the morning of the 4th, I had the idea to take a horse drawn carriage from Central Park to the gig. Juliette and Jenny were up for it, though I did have to work hard to inspire them. We were dressed in our usual New York City finery and embarked upon our adventure in the open carriage. Rick and Juliette's son, Jamie, sat up front with the driver, exuberant as a young boy would be. It was super riding down the Manhattan streets and the weather was perfect. My favorite movie clips of couples in love, circling Central Park, sparked my imagination, as we rode along under the leaves of the trees. I just loved NYC.

As we got closer to the venue, the crowds started to build up towards the entrance. The NYPD were performing searches for fireworks and other unacceptable items. Of course! I hadn't thought about this situation the night before. Crowd control was keeping the tension checked. At least, we hoped. Unfortunately, it became more difficult to penetrate the crowd with our carriage. We found ourselves stuck amongst them, feeling a bit vulnerable as their agitation grew. Packed like sardines in the heat, worried they would miss the start of the show. Some started to whistle and make wise cracks as we inched along. The horse got nervous along with us. Gone was the security of our limousine. Our eyes reflected our concern behind a brave face and a smile.

We finally reached the backstage entrance all a tremble, still in the carriage, for we were too frightened to leave it amongst the crowd. Juliette and I both agreed that never again would we let our heart fantasy put us in such a situation. We were just grateful to have gotten to the gig safe and in one piece. I often wonder how the journey home was for the carriage man and his horse.

I sat at the mixer as usual, but could not stay long as my nerves were a bit shot. The audience seemed so on edge it sparked mine further. The mischief the night before and our carriage experience, left me unsettled. Feeling the fervor in the hall being between excitement and frustration, became too much. So I left to find sanctuary back stage. Brian Humphries, their sound engineer, told me later that just minutes after I had left, a mini-firecracker exploded close to where I had sat. The one firecracker that got away, Heh? What grace that was. Time and time again, I have been protected even from my own folly.

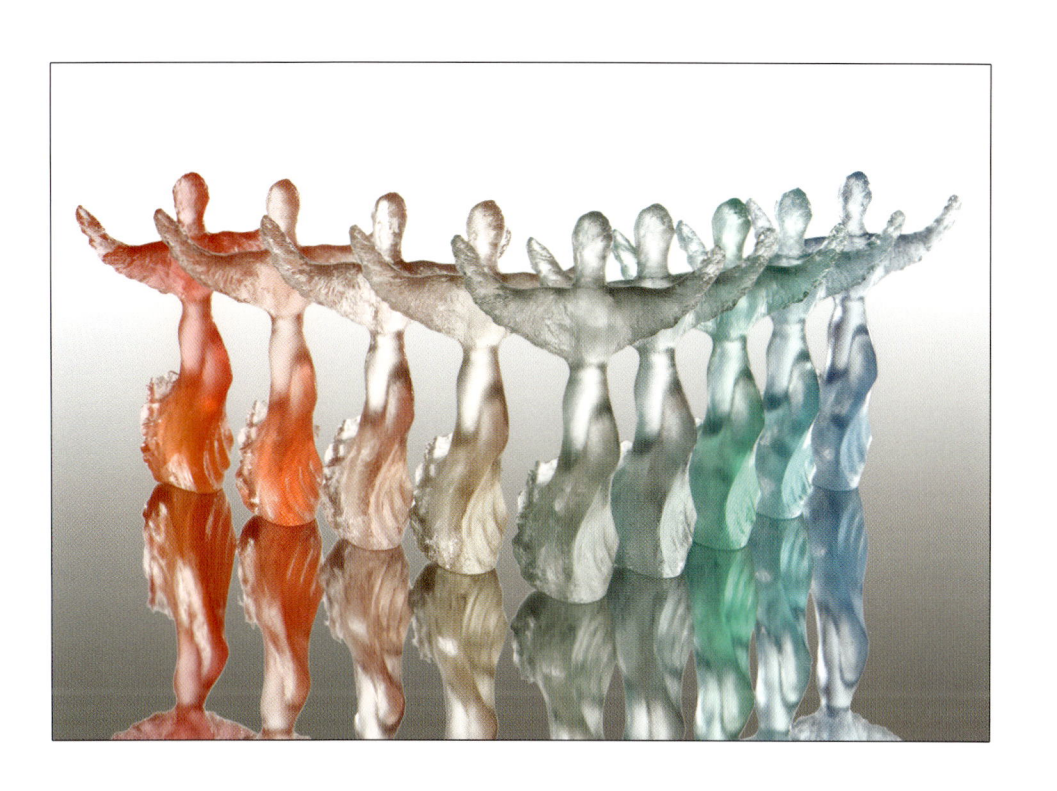

'AERIEL MINIATURES'

2006

Dr Sharma & Companion

CHAPTER 28

IS THERE ANYONE LISTENING?
MONTREAL

6 JULY 1977

It was during the latter part of the tour that the sizes of the crowds were getting Roger down. In fact, in Montreal, he actually spat at the audience because he felt that they were only there to party and not listen. I have to agree with him up to a point. Sitting out at the mixer gave a different perspective. Most of the audience was there to listen and did. The Unruly ones up front made most of the commotion. During the recording of *Animals*, Roger started to act as if he was the sole writer and master of ideas for the band. In addition, he was the only reason that the band could keep going. Gone were the days of unity with the *Dark Side of the Moon*. He was starting to treat the others as hired musicians sadly forgetting how the Floyd came to be.

I always saw Roger's frustration, but he was becoming more narcissistic. I firmly felt that he did not realize the energetic and creative parts that David and the others contributed towards balancing his character traits. Or realize how much they were a gestalt and that their music formed through their alchemical process. It might just be his soul, calling him to leave the band. He was a tortured man. Our challenge was not to go down the slippery slope with him. Time would tell.

Roger had divorced Judy, his first wife, in 1975 and had fallen in love with Lady Caroline Christie. They married in 1976. Their bond seemed to reinforce Roger's ego trip or perhaps encouraged his path of his own creative realization. The process did stir the waters. All the wives stood behind their man but each had different ways to do that. As the families grew, the gestalt of the Floyd had to adapt. Whether that was good or not, it was what it was. Roger was always taking much of his frustrations out on Rick and I slowly observed Rick's resolve breaking over the years. Somehow, I don't think he liked being a punching bag. Who would?

    I remember when each of them had been gifted Cartier watches. Later, we were all sitting by the pool, having lunch at Roger's house in the South of France, while the band was there to record *The Wall*. Some of us rented a home while the Floyd recorded their next creative cycle for the album. Roger was in one of his moods, and he asked if he could look at Rick's watch. As Roger was holding it in his hand, he leaned over the pool and dropped it in the water. Rick said nothing. Roger's expression on his face was one of silent satisfaction. He had won that round.

    I think on that day, I began to lose my tolerance for the psychological games they often played between each other for fun. David often stayed quiet and even today his guitar is where he expresses the depth of what he feels. Unfortunately, our life together was changing, as the music changed its emphasis into transforming Roger's archetypical struggles. Or were they ours as well?

    In that last gig in Montreal, David held a silent, stubborn stance and walked off the stage because the band did not perform well. He refused to do an encore because he felt it was a lie of honor. The gigs were getting so technical. The music was becoming lost in the tension. He used to be in his creative world, sometimes standing with his back to the audience feeling. Now he had headphones. They all had headphones. And the freedom to feel the music was disappearing behind the click track.

David had had enough that evening. Snowy White, the second guitarist hired as background support, had to take over during the encore as David had left. In fact, David went out to the mixer to access the situation. My heart leaped to see him standing there. I didn't know what to do, hug him or hold my distance. I chose to wait for I felt a storm brewing. Snowy remembers the moment that he was in the freedom of his guitar. Unfortunately, it was right when the road crew started to dismantle the gear. It was the same night that Roger lost his temper and spat at one of the obnoxious punters below.

We returned to the UK exhausted and needing a break from that part of our life. But such a gift was not forthcoming. One morning I awoke paralyzed in pain from the waist down. I pleaded with David to contact Dr. Sharma. During the tour, Pauline White, Snowy's wife had told me of him and recommended him highly. I had no idea why I wanted to see him. I just did. Later, I was to find out that Dr. Sharma was not only an orthodox trained doctor, but also was an Auyervedic, Homeopath and Naturopath (all alternative healing methods). Of course in those times I had no idea what that meant. I only knew that Pauline said he was brilliant! David found him and arranged an appointment immediately, but he first took me to an osteopath whose treatment eased the pain enough to get to London.

Dr. Sharma's practice was in Seymour Place, London. He was from India and in his office hung a painting of Ramana Maharishi, his guru. He took my pulses and looking at us from behind his glasses and white beard he said, "She should go to my private Naturopathic hospital, Ludshott Manor. IMMEDIATELY!" This was located in the Surrey countryside. My time there was to be an experience that opened a doorway to my higher self, my path to God. To realize that such a thing existed was enough to cope with at that stage.

Dr. Sharma put me onto a diet of grapefruit, chamomile tea and other therapies that were extremely new to me. In addition, I was not to have any contact with the outside world, which included David. I had no idea this was part of it. Had Pauline experienced a separation away from Snowy? I wondered, as I waited to hear from David. Why hasn't he called? Was Alice all right? Not knowing he had tried. At the same time, I was in pain and trying to cope. Later David told me how much this worried him. He felt powerless.

I felt like a shivering rabbit caught under a barbed wire fence not knowing how to get away. Apparently, I really shocked my body when I became a vegetarian so quickly, coupled with me stopping drugs without the supervision of a qualified doctor. I was in major Detox! I learned a lot about this process as a result (Unfortunately, the hard way).

Ludshott was a haven of peace. The garden surrounded by multiple evergreens whose scent filled the morning dew as I walked amongst them. Many mornings I sat alone in my room watching the raindrops on the window in the silence. I had regular Shiatzu treatments with Michael Skipwith, who has become a close and trusted friend. Some of the pieces of the puzzle were beginning to link together as he guided me in how to meditate. Each morning I would go to the small chapel and listen to that small voice, which was starting to awake. The sunlight was returning.

During those treatments, my heart opened, freeing me from the tensions I had collected. Michael referred me to many sacred teachings, especially Ramana Maharishi who was an influence in his life. Michael had spent many months in Ramana's ashram (spiritual retreat) and knew its quiet truth. Ramana's main premise was for us to ask, "*Who am I.*" It emphasized that there was a place beyond all thoughts of such Beauty, but was covered with veils of illusion.

Once one touches that place, all beliefs of what is important, change. Your values and priorities change, influencing and inspiring your choices. You no longer need to seek to be kind, caring and loving because you discover that is what you truly are. Instead of being a human "doing," you become a human "being." "Who AM I" reveals that kindness and compassion is the true nature of us all.

Later, with my health restored, Michael took me to a lecture of Sir George Trevelyan, founder of the Wrekin Trust. Sir George is considered the Father and Herald of the New Age that we know now. There he stood tall, gray hair, chatting with someone. He had an aura of such purity and majesty of heart. Michael knew him well and introduced me. Sir George embraced me. I lost my linear awareness within that embrace. I moved out of my body into the universe. Literally, I saw myself traveling through the stars. Where was I? Just in that moment, he shook me out of it. He knew where I had gone and I didn't have my seat belt fastened nor did I know how to land.

We were to meet again many years later at the home of the Baroness Di Pauli in St John's Wood. It was a gathering of great philosophical minds, wise elders. During tea, I found the moment when I could relate the story to him. With a glint in his eye, Sir George said to me, "I so love this modern era. An elder chap is allowed to give young ladies a hug and a kiss on the cheek without it being an offense." He was in his late 70s.

When I returned home from Ludshott, Dr. Sharma put me on a vegan diet with lots of remedies. I was inspired to take yoga lessons and meditate. David was super. I remember how he tried to meditate with me, but it didn't last long. He even stopped eating meat at home. But the troubles with the band were still growing. David started to grow more silent and I am sure my change along a more spiritual line added to his pressure. We were so young and caught in many rounds of growing tensions. He tried to honor all the changes on the practical level because of my health. Something stirred like a little pinprick in his side festering.

No Tomatoes, No Peanut Butter was part of Doctor's orders. Tomatoes are part of the deadly nightshade family and I could only eat them if they were homegrown with no pesticides. Peanut butter is not a nut, but a legume and it clogs the system if eaten in quantity. I had to be especially careful. No more peanuts and beer at the pub. I didn't even take aspirin or have any drinks with caffeine, only herbal teas. Not even Coca-Cola with my pizza. "Pizza? Coca-Cola? Peanut butter? Cheese? What is that?" was the question for years. Then there was the hurdle of asking for a glass of sparkling water at a party. That was a more difficult one for everyone to accept. Looking back, one could say Dr. Sharma was a forerunner of eating organic and so was I. In a land of meat and potatoes, it was not easy.

Meditating was a jewel. It helped me to breathe through any pain that life challenged me with, from headaches to indigestion. It helped me to stay in contact with the breath of Life instead of the shortness of panic breathing. Luckily, a few years later Dr. Sharma said that it was time for me to start eating 10% rubbish foods and return to eating vegetarian since I ran the risk of getting too precious. Too precious, for a Rock 'n' Roll existence, especially as there was limited access to the foods I needed away from home, while on tour, or holiday in foreign countries.

David seemed ok with it all, for he would eat what I cooked at home. Many have made humorous comments that he would eat meat when I wasn't looking. And Emo said that he would secretly go to the pub for a steak and chips. I only noticed this when we went to a restaurant. I didn't require him not to eat meat. I was a great cook. And as time went by, people didn't even notice the difference. It was a difficult period for vegetarians in those days, needless to mention being a vegan. Eating out became more a social affair for me, a gathering of people I loved. I was healthier and that is all that mattered.

Most people, including David, had little understanding of its virtues. Even David's parents, Doug, a geneticist, and Sylvia, a film editor, both from Cambridge came to me upset one day. They said that I was going to kill their son and their granddaughter, Alice. We had on-going discussions. I give them credit for they did their research and eventually adopted a very similar way of eating. Time passed and I became more knowledgeable about food combining and a more balanced way of living. Sadly, it did start to weigh upon our relationship.

At first, I think I was so excited and full of beans that perhaps I was rather too much to handle for others who still were into drugs and hard living. I felt I had found the elixir of life and wanted to share. I wanted to tell the world, which Americans tend to do when inspired. The British and Europeans are different, and Life kept showing me how to walk the talk in their world. I was learning how Silent proof of harmony, peace and joy really sells the story. But at the time in England, being inspired along a spiritual path, including being vegetarian or vegan was rather challenging for most except for the Beatles, who we were to get to know many years later.

I find it amazing, while writing this book, what Beauty and yet what Challenges we experienced. Amazingly, we are still alive. With each page, I have a greater understanding and Love for life, for the journey. And I am grateful for all the moments we shared together including the band. I have come to know that the path I follow is an ART. It is beyond the need for words until someone asks. Even then, "Talk doesn't necessarily cook the rice!" So I am sure I broke a few eggs along the way. Sorry.

As I looked at a photo of the band this morning, I had tears and an ache in my heart for the Love that is still there despite it all. We shared so many moments. I appreciate them and don't miss them.

How could I when it was my life? I am just grateful. In addition, I am also grateful for what I live now. I am grateful for my own creative flowering, which finds earth, water and sunlight to grow within each moment. And writing this book of memories is only the beginning of another cycle being born, showing me the way to my soul purpose.

'ANGELIC BLESSING'

2005

Lindos B4 the 'Wall'

CHAPTER 29

THE BUILDING OF THE WALL

1977-1980

We returned to the UK to discover that the Floyd was in a potential financial disaster. Norton Warburg was proving not to be the best advisor for our financial affairs. Since *Dark Side,* we were in need of advice and turned to Andrew Warburg. I remember David saying once that he really didn't want to go into having investments. He preferred just to bank the money and wanted to keep it simple. However, the sums got too great to keep it humble. Therefore, unlike other bands who were taken by their managers, which the Floyd had under control, their accountant took them. It seemed to sneak in under the floorboards catching them a bit off guard. Norton Warburg eventually crashed and Andrew left the country ASAP.

The band had to find a way out of the mess and they were unprepared. In the past, they had a rhythm of touring, recording, touring and time off for writing. They would come together and an album would be born from their collaboration. This time it was different. David, Nick and Rick had worked on solo projects previously to *Animals*. Roger was the only one with ideas on the back burner that were ready for use immediately. He had two suggestions, which might be possible for album projects: *Bricks in the Wall* and *The Pros and Cons of Hitchhiking.*

They met at Roger's for days. All they did was argue. "No, that is awful. No, that one is terrible." I can't speak for the others, but David returned home grumpy. I don't blame any of them, as it was a huge problem to resolve. They were on the edge of a sinking ship worth maybe £12,000,000, payable to the taxman. And the bank balance was low thanks to Warburg's bad investments. Finally, after much discussion and debate, they decided to work towards developing *The Wall*.

We returned to Lindos that summer. We stayed in Auntie Mary's house, the Museum, in order to oversee the conversion of our house on the other side of the village. David had been playing the demo tape over and over throughout our holiday. It was excruciating. Roger's pain was so deep. I will never forget when, one afternoon, David emerged from the sala (a Lindian living room) shaking his head saying, "I don't think I can really work with this. I have no idea how this could become something people would enjoy listening to. It is just Angst!" But he had to in order to rescue us all from our financial predicament. He had no choice. We thought. So the real work would begin back in the UK in the autumn.

One of the highlights of that summer was when Simon and Garfunkel along with Carrie Fisher and friends, arrived into Lindos bay in a HUGE cabin cruiser. Carrie and Simon were on their honeymoon. Garfunkel gifted them with a Mediterranean Cruise so they headed for Lindos to visit Melissa who was their good friend. Dixie and Alice otherwise called Dixie and Pixie, were waddling up the hill from the beach behind them chatting under their breath, "She doesn't look like Princess Leia!" "No, she doesn't have any buns!" Oh, out of the mouths of babes!

We were all invited to hang out on the boat each day. Carrie wanted to go shopping in town so Emo volunteered to take her around. He was staying with us that summer at the Museum. Like us, Lindos was becoming his home in the summer. Rick and Linnie Wills (David's bass guitarist from Joker's Wild) were also staying with us with their first child, Nicky. As Emo and Carrie were turning one of the corners, they all met. Nicky exclaimed pulling on Linnie's skirt, "Oh look Mommy. It's Princess Leia!" Someone recognized her without her buns and white dress. Emo said they all smiled and said, "See ya later at dinner," and walked away on their shopping adventure. Carrie commented to Emo later, "I haven't been called that for a while."

So *Star Wars* had come to Lindos. We had a very grand dinner to celebrate their arrival and our growing friendship. Emo sat next to Carrie. Being a *Star Wars* fan, Emo raved how wonderful the movies were. How David and I had gotten him premier tickets when it first came to London. It meant so much to him to think there would be two sequels. He said she freaked! She felt trapped. She went on to share a lot of stories of how that movie had compounded upon her life. Some good, but most troubled. Here he was expressing his love for the movies and instead came face to face with the reality of the star who brought so much joy in his life. It was sad.

As I relate this story, I feel this too has been our challenge as it is with most people launched into fame. The story plays over and over. The temptation to go down with the pressure, the adulation and the lack of your own life is great. We were sometimes drowning trying to hold on to the Beauty and Love in our heart. We walked hand in hand in front of the adoration caught between the glamour and "Who am I?" Caught between the ART and the LIE.

Turkish Delight
Christian Mouzon, our skipper

CHAPTER 30

ANCIENT HISTORY UPON THE SEAS

SUMMER 1978

This year we made a trip to Turkey at the invitation of our dear friend Christian Mouzon. The idea would give us some light relief from the pressures that were building back home. Christian was in charge of getting Sandro Somare's boat, "Plimiri," ready for the summer when he and his family would come to Lindos. He was like a member of their family and usually spent his winters with Sandro in Tuscany, Italy.

We had wanted to go to Turkey for years, for our friends in Lindos shared many stories filled with sparkle in their eyes of great adventures. Alice was safe with our trusted nanny, Jeannie Bell, at Aunty Mary's in Lindos, allowing us to go away for a week. So we said, "Yes." Our plan was to leave from Rhodos and go down the coast of Turkey, which we could see on a clear day. Its magic called to us. Our first port of call was Marmaris for that is where we had to have our passports stamped before entering Turkey, even by water.

Marmaris is considered the Saint Tropez of the country, and at night, the bay is lit with the bright lights of many restaurants, hotels and discos. Eastern music mixed with Western songs traveled together through the warmth of the air as we ate on the waterfront, on the night of our arrival. Christian was familiar with the city and took us deep into its heart to its marketplace. Carpets and embroideries hung from the stalls floating in the light breeze. The air smelled of spices, dried fish and the dung of chickens and donkeys. Turkey is a feast of colors, even the boats. The vibrancy of each color was different from Greece. I got high just looking at the blue paint of the tables mixed with Turquoise and yellows on the chairs.

There was a man begging, sitting on the dirt below one of the stalls who had his fingers cut off since he had been caught stealing. I felt pity and wanted to help but David pulled me away speaking under his breath, "Don't. You can't do anything" as he led me in the opposite direction. I whispered in a tone that expressed my feelings, "But it's tragic! It's awful!"

I really don't know what I could have done anyway. This was just one of the ways the law dealt with crime in Turkey. There are worse stories, I was told later. It was a shocking eye opener, especially as this occurs in many cultures. It was such a condemnation of a person's future. What future? A life without fingers? These things really disturbed me. An inner voice shouted, "Humanity needs to find more Compassion, more Wisdom! We need help!"

As the sun grew higher and mid-day approached, we found shade in a café. We ordered the traditional sage tea, Ata-chi, which came served in a metal teapot the shape of Aladdin's Lamp. The waiter first brought us little narrow glasses about two inches high embellished with gold designs and a plate of Turkish delight sweets. Lifting the teapot high above the glasses, he proceeded to pour the tea without losing a drop. This custom enhanced its flavor as the tea descended from above traveling through the air greeting each glass. It was so refreshing that I bought the teapot and glasses and have made it since often.

Before we left the market, we filled our baskets with fresh vegetables, eggs, water, bread, and all the extra staples we would need for our journey. We bought a few carpets to take back to England, and a painted blue basket with flowers. Haggling in the market was a custom in which I was not skilled. In America, the price was the price. In Turkey, you gained favor if you did succeed in securing a cheaper price especially if you were good at it. If not, the price went up or the sale did not happen. They had a skill on how to play the tourists. Christian was our captain and kept us straight in matters of bartering. He had been there on many adventures in the past and knew the ropes.

Christian had invited a dear friend, Linda Shorten. She was so beautiful and such a kind person. Her hair was long cascading waves the color of amber. She was easy to be with. I dressed modestly, hair tied back with a large straw hat, as did Linda for I had learned to respect other cultures after some of our other adventures. The four of us made a great team, which is so helpful when on sea adventures in close quarters. David and I loved being on the sea. I often took my place up at the bow watching the water as we glided along with the wind. David helped with the tiller, as Christian changed the sails.

The water was clear as blue crystal and we would often moor off the coast to have a swim. We dove off the boat into its refreshing coolness. It felt like silk caressing my body as I dove deeper twirling like a dolphin. My blonde hair was moving around in the water like a mermaid within the sparkling lights. All my life I sought to be one with the water, graced by its wonder. Last year I was inspired to write a piece of prose seeking to capture the essence of this experience where silence touches my soul in the watery sunlight.

BREATH OF LIFE

As the waves approach the shore

I breathe inwards and enter within the crystal waters below

It washes away the tensions held deep within my heart

I dive deeper and deeper into the sparkling lights

As the waves encourage my return

I breathe outwards to be touched by the sunlight

Again and again I breathe rhythmically to the movement

Below and above

As the Beauty of my Spirit is revealed

Once again touched by the Breath of Life

© Ginger Gilmour

One evening we sailed into a small sheltered harbor only reachable by boat. It seemed lost from normal time and tourism. Ladies in simple Turkish dresses approached us in little wooden rowboats captained by their son or husband. The bay seemed asleep as we entered between the cliffs that hid its presence. So it was like magic when they appeared out of the blue.

There were lots of them. How did they know we were coming? Within moments, they surrounded our boat waving scarves with starched embroidered flowers on the edges, speaking in their mother tongue, hoping for a sale. Their skin dark, cracked from the sun but their eyes glistened. At first, we could only see mushroomed shaped rocks near the shore and a small-pebbled beach. So where was their village? Then we noticed there was one café store that sat just back up on the slope, indicating that there was life beyond.

After dropping our anchor, we prepared to go ashore. There were curious mushroom shaped rocks about six foot high, worn by the winter storms in the distance marking our way. They were like monoliths emerging from the water. We got closer, stirring our little zodiac between them. We noticed that upon the top of each was an ancient coffin. Each coffin had carvings and was made of a different stone than that of the mushroom. They seemed melted together, joined perhaps from the calcification of the seawater over time, set into the cliffs above the water's edge and scattered around the village. I wondered and still wonder how this came about. It was a curious mixture–a mausoleum honoring the dead and the villagers who were alive.

In the morning, we wandered around the village, which lay hidden from view behind the monoliths. Life was in full swing as we followed the smell of bread baking. There was a woman sitting on the ground next to an open fire between two of these tombs. She had a metal plate placed upon the embers of the fire and was cooking bread very similar to Naan from India. They were larger and she kindly sold some to us once she realized what our hand gestures meant.

After breakfast, we set off again upon our adventures in the uncharted waters. (For that is what it felt like when out at sea.) It was just the sky, the sea and the boat. Christian often looked like the Christ silhouetted against the sails as he took them down. The clanking sound of the anchor rising from the water, clicking of the metal ropes in the wind and the flapping of the sails became familiar sounds close to my heart.

Further down the coast, we dropped anchor in a quiet corner of Ekincik Bay. It was a desolate place and its land covered with green pine forests. We moored there for the night. Christian planned for us to visit Kaunos the next day, which was not far away. He wanted it to be a day of Ancient discovery of the power of the Roman Empire, but we had to wait like little excited school children.

As the afternoon temperature cooled, Linda and I sat on deck preparing vegetables to accompany dinner. The sun was setting, reflecting its golden colors intermingling with the greens and blues of the still waters, when suddenly, one after another came a swarm of wasps. Christian shouted, "Quick! Get below!" We gathered our preparations just in time to find safety behind the doors of the cabin. Apparently, this was a usual occurrence at that time of the year, especially when there is the smell of food.

That evening we took sanctuary in the kitchen until dark. Christian cooked a wonderful dinner and we ate by lantern light, played cards to the Eagles, the Beatles, the Stones and many others. David had brought along his summer compilation, which he was extremely good at making each year. Summers in Lindos would not be the same without it. We slept as if babies until Christian tiptoed into our cabin.

Whispering, he nudged David to come with him, holding his finger over his mouth, "*Shhh*! Come quickly." David did what he said putting on his jeans and followed quietly. A boat had dropped anchor rather close to our boat. It was still dark, but the sun was showing a wee glimmer upon the horizon. It was too close for comfort and gossip had it that pirates still roamed the seas in that region. I peeked out the little window shivering, worried.

The lads made small talk while raising the anchor. The pirates were not pirates but rather part of a cooperative of villagers who would take people from their sailboats around the corner to Kaunos. We still found it a bit suspicious as it was rather early so we set sail for our next destination rather sprightly. We dropped anchor again, closer to the ancient site where all the tour boats moored along a wide and white sand beach. We made our way in our own little powered zodiac up through the narrow silted delta, slowly, mouths wide open, as the wonder of this ancient place appeared.

Lost in Time
Kaunos, Turkey

CHAPTER 31

LOST IN TIME AT KAUNOS

So there it was, the adventure Christian had planned for us to experience, the ancient seaport of Kaunos. Today, it is a magnificent ancient example of a day gone by of when the Romans conquered that part of Turkey. One's imagination could easily return to Troy and the Trojan horse despite that this was not the place. It was truly breathtaking and is an incredible experience of the passage of history as one wanders from one site to the other.

Kaunos was once an important seaport and is a mixture of Greek, Roman and Byzantine ruins dating back to the 10th century BC. It had two ports originally, but due to the silting of the delta and the ports by the Hellenistic period, Kaunos had long lost its important function as a trade port. Further on, in the 15th century, it was totally abandoned due to a malaria epidemic and Turkish raiders. Then a severe earthquake totally devastated it and buried the city under sand and dense vegetation. Forgotten until an English archeologist (Hoskyn) discovered a tablet during a dig in the area in 1842. His discovery brought Kaunos back into the public eye.[1]

There are still remains of the Acropolis from which one can get a feeling of the city's size and original greatness. The vista took my breath away while we sat on the top row of the huge amphitheater, which was on the slope, just below the Acropolis. It is one of the largest that I have ever visited. Being 75 meters in diameter and could hold 5000 spectators in its day. I remember looking up at the top where David was standing like Colossus, his long hair blowing in the wind, his bronzed body revealed above his blue jeans, as he had taken off his T-shirt.

There were so many other sites. No wonder Christian wanted for us to spend the whole day there. The palestra once had a Roman bath of such proportions that it spoke of the opulence of the time. It was eventually dismantled and a church was built with the fragments as Kuanos was Christianized. Eventually that too collapsed and was replaced by a Byzantine Basilica, which still stands along with the most beautiful mosaic floors. I was inspired by their intricate designs made visible through the delicate work of the archeologists.

They had excavated six temples by the time we were there. Six rock tombs with two Ionian pillars, a triangular pediment, an architrave with toothed friezes, and a criterions shaped like palm leaves; including many pedestals which most probably were adorned with bronze sculptures of Roman noblemen. There was a huge wall surrounding parts of the city including the Agora Fountain. How all of this was hidden for centuries amazed me. The sheer immensity was staggering and all due to the ingenuity of the Roman times that allowed the city to prosper.

Compared to the little coastal village with the coffins scattered around in close proximity to daily life, Kuanos was different. It is surrounded by ancient necropolis, because the ancient Greeks and Romans always buried their deceased at considerable distance from their homes. Further, beyond the archeological site of Kaunos, there are also tens of niche tombs hewn from the rock. It is said that the ashes of the deceased were put in urns and then placed in a niche. This was the most common practice amongst the people unlike the rich who had more adorned tombs as mentioned above.

Many of which have stood the test of time. This custom makes me wonder about the history of the other village.

So our journey had reached its height and it was time for us to return to Lindos. Our sail back home was with the wind, which is my favorite way. Running with the wind, the boat glides as though lifted from the surface of the water and just the *Shh-ish Shh-ish* of the boat greeting the waves is heard. Often, we were graced to be escorted by a pod of dolphins, which lifted our spirits as we headed home to be reunited with our Alice. Love, Love!

Ginger & Alice
Lindos, Greece

CHAPTER 32

TAX EXILE
SILENT BEAUTY DISAPPEARS BEHIND THE WALL

1979

It was around March-April, David came home and said that we had to do a tax exile year. English tax laws were such that this would be the only way to get out of our mess. With our income bracket and the possible income tax liability from the Warburg affair, we had no other choice. The word Exile made us tremble. The thought of not being able to return to our home without David for a year was weird. It brought an understanding and more compassion for my mother. It reminded me of the times Ron, my stepfather, had gone on isolated duty in Libya with the Coast Guard for one year. It reminded me of when he went again to Alaska for one year. The tension in the family was not something I wanted to relive. We had to go with David.

Overnight, we found ourselves packing and leaving the country A.S.A.P. We went back to Lindos, as our house was nearly ready to live in until other plans materialized for where the Floyd would continue to record. I interviewed several ladies to be our nanny for our year away. Sue Turner entered the fold. Eventually, we would re-locate in a home near Super Bear Studio in Berre-les-Alpes, France, where the creating of *The Wall* would further manifest.

In addition, we asked our dear friend Christian Mouzon to come as family support while David was working. We had grown very close during our time in Turkey and we thought he would be a perfect addition to our team. He was French and as only David spoke French, he would be a great asset to us at home. The process was swift as I recall. By the time we settled in Lindos, to my surprise, I began having not only morning sickness but also afternoon sickness. I was pregnant with our second child.

Our home in France was a lovely ground level French stone structure amongst a forest of pine trees. It was hot, but we were graced with a swimming pool to cool us down from the summer heat. Alice and I often played on our rubber rafts in the late afternoon sun splashing about like little kids. I was getting rather pregnant and often sought refuge in the shade.

Some afternoons we would have rain showers. Waiting for the rainbows, Alice and I could be found in our bikinis, lying in the garden at the back of the house in the rain, arms out. I told Alice that the rainwater in the mountains was good for our hair and our skin so we would lie there happily getting soaked. We would giggle and laugh together. Sometimes she would put her ear upon my growing tummy and speak to her next brother or sister with loving words.

Some days I would go with David to Super Bear. There were very special walks down the road from the studio. The air was always full of the scent of pine and mimosa. The branches hung down over the path laden with yellow fluffy flowers and the morning dew would wet my face as I parted them along the way. There was a moment during my first walk amongst this wonder of nature that I had such a fright. Bathed in its Beauty as I was, I parted the low-lying pine branches when unexpectedly the path abruptly stopped. There I was teetering on the edge of a deep ravine. I felt off balance with my pregnant tummy hanging out before me. Leaning against the rock face next to me, taking a moment to stand still, I regained my composure.

To continue I had to walk carefully along a narrow path to the left. I felt like a mountain climber minding each step for fear of falling. It was majestic. Over the years, the winds created bonsais amongst the rocks below and across the cliffs on the other side. Eventually, I found a place to sit and bathed in the silence surrounded by this breathtaking beauty.

I meditated, chanting sounds of peace and love for my baby growing within. I felt I was in a Zen temple molded by nature hidden away from the ordinary passerby. When I could, I would visit my secret place where I found peace with Mother Nature. It seemed Heaven was upon Earth there and it nurtured my soul and my baby.

It was not so within the Walls of the studio. The contrast between the calm of nature's temple and the creative process amongst the band made it rather difficult to be there for long. As time went by, I especially found it painful to witness Rick losing his self under the pressure of Roger's growing domination. Since *Animals,* there started to be no room for Rick to express his innate qualities, nor David, but David persevered and found a way.

Others have written that Rick had nothing to offer, but I feel there was another contributing factor that created this difficulty within Rick. There was no room for his true soul to enter which I will explain later. What also made it difficult was the fact that he was often the punching bag. The camaraderie of the band's relationship was always boy tease boy, but for me this was getting to be too cruel. Rick buckled. It was heartbreaking to watch. Nevertheless, I feel there is another invisible aspect that turned off his creativity.

In writing this, I have discovered that Rick was inspired by Stockhausen, a German composer, who's known to be "One of the great visionaries of 20th-century music."[1] He was known for his groundbreaking work in electronic music, aleatory (controlled chance) in serial composition, and musical spatialization. I can see his influence in a lot of Rick's compositions and playing.

But as Roger's need to have his vision dominate, his inner turmoil increased, it did not make fertile ground for such music to grow, or for David's intuitive way to bring forth that silent flavor. The flavor, which both contributed to within the sound of Pink Floyd. Upon reflection and some research, I was unearthing an invisible aspect of this time, which I had never considered, buried under the Wall.

From an energetic and spiritual understanding, the force of such deep angst (ONLY I AM, THIS IS MINE) closed the doorway to the Beauty they had created in the past. Consequently, it was quite a task to create Harmony, a struggle to transform such negative emotions. It was often said that Roger was determined to get his way, often in sacrifice to the music. Out of desperation, the band became involved with transforming Roger's shadow instead. It was an uphill struggle. Things had to change and did eventually. However, it did leave its mark on all of us.

***

The reason why I wanted to bring this into the story of my journey with the Floyd is that in 2006, Blessed Father John, a Cathar Master from Spain, asked me to paint a piece of artwork. He felt that I was an artist that could paint the spiritual energy, which radiated in his work, which seeks to uplift humanity. He believed strongly that Art is a universal medium that can speak beyond borders, especially, if it is born from an intention of Love and Beauty.

It had been my wish for years to do artwork for spiritual teachers, whose philosophy uplifted humanity in this way. The opportunity arrived on the wings of a messenger who was a dear friend, Hans Guenther. He said that Father John wanted to see me. I traveled several times to Spain to spend time with Father John so that I could capture his resonance. He believes strongly that there is a light within each of us, which can't be put out. He encourages each of us to know the God Light in our hearts.

During those meetings, I experienced the work of Stockhausen but I didn't know it. Father John was also a concert pianist famous in his motherland Russia. Today he not only is considered a prophet, but he also inspires musicians and singers who are on a spiritual path to open to the celestial sounds of the heavens. There is a group who work and study with him called "Consolomente."

One night I went to one of their concerts in Spain. Throughout the evening, sounds that were familiar in many ways bathed me. What I heard was so similar to the Floyd, but more angelic. The notes seem to travel across the stage, from the instruments to the voices as though it was one continuous fluctuating sound and then back again. It traveled over the audience uniting us together in its Beauty.

After I went backstage, I complimented them for such uplifting and beautiful music and asked how they played the way they did. Where did they learn to be so at one, together in their music with the space, and then merge all of us in the audience? I had experienced this merging many times before at the Floyd gigs, especially at Earls Court. But this was even more special. I was fascinated. My inquiry kept going as more questions appeared bubbling from the elation of the evening. I have done that often before. Bubbled! Who inspired them finally came forth? They said Stockhausen and Father John. I had no idea who Stockhausen was then, but I do now. I was curious to find out more, but until today, I did not know of Rick's interest.

***

Many Floyd books reference Roger this and Roger that. They all seem to talk about him being the visionary and yes, he did carry those elements. In his banter, the world forgot that the Floyd were a creative gestalt, within which, were many aspects needed to have made their music happen. Some are visible, some invisible. All that we have read built the image that Roger was the main force keeping the band going forth. The stories do not acknowledge another level of vision, which transformed Roger's melodrama into something of Archetypical Beauty. It came through the work of the whole of the group. The suffering turned to Hope hovering in the darkness.

Somewhere I read about Roger's excitement—about how the audience would be able to experience the show from all angles, sound wise as he stood high up in the auditorium. "Sound in the Round" was one of their wonderful qualities. This special aspect always touched me. It so brought the audience into a union with the music. I am taken back to Ann Arbor when I first heard them playing. Great sound traveling around in the space where we sat creating magic.

In fact, not many groups then even had a good sound balance. I would ask David, "Why were there not more groups using it? Why don't they have good sound mixing? Surely they must realize that we want to hear what is on the albums!" It was always one of my niggling comments after many concerts that we went to throughout the years. I definitely had a high standard I suppose.

While referencing Stockhausen I came upon something else I that I would like to share with you.

> *"In 1958 Stockhausen called for new kinds of concert halls to be built, "suited to the requirements of spatial music." His idea was a spherical space which is fitted all around with loudspeakers. In the middle of this spherical space, a sound-permeable, transparent platform would be suspended for the listeners. They could hear music composed for such standardized spaces coming from above, from below and from all points of the compass. His*

music dealt with the integration of all concrete and abstract (synthetic) sound possibilities (also all noises), and the controlled projection of sound in space" giving the impression of movement in space. Towards the end of his creative life he finally achieved isomorphism of the four parameters of pitch, duration, dynamics, and timbre."[1]

As I read this, I thought goodness that sounds familiar. That perhaps intuitively this too was the driving and inspirational force, which made the essence of Pink Floyd pre-*Animals* and *The Wall*. Did they know? I never heard it discussed and if they did, it was behind closed doors or perhaps before my time. But honestly, it probably would have gone over my head then.

What spoke to me was between the lines in the silent spaces of their music. It continued to be over the years. Time and time again, it elevated their audience and me beyond ordinary existence in those concerts and albums. It certainly touched my paradisiacal heart. Repeatedly we fell into the timeless euphoric blending within the drama of the lyrics. The silent message of Beauty beyond the conflict, offering a way to transform the challenges of the treadmill we have created. Did they know?

There is no need to have any understanding of any theory. For me, it does not need any explanation. Beauty just is. It has the power to unite. What David and Rick brought to the table, started to be compromised more with *Animals* and then *The Wall*. It had become our life, the conflict. It was in our tissues in the air that we breathed. We were to become like the frog who, when put into cold water and the heat is turned up slowly dies. We didn't jump out.

As we went deeper and deeper into the birth of those albums, we all succumbed little by little into being those albums. I do not think Roger's viewpoint, quoted in many books, is truly the Only explanation of the creative process for those two albums. He felt

David wasn't interested, Rick had nothing to offer and Nick was just a good friend and more interested in his cars. Quite often, he expresses that He worked through the Floyd banter because he wanted to help the others through the difficulty. I think there is another side to the "*Wall*" not mentioned. It was really our soul struggle to "BE what we were born to BE." To clear the way so we could live the highest potential and Shine!

    For sure we did work through difficulties together, The Band, Bob Ezrin, James Guthrie, Steve O'Rourke, and the Families, as we went deeper and deeper into the transformation of Roger's troubles and his visions. So often, the pressure in the room could be cut with a knife. So often, there were days our hearts silently wished not to have the wall.

    I watched David's quiet and sometimes not so quiet influences bring music to us that spoke of hope, outside the lyrics. I saw his struggle. He tried so hard. I watched Rick's withdrawal give a podium for a victim within the subconscious aspects of the story. I watched Nick's struggle between friendship and finding his voice. Ultimately, they each served in their own way to make those albums an archetypal transformation, of what challenges we all have in life; i.e., to truly find freedom, peace and beauty.

    It may have been Roger's visionary story and perhaps Roger should have had the courage to go it alone. Perhaps so much of his inner conflict was actually his trapped soul trying to get out. Perhaps it was God speaking to us. It was certainly evident, but we turned away. Roger and Caroline hid in their own limo, chose a different hotel, and a different caravan while the torment continued. Realization was waiting but didn't come. Perhaps the process was all of ours, which is why we are still not released. The struggle, the conflict, the pain, the beauty, all became our lives even now. We, too, became the gestalt hitting against the wall and blindfolded.

Rick left the band on paper, and in secret agreed to do the gigs (Broken to some). Unable to confront the ever-rising tide, Rick disappeared into history after *The Wall* tour. However, his essence remains on those albums that went before. The drifting silent beauty of his melodies carried on in other ways with other outlets. He wrote *Broken China* dedicated to his third wife Millie and collaborated with Dave Harris on the album *Identity*. In 1994, he was officially reinstated into the New Pink Floyd so the sound began to fly again. His last performance was 6 September 2007, the Premier of David's concert "Remember that Night" at the Odeon Leicester Square, London.

In September of 2008, at the age of 65, Rick died at home of an undisclosed form of cancer, leaving an unfinished solo album, supposedly comprising of a series of instrumental pieces. Did the music of his soul come just before his spirit called? I wonder? David was moved and published a Tribute to Richard Wright on 15 September 2008.

> "No one can replace Richard Wright. He was my musical partner and my friend. In the welter of arguments about who or what was Pink Floyd, Rick's enormous input was frequently forgotten. He was gentle, unassuming, and private, but his soulful voice and playing were vital, magical components of our most recognized Pink Floyd sound. I have never played with anyone quite like him. The blend of his and my voices and our musical telepathy reached their first major flowering in 1971 on Echoes. In my view, all the greatest PF moments are the ones where he is in full flow. After all, without "Us and Them" and "The Great Gig in the Sky," both of which he wrote, what would The Dark Side of the Moon have been? Without his quiet touch, the album Wish You Were Here would not quite have worked. In our middle years, for many reasons, he lost his way for a while; but in the

early Nineties, with 'The Division Bell', his vitality, spark and humor returned to him, and then the audience reaction to his appearances on my tour in 2006 was hugely uplifting and it's a mark of his modesty that those standing ovations came as a huge surprise to him (though not to the rest of us). Like Rick, I don't find it easy to express my feelings in words, but I loved him and will miss him enormously.[2]

As I write this book, I have awakened to just how much the journey still exists inside. And as I awaken the memories, it is like there is a separate video running 24/7. It seems to have always been there in my subconscious, as a parallel existence to the one I am living now. Such a revelation. I am so glad I have chosen to do this. For I have been given an opportunity to let go of the pain that closed my heart during those years. And see the Love that led us on which now fills the space.

But equally, to realize what seeds were planted, which have inspired me to know "Who I AM." I am becoming a gardener choosing what I want to plant. Learning to put just the right amount of water and sun. Through this journey, I know there is another way, which I seek to live, through the *"Art of Creating Beauty"* but most of all through the *"Art of Living Beauty."* Thus, I am being led closer to finding *the Bright-Side of the Moon*.

So on with the Journey.

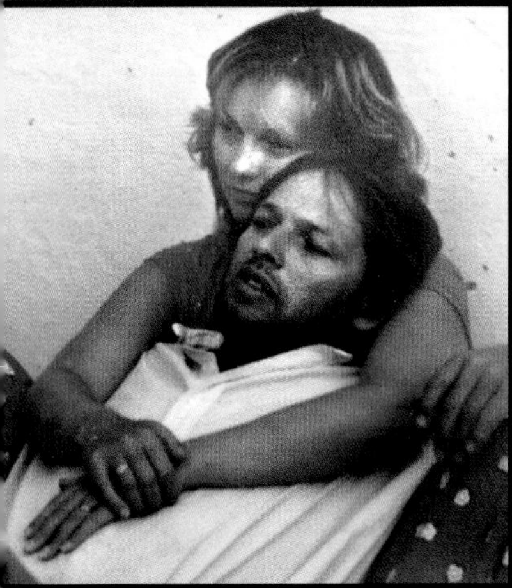
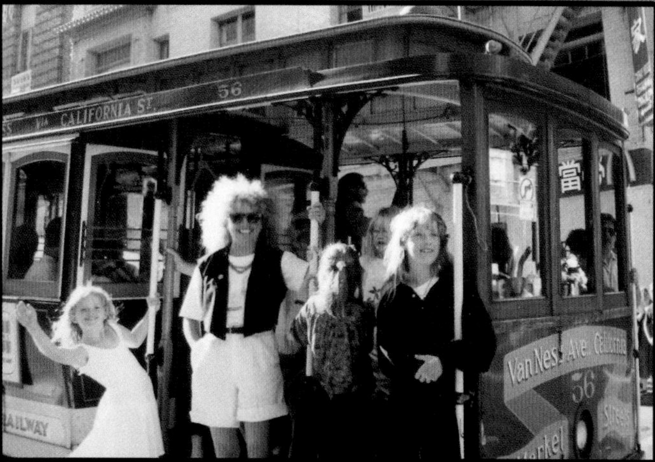
CALIFORNIA ST.
56
Van Ness Ave. California
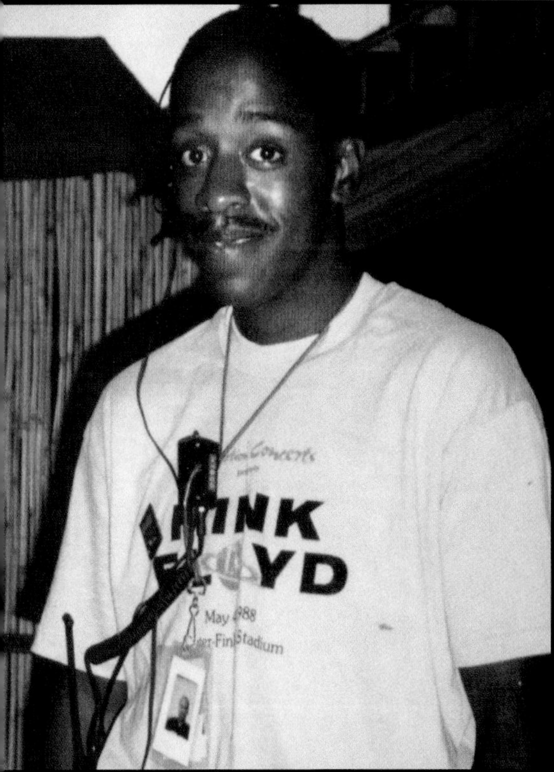
Stadium
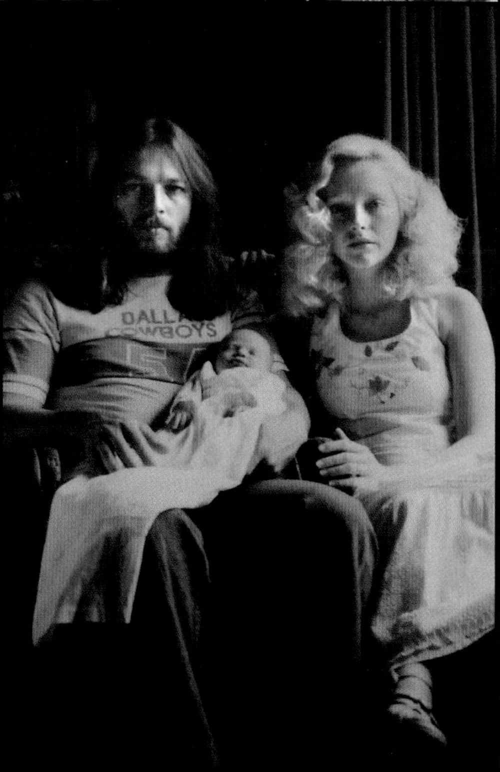
COWBOYS
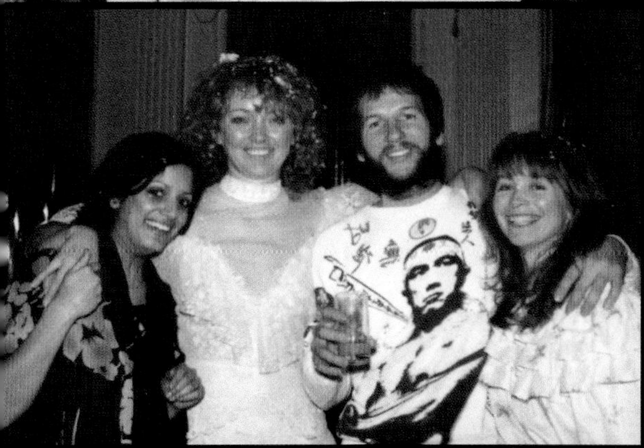
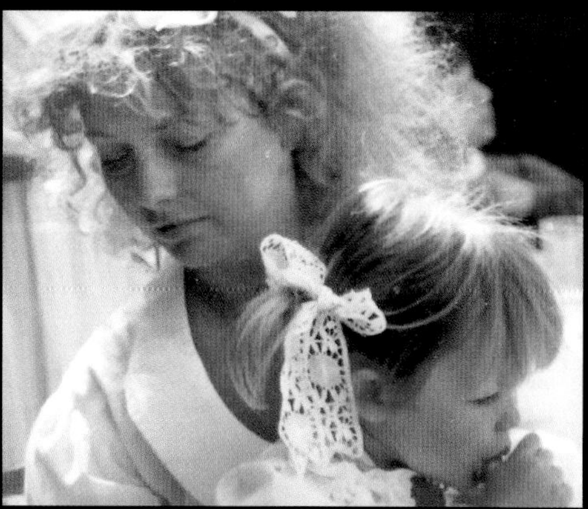

David singing to Alice & Dixie
Lindos, Greece
Effervescent Elephant

CHAPTER 33

MIRACLES DO HAPPEN

While in France, I was in my sixth month of pregnancy. I was lying on our raft in the pool and there were many wasps flying about for that time of the year. When they do, they tend to hang out near the water to get a drink. In this case, it was our pool. I went into the water for a dip and when getting back onto the raft, I was stung. (Not once, but twice.) Within the hour, I went into an allergic reaction and I took to my bed with severe pain in my right kidney.

When David came home he took charge. He called Dr. Sharma in London for advice. He said, "First you must bring in the paramedics and then let me know what they say." France is very sympathetic to homeopathy but my condition had accelerated beyond having a remedy. Two paramedics wearing dark blue entered our bedroom and examined me. They said to David that he should get me to the hospital quick. That I should have my kidney and my baby removed otherwise I would not survive.

I had never experienced such pain in my life. I held on to the bars of our headboard each time the spasms came. I cried, I screamed, I hoped Alice would not hear. David called Dr. Sharma back and gave him the report. He said, "Get her on a plane tomorrow. Give her one shot of Champagne and one shot of Brandy every hour until she gets on the plane." I did not drink in those days so I got a bit tipsy. It did the trick so that I could make the journey back to the UK by myself.

David drove me to the airport and took me as close to my gate as possible. He had such concern on his brow and I could feel his heart was aching. He had to stay and needed Sue and Christian. I was not worried for Dr. Sharma was to meet me at the airport when I landed and could feel my angels. He took me to his clinic on Seymour Place in London, which had two adjoining houses. One was the clinic and the other was his home. At the top of the clinic was a spare room reached by a connecting door, which became my home for a few weeks.

He put me on a drip of a special mixture and other remedies. I have no idea what really happened since I was numb with pain, delirious. At the end of the week, he told me that I was off the critical list. I would be able to keep my kidney and my baby, but I would have to take care for a long time even after the birth. By the end of the second week, he said I could leave and be with David and Alice. They had gone to Lindos, while the recording was in the process of moving to LA.

Dr. Sharma had a flat in Dublin, Ireland and said we could all go there, as he wanted to monitor me for a while. David could come to Ireland, because it did not interfere with his tax exile requirements. Primarily, Dr. Sharma wanted to see how I would cope with being in a city and not having daily medical care. I think we stayed there for a week or two. I was very weak, but happier to be on the mend knowing that I kept both my kidneys and my baby would still be born in late October.

During our stay in Dublin, David was in regular contact with Dr. Sharma until my final checkup. We had lunch at his favorite restaurant near the flat while we reviewed the situation. Alice was used to having the freedom to walk into the kitchens in Greece and so were we. She was brought back to our table by the Maître d' kicking. We apologized and made sure she didn't roam again.

Dr. Sharma gave me the OK to go to L.A. with David on the understanding that I stayed in my bedroom most of the days. L.A. did not have the best air for me to heal or live in under these circumstances especially as I was pregnant. He let me go under one condition, I had to have an air conditioner, ion machine and air filter.

An additional surprise gift to us was that Dr. Sharma said he didn't want payment for his time. He thanked me for putting such trust in him, because he learned so much through the experience. He only wanted us to pay for the medicines and the medical tests. David and I left smiling as we set off on our next adventure to Los Angeles and the birth of our second child.

Clare Born
2 November 1979

CHAPTER 34

ANOTHER CHILD IS BORN
CLARE

1979

The entire band, including our manager rented our own houses. Ours was 712 Rodeo Drive in Beverley Hills. Most of our homes we rented belonged to very rich people, some stars, some CEO's. It seemed this was the usual way to do things in L.A. They were full of paintings, sculptures and precious furniture. We had a maid named Louella and community gardeners. Louella looked like Aunt Jemima from the movies of the twenties and had a heart of gold. She became invaluable to our daily life, especially her smile.

Life began to fall into place after a few weeks. David went to the studio, I stayed in my mountain air retreat upstairs and we enrolled Alice in the local Montessori school. Sue and Christian were still with us and would drive her there and pick her up. The children would be playing on the playground when they arrived each day at midday. Alice's face lit up, happy to see them as she ran across the playground. She was so cute with her blonde bunches flipping in the air. The heart of our home was growing each day.

We fell in love with the Wholefoods shop. It was heaven for a vegetarian like me, so much choice. They would spray all the fruit and vegetables with water each night to keep them fresh. There were so many sprouts to choose from that I had never known existed; alfalfa sprouts, buckwheat sprouts, fenugreek sprouts, mung bean sprouts and the list went on and on.

Other new delights, which expanded my menu, were soya burgers, soya bacon and many other vegetarian surprises. After having nearly six months of this luxury, I must say, "I went into withdrawals when I got back to the UK." Fortunately, many years later things have changed here in England. There are health food shops in every town AND Wholefoods has come to London.

The band had quite a schedule and problems were stirring in regards to Rick. A decision came forth that he must leave the band. A deal was made, which allowed everyone to save face and complete the album that they started. Its intention was a gradual withdrawal from the unsuspecting public. In addition, part of the deal was for Rick to continue to do the gigs for a pretty sum. He agreed.

Then discussions about royalties came…this is my memory of the event. I was in my last month of pregnancy when we all had dinner at a Japanese restaurant. David was in a *mood* when I arrived, with everyone's tensions riding high. Roger wanted to remove "Comfortably Numb" from the album. It was one of the only songs, which David had a major credit for and he *exploded*. I think if he had known karate the table would have split in two! I will never forget the look of shock on everyone's face especially Roger's. I have only seen David lose his temper once and I hoped never to do so again. In the end, "Comfortably Numb" stayed and to this day, it is considered one of the best songs on the album.

I have said it before and I shall continue to say how hard I find it to understand the way royalties work. Having watched the transformation of Roger's angst into something that *Animals* and *The Wall* albums have become, David and the others deserve more acknowledgement. And these are not just the words of a devoted wife. "Comfortably Numb" symbolically represented the release of all the tensions built in that album. Without it, we certainly would have gone down under the weight of the stone. Needless to say,

David and Rick's intuitiveness as musicians influenced the whole album.

David soared to the heights of Beauty when he let go, playing "Comfortably Numb" with the rays of white light behind him. That moment proclaimed from the top of the Wall sending us Hope! I know that many lead guitarists feel that it is the best song on the album. I have to agree. Every time I was at the mixer at the gigs of *The Wall*, it was "Comfortably Numb" that took my breath away and uplifted my heart. It was a relief, a testimony that we can be free from the stone.

During the first few months in L.A., I found the book *Spiritual Midwifery* in the Bodhi Tree, which was the most wonderful bookstore dealing with every possible metaphysical and religious philosophy that existed. I have spent many hours there over the years, but sadly, it has now closed. For me, L.A. is not the same without it.

The concept of that book kept me captivated as I read each page. It was like reading what was deep in my inner world of being pregnant. Therefore, I went on the hunt for a midwife who was ok with delivering at home and had the same vision. Some states were not in agreement with this. It seemed it didn't matter that having a home birth existed for centuries in the backwaters and in most European countries.

Of course, the current orthodox medical story is that there are many fatalities having a home birth. In fact, statistics show that there are many fatalities giving birth in the hospital these days as well. Certainly, there are many painful births in hospitals due to us having to lie down on our backs. Luckily, California is a nest of many new and alternative ideas so it was not difficult to find a midwife and a doctor to approve. So we set to work on our vision, to have our baby at home inspired by Leboyer, again.

Somehow, we came to meet Yogi John, who would eventually come to the house and give us yoga lessons. He and his wife, Bella, became friends and introduced me to Tibetan Buddhism. Initiated into Chenrzig, I was given a Tibetan name which, when translated is "The auspicious lamp of the Dharma." I suppose that auspicious explains me—prosperous and favorable. Within this name, I could shine brightly where ever I went. My shyness and insecurities seemed to fade as I began to know who I was from a soul perspective. I felt protected in the Sanga-followers who seek self-realization.

I became aware that I was no longer alone seeking the path to inner Beauty, Goodness & Peace. I had joined an invisible group of good people around the world called the Sanga. Upon reflection, Life has always touched me with the wand of Grace through all of my challenges with different levels of prosperity both inward and outward. I discovered more of my blessings and how much I am protected; I discovered it is there for all of us. From then on, each time I would fall, I would get up with an emerging smile of gratefulness to be alive. I was ready for my next step, my path, to guide me...There was a light at the end of the tunnel.

Here is a Zen story that guided my path to Harmony and Peace:

There was a woman who, every day, brought flowers to decorate the altar at the temple. One day while she was decorating the altar; she met a certain Zen Master. The Zen Master said to her, "You bring flowers and decorate the altar every day. It is said that because of this your life will be very wonderful and beautiful." She said to the Master, "Master, when I am decorating the altar, I'm so peaceful and happy. But when I am at home, I have unrest, worry and anxiety. What can I do to be peaceful and happy?" The Master replied, "To be peaceful and happy is like how you decorate the altar."

The woman asked the Master to explain this more. The Master explained, "You are like the altar. Peace and happiness are comparable to the flowers with which you decorate your life. So you have to keep them fresh. Do you know how to keep the flowers fresh?" She answered, "Yes, sir. That is easy. To keep the flowers fresh, I just cut off the bad stems because they cannot suck clean water, and I put them in clean water, which keeps the flowers fresh." The Master said, "That is right. You can use in your life the same method you use to keep flowers fresh. Let go of bad thoughts and cultivate good thoughts instead and then you have a purified mind, which is without unrest, worry, and anxiety and so on."

The woman thanked the Master and said, "Thank you very much for your advice and allowing me to come to the temple to learn Dharma, practice meditation and to listen to chanting." The Master said, "You are welcome. That is good for you", and added, "You should see your body as a temple, Dharma as a way of life, meditation as being like your breath leading to peace and happiness and chanting as the sound of mindfulness." She again thanked the Master for more advice and more than that, she put the Master's advice into practice in her life. As a result, her life became peaceful and happy just like the fresh flowers, which decorated the altar so beautifully.[1]

I finally found a midwife. Her name was Merina and she was gentle and angelic. I particularly liked the fact that she was still breast-feeding her child of three years when we first met. I was happy for she was a true Spiritual Midwife. We met regularly and practiced our breathing exercises, sharing our mutual vision. We made a great team ready for the day our child would enter the world.

David and I waited and waited for that moment to come as I was ten days past my expected due date. The Floyd kept working and working to finish the album. On the evening of 1 November 1979, David returned home and said, "The album was finished." No sooner did he say that I went into labor. It was clockwork. The gates were open and she was born in the wee hours of 2 November 1979, full of light.

To this day, I know the baby waited for her dad to be there (and the album finished). It wasn't a long labor. It was a girl. We named her Clare for a radiant glow surrounded her. David went and fetched Alice into the room to greet her new sister. Together, David and Alice took baby Clare into the candle lit bathroom and had a bath together. In addition, Alice took with her a life-size doll we had given her as a present. I think it was a bit crowded.

While they took care of Clare, Merina finished dealing with the placenta, later buried under a new lavender colored rose bush in the garden. We were all tired, especially David, but joy overcame us as we held our wee Clare in our arms. Within hours, flowers, cards and telegrams surrounded us and the phone didn't stop ringing. The house filled with the sweet scent of hundreds of flowers.

Little by little, our life integrated another child to care for, while the Floyd had a breather preparing for the next cycle, the gigs. We rented a large camper van and we gave Sue some time off. Kids in tow and Christian by our side, we set off up the coast of California, destination Big Sur in a large American camper van. As I chose to breast-feed, it made it easier to travel with a young baby. We met up with Crosby of Crosby, Stills & Nash who lived up that way. We walked on the beach of Big Sur at sunset. Alice followed her dad walking in his shadow as I took pictures of the moment with Clare carried close to me in our baby sling.

We had relief from our small quarters for a few days in a wonderful log cabin Hotel just beside the road near Big Sur. One day we took a walk in the woods and came upon the mushrooms that looked like the fairy toadstools from our children's storybooks. They were red with white polka dots. Goodness, they are real! I thought as I went to touch them. David motioned me away and in a concerned voice said, "Don't pick them! They are highly poisonous!" He knew a lot about mushrooms.

When we returned to Los Angeles, I was tired, so we hired a vegetarian cook named Akasha. She made the best corn bread and aduki bean stew with Hijiki seaweed. I learned a lot from her as we explored the world of vegetarianism together. Clare started to cry a lot, especially after midnight. David and I took turns walking around with her. During the day, Louella was a great help for she was a real MOM-MA. She had had nine children of her own and she would walk around the house with Clare in one arm and dust with the other. It gave me time off to rest.

It became obvious that Clare did not accept being held by many other people except her immediate family and especially Louella. Anyone who resembled hard Rock 'n' Roll and into drugs caused her to holler until we took her out of the room. The reaction time and time again was too much to be a coincidence. I made excuses so no one's feelings were hurt, but silently I saw her sensitivity and protected her from any misunderstanding. In those days and in that environment, how would I say, "My child is sensitive. She is straight from Heaven. She knows you are not happy and take drugs and are wasted." How could I say that and hope they would understand?

Her screaming became rather disconcerting. Maybe there is something wrong. Eventually, I found a homeopath and an alternative doctor who helped me with a way of eating as an experiment. He hoped we would discover what was bothering Clare as I was still breastfeeding her. We started by me stopping dairy products for one week and then introduce one thing for a few days and see her reaction. Then I would go on to excluding Wheat. The first try proved that it was dairy, but it was not her having difficulty. My kidneys were not digesting dairy well and it was going into the breast milk. She was fine after I stopped eating dairy.

    I personally feel that as we had that near death experience during my sixth month of pregnancy, she too was behind in the development of her organs. This would come to light later when she was around two, for she could not tolerate milk. She is fine now, she says. Later, back in the UK, Dr. Sharma suggested that we should put her on to soya milk, which was organic in those days. GMO was not in our vocabulary then. We were just not aware of it.

    As David's schedule was very demanding, I took on the total responsibility of breast-feeding Clare without him giving her a supplement bottle as he had done with Alice. This meant that Clare came everywhere with us. She was a wee one going to all the Hollywood parties. I was in a back bedroom feeding her once when Andy Warhol walked into the room. We sat on the bed chatting for some time and became friends. He said for me to call him when we got to NYC and we could go shopping together. I particularly wanted to see his studio.

'ABSTRACT MOTHER & CHILD'

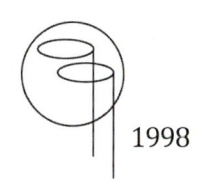

1998

Up on the Roof
Hollywood

CHAPTER 35

THE WALL COMES ALIVE

The months of December, January and February involved creating the next step of Roger's dream. *The Wall* was to become a multi-media theatrical production. Some have referred to it as a "dramatization of angst." Really it was a "dramatization of how to transform angst" for me. Rehearsals began and day after day, over and over, the Wall came down. On one occasion during rehearsal, I said to David, "Wouldn't it be nice to have a positive ending amongst the rubble?" The next time I saw the run through, all the band were stepping out over the rubble playing acoustic guitars or other simple instruments. Lovely.

The Wall gig consisted of only two venues in the States, Los Angeles (seven shows) and New York (five shows). The idea of taking it on the road just wasn't a possibility anymore. Thus, the way the band toured changed. All of the shows were full of everyone we knew and didn't know, from ticket holders to Hollywood stars, from record companies to musicians. David's parents came over from England to be with us and hold their new grandchild. It was a family affair. Lots to organize regarding concert tickets, backstage passes, cars to the airport, cars to gig, babysitters, restaurants, who sat next to who but the most challenging of all, for me, was the night the grand-nephew of Kalu Rinpoche (a Buddhist Lama) came.

I had taken *refuge* with him several times while he was in Los Angeles. In the Buddhist tradition, the purpose of taking refuge is to awaken from confusion and associate oneself with wakefulness. Taking refuge is a matter of commitment and acceptance and, at the same time, of openness and freedom. By taking the refuge (vow), we commit ourselves to freedom.

Yogi John had suggested that I should offer Lama passes to come. "Do you think he would really like to come?" I asked. He was sure that he would like to come, for he had had a private conversation with Lama the previous day. The Lama was only in his mid-thirties and interested in other aspects that influenced the hearts and minds of the young. Despite that, I was still quite surprised when he said yes. I wondered to myself, "What does a Tibetan Lama need, in regards of care from me, in order to witness the Floyd Concert *The Wall*?

We picked him up within the appropriate time. I escorted him to the mixing desk. I had arranged seats for us, thinking that he might prefer to be in the center of it all. The mixing area was like the helm of the Star Trek Enterprise. The one mixing desk had expanded to two: sound and lighting. Now the WALL was beyond description except by a technician and there are books about it. There were sections of command modules for each aspect of the production, which took up LOTS of seats in the middle of the hall. Production managers, plenty of assistants lined the desks with headphones, their fingers poised to begin the show. Bottles of Evian water were everywhere.

Lama walked through the audience in a cloud of unending Peace, observing, feeling. The Peace was contagious and entered my being softly. I felt like I did as a child always trying to do my best for my parents. I was over excited, honored and at the same time fearful that I might trip catching my high heels on my long chiffon dress right before him. At the beginning, I offered Lama some earplugs. He shook his head, "No, it is ok, I will be fine." Then the music began.

The surrogate band in masks, made in the likeness of the band, first led us into a euphoric state as brick upon brick built the wall. The Wall representing symbolically the alienation Roger had been feeling on the *Animal* tour and within his life. As the last brick was put into position, his voice echoed throughout the hall, a farewell. Many words kept screaming over our heads song after song. God, it was loud! Painful!

I looked over to Lama to see if he was ok. The stillness of his focus maintained within his being. Words of desperation called out to us from the wall as the drama unfolded, searching to be heard. The Wall was complete. We were Isolated from being one together, the band and the audience. No longer unified within the music. This time we were just alone in another's projected anxiety. Anguish of a person's pain hung in the air.

Spellbound and overtaken by the grandeur or perhaps the incredible majesty of the production, the audience was still. Numbed, held by the drama of the journey of self-indulgence into the shadow, into the pain of existence. We succumbed to the imagery and the *Sound of the Round* and the theatre of it all. The drama still plays in my head. Just the sheer volume pierced every cell of my being. It was quite a feat. Where were we going? Were we being dragged down by it all. Was this our reality as well? Were we blinded by the glamour of it all and yet held in such Beauty. What was it? Held in the crossfire? Numb?

Finally, the moment of release arrived. The lights dimmed. Stillness filled the air. David appeared on top of the Wall. His playing came from his heart. It reached beyond, piercing the fog. In that song, we transcended the angst and brought Beauty even though the lyrics led us to believe otherwise.

The audience held in rapture as the notes took us higher and higher and higher, releasing the tension. David, silhouetted by rays of light behind, moved with the sounds as his playing pierced the air from above. Waking us up from the spell of destruction, nurturing, freeing us, taking us to our resurrection. Transcending the angst within us all. No wonder Roger didn't want the song on the album. Maybe he was not ready to transcend his own pain. Yet, maybe he listened to his soul telling him this was the way?

The fervor increased as Roger screamed out to the audience, asking us to enjoy ourselves. Did you really mean that? He was so sarcastic. The pace increased. Sounds of primeval screeching, drumbeats, repeating, took everyone further. They stood and danced hypnotically clapping to the beat. Surprisingly, Lama stood with them, his poise captured in the colored lights. And when it finished, he honored them and clapped too, but it was silent. I understood that evening the term, "One hand clapping," for there was another energy that emanated from his gesture. It was a deep appreciation from his heart that brought tranquility to us all within the frenzy. It was a creative force lifting and transforming the vibration already there.

I motioned for us to leave during the last song just before the Wall came down, so we were not caught in the audience leaving the stadium. The imagery spat out its vile throughout the hall as we walked down the aisles of the seated audience towards the backstage. Their heads were focused on what was happening on stage, but as Lama passed they turned. One row after another turned and saw him.

I will never forget the expressions that lit up their faces in contrast to what they were witnessing. It was as though they saw Christ. Their hearts opened with the thought that he had graced them by being there. Rock 'n' Roll concerts were up until then a place where we were free to rebel, to hide out. A secret place just to be, to contemplate, to express, we thought, but Lama came. He entered their sanctuary and made it acceptable. He honored us all that evening with his silent presence of compassion. The madness stood still for a while.

While we watched from the sidelines, shouts of destruction resounded around the hall, over and over. The Wall collapsed against explosive sound effects and smoke. It was over. My head rang from all the screaming in the last few songs and from being so close to the explosion where we stood. Was it the end of the world? And there from the rubble came all the musicians playing the final song with acoustic guitars, mandolin, clarinet, and accordion. The calm after the storm.

Animal Farm State Side

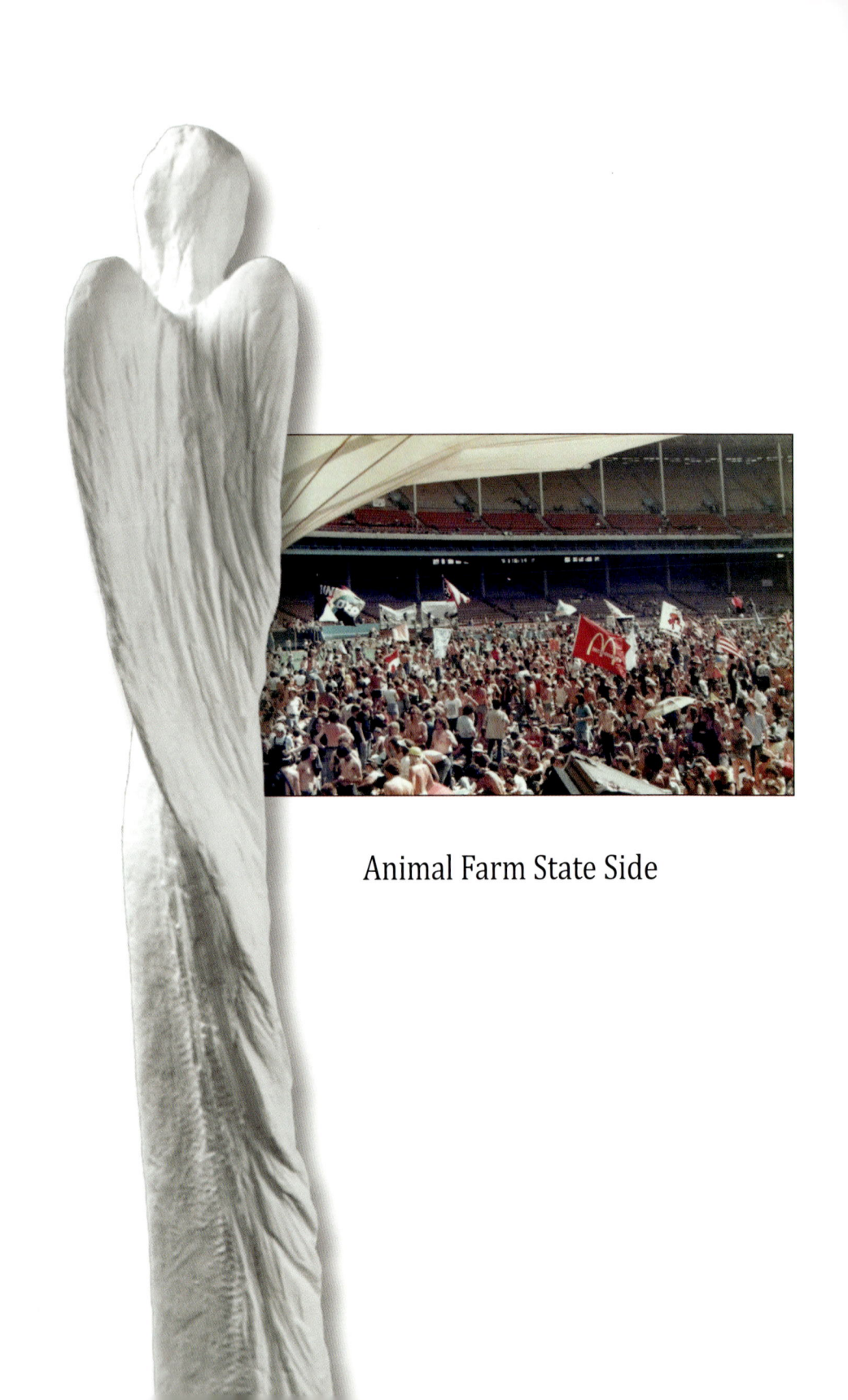

CHAPTER 36

NEW YORK, NEW YORK

FEBRUARY 1980

Next stop, New York, New York. The flight from Los Angeles was full of celebrities. Juliette Wright secured the seat next to Rudolf Nureyev. Joan Collins with her large sunglasses sat in the row behind us. Dudley Moore was sitting in David's seat when we were boarding. We had a moment of laughter as David said to Dudley, in a Dudley voice, "Dudley, I think you are sitting in my seat?" Dudley looked up from behind his newspaper and in a Dudley voice said with a smile across his face, "Really? *OOOH*, Sorry David." It was a real English moment.

Just before take-off, I had to go to the ladies room while the stewardesses were busy making us all comfortable in first class with drinks and menus. I was walking down the aisle when a man wearing blue jeans, a cowboy hat and boots was coming towards me. He was tanned and extremely handsome. He had a glint in his eye and emitted a very strong energy of desire. Our eyes met as I felt his magnetic energy coming closer. Did we know each other? He looked so familiar. I smiled in response as I searched my heart to understand the connection. Closer and closer we came to the moment of acknowledgement and just as we almost fell into each other's arms like long lost friends, I knew who he was…*YIKKEES!* It was Richard Burton! I didn't know Richard Burton! I closed the door of my heart quickly and coolly brushed by him like two ships in the night avoiding the crash. He turned with a perplexed look as he watched me disappear behind the drawn curtain of first class. Goodness, everything written about his charisma is true. I had a narrow escape.

I so love New York, the smells, the taxis zooming by, the fairy lights in the trees no matter what time of year and especially the soft pretzel stand on the corners. It was February and touches of winter still lined the streets, but the air gave a hint of spring. The hotel we were staying in was also booked for a Sumo Wrestler Convention. It was a rather *close* moment one day when Alice and I, with Clare strapped to my chest, had to share a lift with two of them. They are soooo tall and big.

They were in their full gear. Actually, they were only wearing their *Mawashi* wrestling belts. One does not usually come so close to them in their ceremonial belt only, at least not in Rock 'n' Roll. I could feel their spirit of silent control and purity of heart. This quality was beyond the competitive presence of normal wrestlers. They had dignity in their demeanor for they are devoted to their native religion Shinto.

While in Japan on the *Dark Side of the Moon* tour, I became aware of Sumo and Shinto rituals and the sacredness behind their history. In a way, I felt honored to share these few moments with them. Alice was dinky next to them as they made room for us to come into the lift. In her innocence, she kept looking up at them as we stood next to each other. I had a smile on my face as I held her hand with assurance that all would be ok. She had never seen anyone like them not even in a circus, which is far from where one might find them.

On one of David's free evenings from rehearsals, we visited Auntie Mary, from Lindos. She was staying in their New York family apartment and organized a wonderful dinner in her favorite New York restaurant. Andy Warhol was one of her guests, we sat next to each other and I felt at home chatting with him. The feeling of friendship that we had felt in Hollywood was still there. I had Clare with me carrying her in a Moses basket and had to breast-feed her during our evening. Andy was very open to discuss the nature of breast-feeding. Looking over to Clare suckling he asked me how it felt. I said that it was wonderful and created a special bond between baby and mother. I added that I wish this could be true for the dads.

He sat still in thought, when he came up with the idea that we should make a plastic brassiere, which could hold milk with nipples. The idea would be so that the dads could wear it and feed the baby. One of the bonuses would be that the milk would stay warm at body temperature. He paused for a moment, and then added, "Darling, it must be pink, of course! What should we name it?" I was not good at naming these sorts of things so I shrugged my shoulders putting my focus back on Clare. He then said with the glee of insight, "I have GOT IT! We shall call it PINK FLOOD!" We so laughed at that one. How great…PINK FLOOD!

During the evening, he asked David if he would let me go shopping with him. We shared a love for Art Nouveaux. Cheeky, Andy said, "Don't worry David I will only take her to the best antique shops! Hee Hee." I reassured David that I would just buy little things. In the end, Andy and I never had the opportunity for our adventure.

We did meet up in the helicopter going to the gig on the night that we gifted him tickets. Clare came with me in her Moses basket and surprisingly slept through the sound of the chopper. The gig was outside of NYC in Nassau Coliseum. It was initially booked for two dates 25–26 February, but there was such a demand that two more dates became necessary. We took the helicopter from the New York City Heliport. It was my first ride in a helicopter and it was exciting! I was so grateful that we did not have to sit in rush hour traffic to get there. We just hovered over it.

Things were different back stage. There was a Sushi Bar! Traveling with the band was becoming more civilized. No more dried cheese sandwiches and potato chips. Even the road crews enjoyed a fabulous spread. There was a time when they all took alcoholic beverages out to their stations. Now they took Evian Water. In the last shows, I spent more time backstage with our little Clare for the volume and the subject matter was getting to me. It had been an amazing journey in many ways, but I was tired. I needed to get home. Lyrics repeated in my head as "Wish You Were Here" was playing and penetrated through the walls of the dressing room.

I was beginning to know Heaven from Hell and this was my life. This was all of our lives. Wish You Were Here! Our marriage began during the "Wish You Were Here" recordings. Now it had become truly our journey. Sitting backstage on the large couch breastfeeding Clare, I asked myself, "Where will this journey lead? Or are we two lost souls?"

'SPIRITUAL SUN'

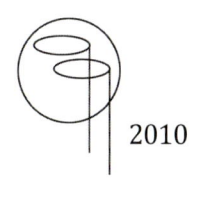

2010

Hook End Manor
Checkendon, Oxon, UK

CHAPTER 37

HOME AGAIN
LITTLE NAOMI

I flew back to the UK alone on Concorde with Clare in her Moses basket for David had to finish his year of tax exile. The flight was amazing and my first. It would be the last for many because Concorde was to be taken out of the air soon after. We arrived in just over three hours without a feeling of jet lag. The plane is testimony of grace in aerodynamics. Sadly, it no longer flies and if it did, I would have to ask for the seats to be rectified. They were very uncomfortable, like metal lawn chairs. However, I am truly grateful to have had the experience.

David and I decided that with our growing family, we would buy a new house. So I began our search in the UK with the help of Perry Press. Eventually, we bought Hook End Manor, the home of Alvin Lee in a village called Checkendon in Oxfordshire, which was six miles west of Henley-on-Thames. It was a Tudor farmhouse from the 15th century with many outbuildings and a pool. Just right for David, he could have plenty of room for his studio. And certainly lots of room for a growing family. David had always said he wanted six children. Well, wishes do come true and sometimes become eight.

We were familiar with the area for we had visited George Harrison's home, (Friar Park), in Henley with Terry Doran the year before. Friar Park will be an experience I shall never forget. I felt so honored to be there. As we entered the large gallery hall, I just didn't know where to look first. There was so much beautiful art everywhere. The walls were carved with images of friars by the original carpenter. An original Tiffany standing lamp stood near the high back couch before the large fireplace. The dining room had William Morris stained glass windows and wallpaper with peacock reliefs. My eyes and mouth were in awe. Even the light switches were the faces of monks in brass, the switch being their nose.

We had stayed the night and in the morning, while having breakfast, there was Ravi Shankar music playing through the speakers. George entered since he had come home in the night while we slept. I complimented him on the music, for Ravi Shankar was one of my favorites, when he said, "Would you like to meet him?" I said in amazement, "Sure but how?" He said, "Come with me."

We had finished our breakfast and got up to follow him. Room after room we followed him, my head spinning in all directions, taking in all the artwork and beautiful lamps while the music got louder and louder. Finally, we reached the last room. As George opened the door, my face took on a rosy glow with the reality of what I was seeing. There, sitting on the floor all in white was Ravi Shankar and his entire band. That was a moment to remember.

Once the purchase agreement was complete and Hook End was ours, we took Warwick on board to help with re-decorating. We trusted him enormously. The majority of the house had wood paneling and 15th century lead light windows, so it was mainly the painting of Alvin's color palette and installing an electric oven in the kitchen. In the midst of it all, one of the builders installing the cupboard for the oven approached David and Warwick. He had sought them out in another part of the house and in his Irish accent said, "Excuse me Mr. Gilmour, Mr. McCreddie, I couldn't help but overhear you wonderin' who had built the property. And may I say

I 'dink I know. Come along with me. His name is written on a board I was removin'. His name is Mr. K. Itchen." They both said, "Really? Can you show us?" They followed him to the kitchen where he showed them the board. There on the back of the board it read, K...itchen.

Fortunately, they waited until leaving the room before bursting into laughter. I never quite understood the way the British had Irish jokes, nor did I ever understand the Polish jokes in the States. But I think I was getting the drift, though I still do not favor making fun of others. In a way, the story was quite charming and precious. I hope he wasn't local for it did go around later at our local pub.

There was an Aga cooker, which took a little adjusting to, but it wasn't long before I fell in Love with it. I think the baked potatoes were the best! But baking cakes was another matter, one that I never mastered, at least in the Aga. I had to have a larger oven for we really needed one to manage the HUGE turkey for Christmas. There just wasn't enough room in the smaller oven. We fed many over the holidays.

Our first Christmas was a very special time and we were planning to celebrate our new home in a classic Victorian style. Many friends and family would be coming to share in the festivities. Miv Watts with Naomi and Ben, her children, came and stayed with us for a few weeks. She helped me decorate the whole house with garlands of evergreen, Victorian ornaments and red ribbons galore. Dried red apples and holly decked the hall. Miv was always amazing in finding special baubles to add to my collection. My children, now grown, have already decided which ones they want, if I ever let go of them.

Each day the fires were lit casting a glow of warmth in every room as we ate mince pies, stilton on crackers, and the occasional cob nuts with our tea. The children played with the dogs and cats in the garden while we decorated with Joy. What a family affair it was, always.

One morning Naomi, who must have been eleven, came up to us after breakfast with a pout. "Mom, I so need to earn some money so I can buy some presents. But I have no idea how I do that?" Miv and I looked at each other, and I came up with an idea. She could help wrap my Christmas presents, which were hidden away upstairs in the attic. Her eyes lit up with excitement and relief that a solution had been found.

I took her up the many stairs into the attic rooms where piles of presents lined the walls with rolls of wrapping paper and ribbons. David and I always gave presents to all our friends, family and business associates not to mention our children. So you can imagine the size of the task. Though I had not expected for her to do it all nor did I think an eleven year old would have the stamina. As I closed the door the last image I saw was her blue eyes sparkling and a smile that revealed the sweetness of her heart.

The day passed by with all the decorating and preparation keeping us occupied. Our nanny kept an eye on the children but at some point, around eleven in the evening, Miv and I decided to put our feet up in the telly room. As relaxation took hold Miv suddenly said, "Ginge', have you seen Naomi?" I shook my head "No." "Where do you think she could be?" "Oh, no. She couldn't still be in the attic!" We bounced from our comfy chairs and went swiftly to find her. What we discovered was heartwarming. There she was covered in bits of ribbon, sitting amongst scraps of wrapping paper, cellotape stuck in her hair, engulfed amid a pile of presents that Santa's very own team of elves would have taken a week to get through.

It was so touching. She had worked all day, determined to get through a room full of presents the size of the gift-wrapping department in Harrods. Resisting defeat, she confessed that, curiously she had not yet discovered her own gift in the milieu! Perhaps this was her motivation, but never one to lose focus, she finally conceded it was off to bed for her. And so, with a hug from Miv she wobbled off to bed... with the picture of the sugar plum dance in her head. Tomorrow was another day and there was a good deal of shopping to be done. Her own present sat wrapped and ravishing, already under the tree.

As spring arrived, we were to discover the beauty of the garden. Flowers appeared around every corner, little snowdrops, crocuses and primulas silently waiting for the daffodils and tulips. A wall garden in the back lined with herbaceous borders, full of perennials (especially Dahlias), greenhouses full of vegetables, and a forest of pine trees next door. We took on the service of a fantastic and jolly couple named Jack and Rita, who had worked for Alvin Lee, as well as Henry, the gardener. They soon became part of our family. Joe, Lisa and our cats eventually adjusted to all the space. Unfortunately, Blue, our peacock did not. He flew off when we let him out of his cage. We had been advised to give all the animals a period to acclimatize but in this case, it did not work. I often wondered if he found a safe home somewhere for we could not find him. I hoped to hear his call on my morning walks but such was not to be. I did love those long walks in the forest with the dogs each day and the family bicycle rides down the country lanes once the snow cleared. Winter was full of wonder too as the white snow fell onto the hedges. With the cool air full of the children's laughter, frolicking, throwing snowballs and sometimes lying in the snow flapping their arms and legs making angel impressions. All the seasons touched our hearts with its beauty unveiling the changing faces of the English countryside. Our new home suited us well.

"The Best are sent to War"

CHAPTER 38

THE CLASH OF THE TITANS

The Floyd had moved on to making *The Wall* movie with Alan Parker. Well, really, it was Roger, Gerald Scarfe and Alan Parker in the end. The stories that filtered back were like the clash of the Titans. David did not agree with the whole way things were developing during the making of the album. Little by little, he saw a democratic relationship in the band change to "You are working for me. I am your leader." There was no space for anyone to contribute under those conditions. It was really a Roger Project and David withdrew from having much to do with the film. Until one day, Steve O'Rourke called and asked if he would be a referee.

    I really don't remember much of what went on because I had become pregnant again with our third child. I had to focus on my health, as my kidneys were weak from what happened during Clare's pregnancy. We were still settling in the new house and something about it was unsettling. I did worry about the house becoming our home for I felt uneasy. Normally, an energetic sparkle appeared shortly after redecorating. It wasn't the case at Hook End. The sparkle never came even by the time we had our open house party. How could I say to David that there was no sparkle? We have to move? He probably would think I was mad.

    At our party, Alvin Lee shared with me that he felt there was a hex on couples who lived there. I wish he had told me that before.

Historically, since the 15th century every couple either met their death, divorce or separated. Gosh. Why did I not see that? Dr. Sharma came often and said there was a ghost that walked around the garden and another upstairs. I have to say I had to put those stories away.

Until one evening, just outside the doorway where Alice and Clare slept, our white Alsatian, Joe, started growling into the air in the Hallway near the door. His hair raised and it was hard to get him to move. The girls awoke and I took them into our room to sleep. David was working so I asked Michael Skipwith if he could assess the situation the next day. It was spooky.

David would often return from a day filming with photos of the war scenes. These images often triggered off memories of Vietnam for me. Roger revealed his father's story and this reminded me of the only war story in my life. My stepfather was a medic in the Coast Guard and was on isolated duty during "Nam." He was away for a year. We could not avoid hearing stories on the news as to what was going on over there. We watched the anti-demonstrations and the world's disapproval. While we, one of the soldiers families, suffered and worried at home suspended in the emotional dilemma.

On April 4, a year before his assassination, Martin Luther King spoke about the war at the Riverside church in New York. King stated:

"Surely this madness must cease. We must stop now. I speak as a child of God and brother to the suffering poor of Vietnam. I speak for those whose land is being laid waste, whose homes are being destroyed, whose culture is being subverted. I speak for the poor of America who are paying the double price of smashed hopes at home and death and corruption in Vietnam. I speak as a citizen of the world, for the World as it stands aghast at the

path we have taken. I speak as an American to the leaders of my own nation. The great initiative in this war is ours. The initiative to stop it must be ours."[1]

But the war went on and on. Demonstrations and protests continued. One thousand women marched on the White House. Students were arrested for being conscientious objectors. Students for a Democratic Society, demonstrated in Chicago and I watched in disbelief as the police on National Television, hit the cameraman who was filming them beating the students. I watched. I saw it happening! And I just couldn't believe that there was nothing about it in the News the next day.

While at a White House luncheon, singer Eartha Kitt, spoke out against the war and its effects on the youth, exclaiming to her fellow guests:

"You send the best of this country off to be shot and maimed. They rebel in the street. They will take pot... and they will get high. They don't want to go to school because they're going to be snatched off from their mothers to be shot in Vietnam."[2]

But the war went on. No one was listening in power. My mother prayed each evening for his safe return. She waited each day for a letter, which did not tell us much except we knew he was alive. He kept the truth away from us. He had to as a soldier in combat. He was a Chief Petty Officer, a leader of men. The only way for us to keep our sanity was to stay away from listening to the news about the war. It is only now I realize how he often must have walked on land in the aftermath caring for the dying and the afflicted.

Seeing the images now I just wonder how he dealt with the atrocities he witnessed, especially in the night when he got home. Agent Orange did not discriminate. It not only destroyed the underbrush, but maimed children, mothers and the elderly. It destroyed their homes, all the people in the way. In addition, pregnant women gave birth to deformed children. I still don't get why we were there. How does one live with those images? I cried today as I looked at them. Ron was there. He breathed the air. He was a witness of the devastation of a people, of his men.

Over the years after he returned, Ron would often have lung problems. My mother kept on him to stop smoking cigarettes, but he didn't. On 19 MAY 2002, he passed over diagnosed with Lung Cancer. It was not until afterwards, when my sister, Donna, was helping my mother with the financial closure that we discovered something which made us weep. Apparently, he died, luckily they said, just a year before the government's allowance for families of servicemen, dying from Agent Orange could claim compensation. What? Oh My GOD! He really died from Agent Orange. It was too late to question his treatment. It was his time to pass over. But families still are in a process with the government to get more help. Tragically, they are being ignored.

And so it is today. The War goes on amongst men. Why do we not value the preciousness of life? The love of power seems to be more in favor than the power of Love. As an artist and as a human being, I constantly seek to question the ripples I create with my images, or forms or even with my actions or my voice. As much as I tried to understand Roger's vision of the Wall and as much as I can see how art sometimes must shock to awaken the sleeping dinosaurs it is not my way, for I know *we become what we contemplate.* I choose Divine Beauty. I choose Love.

DAVID GILMOUR
IN CONCERT
TICKETS AVAILABLE AT DOOR
BAR
SMITH
ODEON
HAMM
JEFFREY OSBORNE
JEFFREY OSBORNE
motörhead
motörhead

Zealand

Ponji

CHAPTER 39

PONJI DIES

SPRING 1981

Andrew Warburg's company had crashed and potentially taken almost all of our investments with it. Other issues compounded the pressures we were living under, our personal life and the shifting ground with the band. It wasn't until March 1981 that the full extent of our losses became apparent. Until then, the top floor of Britannia Row was full of accountants working hard to reduce our enormous tax exposure. I don't think any of us knew or could have possibly predicted the outcome. The pressure was enormous. Our lives seemed to be held in a precarious balance, waiting.

There were several incidents that intensified it all, which came Out of the BLUE. On the last tour, our Pyro-technician stored the explosives in a farmer's barn in the States. The intent was to save the costs of carting it all back to the UK, as they would be used later. It came to pass that the barn caught on fire. As the firemen drew closer to extinguish the flames, the farmer came running towards them shouting, waving his arms, his words disappearing as he said, "DON'T!"… Kaboom! His words were too late. The barn blew up taking the firemen with it. The wives, of course, sought every option to sue someone and get compensation, including the Floyd. I don't remember how it turned out, but the Floyd were absolved of any responsibility.

One day David returned home, white as a sheet and in deep remorse. One of his childhood friends from Cambridge committed suicide in the London Underground that day. He jumped in front of the train. His name was Ponji and I knew him well. Out of all the Cambridge gang, he was the only one that took up the white robes of spirituality. He followed the teachings of Charan Singh who became his spiritual master. Charan Singh was also the guru of Emo and many others that had come into my life living with David.

At one time, I had seriously considered becoming initiated, for all the disciples were of such tender hearts and full of light. I was so comfortable being with them, they were more than family to me. Visits to their houses were a joy for me as they were vegetarian. Often they came to our home where I could prepare dinner with the highest intention, without judgment or pretense and would be well received with appreciation. Emo said to me that David was not too happy with his influence upon me regarding Sant Mat. Emo said to him, "David, Ginger is a grown woman and can make her own decisions, surely? Besides, it is about learning to Love more. And that means you will benefit."

This tragedy really threw another cloud over our lives. David seemed to be lost within a very hurt heart. At home, in Gilmour land, the story was a closed book, but the suffering worked its way subtly, making a very poisonous cocktail with all the rest. The Floyd story was obvious and huge. This took it deeper. To compound Ponji's passing over, I knew David was having issues with my spiritual awakening as well. I am sure it was difficult as I withdrew from the more negative aspects of a Rock 'n' Roll life, i.e., drugs, drinking, late nights, etc... Initially due to illness. I know his logical mind tried to understand and go with it. But it added to the pressure, especially when Ponji committed suicide.

I recently spoke with Emo and Matthew Scurfield, Ponji's brother, to understand more. Matthew shared with me David and

Emo's adoration of Ponji, who was three years their senior in Cambridge. He was the big boy they looked up to as little boys. He was the one who dared to build a bridge between two trees, fell and walked away smiling. David grew up with many friends who all stayed connected with him throughout life's journey, but Ponji dared to question the status quo.

Cambridge was a place for the young to grow and develop. The Gilmour family and many others were highly academically and creatively focused. The community was that way, producing many great minds. However, unfortunately, it did not include spiritual paths that led to God Realization, which were not Church of England. Throughout his life, Ponji always stood out from the crowd daring to question the norm. I think that was one of the qualities, which inspired the younger boys to dare, to be courageous during their adolescence.

Then one day Ponji discovered the teachings of Sant Mat. In 1967, he went to the Punjab to be with the Master, which is in the North of India in Mariza. Emo said that when Ponji returned, he was full of such light and love. He was glowing! I know what that looks like for Emo was like that when he returned in 1979. Ponji shared stories of such beauty that Emo said, "It was like listening to a fairy tale."

They were unbelievable, yet true, because the living example of the person telling the story was before us. It was Ponji, a person we loved and respected. In fact adored. Apparently, David sat on the floor spellbound, mouth open, listening, captivated. After three hours had passed, they were teleported to another possible reality of what life could be. It wasn't just a story but a reality. David commented, Emo recalled, "If I had the money I would jump on a plane now and go be with the Master!" But he didn't. From what Emo said, that evening left a deep impression on all of them.

Part of the teachings of Sant Mat, requires each person to go back into the ordinary world. The master takes his disciples up to the Light and Audible Sound of God then says, "You must go back home and share it with others." Unfortunately, Ponji was up against social condemnation most of the time when he returned. That seems to be the struggle for many on a more conscious spiritual path. The sixties opened a doorway, but we had to walk the talk, we had to manifest Heaven on Earth. It didn't come on a golden platter—most did not believe. The churches were falling to the side and Eastern culture was considered threatening (despite the Beatles). "The Times They Are A-Changing," but we had far to go.

    It was obvious to me that many from their Cambridge group, including David, held a high regard for Ponji's decision to take up the white robes, even if it was not their path. This, David kept very silent to himself. I understand more of the inner process of this story as I ponder its background. Matthew, Ponji's brother, shared moments of their past with me. He watched them grow up and years later used to visit us as well. I felt they were family. Matthew felt David teetered between resistance, regret and believing. He said to me that during one of David's phone calls many years ago, David said, "Oh, I am really tired of this spiritual stuff." Personally, I wonder if within the corners of his heart he thought…if it works for you perhaps it would for me. Show me.

    What added to David and Ponji's challenge regarding spiritual matters was that their parents did not believe in God. They were not religious in the traditional sense. Perhaps they believed in a greater power, but daily life and academia was their inspiration, their God. That was their way to touch the Beauty of life.

    To compound the situation, David now had a wife, me, who brought the subject closer to home. He could not escape having this concept around. Our home became a magnet for spiritual concepts and many people with a similar vision. Sorry David, I felt it was a way to happiness, joy and a healthier life. God put the path before me to follow, I was shown the way, I had to go. I thought it was for the best. I did not question it for what we lived was the way of Kindness, Love, Goodness, and Charity. This made Peace and Hope possible in a dying world of conflict. It was the Bright Side for me.

Then it happened, Ponji gave up living. Apparently, John Lennon's death in December of 1980 really affected him. He lost his reason to live even with having a spiritual master. He was finding the chaos of the modern world of dog eat dog too grueling. He ran out of the strength to continue. His light was growing dim. We all found it difficult that he was gone and to reconcile the reason and the way. Perhaps his time had come, to return to God. I wish he could have found the strength and insight to continue his courageous journey with us as a child of God. Who am I to question, I suppose.

I feel certain that this cycle really had a strong influence of what was to come into our lives. Finally, the accountants came up with a sum that we owed. It was a very dark cloud needing the sun. We needed a miracle. Looking back from the perspective I have now, God was looking after us and created a miracle for one day the postman arrived with a letter. Hook End had an inner back courtyard where the little red mail truck, would arrive each morning. David was in the courtyard and was opening a letter when I approached. As he read it, his face lit up with a smile that I loved so much, I had not seen it for ages.

We received a royalty check down to the penny that matched the amount we owed the Internal Revenue. And I mean down to the penny. Looking back, I know that Miracles do happen. We so often forget to see them when faced with the difficulties of life. Needless to say, we were still walking on eggshells emotionally and financially, but at least there was some slight relief for a while.

Pregnant with Sara in Lindos
Easter 1981

Background People
Christian Mouzon & Clare Gilmour

CHAPTER 40

ISN'T SHE LOVELY
WALL CONCERTS EARLS COURT

1981

The Wall concerts at Earls Court were about to begin. The month was June and I was pregnant, not far away from the day our next baby would be with us. The countryside was a bit warm and muggy, the air rather close so I stayed in the coolness of our home drinking homemade ice tea. David was rehearsing during the day and sometimes into the night.

One evening, "Happy Birthday" by Stevie Wonder was playing on the radio as I prepared dinner. That song always gets me dancing. It is such a happy song. I never knew that Stevie had written it as part of his campaign to have Martin Luther King, Jr.'s birthday become a national holiday. In fact, he was one of the main organizers and decided to create this single to make the cause known. The holiday, he proposed, would facilitate the realization of Dr. King's dreams of "integration, love and unity for all of God's children."

An interview with Stevie took place that evening on the news. He was in the UK to promote his new album *Hotter than July,* on which was "Happy Birthday." It was a great interview. He has such heart, joy and a sense of humor. The interviewer asked him, "Stevie, how does it feel being blind?" He responded, "I don't mind so much being blind. I probably would mind if I were black!" Then he laughed. The facetious twist held our laughter in thought. "Wonder," what he really meant?

There were six concerts. I was rather big, so I didn't go to all of them. Furthermore, the atmosphere amongst the band had reached an all-time high; to such a degree, we each had separate Portakabins (modular building) back stage. To compound the dividing wall of separation, Roger and Rick had theirs turned away from the center of the hospitality circle. Long gone were the days we shared dressing rooms together, greeting friends and family. Unbeknownst to the waiting people, it would be the last time the Floyd would play together again for nearly twenty-five years. It would be at Live 8.

The center of the hospitality area was carpeted, had tables with white garden umbrellas and flowers, as though we were backstage at Ascot without the woman wearing hats. Many people were congregating around one of the tables. I wandered over to see who was sitting there. It was Stevie Wonder. He came to the gig and was a magnet for everyone.

Somehow, someone offered me a chair to sit down next to him. Maybe it was because I was rather pregnant and needed to sit down. Many were envious for we chatted for quite a while. Can you guess the subject? Babies. He put his hand on my tummy, bending closer and quietly sang, "Isn't She Lovely" for a few bars. My tummy tingled. Did he know it was a girl? We didn't. Now every time I hear that song I remember the night Stevie Wonder blessed my baby. Isn't she Lovely? Yes, she is our Sara.

'BEAUTY'

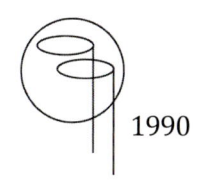

1990

Baby Sara in Lindos

CHAPTER 41

SARA IS BORN

JUNE 1981

Then there were three. During most of my pregnancy, as I mentioned previously, I had to be careful with everything. While one is creating a baby, their kidneys go through changes and need close attention. Mine especially. Consequently, I was tired most evenings. David hung out with Mick Ralph's when he was not involved with the filming.

By my third pregnancy, I was more and more inspired by how important it was to create an environment of Peace. I wanted to allow quiet to penetrate my baby in the womb. I had a little room at the back of our suite where I would meditate each day. Again I had nausea. I remember always having a bowl of fennel seeds and cardamom on our bedside table to ease any indigestion in the night. It was in many ways an easy pregnancy. I loved being pregnant. I always felt at one with Life with a baby inside.

I had found another local midwife named Melony. We shared many hours together in the last few months insuring we were on the same page. She seemed totally at one with my vision of natural childbirth. It was on midsummer's night eve that our third baby called for it was time to enter the world. It was just around 8:30 p.m. on 20 June, when we had another girl whom we named Sara. I remember the time because there was a program I wanted to watch about Krishnamurti. I was interested in his teachings and had read many of his books.

I watched the program as the golden sun set with me having contractions. When I close my eyes, I still feel its rays filling the room through our leadlight windows. This delivery was very different from the previous two. It was faster. As I recall, I could not stand anyone touching me except on my feet. I am sure David was at a loss after his helpfulness with gently rubbing baby powder on my tummy before. It was such a surprise, especially for me. It was so fast and intense that all I could do was to breathe and stay focused.

There was no time to educate anyone on how to approach me. Even I was at a loss. It was so intense. There was no space to speak except do my breathing and go with the birthing of our child. I just wanted to say, "Melony, Please, you are so kind hearted, but don't touch me," as she continued to stroke my forehead. Somehow, I don't think it would have come out that way. Therefore, I just grinned and bore the irritation. Her and David's feelings were more important to me.

Actually, it did go smoothly and we had a perfect little baby girl. The rays of the setting sun filled the room with golden light along with the smiles in our hearts. David was wonderful as always with our wee ones. He was and is a natural born father. I adored watching them together. Their hearts uniting in Love.

In those moments, we were so happy. The birth of a new soul to one's care is wonderful. Unfortunately, the afterbirth pains weren't so wonderful. With each subsequent pregnancy, they got stronger and stronger as the womb sought to contract. They were awful! When it came time to put her to the breast they intensified. I knew that was part of the purpose, to contract the womb, but it was painful. The delivery contractions seemed far easier in comparison.

Dr. Sharma said to take Magnesium Phosphate and Arnica, but it didn't help much this time as with Clare. Michael Skipwith came to see me and gave me a Shiatsu treatment, which was the only thing that alleviated it a bit. I cried a lot each time I put Sara to the breast for that is when it was the worse. Breast-feeding brings things back into shape. It creates contractions of the uterus, but I often wonder, maybe it was also something to do with my kidneys? Dr. Sharma did say that pregnancy does tax all the filtering organs. Maybe giving birth and contracting of the womb did too. Fortunately, it was over in a few days. *Phew*!

Family life went on. I remember the early mornings in the kitchen next to the Aga preparing the kids breakfast and packed lunches. The House had not awakened yet. I would be up very early with the sunrise, listening to the early morning chorus of the birds with Sara. I would feed her and then sit her in her little reclining bouncer on the floor next to me warmed by the heat of the Aga. It was special times together in the stillness of the dawn.

I would prepare the school lunch boxes. I made whole wheat bread sandwiches with cream cheese, cut into shapes of words. LOVE was my favorite. The "L" topped with a carrot, thinly sliced. The "O" was a slice of cucumber. The "V" might have Nori-Seaweed, but I have forgotten. The "E" was more of a challenge to cut any vegetable. I had to make little pieces. Each day I would spell a different word. Their lunch box would have fruit and cartons of apple juice.

Then of course, was the story of the Homeopathic remedies they took to school. Apparently, someone revealed to me many years later that Alice would exchange them for sweets with the other children. She would give them a few pills for a piece of their Mars bar. Fortunately, this did not seem to affect them as much as the sugar did with Alice.

So there we were Sara and I, each morning with me being creative by the dim light of the kitchen. Everything was an opportunity to be creative. Sometimes Sara was so quiet that I almost forgot that she was there. She would just sigh and giggle. She had and still has a very placid and deep meditative nature, which I treasure. All our girls were blonde beauties with pigtails and bows, still beautiful as their blonde locks have darkened. Their tender hearts remain precious to me despite the challenges that make them cry or angry.

A few days ago, I was looking through all my photo albums for pictures to complement this book, when I came upon a blue folder, which said "Kids Menus." They were from 1981 during which time I was still pregnant with Sara. I had forgotten that I had written these menus to insure that they got a balanced diet. I had often told the kids, that there was a time I made sure they ate three raw vegetables and three cooked along with a variety of proteins and fruit.

Our pantry was a health food paradise. I had to go to London to Neal's Yard regularly to get most of my vegetarian needs. Round jars lined the shelves filled with many staples including beans, nuts, rare seaweeds, mixture of grains and muesli (an oatmeal dish). We ate whole grain pasta and breads. Dr. Sharma said it would be better for us to use Butter than processed margarine, which was a relief, as English butter is so yummy.

I had forgotten about these written menus. Alice and I had quite a laugh the other night as we read the reality of my family stories appearing before us. We went back in time. Alice could not believe its reality and exclaimed, "I really ate like that when I was five! God, Mom how super!" My Osteopath commented, "If I hadn't known you for the last 15 years, I would say you were a control freak! But I know this was born from inspiration and love." I just had to share them with another friend and she said, "OH my God! You did that in the 80s!—In England?—Goat's milk, Lecithin, Seaweed, Yeast Powder?" I must say, I knew that I was committed and inspired, but before finding the menus, I had forgotten to what degree.

Some of the recipes and comments were such a giggle. One said, "NOTE: Let me know what Alice ate from her lunch box. If nothing, do not let her eat anything until dinner. Try to tell her how important it is to eat her lunch." Other comments were to let anyone who was cooking to know about the little things: Alice likes thin cut bread. Clare has to have Goats Milk. Wash Alice's hair today. Clare loves avocado in pieces. In addition, some pages had little Alice people drawn at the bottom.

These menus certainly were like looking back into history of what I truly did for my children. Unfortunately, as our flock grew in numbers and we went on tour or holiday in foreign countries, nutrition at this level was difficult. I, at least, was gaining knowledge as those were the days of focusing on learning how to care for our physical bodies. It was like going to a university for a degree in nutrition, but a home course. I bought book after book.

Upon reflection, life continuously gave me opportunities, which would help me to live *What I was Born to BE*! I have had cycles, which focused first on the health and maintenance of the physical body. Then there came a cycle, which stabilized my emotional body, followed by training to develop my mental focus. All laid the foundation to discover that we all hold a divine spark of God. Cycles encouraging me towards the highest in me and passing it on to my children.

Dagoba in Anuradhapura
Sri Lanka
1972

CHAPTER 42

THE LAND OF SMILING PEOPLE
SRI LANKA TRIP

1982

Every year, two very dear friends, Mary and Melissa went on adventures to India, often with an entourage of friends. We had spent almost every summer and some Easters in Lindos together since 1973, during which time they shared all their stories. It had always been my wish to go with them, but I was either pregnant or was with David on tour. I had Sara in June and was in the process of weaning her when the opportunity arose that I could finally go on their next trip. Unfortunately, Mary said that she didn't think India was for me as my constitution was too weak. Her comment hurt since they always said that it would be wonderful for us all to go together one day.

The disappointment set me back for a little while when it came to me that David and I could go it alone for he had some time off. So that is what we did once I was sure Sara was weaned and happy. We chose to go to Sri Lanka, formerly known as Ceylon until 1972. It is an island country in the northern Indian Ocean and was of great strategic importance since the time of the ancient *Silk Road*. What attracted me most is its nickname, *The Land of Smiling People* and its heritage is primarily Buddhist. Having been initiated into Tibetan Buddhism since our time in Los Angeles, the thought of being amongst thousands of people that found this ordinary was very appealing.

There was a wonderful antiquarian travel bookshop, just off the Portobello Rd in London. I bought books about their culture and interesting sites to visit. I was totally vegetarian by this time and was relieved that I would not have a problem with that aspect either. To be able to have more of a choice on the menu than rice, salad and chips would be a luxury though I never complained about the limitation when eating out. I felt good in this way of eating so it became more of a social gathering for me. It became a way of celebration of friendship. Besides, I felt healthier choosing to be a vegetarian. However, it did cause problems with many in the meat and potato society.

I wondered how it would be amongst a culture that supported this "Way of Eating." A culture that didn't snide at the thought. Most of the time, I felt as if I was on a battleground of insults and misinformed judgments. It was my litmus test when I look back at it. Something in me kept me committed. I knew it was the way to a healthier Life, at least for me. I was grateful that George Harrison and Olivia were friends because having a neighbor who understood was a comfort, a neighbor who had walked the path for much longer than I had.

Another bonus that made the decision easier was that Dr. Sharma was from India and practiced Auyervedic Medicine and Homeopathy. So I sought his advice for our trip from a medical point of view. I told him where we were going and inquired about inoculations. He had another opinion. In other words, he was very adamantly against them and said that we did not need them. He felt strongly that inoculations lowered the immune system and there were remedies that he recommended instead.

The Ayurvedic philosophy is to treat symptoms when they arise not before. In addition, he advised us not to drink water from the tap or eat anything raw like salads (most likely washed with water). Most of all wash your hands whenever possible. Luckily, this we already knew from Mary and Melissa's list of "what to do and not to do" that we gathered over the years. To hear it from our medical advisor who was born and raised in India put me at ease.

We flew into Colombo and stayed a few days, travel guides in hand. Our hotel, built in the Colonial period was absolutely wonderful. Walking around in the hotel gardens, I noticed the gardeners all worked the soil and tended the borders squatting. Traditionally, the men wore sarongs and a shirt held up with a belt when working. The women wore colorful saris very similar to India.

Having done yoga for years, I knew how beneficial it was to work in that posture, though very few Westerners could do that as a matter of practice. In addition, unbeknownst to us in our culture, the sitting in chairs has undermined our general health and posture. According to many alternative practices, the squat position keeps the energy flowing through our spine and our bodies.

I had brought some art materials with me and my first water color was of the Sri Lankan sunset, from our balcony. There was a decorative balustrade forming the railing that gave a flavor of the time when the Portuguese and British ruled. As I recall, David immediately came down with a stomach problem and lay in the shadow of our bedroom while I painted. Perhaps it was because of the meat he had eaten the night before. It was hot and meat can go off easily. The locals, I am sure, have the constitution to deal with it. I was happy and relieved that throughout our trip I did not have any tummy problems. What I chose to eat and my remedies must have helped.

Eventually we were on our way. It was customary for tourists to hire a taxi driver who would stay with you throughout your road journey unless you chose to stay a few days at various sites. I felt very at home as we drove along in the green rolling hills of Sri

Lanka. The green glimmered like jade from the sun's rays revealing their bountiful shape. They were like the soft breasts of your mother offering safety and nurturing your heart. There was a very strong feminine quality about this country caring, protecting.

Tea plantations were everywhere and are one of the main crops for export. It formerly was coffee until the country had a blight (disease) killing all the crops. Curiously, a farmer told us that the Brits bought the leaves and the Americans bought the stalks. No wonder the tea in the UK was so strong and ours so weak. Often, when in a restaurant in London ordering a cup of tea, I asked the waiter to wave the teabag over the water. I was joking, of course, but, truthfully, I would ask them for a single dunk of the teabag. Sometimes if it was appropriate, I would ask if I could do it. PG tips were David's favorite and many of our friends. It was too strong for me for many years. I have adapted, "Cup of tea, Love?"

Sri Lanka is a famous and archeological reminder of a rich civilization dating back more than 2500 years. The brochures emphasized that there was a Cultural Triangle, which we could follow on our Sinhalese adventure. Most of the sites were further north. We traveled along the east coast and stopped along the way at a beach resort. We found a Sinhalese local newspaper in English that I remember reading on the beach. Most of the stories were happy. Many of the articles brought a smile to my heart, not clouded by all the world conflicts like ours. It was so different.

As we went deeper into the countryside, the surroundings became littered with small huts with smoke coming from their chimneys. Beautiful people standing in the doorway, wrapped in colorful fabrics with their children at foot waving as we passed. They are an elegant people sylph-like in their sarongs and saris smiling from behind their dark eyes. Such a soulful presence filled the air everywhere we went. It seemed that they found happiness with so little.

My most favorite city there was Anuradhapura. Its history goes back to 3 B.C., pre-Christ, considered the most sacred and developed city in its time. But it had been lost to the jungle until the 19th Century when some British explorers discovered it. Hidden within the jungle after cutting away the vegetation there it was. They thought they had found the mythological "Lost City."

At present, it is quite restored and thriving. We decided to stay the night and found a sweet but modest hotel, which had mosquito nets over our beds. Something I, as an American, had only seen in the movies. I felt that I was within the movie *Gandhi* as I entered the room. It was sunset when we arrived so we ate in the hotel restaurant. I had veg curry; it was so good. Their spices were a mastery of blends that is so Indian. My taste buds floated from the cumin to the coriander to the garam masala and onto the vegetables, still crisp and fresh with other flavors yet for me to know. That meal was such a luxury.

The next day I rented an old fashion bicycle and set off in the morning to meditate under the Bodhi Tree (sacred fig tree) while David slept. I wore a long khaki linen skirt and a short white cotton blouse with white espadrilles. I pulled back my hair in a modest ponytail, put on my straw hat and set off across the town bicycling back into history. The bicycle had a little bell, was black, rusty on the edges and a straw basket. It was not too dissimilar to the one we had back in England. It was easy to find my way about the city bicycling around. Tourist maps were abundant and the people were extremely helpful.

The Bodhi Tree in Anuradhapura is believed to have been propagated from the original Bodhi tree in Bodh Gaya, India. According to Buddhist texts, the Buddha, after his Enlightenment, spent a whole week in front of the tree, standing with unblinking eyes. This Bodhi Tree really interested me for while the Buddha was on his deathbed, he had resolved that a branch be taken to several places around the world. Ceylon was one. I discovered later there was even one sent to Honolulu, Hawaii. Nowadays one will find younger Bodhi Trees growing next to most Buddhist monasteries for it became a tradition.

The original, called Jaya Sri Maha Bodhi was the most sacred Bodhi tree and known to cause rain to pour and heal the sick. It is written, that when an individual became ill, one of his or her relatives would visit the Bodhi tree to water it seven times for seven days and vow on behalf of the sick for a speedy recovery. The Bodhi trees that grew in Sri Lanka also had great significance in the history of Buddhism and I wanted to experience its sacred power. I felt fortunate to be able to do this for it was not from a book inspiring me to dream. It was real.

One had to enter through a temple up many steps. The room was full of colorful flowers placed there as offerings with little candles and little bells tinkling. Women and children in their colorful saris praying to Buddha added to the picture. Most people gave honor to the shrine before going outside to meditate under the Bodhi Tree, which was in the back garden. It was full of devotees and tourists, so it was a challenge to find a place to sit in the shade. I was a bit shy and timid, as I stood out as a foreigner and a woman alone. Eventually, I found a place in the corner against the wall where I could sit and meditate, hoping not to be noticed.

Normally, when I meditated, I did all my shopping lists, reviewed all my thoughts for the day, never until this day did this stop. I have no idea how long I had been there, but when I came back to the present reality, Indian women had surrounded me. They were in a circle staring at me smiling with acceptance. With approval, some were nodding their heads side to side in the gesture typical to their culture. Curious I suppose, of a western woman holding meditative focus without knowing they were there.

One elder woman who was sitting the closest took my hands and put them in a gesture of a particular mudra. Pointing to me and then doing it herself while closing her eyes for a moment and speaking in her native tongue. The entire group of women began to speak as well. It felt like it was a welcoming into their culture.

The leaves of the Bodhi Tree are very distinctive because they are in the shape of a heart. Many had fallen on the ground and I wondered if it was appropriate to take some home. I motioned to the woman, in a sort of sign language, if it was all right to pick up several to take home. I didn't want to do anything that dishonored their culture or the moment. One was for Dr. Sharma, David's Mom and Dad, several other close friends and me, which I had framed for my meditation room. Symbolically, to this day my Bodhi leaf holds a special place in my heart. It reminds me of the first day I really meditated and found deeper peace.

We went on to visit many other archaeological sites and treasures of Sri Lanka. With every day with every place we visited, Buddha statues of all sizes surrounded us. The energy of tranquility filled the air. The most impressive Buddhas were actually in a place called Polonnaruwa. In the 12th Century A.D., two sovereigns endowed the city with Buddhist sanctuaries, palaces and monuments placed within a triple-walled enclosure of a fabulous garden city. We came first to a standing Buddha of 7 meters. This was beautiful, but I was taken to my knees as we stood before a 14-meter lying Buddha. Its size made me feel very humble, not only from an artistic point of view, but also from a spiritual understanding of the power it represented. We stood there for a long while taking in the majesty of what we were witnessing.

Next came Damhulla, the Golden Temple, which had over 100 steps to climb before witnessing its splendor. The Sri Lankan steps were a different height and width to steps in Europe. As Westerners, we had to find a different rhythm to climb them. Upon entering the series of caves, which was the temple, I was captured by the magnificent splendor of an era gone by. One gold Buddha after another lined the walls in the shadow of its cave, occasionally catching a ray of sunlight upon its form as we passed. Donating a Buddha or in fact, several was considered a way for the Royalty and leading sovereigns to gain support of the people and their treasured Buddha in the invisible world. This was the case at the Golden Temple. In fact, one of the sovereigns donated the 100 steps in this way.

Our next adventure was to be in the Valley of Rubies, Nuwara Eliya. Our driver told us there was a possibility to go fly-fishing because the British colonialists in Ceylon first introduced Trout in 1882. Originally, the English built a Private Club House for them, now converted into a Hotel, called the Hill Club. It was truly of a British Colonial Flavor and further brought the movie *Gandhi* alive for me.

The Power of the British Empire created an exclusive beauty at the cost of the people who served them. The waiters were tall and Sinhalese. They wore black uniforms and served us tea in white gloves. I traveled back in time as we sat outside under the umbrellas having High Tea and little cakes, the early evening smelled of exotic scents. As David read the newspaper, I sat dreaming under my straw hat as the sky was full of pale yellow butterflies who flew all around from flower to flower.

We had a lovely night's sleep under the white sheets and big pillows with a circulating fan above. It was easy to surrender to this comfort. It was slightly cooler when we awoke and David wanted to go fishing to have a bit of home. The hotel arranged for us to have a guide who would take us deeper into the valley on foot. He would bring with him the necessary rods so David could have a go. Nuwara Eliya stream flows through the grounds of the

Club and into Nuwara Eliya Victoria Park, which is the prime trout fishing location of Sri Lanka.

We walked for miles along the path. I do not remember our guide's name but I do remember his face and kindness. He almost looked aborigine. His skin was the color of dark chocolate, deeply lined from years in the sun and his eyes were pools of heart. At one point there was a mist, he grabbed my arm and said for me to stay close. Apparently, to our left hidden by the fog was a cliff edge miles deep to the valley below. We would surely reach our demise if we fell. Eventually, we got to a valley where they would fish and I stayed up on the hillside to paint.

I had a good view from there. The midday sun approached while I was held deep in creative focus. I had my little watercolor box, miniature brush and water container. I was in my element. Suddenly, from across the valley, near the jungle, came loud sounds of gorillas. I looked up to call out to David but they were gone. Time had passed by as the colors, tinted my paper. Quickly, I bundled up my things, holding up my long skirt and ran down the hill to where they were. Our guide (I do wish I remembered his name) said that there were no gorillas in Sri Lanka just monkeys. Well then, they were rather large monkeys to sound like that! I was in the grip of my imagination and fear. *Gorillas in the Mist* was not far behind, the movie did not come out until 1988.

One thing I forgot to mention is that many of the Sri Lankans chew Betel Leaf in what they call a "paan" or "quid." As we drove along the countryside, many of the villagers waved and smiled as their mouths were drooling red. With eyes glossed over, they were not really present. It was a curious thing to observe. Where did their "smile" really go? I asked our driver why their mouths were so red. He said, "That's Betel Juice, Mar-am." Apparently, it is a mild stimulant and known for its medicinal properties.

With or without tobacco it's an addictive psycho-stimulating and euphoria-inducing formulation. The betel quid normally contains a combination of substances, including betel leaf, areca nut, slaked lime, opium, and may contain tobacco and spices. It has adverse effects on one's health for regular users. Very often, their mouths turn red and when they smile, they are usually without their front teeth. There is evidence that originally this was used both in ceremonies and had a highly symbolic value since ancient times. When it became an addiction is not sure, but there is a rise of oral cancer throughout the rural areas as a result.

Down from Nuwara Eliya was a pilgrimage called Adam's Peak. The road to Adam's Peak took us past spectacular waterfalls as the road wound through the heart of some of the finest tea-growing country in the world. We stopped at one waterfall for me to bath under. I had never been under a waterfall so here was my chance. In my white dress, I waded out into the pool until I met the gentle waterfall. Its crystal water washed over me like silk. David waited at the shore taking photos. I did wonder if there was any chance to catch something from the water while I swam. I didn't.

We had heard of a walk up to Adam's Peak that David wanted to try. By late afternoon, we found a hotel near where he could start his climb to Adam's Peak. It was something he was sure he wanted to do. The climb up consists of steps most of the way, about 5200 of them, would you believe? I couldn't. He was assured that there were plenty of rest stops along the way. The estimated time it would take him to get to the top would be 2 1/2 to 4 hours. A 2:30 a.m. start would easily get him there before dawn. It would be just in time to see when the historic "Shadow of the peak" takes place.

At the top, there are some breathtaking views across the surrounding hills. Steps lead up to the sacred footprint, on top of a 4-meter rock. Pilgrims cluster round, throwing offerings into the 1-meter hollow before moving to the Saman shrine, up another flight of stairs where thanks are traditionally given. Pilgrims, who have made the trip more than three times, then ring one of the two bells at the summit, each chime representing a successful ascent. Each climb brings special blessings.

I stayed back at the hotel because I did not have the physical stamina to go the whole way. Plus, the endless steps can shake the strongest knees and mine were not strong at all. Therefore, David went alone. Somewhere along the way, he met another European. There was a moment both of them, he told me, were pondering on stopping and going back down. When an elder woman passed by in a rather quick gait carrying a crate of soda, they looked at each other and decided to go all the way. They just had to for their masculine pride was facing them.

David said the view was spectacular and when the sun rose, a pyramid symbol was cast against the mist across the valley. Many were ringing the bell for they had been there before, as the guidebooks said would happen. The Sri Lankans have many rituals of giving thanks and blessings for a good life. There is nowhere one could not find this quality. To live each day with gratitude I believe is a key we could benefit to incorporate into our culture. Rituals to remind us not to forget God is there keeping a watchful eye with Love and guiding protection.

When he returned he was not feeling well. I believe he had a mild concussion from descending down the 5200 steps in an alternating thumping motion for three–four hours. He was a bit sunburned as well, as the sun rose quickly upon the mountain and he did not have a hat. I gave him a strong dose of Arnica. He slept through the day and we left for Kandy in the morning. We entered back into a metropolis, which was a huge difference from the places we had been.

Kandy is the capital of Sri Lanka and is its cultural center. It is still the home of the arts, crafts, music, dance and song, which flourished under the patronage of the Kandyan Kings. The great royal city fell to the British in 1815. Despite their influence, it was and still is the seat of much of Sri Lanka's culture. Kandy is the sacred city for the Buddhists. Its focal point is the Dalada Maligawa also known as the temple of the tooth, where the Sacred Tooth Relic of Lord Buddha is enshrined.

We stayed in a wonderful ancient yet modern Hotel. It was a return to the luxury of home but more special. I must admit to being happy to have a real bath in such comfort. I appreciated more from where I came. Yet, poverty surrounded us. India is such a contrast on all levels. The smells, the colors, the food and most of all, the people sleeping on the sidewalks in the cities are quite a paradox.

During our stay in Kandy, we walked from market to market place. There were Snake charmers with baskets, which held their cobras. The sound of their flutes drifted between the tourists and the traffic. The quiet was gone. Commercialism had returned. Humanity's suffering was evident. I was not sorry to leave this thriving yet sacred metropolis and return to the countryside. My rose-colored glasses were being tested.

We drove through their national parks on our way back to Colombo. Along the roadside were small straw huts, which sold Buffalo yogurt and homemade smoked cane syrup in tall brown bottles. No labels, just freshly made and bottled beside the hut while the Buffalo grazed in the fields behind (snorting). They are magnificent animals standing with such held poise. They are huge. In addition, even though I am an American and part Cree I have never seen a Buffalo on the prairie. Never mind one in Sri Lanka! I sat in silence as I ate the yoghurt, which was extremely delicious with the syrup poured over the top.

At some point, we took a ride on an elephant before we returned through one of their National Parks. I love elephants! But our time in Ceylon was drawing to a close. We made our way back to Colombo and had our last Sinhalese curry. I am glad to say that we returned to England without malaria or any other chronic illness. Dr. Sharma was right when he said we didn't need inoculations at least not to go to Sri Lanka. Instead, we focused on strengthening our immune system with his course of Homeopathic Remedies. I returned grateful for the peace and beauty we found amongst the Sinhalese.

Upon our return, I had spread the news to all my friends of how peaceful Sri Lanka was. However, the story clouded as we were watching the news before dinner. The report stunned me. A rebellion broke out between the Tamils and the Sri Lankan government in the north. It actually started just before we left the UK on 23 July 1983, and has gone on for twenty-five years since. Today, I am in Lindos, Greece at an internet café writing this in 2014. To my surprise, I have just discovered the news of this Civil War as I was searching for the spelling of some sites.

I just shook my head in awe as I read all the reports of that time. We had been traveling in a war zone and didn't know it. I feel very fortunate to have had such a wonderful time there when we did. A thought comes that perhaps the Light of Buddha protected us—Perhaps our guardian Angels surrounded us—Perhaps God was keeping a watchful eye. Whichever it was, I am grateful we made it home in one piece.

New York, New York

CHAPTER 43

"WHAT WAS THAT?"
THE WALL PREMIERS

1982

Finally, the film was finished. We all traveled to Cannes and hung out on the beach during the day, watching all the people pass by, waiting for the moment to see the show. *The Wall* was one of the last films shown in the old Palais; it had seen better days. The Floyd had up-graded the sound system and it was so loud that the paint literally fell off the walls. It fell like fine snow onto our heads, leaving a distinct impression of dandruff on us all. Alan Parker, the film director, is quoted as saying, *"I remember seeing Terry Semel, there, who at the time was head of Warner Brothers, sitting next to Steven Spielberg. They were only five rows ahead of me and I'm sure I saw Steven Spielberg mouthing to him at the end when the lights came up, "What the F*** was that?"*[1]

David and I spent a lot of time together with Bob Geldof and Paula Yates while we were in Cannes. I so admired their dry sense of humor full of intelligence of World Affairs and Philosophy. They were so sharp with their wit and at the same time very down to earth. You couldn't pull the wool over their eyes. We had such a lark cruising the after show parties. When we returned to the UK, Bob and I had regular phone conversations. I remember sitting in our telly room at Hook End Manor slumped in our navy blue comfy chair, feet over the arm, having long conversations with him on the phone.

The Floyd had several premiers to attend and Olivia Harrison was very kind in helping me to get some dresses, especially for NYC. She took me to the workrooms of Liz and David Emmanuel, who designed the Lady Di's wedding dress. Liz was there waiting for us to arrive. The afternoon took me into her world of Beauty with each dress. She showed me the collection just recently created for the movie *Barry Lyndon.* It was a period film and my favorite dress was a ¾-length lace dress with puff sleeves and bows. Liz organized everything from hairgrips to shoes.

I had hoped to find a couple of dresses. Therefore, Liz took me further into the fantasy when she appeared with a dress that Carmen Miranda would have worn. The shape was very flamenco with a kick skirt on the bottom. It was scarlet with a fuchsia lining which appeared as I walked. I loved it! I was set. Two fabulous dresses for the premiers.

Unfortunately, I went into shock a few days later when Liz presented me with the invoice. It was over £5000.00. I had to let go of Carmen Miranda. Barry Lyndon was much more affordable. The dress had already been custom-tailored for the film. It fit me and was on sale. Carmen was a new creation needing adjusting. At the time, and still, I am not used to having a designer of her fame make a dress for me. Nor could I justify spending so much on a dress for a few evenings no matter how beautiful! I had to turn it down before she started to work on it. I was rather embarrassed, but she totally understood. I think that one of my daughters still has the Barry Lyndon.

Wonderful dresses were important to me because over the years I found it difficult to deal with all the women who fancied David. Women always projected their Goddess onto him while at the same time would project psyche daggers of jealousy at the woman in the way, in other words, Me. In the process, they would analyze me first to see what they were up against, then, judge what their chances were and how to destroy the love connection—hoping David's eyes would shift to them. Fortunately, David seemed oblivious to them. But I knew the energetic game women on the hunt play. I was sensitive and very aware to the feminine wiles. Shocking at first being a small town girl. However, eventually I discovered a way to insulate our relationship and myself.

I started to empower my own beauty with divine dresses. I put myself high up amongst the stars in the heavens beyond reach. I loved the period of Fred Astaire and Ginger Rogers. They were my role model. As a young girl, I used to dance in front of the telly dreaming of the day that I would dance with Fred Astaire. I so wanted to be one of the dancers in a Busby Berkeley production as well, but I knew that time had passed as it was the 80s.

On many afternoons, gliding in my dream, I practiced around the living room floor on Saturdays when my family was out, learning the steps. My imagination was so good that I could feel his arms holding me with his gentle yet guiding support. These movies were my secret life taking me through my teenage years, tap dancing along the way.

My vision regarding the groupies was an easy task to achieve. London was full of amazing antique dresses of the twenties and my collection grew. And it was affordable! I was still sylphlike and they worked perfectly. One day I found what I felt was simply the best, at the Antiquarius Antique Market on the Kings Rd., Chelsea. It was such a find.

It was a dress that made me feel like Cinderella, somehow I felt safe within its gentleness. I loved this dress so much; I could almost sleep in it. It was to the floor, in a most delicate fabric, pale pink with applique blue lace flowers. The cut flowed like a tulip in the wind. I would always put a Ginger touch on my outfits bringing them into the twenty-first century Rock 'n' Roll look. In this case, I wore a mini blue jean jacket and platforms, which allowed me to tower above the groupies and yet be elegant.

It was to become a challenge later holding up the image as my inner journey began to call me to ask the question, "Who Am I?" It was one thing to create a wall of protection and yet another when it began to separate me from David and myself. It seemed as time went on all of us went deeper and deeper into the story of the making of the Wall.

Our own walls were being built, that not only isolated the band from each other, but also within our personal lives. Sometimes I just wish I wasn't drowning in it at the time. Perhaps things might have been different? A friend once said to me, "Ginger, when those thoughts arise, Take life as it is—then make it special." That wisdom has helped me so much to accept the twists and turns in life and create Beauty as the journey still goes on. Wish I had known that wisdom at the time.

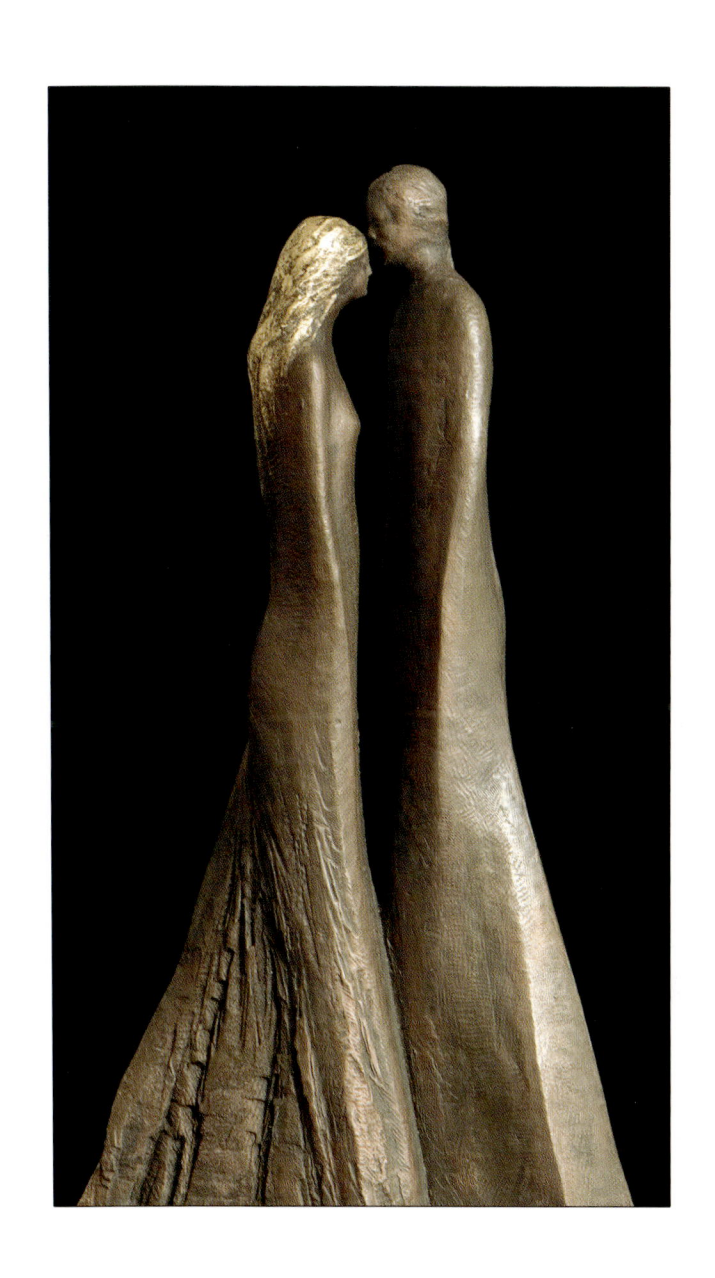

'MOMENT'

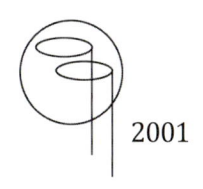

2001

Walks in the forest
Lisa & Joe

CHAPTER 44

GILMOURLAND
AT HOOK END MANOR

Back home in Gilmourland, it was time to readjust and reflect upon our future. We had a full family life and many outside stresses to harmonize. My meditation room was my retreat each morning after the children went to school. I tried to establish at least thirty minutes to myself every day, which Dr. Sharma recommended. At first, it was hard for the household to adjust to not having twenty four-seven access to me. Eventually they did and I got used to not feeling guilty.

One of the sweetest moments happened on the weekends when the children were home. They would often sit outside of the door. Sometimes whispering. Sometimes not speaking. Just sitting, waiting, quietly, but I knew they were there. I could hear their breathing. I could hear them shuffling. Alice would try to silence Clare and Sara when they started to talk.

She would whisper, "*Shhh*. Mom is meditating!" Then Clare would repeat it to Sara but a bit louder, "*Shhh,* Mom's Med…di…dating." I could feel that came with a nudge of command from an older sibling. But she didn't quite get the pronunciation right. I had to smile and continued to hold the space of respect despite that it had broken my meditative focus. Sweetly.

When the weather was warm, I often took Sara for a ride on my rather old Victorian-like bicycle, which I loved. It was black, rusty, with a wicker basket and bell (as I have mentioned before).There was a wonderful tree lined road, which led further into the countryside. It was as though we were riding back in time in a Beatrice Potter book. Sara with her blonde hair and striped scarf blowing in the wind, as we rode along weathering the chilled wind. The fresh air and the beauty of the lambs in the field touched me, happily. One day she asked, "Mom, are you a side kick?" I held my chuckle within as I answered her question. "I don't think so Sara," grinning like a Cheshire Cat. I have often wondered where she got that one from but the memory always returns with a warm tender smile. Children say the darnedest things.

When we were home, bicycling on the weekends to a family lunch, with friends, at the local pub became a regular affair. Sometimes we would walk if there were many children over. Sometimes we even took Joe and Lisa with us because dogs were allowed outside. Some English pubs allowed them inside too. When I first came to England, I loved English beer on tap. I grew to love a pint with Roses Lime juice on a hot day, but No longer could I drink any alcohol just Perrier with Lime.

Bluebell season was my favorite time of the year. Their electric blue bells lined the roadside amongst the fading daffodils. Flowers, flowers were everywhere in our garden. Our gardener, Henry, filled the beds near the greenhouses with almost every Dahlia imaginable and we had so many vegetables I often ran out of room in the freezer. So I took up making jam, preserves, green tomato chutney and pickled onions in order not to waste anything. I was re-creating Nannan's pantry of my childhood without realizing it. I would like to find her recipe for Rivel cake, but I fear it went with her to heaven.

On mornings with dew, I walked barefoot creating patterns in the grass. Dr. Sharma said it was good for me as it stimulated my energy systems. After Clare's pregnancy, it was a way to maintain my health. Each morning before breakfast, the girls would sit at our telly window in their nighties watching me. Some days, I walked fast because it was so cold! Other days I could walk in a Zen fashion feeling each step as my foot touched the earth. Other days I would frolic just for them, in the morning dew shining in the sunlight.

Today this is normal amongst many people for there has been a lot of study, which has changed our awareness about our connection to the energies of Mother Earth. Walking on the grass in the morning and hugging a tree is highly recommended because the earth not only gives but also takes. It takes our stress levels and fills us with clear healthy energy. I dare say many thought that I was crackers then! *Ho Hum*. The life of a forerunner. But the memory of my blonde beauties sitting in the window is special to me, and we often chuckle together about their Mom's antics.

Mrs Tweedie

CHAPTER 45

MEETING MRS. TWEEDIE

1983

I had been having regular Alexander Technique Lessons with Diana in Nottinghill Gate. Alexander lessons strengthened my posture from the weight of my pregnancies. I would walk from our flat on Mc Gregor Rd. to hers each week. In the spring, I passed a typical English Rose Garden. I would stop for a moment to allow the fragrance to soften my heart. I was allergic to most perfumes, except that of roses. I had worn the essential oil of roses for years. One afternoon as I was taking in their fragrance, I realized that each time in the future when my children smelled a rose they would think of Mom. Sweet thought. So I would wander in this sense of Beauty to my appointment.

The Alexander Technique is an educational tool, which helped me identify and release areas of tension and imbalances that were restricting my freedom of movement. In doing so, it allowed my whole body to realign itself. In fact, these lessons went further through the act of directing the body to release muscular tension, it actually helped me to let go of habits of thought, which contributed to build up of tension in the first place.

With the Alexander Technique, I felt a new sense of lightness coupled with increased freedom of movement and a sense of easy contentment. Often, they gave me a sense of renewed happiness. Becoming aware of myself in action was a most rewarding and fascinating experience. Alexander is quoted as saying:

"Stop Doing the Wrong thing and the Right thing will Do Itself."[1]

As I was about to leave one afternoon, my eyes noticed a book lying on Diana's table called the *Chasm of Fire*. I asked her about the book as I picked it up to read the back cover. She said it was about a Russian woman, Irina Tweedie. It was her spiritual journey with her Sufi Master Guruji. The hairs on my arms stood up while I listened, which was an indication for me to inquire further about her. She lived in Willesden, on Teignmouth Rd., in North London, and she allowed people to come there in the afternoons to meditate and have tea. Diana said that she goes there every Wednesday. I asked if I could go with her, but she said that I should go alone. Later, I discovered that this was a spiritual test, that is, for me to make the journey to see Mrs. Tweedie unaccompanied.

So that is what I did. I went alone. To my surprise, just as I was about to knock at the door, Mrs. Tweedie opened it. She was an elegant woman with gray hair neatly gathered behind her head. She had the deepest blue eyes that if one looked long enough one could touch heaven. I was held for a moment in the presence of her radiance and depth of her greeting. I knew a truly *great being* stood before me and a new cycle in life was about to begin. She looked at me with a slight smile, gesturing with one of her hands, making room for me to enter. She said, "Welcome, Please come in, We have been waiting for you." At first, I thought this was a bit strange but my mind stood captured and did not question her statement.

Mrs. Tweedie was gifted the use of the downstairs flat of one of her disciples, Llewellyn and Anati Vaughan-Leigh. It was a semi-detached home composed of two bedrooms, kitchen, sitting room, and bathroom. As one entered there were two bedrooms, one either side of the entrance corridor, which then led to a larger room full of light from the garden windows. On the left was a smaller room, the kitchen, where tea was served after meditation. When I entered, it was just 3:00 p.m.

Everyone was lying on the floor in most of the rooms with blankets covering them. I was having trouble finding a place to sit, stepping carefully amongst all the people. I was a bit lost as to what to do when Mrs. Tweedie offered me the empty chair next to her. "Sit here Love," she beckoned graciously. She always sat in a swivel black leather chair. There were two. I was rather shy and trembled a bit as I sat there meditating while everyone else was lying on the floor. It had taken me years to be able to sit in lotus so this was rather different. But I got used to it over time. Mrs. Tweedie would say that we would be freer if we laid down.

Anati and Llewellyn lived upstairs with their two children. Every day while meditating the children would come home from school. They had a metal spiral staircase leading up to their bedrooms and we could hear stomp, stomp, stomp, as they went up and down. At first, this was disturbing but after a while, it proved invaluable. I say invaluable because I could meditate anywhere after that experience, i.e., on the train, in traffic, on the bus with children screaming. Invaluable.

After meditation, Mrs. Tweedie would ask people to share their dreams. Historically, in the Sufi Tradition one learned from parables handed down through the ages. In this era, teaching stories, are told from dreams. She said that there were four dreams:

1. Dreams that would give you hints as to what you
need psychologically to focus on or let go.
2. Dreams that were from your soul and guide you on your
path.
3. Dreams of the collective, which might also include future
events for humanity.
4. Finally, Dreams, which were teaching dreams from a

higher source, i.e., God or his messenger who might be a living master visible or invisible.

The afternoon would finish with Tea and biscuits or special cakes that others would bring to share. I was sitting in the kitchen when Mrs Tweedie came in and sat down with me. "Ginger how did you know to come see me?" she asked. I told her about Diane and my Alexander Treatments. "Please tell me more about yourself." I told her I was married to a guitarist in Pink Floyd, after which, she called over Miriam Freedman, one of her disciples, to join us. "Miriam, this is Ginger Gilmour and she is married to the Pink Panther." Miriam was confused, as she knew that Peter Sellers had died in 1980, but later we straightened that out. We have chuckled over that one through the years.

Miriam Freedman was graced to receive many dreams for the collective. Mrs. Tweedie said that she should compile them into a book so mankind could benefit from them. Years later, when they were complete, Miriam asked me to do the illustrations, and the book was published. The book's title is *Under the Mango Tree,* in which there are many dreams that serve as modern day parables. One of my favorite stories from that book and illustrations is called "A Lion and a Rabbit." Here is a synopsis:

> *Once there was a great Lion who roared and brought fear to all of the animal kingdom because he would eat them for his dinner. The animals would scurry under the bushes whenever they heard him coming. One day a little rabbit approached him. He roared and roared but the little rabbit was not afraid. He just sat there staring up at the Lion. The Lion said to him in a very stern voice, "Why are you not afraid of me. I could eat you for my lunch!" The rabbit replied, "Oh Great Lion. Please do not eat me. It is not necessary." "And why not," he exclaimed getting a bit angry, "I am hungry!" "Well, I am not afraid for I have a way*

that we could all work together in harmony without eating us." "'Well, how is that possible?" the Lion inquired rather loudly. "Well, we could bring you your food from animals who had died naturally and in return you could protect us." The Lion raised his head in thought. The rabbit continued, "As a result, we would no longer fear you killing us and we could work together insuring the forest would be a safe and happy place to live." And so it came to be. The Lion agreed and all the animals lived together in Peace.[2]

I once had a dream where I was in a marble catacomb lying on a raised altar. There were maidens in white, chanting while walking around me in a slow rhythmic procession. I seemed asleep adorned with flowers and dressed in a similar white robe. At some point, I awakened. They rejoiced for I had returned to the land of the living. They wept with Joy as they helped me sit up. As I got down from the altar, they said in unison, "WE are so happy you have returned to us!"

When I shared this dream with Mrs. Tweedie we were sitting on the bed in the main room, she put her arm around me and said, "Ginger, you and I have something in common. Neither of us wanted to be here. The world is so cruel at times, but we have a purpose. We are meant to be here. We have work to do." She put her hand on my back for a few moments. She would often do that to me. I felt such warmth and love, which seem to take away the hurts in my heart that I carried. Her hands spoke to me that all would be ok.

After that dream, many things began to change within me. Life's challenges became a great divine adventure. It was full of hints for me to listen and then respond. My challenges were no longer a breaking down, but a breaking through. They were a means to reach Heaven on Earth. The hints keep coming, guiding me all along the way to finding what "I was born to BE." I was One with our Creator. Life became more of a painting whose finished picture would be full of bliss. My fear and resistance of being on the Earth was changing into being a wonderful journey and I was the conductor! I had a choice to believe the spin around me or to believe that we were Divine children of God with a purpose.

Often Mrs. Tweedie would give us a private moment with her in one of the side rooms. I had been writing and illustrating a children's book and brought the drawings along to show her. She led me into the room so that we could be alone. We both sat on the bed while she took her time and looked deeply at each one. She lifted her head and looked at me with her blue eyes then shifted her gaze going inward.

Then from a place of deep thought, she said to me, "Ginger, I have known three enlightened men in my lifetime. One was my spiritual teacher Guruji, the other I cannot name and the third is Cecil Collins, who teaches Life Drawing in the City Lit and the ILEA here in London. I would like you to take his class." "Yes, Mrs. Tweedie, how do I do that?" She said, "Well I suppose you go to the City Lit and sign up. And may I tell you that after a while between him and me there won't be much left but rice paper!" She laughed her blue eyes full of sparkles. I replied as she ushered me out the door, "Well, at least it will be eatable!"

My days were full being a mom of three, David's wife, and head of running a large household, including several holiday homes. Nevertheless, I found a day to get over to the City Lit admission office to fill in the form. It would take a few days for them to reply so I continued to work on my book. I continued doing what my day required me to do waiting with anticipation.

Finally! The notification came but it was not of acceptance. His classes were full. I went off concerned to tell Mrs. Tweedie. She just said, "Oh?" with a puzzled look on her face and went into the other room. However, within a few days, I received a second card, which was of acceptance. Years later, I found out that she had sent word to Cecil via Miriam Freedman saying that she really wanted me to do his classes. She had pulled strings as we say in Rock 'n' Roll. Therefore, a new cycle was beginning for me creatively.

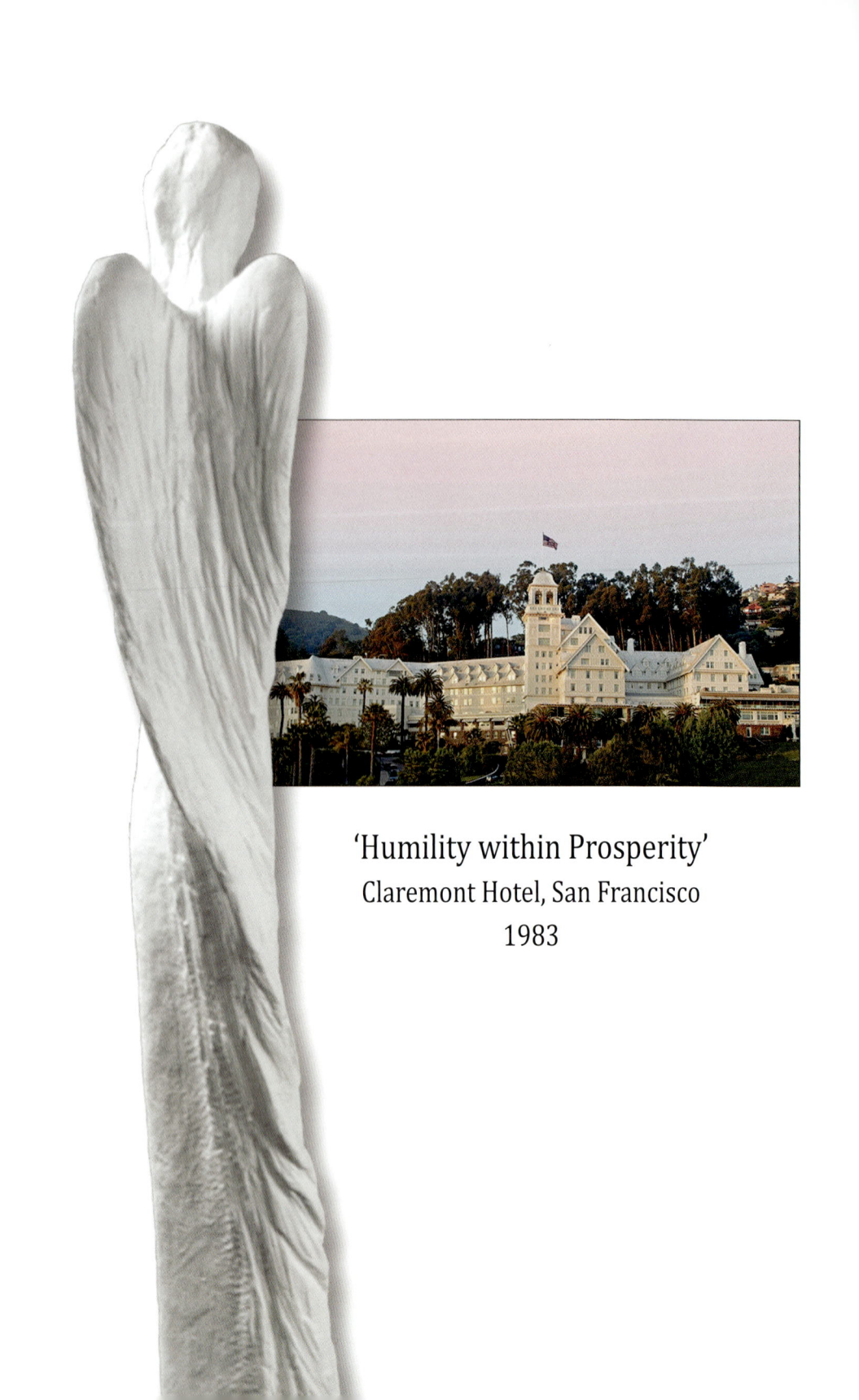

'Humility within Prosperity'
Claremont Hotel, San Francisco
1983

CHAPTER 46

SEARCHING FOR HUMILITY

1983

My path was leading me more into conscious awareness of my humanity. I was becoming aware that the ripples that I created either separated me from the world, or joined me together in community spirit with everyone upon the Earth. It was important to feel the gentle breeze of my thoughts as I walked down the street sending a smile to passers by. A smile, not in need of acceptance, but from a desire to give because everyone seemed so beautiful. Life was hugging me each day and I wanted to share it.

Sir Paul McCartney and Linda were creating a film based on his love of Rupert the Bear Stories of his childhood. It was a short film, *Rupert and The Frog Song,* which had its first release in 1983. Sir Paul sought to capture the sense of wonder and adventure in childhood that never dies within us all. Perhaps it awakened a memory forgotten? The innocence of the animation and the music certainly captured my heart, especially the theme song called the "Frog Song" also known as "We all stand together." In 1986 it became a hit and the animated film received Best Music Video at the Grammy's. To this day, the joy in the film has often found myself and my children holding hands singing, along with the frogs on the telly, dancing and rejoicing together. Now it is our granddaughter's turn. Thank you Sir Paul and Linda.

While Paul and Linda were in the final stages of its completion, they asked David to play on the song during the final credits. The video was released in 1984 and we were invited to attend the premier held in Soho. I decided that I wanted to dress low-key and work on my humility in the public arena. The quality of humility was coming more into focus, on my Journey and path of return to God. Could I handle not being noticed, standing out in the crowd, standing by my famous Rockstar husband, humble?

So I wore a long gabardine white skirt, white boots with a white jumper with tiny embroidered flowers knitted for me by Rita who cared for our house. The Premier was held in a club that seemed very dark inside. Everyone was wearing black, which was the fashion at the time. I was astonished as I walked to our seats for my plan did not work. I stood out like a light bulb, as I was the only one wearing white. I was extremely noticeable as the spotlights panned over the crowd of famous and not so famous people. The story went on into the next morning. Johnny Walker on his morning radio show spoke of the evening and the lady in white. I would have to try harder to be less auspicious, if that was my wish.

My next attempt was on a trip with Mrs. Tweedie in 1987 to San Francisco. I was traveling with Matthew and my sister-in-law, Catha Gilmour. Most of her group booked a room at the Holiday Inn across the Bay. So I decided to book into the same hotel to insure we were part of the group. I did not want to be set apart from them.

I rented a car from the airport and drove to the hotel despite being tired with jet lag, with a young child and not knowing how to get there. It was long before having GPS but we made it. I had requested joining rooms for I was very much the Mum. My nannies were really substitutes for the family I did not have living across the ocean. There we were, checking in ready to go to bed after a ten-hour flight when the registrar broke the news, "Sorry, Mrs. Gilmour, we have your rooms on separate floors."

My mind went into a spin. I had specifically booked adjoining rooms as I wanted to be close to Matthew. *"Sorry Mrs. Gilmour, but we have a conference staying with us,"* he said apologetically. I was annoyed. What else could I do? I had to surrender. I signed in and went to my room with Matthew and Catha in tow until we figured out what to do next. I was steaming with irritation, pacing the room, waiting for our bags. Hands on my hips I parted the curtains to look across the bay. At least we had a view when I noticed this beautiful white German-like castle sitting upon the hill opposite.

I phoned the front desk as our bags were late and we needed to change Matthew's nappie. *"Excuse me, Kate, I have not received our bags yet. Do you know when they will arrive? Also, Can you tell me what the white castle is across the bay?"* She said it was the Claremont Hotel. I immediately called them to see if they had a room, which they did. The desk allowed us to cancel our room with no charge. Back into the car, we went jet lagged, bags and all. One advantage to being a Rock 'n' Roll wife was having the ability to turn on a dime even with kids.

When we arrived, we were greeted by a rather concerned registrar, *"I am sorry Mrs. Gilmour, but the person dealing with registrations got it wrong. We don't have a room."* My inner calm left me in that moment, pleading, struggling to speak with a tear, *"OMG. What are we going to do? We have just flown in from London with my young child. We cancelled our other reservation and we need a room."* She went to speak with her manager and returned with a solution. As it was their mistake, they would give us one of their suites.

I was so grateful. But a thought lingered. How could I live as Rock Royalty when I saw so much poverty around me? The Lama did call me *"The auspicious lamp of the Dharma."* The question would surface again and again. What is it to be humble? My inquiry led me to discover that there are three spiritual paths. The first is complete surrender of material things. The second is to live in a community where everything is shared. And the third, is to accept material prosperity but use it to help those in need.

 In the end, it did turn out rather well as many of the group and Mrs. Tweedie often came for tea. Once again, I felt that God had his plan and we were being looked after. What my service for humanity was to be—had not yet been revealed. I just knew "We All had to Stand Together" in Peace and Humility.

'GRACE'

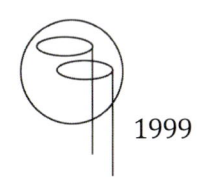

1999

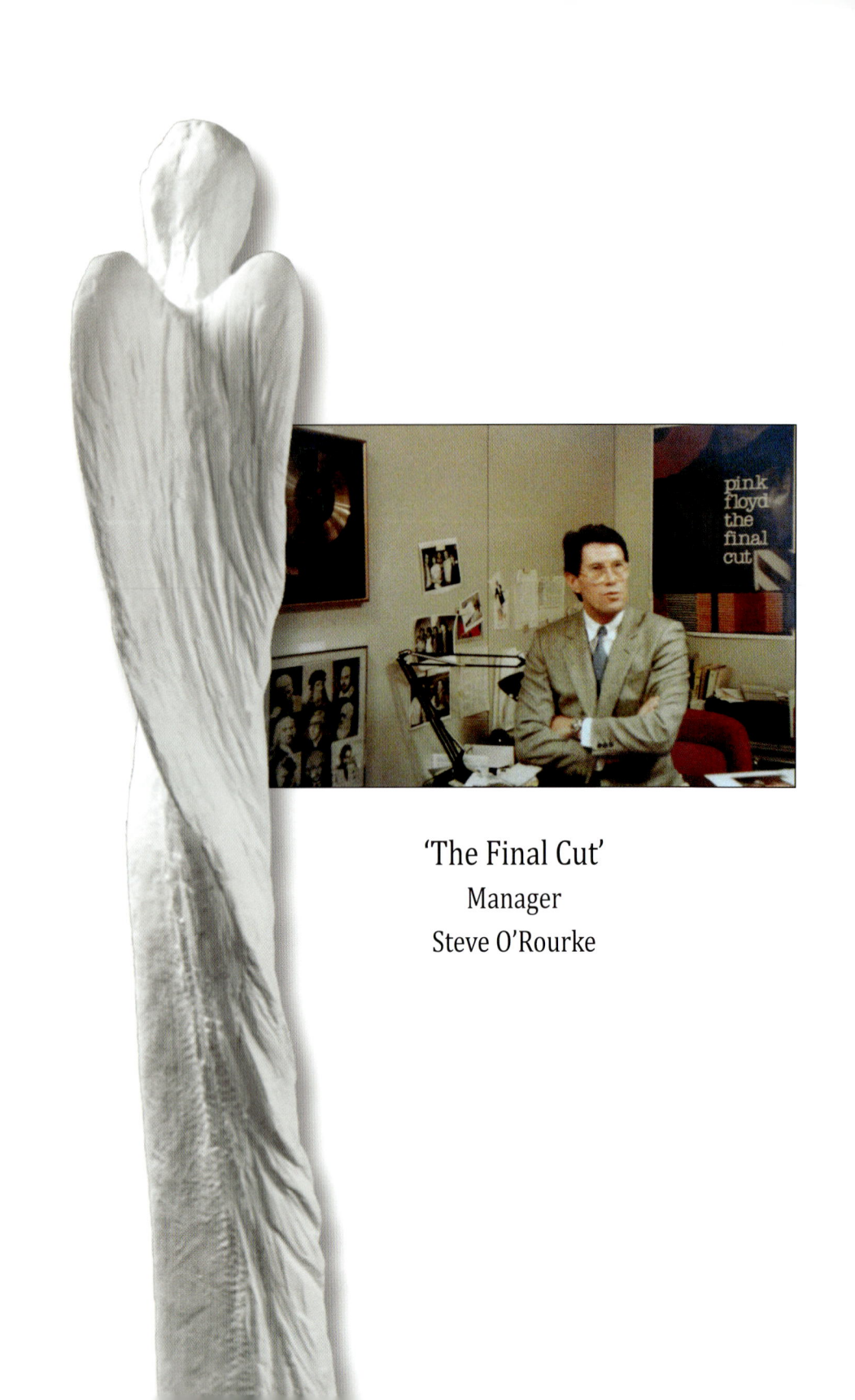

'The Final Cut'
Manager
Steve O'Rourke

CHAPTER 47

FLYING AGAIN
ABOUT FACE

1984

After the recording of *Final Cut,* it seemed like there was a final cut in the relationships within the band. Rick had already left, not amicably, during the Wall. Roger had turned further to dominate, trying to exclude David from collaborating with the concept for the *Final Cut.* The theme primarily focused on a critique of the Falklands War as well as Roger's personal betrayal from his father again.

The Floyd needed to produce another album to comply with their record contract. Roger's vision and his one pointed drive after *The Wall,* pushed him on. He thought the Floyd was his. Consequently, this did not leave much creative room for David to participate. Nor inspire David, for Roger's energy was like a little boy clinging selfishly to his toy (It's mine, It's mine). Besides, what for? Why should David contribute? The original way of creating an album was gone. In fact, how could he under those circumstances?

During this cycle, I felt that Roger should have gone it alone in his own creative process, but the ties that bind still held on. Did he use the lads when he should have had the courage to let go? He insisted he was doing them a favor. With strings? Who can say upon reflection? Tensions ran high. Neither David nor Nick felt it was over, even as Roger treated them as though they were not there at times.

The album was not the Floyd we knew and loved. Nor was it reflective of group metamorphosis. The delicate sounds of Rick's piano and David's distinct voice were almost gone. Roger's angst once again appeared without the balance of the others. But David held on. The Floyd was part of him. After so many years Roger could not just say, "It's over!"

I supported this in whatever way David deemed necessary to maintain his honor. Bob Geldof said during the filming of the *Wall* "Democracy on the set is a hundred people doing what I tell them!" That statement was true on the film set. It was about Roger and Alan Parker then, but the truth of the comment also applied while recording the *Final Cut*. It was apropos for Roger was freezing David and Nick out. It was far from a democracy.

I stayed away from the studio most of the time. Life was full of family life at Hook End. In fact, I don't think I have ever listened to the album. I had had enough of the sound of war and conflict as the sound of Beauty was disappearing behind the Wall that still stood. I could feel the winds of change and prayed for a fruitful one.

David spent a lot of time over at Mick Ralph's, formerly of Mott the Hoople and Bad Company. It was boys together smoking and drinking, playing guitar and laughing for a change having fun. He had decided to take some time to reflect and do a solo album. Over time, it began to manifest and Pete Townsend helped with its birth as a co-writer. Bob Ezrin, Michael Kamen, Andy Jackson and James Guthrie came on board once again.

This meant that there was some semblance, some continuity of what went before, but with more space, more freedom for David to create. It was an opportunity to step out of the part he had been forced to play with the Floyd, to dare to open up again. It did not mean he was giving in to Roger's belief that it was over. He just needed to fly, to breathe again. It was a very joyful phase. His team were so supportive not only creatively but also in heart.

David said in an interview from the *Source*, "Doing this album I wanted to make a really good record. I did not want to do it very, very quickly, and I wanted to get the best musicians in the world that I could get hold of to play with me. So I thought I'd just make a little list of all my favorite musicians, you know, best drummer, best bass player, best keyboard player, and I'll work through the list to see who I can get. Jeff Porcaro was top of my drummers list, Pino Palladino was top of my bass players list, and Ian Kewley, or the Rev, as he is known, he actually came and did the bulk of the Hammond and piano playing and he was terrific. Steve Winwood was top of my keyboard playing list but he couldn't do most of the album, but I got him to do a bit. He played Hammond organ on "Blue Light." I had a bit more time and was feeling a bit freer about things on this album...just more "accidents" tend to occur."[1]

At the same time, it did feel like we were walking on eggshells. Roger had announced that he was leaving the band and for sure, he felt the band was finished! We were in shock as the story began to unfold. David was caught between self-preservation, being driven by his determination and right to go forth. Plus, wondering can he do it alone? Was he too stuck in the formula? Was the formula actually his way forward? Time would tell.

Right now, he had to focus on *About Face*. Questions floated between the creative lines of his thoughts; what would my listeners think? Can I play to smaller audiences, in smaller halls, without a huge production? Who am I? Many thoughts that were kept silent—came and went as he focused on the birth of *ABOUT FACE*. Some he shared. Some he did not.

'My Icarus'
"The next time she flies,
Her wings will not be made of wax"
Artwork by Ginger Gilmour

CHAPTER 48

CECIL COLLINS CLASSES

1983

Days went on. The children went to school. Dinners were shared with friends. I started to paint in the little room off our bedroom. Before long, I began art classes with Cecil Collins. When I entered the classroom on my first day with Cecil, I felt as if it was a homecoming. After attending a few classes, Cecil asked me to bring in a few samples of my artwork. There was one particular painting, which held his attention.

It was a watercolor of a winged being, crouched in a fetus position. The figure sat upon the water's edge below a Greek-like mountainous scene. It was one of a being, broken and waiting in contemplation, forlorn. Cecil, peering straight into my eyes from behind his glasses, said with such clear compassion, *"The next time she flies, her wings shall not be made of wax."* I decided to call this watercolor "*My Icarus.*"

Further, into the term, Cecil said that he did not want me to do any artwork for two years except to come to his classes. So I did this as per his request. It proved interesting to wait and allow something new to grow within me. These classes were like the apprenticeship of old working under the tutorial ship of a master in many ways. As it came to pass, I continued to come to his classes one afternoon per week for nearly eight years. I am so grateful to have experienced so many formative and inspiring moments with him and the other students. It tingles and fills me with a smile as I remember them.

One afternoon I came to the class with my abundant American spirit and smile. Cecil was sitting there just by the door in his tweed suit, yellow wool waistcoat and tie. His arms hung loosely across his chest. He sat there in his usual meditative look from behind his tortoise-shell glasses waiting patiently as we all went to our desks. Just as I came into the room, he ducked. With a Cecil chuckle laced with wisdom he said rather directly, *"Ginger, you shall have a real smile on your face one day!"*

Boy! He put me through my paces from then on! Usually, no matter what instruments, tones, pace, or positions he put us through, my drawings were always perfect, something petite and cute. Then one day he worked us hard. He had us moving with the model, and then quickly—drawing faster—faster. My head was in a swirl! I had to let go! I struggled to hang on but there it was ONE BIG FAT BLOB of black Yuk! A new beginning.

To make matters worse, we had a male model that afternoon instead of our usual female model. I found myself working through some extra issues. I had no trouble going into the creative relationship with a female model. But a male. Gosh! I didn't know where to look. Cecil was laughing from the back corner as he often did. He remarked that on some days little gremlins popped out of our mouths, scurried across the floor and out the door. With a chuckle and a glint in his eye, he said that he wondered where they went.

'EMBRACE'

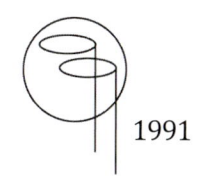

1991

Elizabeth Collins & Ginger
at Anthony d'Offay Gallery
London

CHAPTER 49

MEETING ELIZABETH COLLINS

1983

We were living in Los Angeles during the creation of *The Wall* and I had gone to the Bodhi Tree Bookstore off Melrose Ave. It was always an uplifting breather to spend time there. Stained glass and crystals hung in the window, casting rainbows across the room. I would often walk through the aisles of bookshelves, category to category, waiting for a book to call out for me to read. Way in the back, in the dim light something attracted me to pull out two paper pamphlets from between the hardback volumes. They were two rare documents with the final words of Madam Blavatsky, on her deathbed.

    I did not know much about her at the time, but trusted the process. I added them to the pile of my other choices I wanted to buy. Putting the pamphlets away on my bookshelves at home, I forgot all about them. When packing for our move to Monksbridge they re-appeared. I sat on the floor and started to read them as an inner directive thought passed through my mind, "give these to Elizabeth." The only Elizabeth that I knew was Cecil's wife, whom I didn't know. I wondered how I could do that? I would love to meet her since I had heard such wonderful stories from the other students about her beauty of Heart.

    Mrs. Tweedie often mentioned of how Cecil painted Elizabeth, that she was his muse and inspiration. I loved his wisdom I was beginning to know. I loved how he touched us within our classes awakening our innate creativity. So Elizabeth was the woman behind the man. In one of his BBC documentaries sitting in the corner of the pub he commented, *"One day I discovered, as I listened to the songbird from my window in the early morn' that the song and the bird and me were one"*. Further along in the documentary there was a shot of Elizabeth and Cecil walking together. I felt their union. They were the songbird, the song and were one.

My desire to meet her increased so much that I decided to give the pamphlets to her. I wrapped them in brown paper with a string tied bow and a rose from our garden. I carefully put them into my leather art satchel and set off to class. I was still a newcomer to the classes, but I overcame my shyness as I approached Cecil. His eyes always penetrated from behind his glasses as he listened to my request, *"Cecil, may I ask if you would give this package to Elizabeth for me? It is something I bought in Los Angeles and feel strongly I need to give it to her"*. He looked down at the parcel attentively, *"Certainly, it would be a pleasure."* My face flushed as I walked away. I did it!

I forget how long it was for Elizabeth to respond or who passed on her message to me, but she asked if I could come for tea. I felt so honored, when their private telephone number was given to me so we could arrange a time. The day arrived and I set out for Paulton Square, just off the Old Kings Rd. in Chelsea. I knew where it was for my favorite boutique was on the corner. I asked the taxi to drop me off on the corner and slowly walked down the street to their house. I rang the buzzer and was let in. They lived upstairs and the hallway was narrow. It was quiet, almost too quiet as I was nervous but excited. As I entered, I wondered silently to myself, *"What am I to experience?"* It isn't Rock 'n' Roll but I like it.

Kathleen Raine lived on the first floor. She was a poet, a philosopher, a critic and a scholar who wrote mainly about William

Blake (the renowned British artist of the 17th-18th Century), W.B Yeats (Poet) and Thomas Taylor (English translator and Neoplatonist who was the first to translate into English the complete works of Aristotle and of Plato). The Collins and Kathleen used to be close friends but had a falling out. Therefore, there at the top of the stairs was a white door separating them from each other.

As I climbed the steep stairs, my attention held as I passed from one William Blake print to the next. I was very fond of his work and his philosophy. Elizabeth opened the door to greet me. She was tall, sylph-like and a rather beautiful elder woman. Her hair was graying with an updo Gibson style. She had Parkinson's and her body was frail but her blue eyes shone as bright as the sun reflecting upon a pool of water.

Their living room was on the top floor, another two flights to go. Cecil's artwork covered every wall. There were little canvases and larger canvases, many I was familiar with from his book. Sadly, the narrow space and the amount of paintings hung so close to each other, made it difficult to take in the sheer delight of the moment. Nor could I as I was following Elizabeth and needed to stay focused.

On the first floor, we passed a room filled with canvases and papers piled high in the corners. Paintbrushes of many sizes in containers and paints were everywhere. The energy of creativity and poised inner silence oozed out from the door. I could feel the timelessness that would engulf me had I entered. I assumed that it was Cecil's studio. He was not home that day. I passed the doorway as if a ship in the night, graced, allowed to witness part of their life.

We entered their living room where the sunlight cast its beams of light onto the colorful pillows and carpet. Elizabeth motioned for me to sit at their small table while she made us tea in their little French maisonette kitchen just outside the door. Her first question was, *"So Ginger, why have you sent me these pamphlets?"* I shook my head as I answered her question, *"I do not know Elizabeth. They just called me inwardly to give them to you. Perhaps you might tell me?"* She only said, *"They are curious"* and poured the tea. That day began a special friendship. Over time, she would share many stories about the evolution of their relationship, which gave me insight into mine.

Cecil often told us of how, in his early life, he had a sword that he often used upon his paradisiacal heart. Then one day he awoke and saw its true purpose was to protect his paradisiacal heart, not to destroy it. While speaking to Elizabeth and listening to her stories, I learned her part. She said, *"Ginger, I came to realize that there was a bigger story we were participating in, for humanity. From that day onwards, I sought to do my part creating the vision, that Cecil and I were given to do. As a result, all the little conflicts between our personalities disappeared. We both woke up and dedicated each other to it from then on. That is when our relationship changed."*

She shared with me the time when they were drawn into the teachings of Ouspensky. He was a Russian philosopher who rejected the science and psychology of his time under the strong suspicion that there had to exist a superior system of thought. He felt there was a wall everywhere. Cecil and Elizabeth had also been exploring together with Kathleen Neo-Platonism, along with other great thinkers of past centuries in search of becoming conscious.

One day, Ouspensky invited the Collins to a secret meeting somewhere in London. Elizabeth said that as they approached to knock at the front door, it opened by itself. The hallway was dark and painted a dull red as she recalled. As they climbed the stairs to where the meeting was, she said, *"It was rather eerie. I felt a chill course through my bones."* She went quiet for a bit and went inwards. I sat still honoring her quietude and waited. As she returned from her memories looking at me from her crystal blue eyes, she said, "*Ouspensky is not a path for artists!*"

It was a special afternoon, the sunshine, the cakes, the tea and Elizabeth. On one of the walls, Cecil had drawn in his unique way a caricature of her. He called her Bell. Mrs. Tweedie was right when she said that Cecil painted Elizabeth. Sadly, it was time to depart for I had been there for hours. It was time to descend down the stairs back into my daily life. My mind and soul tingled from being with her.

I was inspired to walk more along the path she walked with Cecil in their marriage. It was wonderful and yet could we, that is—David and I? As I was leaving, she stood at the top of the stairs silhouetted by the light and called out to me, "Ginger." I stopped and turned around to listen. She said, "*don't forget your Angels!*" The truth of her voice held me for a moment. I smiled, turned and left with my heart uplifted. Her final statement was to guide me silently within, as its seed grew over the years.

Cecil Collins

CHAPTER 50

CECIL EXHIBITION
ALDEBURGH, SUFFOLK

JUNE 1984

Cecil was exhibiting in the Festival Gallery in Aldeburgh, Suffolk. Many of his students were going so I got a ride. He was exhibiting 44 paintings and I so wanted to see them in the flesh. During class, he often spoke of the Journey to the Lost Paradise. That within each individual, there is this secret place, often untouched, under-nourished. He sought through his art to unlock the door, to feed and sustain the viewer. He wanted us to dwell within its mystery, within its poetic symbolism and intention. He wanted to catch the soul in its return to Paradise.

His journey had not been easy, but his vision held fast. Within the intellectual and artistic communities, he found he was alone except for Elizabeth. He challenged both the conservatism of traditional religion for he drew Christ's Resurrection full of Light and Freedom. He challenged the iron clad, "Art for Art Sake" with his symbolic images and expressions of the Spirit within us, which they denied its existence. On that day, I stood within the grace of his struggle and the Beauty he attained for us all.

I was especially moved by the painting called *The Hymn of the Night*. Cecil approached and said with a wry tone in his voice, "*This painting always seems to make people pause and some even raise their umbrellas to it!*" I asked "Why?" for the images didn't seem offensive. He chuckled in his Cecil way, which always seemed to put me at rest. He continued telling me in a whisper of confidence, *"I think it had more to do with the Anima."* I stayed longer pondering his words. And as I did so, I felt a mysterious chill about the painting.

Before me, was a young girl standing in front of a bountiful tree, arms crossed between her breasts, eyes glowing beckoning one to enter. The full moon, capturing the time of our entry, guided further by an Angel, while Swans floated below the mountains in the distance. Was this mysterious chill drawing me into the "Woman" in myself? Was I ready to look? Could I dare to go further to reveal what lies deep within? Was my Animus aligned to support this process? I saw and was inspired by the power of Art to challenge the viewer through symbolism and intent to the journey of return and holism.

These questions did not evoke a desire to raise my umbrella and spit at the painting. What it did do was place the experience deep into my sub-conscious memory of the day that someone would raise an umbrella at my work. And they did. My work also created tears of Joy. It has helped me to remember that this was a good response and not to get discouraged.

This witnessing of his work was a very important exhibition for I awoke that day with a strong desire to be open and create artwork, which uplifted and sometimes even stirred the viewer to question. Cecil gave me a tool to weather the storm and create the Light within just a few words, the colors, the images and his chuckle. I bless him every day for daring to follow his soul purpose to serve God through his Art and his life. I am grateful he chose to be our teacher and make his wisdom accessible for us all whether rich or poor.

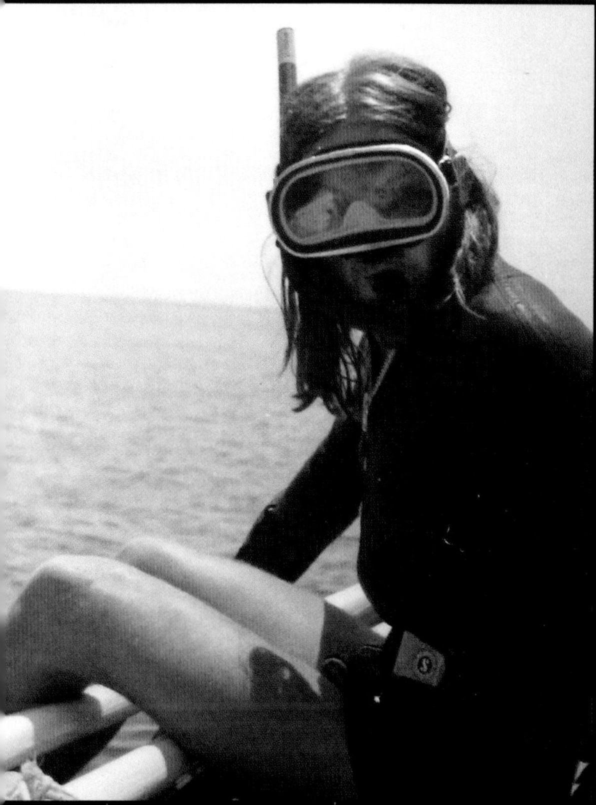

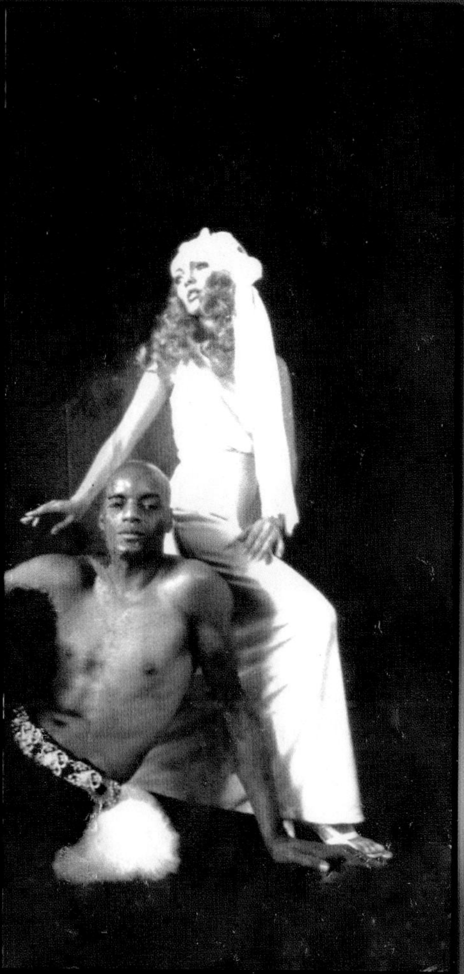

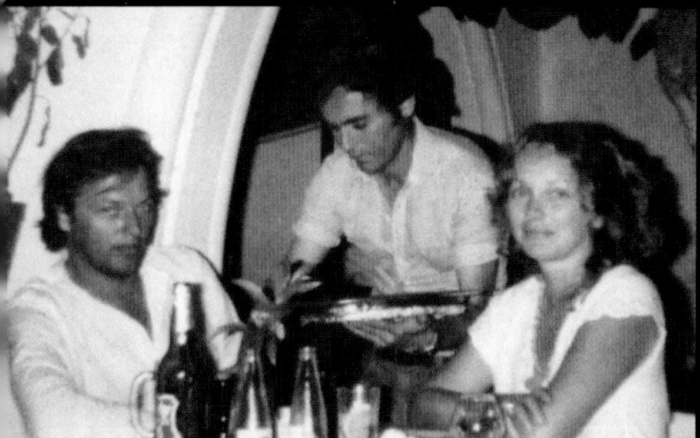

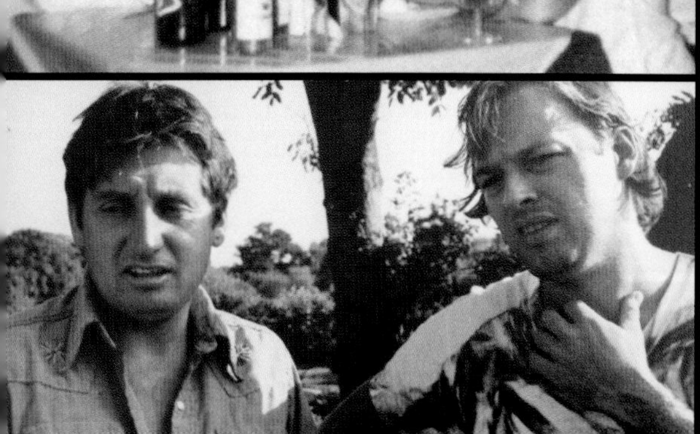
BOY

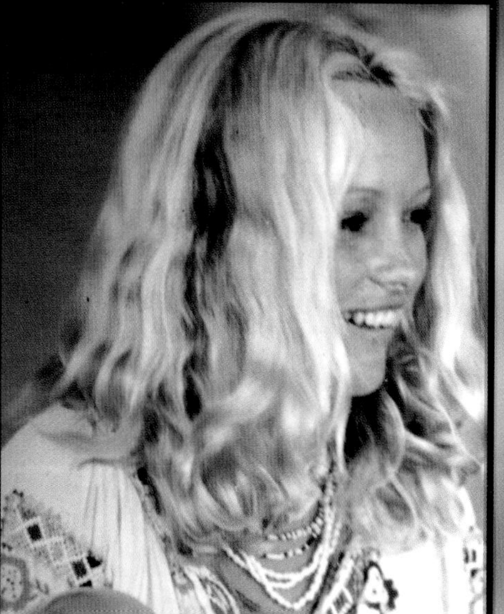

'Life in a Northern Town'
Dream Academy
Guy Fawkes Party

CHAPTER 51

GUY FAWKES

1984

Every November, we had a bonfire party with fireworks. At the time, I never quite understood why, on 5 November, England celebrated the burning of the effigy of Guy Fawkes until years later thanks to Wikipedia. *Its history begins with the events of 5 November 1605, when Guy Fawkes, a member of the Gunpowder Plot, was arrested while guarding explosives the plotters had placed beneath the House of Lords. Celebrating the fact that King James I had survived the attempt on his life, people lit bonfires around London, and months later the introduction of the Observance of 5th November Act enforced an annual public day of thanksgiving for the plot's failure.*

Within a few decades Gunpowder Treason Day, as it was known, became the predominant English state commemoration, but as it carried strong religious overtones, it also became a focus for anti-Catholic sentiment. Puritans delivered sermons regarding the perceived dangers of popery, while during increasingly raucous celebrations common folk burnt effigies of popular hate-figures, such as the pope. Towards the end of the 18th century reports appear of children, begging for money with effigies of Guy Fawkes and 5 November gradually became known as Guy Fawkes Day.[1]

Fortunately, all this had changed by the time I landed in the UK. I also think very few understand the symbolism behind their firework parties. (Around the late 90s, I decided to discontinue having them for I think Guy Fawkes had paid his dues.)

Nineteen eighty-four was a special year for Michael Kamen, a dear friend and composer. He asked if we could make a recording for the latest Monty Python movie *Brazil* with everyone singing in the studio. There were always many friends and children invited so it was a perfect setting for his request. I remember our girls at the edge of the stage in swirly skirts and sneakers, hand in hand bopping to the music of the band throughout the night. Nick Laird-Clowes and his band the Dream Academy played because David was producing their album. Their song "Life in a Northern Town," released later in 1985, still fills my heart with nostalgia as I often listen to it. It was a crisp evening and the lyrics caught the flavor of England and the night.

George Harrison, who had become a close friend, lived in a nearby village and came. We stood by the fire warmly wrapped. Slipping into the joy of the evening, we watched David absorbed with the fireworks. David had been on duty creating the firework display with helpers throughout the day. He loved setting off the fireworks each year. We organized bales of hay in the field next to the fire for people to sit on with marshmallows on sticks waiting to be toasted.

Kegs of Beer sat on the edge of the field next to the coal fired barbeque, which Rita and Jack tended. The smell of Hamburgers, sausages and cooked onions filled the air between the smoke of the fire and sulfur. This was one of David's favorite times of the year. I could see he was full of joy when the fire light touched his face each time he passed to set-off the next firework. There were lots of *Ohh's* and *Ahh's*.

Our house was open to all who came and I must say that over the years nothing was ever damaged or stolen. We didn't even have wine spilled on the white carpets. During the evening, I was walking out from the kitchen with more cups, when a stranger grabbed my arm gently pulling me into the corner. Looking me into the eyes, she said to me from behind her long gray hair, "*Ginger, I have a message for you. I have come from far to tell you. You must start to listen to your American Indian Guides.*" It was a curious moment. All I could say was, "*Oh, Thank you,*" but it did awaken a memory as I proceeded on my way out to where most were waiting for the cups to fill with beer.

***

When I was about twelve, Mom started to tell me some of our family stories of when she was living with her grandparents in Boston. In those days when a family member passed over, their body would be placed in a room so their loved ones could say good-bye. The house was a very Victorian Bostonian house with tall windows and wooden paneling. The rooms were dark with velvet curtains. The light filtered dimly through the room from behind the hanging lace.

Her Great Aunt had died, and in one of the large rooms on a table, lay her body, which was the custom. Mom was a teenager and had just returned from school. There within the dim light was the silhouette of an elder American Indian chanting, the room filled with the smell of burning sage. She stood on the edge of the doorway watching, wondering. She discovered that part of our lineage was of the Cree Tribe. What did they want to tell me? The mystery continued.

***

It was near the end of the evening when we all gathered again in the studio where Michael instructed us on what we were to sing. David and a technician were in the studio ready to record from behind the glass window divide. Mikes were set. The room was full with everyone in good spirits. The recording began. It wasn't until 1985 that the movie *Brazil* came out in the cinemas. Terry Gilliam, one of the Monty Pythons, called it part of a "Trilogy of Imagination" and a testimony to George Orwell's *Nineteen Eighty Four*. It was a satire about the craziness of our awkwardly ordered society and the desire to escape it through whatever means possible. It was not successful at the time, but it's now considered a cult film.

Monty Python has become part of being English. They were our generation of cultural satirists. Many waited each week, we certainly did, to watch their television series *Monty Python's Flying Circus* and looked forward to the release of their films. I still have them all on DVD. Eric Idle became a dear friend and we often had sushi together when we were in London.

When I first arrived in the UK David took me to one. It was like watching a film in another language without subtitles. The humor combined with the accent was beyond me at first. I just sat there in the cinema breathing in all the smoke from the audience's cigarettes. Years later, the *silly walk* and *curry's brain* would become part of my vernacular amongst many more like *nit, nit*. I get it now. And the song at the end of *Brazil* always reminds me of that firework party at Hook End many years ago.

'CONTEMPLATION'

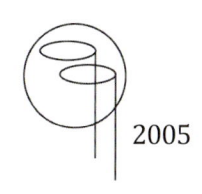

2005

'About Face Tour'
Warwick, Mick, David & Mickey
1984

CHAPTER 52

ABOUT FACE TOUR

1984

The time was approaching for David to form a band and take *About Face* out on the road. With the album set to release in the UK on 5 March and in the States on his birthday, 6 March, David was almost certain of who was going to join him. The general line-up with other guest appearances at individual concerts was: Gregg Dechart (keyboards), Mickey Feat (bass guitar), Jody Linscott (percussion), Mick Ralphs (guitar, vocals), Chris Slade (drums), Raphael Ravenscroft (saxophone, flute, keyboards). I went along for the first few gigs in Ireland.

The first show was in Dublin. When we first arrived, we all went to our rooms for a rest and a shower before going to the hall for a sound check. Mick Ralphs was in the middle of taking a shower when a rather impatient knock came at his door. A man from the hotel was shouting in a rather strong Irish accent as he continued to pound on the door, "*Mister Ralphs, Mister Ralphs?*" Mick shouted back from the bathroom, "*I am in the shower. What do you want?*" "*Well, Mister Ralphs I have ah' telegram for ya.*" Mick shouts as he gets out the shower, "*Can you slip it under the door!*" "*OHHH, NO! Mister Ralphs! I cannot be doin' dat' for it's on a Tray!*" Mick's eyebrows raised in disbelief as he wrapped himself in his bathrobe to answer the door. It was one of those unbelievable moments that marked the story of our journey to Ireland.

The next stop would be Belfast. We had to walk through the check point Charlie barricades to get to the hotel. Ever since I had arrived in the UK, this situation of North and South Ireland was always in the public conscience. There had always been incidents of IRA bombings or killings every year since I arrived in 1971. However, I was never so close to being in the energy of confrontation between groups of people as I was that day. The smell of possible bombing loomed in my mind throughout our stay. Every corner, I tensed wondering is this the moment? The fear of the reality was so alive in me.

Despite being an American and raised with the day-to-day tensions of the four fears: IRS, Cancer, Communism, and Nuclear War, I still could not get my head around this situation. The indoctrination did not prepare me for the possible reality. Any moment there could be an explosion. Any moment a person or many could be dead. Their anger and desperation appeared suspended in the air, saturating the walls, hanging on the faces of the people.

***

Many years later, I was to return with the healer and mentor, Lily Cornford, as her assistant treating patients. In fact, we saw at least twenty people per day. I was training with her in the Art of Mental Color Therapy. It is a form of healing based on the healing power of color and Love. I saw another side of the Irish during that week. Lily was so well received, especially when she spoke about the angels and the wee folk, the fairies. The crowd lit up at her lecture each time she spoke of them. It was special to be in a culture that believed that they existed without a doubt. In the evening, they would share stories of their folklore and times when definitely they met with an Angel or two. It was different to the fear of war.

***

After Ireland, David went on tour in Europe, where they all traveled in one of those big buses from gig to gig. One part of him as a musician needed to be out there sharing his music. He loved the buzz and the interaction. The other wanted to be at home. A great composer once said, *"You can write the greatest piece of music, but if it is not performed before the people it doesn't exist."* This is so true. Performing was and is so very important to the creative process. Just as exhibitions of my art and creativity is essential to me. One is given the ability to create in order to serve and uplift others. For me, it is to remember and to reveal that we are a spark in God's Divine Plan.

After a while of living out of a suitcase, David began to miss his morning cups of tea and the girls playing around the kitchen table with the dogs. He missed his wife and the warmth of his home. It warmed my heart to hear him saying that in his video of *About Face* for I deeply missed him too. I was so happy because he was happier. But I missed him.

At the end of the month, they were to perform in London at the Hammersmith Odeon. We were so overjoyed that he was home again. His lyrics of being Home again captured the truth in his heart. I loved watching the girls jumping into his lap in the morning as he watched telly and read the morning newspaper. Their blonde pigtails catching his face as he tickled them. In fact, our dogs were happy to see him as well.

***

We had two dogs, which we all treasured: our blessed white Alsatian, Joe, and Lisa, a Saluki. Joe was our guardian and friend. Lisa was graceful and delicate, a total contrast to Joe. She could run like the wind, her slender legs reaching forward almost flying along. Historically Salukis were ancient guardians of Egyptian temples. When she sat she would always cross her front paws with her head held high, her long ears gently hanging either side of her elegant nose.

We had wonderful woodland walks around Hook End, which I so missed when we moved years later. The woodland was a cultivated forest of pine trees. The smell uplifted my spirits each day as we wandered through the scattered rays of sunlight between the branches as the dogs frolicked in the underbrush chasing rabbits. Joe and Lisa were quite the couple. Lisa was so sleek and majestic when she ran ahead of us through the fields of grass. Joe's masculine strength held the fort of protection for the women in his life, that was, the girls, Lisa and me. Many said they were like David and I in the dog world.

Lisa would eventually die at Hook End and Joe would not be far behind her. It was the end of an era for me, especially when Joe died. He was always there protecting the kids and me. They would lie on him as he sat on the floor in the telly room. He was my buddy. Dr. Sharma said to me when Lisa passed to feel her spirit in heaven since she was everywhere touching my heart. It hurt so much.

And it was the same again later, when Joe passed over. I felt lost without my canine friends. Something was missing after so many years of them being part of our daily life. Before we all had children, weekends with friends were spent with our dogs walking in the fields laughing as they played with each other. The question was after Lisa and Joe passed, do we start again? We did. We got Lady who was an American cocker spaniel like the one in the movie *Lady and the Tramp*. She was a birthday present for Alice.

***

The London gig was a happy affair. It was an affair of heart with family, friends and most of all Nick Mason and Roy Harper joining David on stage. What I remember the most was how joyful David moved about playing with such exuberance, smiling. Mick was a great partner for him as they inspired each other to the next riff. They laughed together as the sounds reflected their mood. It was a pleasure to witness their friendship through the music as they played.

My favorite song was and still is "Out of the Blue." I remember how touched I was when David first played it to me. To this day, I feel that it's a message from God for us all. It is a message that did come from out of the blue. It holds an archetypal message within its sorrow and pain. It was as though David spoke from the Love deep in his heart as a father and as a man. It is an inner testimony of how he really felt within the shadows of his being. He spoke for all the children, for all the parents, for all of Humanity. Most of all, I wonder was he really writing about the Light?

Next stop was Canada then on to the USA. We would meet when they reached the Big Apple and would play at the Beacon Theatre. We decided to take the girls, Alice, Clare, Sara and Annie Rowland, our nanny. My brother Stephen was to meet us at the theatre. I hadn't seen him in years and suddenly my little brother was no longer little. He was tall with the heart of a teddy bear, plus a huge beard and long hair. Goodness. He took me aside at one point and said *"Charlie, Mom just told me that your father was not my father."* With a lump in his throat he asked, *"Charlie, Why? Why, after all these years did she wait until now to tell me?"*

***

I was rather taken back at the news. It appears that after leaving my father she met the love of her life. (She thought) She was a fragile soul, alone in the world after leaving Daddy. She always had been alone. Her mother, my grandmother, was the youngest of twenty-two children in Boston. During the war, food was short and the girls sold their hearts for extras. My grandmother then went on to have four children, which she eventually put into a Catholic orphanage. She was a prostitute.

My mother was four years old and her stories of that time were rather bleak. She had to scrub the floors, even at four—No time to be held—No time to be a young child. If she wet her bed, the next night the nuns would put her bed with her in it out on the balcony in the freezing winter. As the snow fell, she shivered with panic and fear of freezing. Their intention was to stop the problem. Did it? I wonder.

She didn't get out of the orphanage until she was twelve. There were several tries to have someone adopt her, but all failed. Her life became the life of an orphan scrubbing the floors and going to mass and whipped on the head if she fell asleep. Where was the Christ spirit then?

She has passed over now. Just before, she said that she was grateful for the nuns because they did give her Christ; therefore, she forgave their trespasses. She had traveled far to reach that point of insight and True Christian Love. She had lost her way for a while. Felt guilty about her divorce and having a child out of wedlock. She hated Christianity for a time, but had returned. She could finally find peace.

When Mom met my Dad, he was so handsome and in the armed forces. He and his family gave her the care of a family she had never had. She often says how close she was with Nannan who took her in like Mother Hubbard adding her to her flock. Mom did not have a strong constitution and suffered from colitis. All of life's challenges brought anxiety and fear. A pattern, that became a challenge for her throughout her life.

After she married Dad, her doctor recommended that she got pregnant to stop her bleeding. By the time my sister Donna was born, she felt very isolated. The closeness she shared with my Dad had left. Tired and alone living on very little, she decided to leave. She went to live with her sister, Dot, in Connecticut when she met her next love. He worked in a circus. But it didn't last. He left her pregnant.

    I pondered what Stephen had just told me, as we stood outside the Beacon in the afternoon sunlight. I thought, well at least, Stephen was born from Love. Over the years, more would be revealed about this affair. I partly understood my mother's dilemma for in those days it was not acceptable to have a child outside of wedlock; therefore, she made up the story that my dad was Stephen's Dad.

    Sadly and consequently, for me, the lie made each phone call and vacation with Dad a problem in regards to ever mentioning Stephen. The years of covering Stephen's hurt as he pleaded to speak to his dad came flooding back. I was young but the eldest. He would tug on my sleeve, *"Charlie, Charlie, I want to talk to Daddy!"* My heart went out to him once again as he shared his new heartache.

'About Face' Tour
NYC
"Wonderin' Who's my Dad?"

CHAPTER 53

BABY BROTHER STEPHEN

During a quiet moment in the afternoon, when the girls were having a nap back at the hotel, my mind wandered back to the day in my childhood when we arrived in Connecticut, after the long train ride from Philadelphia. Donna and I had no idea where we were going or that we had a brother. It was late. Donna and I had fallen asleep in the back of the taxi on our way from the train. Mom and Aunt Dot gently woke us up from our slumber carrying us in their arms. Upon entering the small modest house that was to be our future home, a cry greeted us and woke us up.

It was a little baby in another room. Donna and I were looking perplexed, wondering who was in the room. My mother knelt down while holding both our hands and said, *"Girls you have a little brother. His name is Stephen. It has been a long day so let me take you to your room. You can meet him in the morning."* He was a bonnie lad and giggled a lot. We grew quite close, the three of us. The only problem was that my father did not accept that he was his father. This confused us for Mom insisted that he was.

By the divorce agreement, Dad was awarded regular phone calls and visits on school holidays. In addition, in the summer holidays, we were to go with him for the whole vacation and Stephen remained at home with Mom. He and Agnes used to drive up from Philadelphia to visit on Easter and Christmas and stay in a local motel for a few days. Their car was always laden with presents, which brought back memories of Nannan and Poppop. As we got older this giving of many presents eventually got smaller as did the visits, except for the summer.

As Stephen got bigger and could speak, he would often pull on my jumper while I was on the phone with Daddy. *"Can I speak with Daddy, too?"* Every phone call was like that. I became my brother's ambassador with my dad. *"NO!"* Daddy would shout hearing Stephen's plea in the background. *"I will not speak with that Bastard! He is not my son."* My heart hurt with the strength of his words.

My brother would cry as I hung up and I never told him at the time what I had to endure over and over. He never heard those words. It continued for us during the summer holidays. My mother insisted that my dad was Stephen's father. The conflict went on for years until I just stopped asking, listening, or saying anything about it. Now, more of the story is emerging, another chapter in our lives to reconcile on that day in New York.

Fortunately, Mom did meet another man who really became the love of her life and did stay with her. He was a Coast Guard Medic, Italian American and looked like Omar Sharif. His name was Ronald Messura. He became a father to us all, especially for Stephen. We were close. He took on Mom's three children and went on to have two more, Toni and Marcus.

Our family moved each time a transfer came in or when he had to do a new course or his rank upgraded. We went from coast to coast from base to base. He eventually became a Chief Petty Officer and highly respected amongst his men. My special delight was on the weekends when he taught me to play Chess. He taught me strategy with each game. We laughed. I took it seriously for I wanted to win. My mind was activated, which helped me in my school lessons. But of course, this was after the football match.

***

The girls awoke from their naps and David still hadn't left for rehearsals, when the question arose of how and when we could arrange for Annie to go see the concert. David asked Stephen if he would babysit. Stephen said, "*Sure,*" since he was in town for a few days. Later I brought to David's attention that as the girls did not know Stephen I thought it best for Annie to come home at midnight. They both agreed.

Later, David rang to let me know that there would be an after gig party at a place called the Sanctuary. My heart froze with unexpected and irrational panic. The hairs on my arms rose as he continued to tell me the plan and its location. It came as some intuitive warning. These kinds of impressions were new to me. It was so scary and powerful that I had to take notice. I shared it with David, who said for me not to be so ridiculous. It would be fine.

I checked with a few New York friends about the place. It was a converted chapel on 43rd street and 9th Ave., made into a discotheque as part of the global party culture. This dance fever was rampant from NYC to London. The movie *Saturday Night Fever,* went far to inspire and encourage the trend of dance culture clubs. As I loved dancing and in response to David's reaction, I decided to give it a go, but the queer feeling stayed with me.

The gig was good and we got into our cars to make our way to the Sanctuary. There were long queues trying to get in so getting through them required assistance when they saw their stars. We entered the doorway and were ushered up some metal stairs, which previously had been the bell tower. We passed what had been the main chapel. The door was open.

I couldn't believe what I saw; many people gyrating upon the altar with strobe lights accentuating their movements to the loud pulsating music. It was so primitive even blasphemous. When would there be a blood sacrifice, I asked myself, feeling awful at the sight. As we climbed the stairs to the converted clergy rooms on the next floor, I suddenly felt sick.

We continued on to a long room, which was used for private parties. Along one wall were wooden bars, serving drinks and on the other side were half circular cubicles covered with leather and coffee tables. Through the aircon system, they were pumping incense that normally burned during mass. Throughout my childhood, I always associated this scent with going to church. Being used in this way was disturbing. It seemed sacrilegious and the feeling of sickness persisted. It was a long night waiting for midnight, having shallow conversations with people I did not know. I did not drink and the sparkling water did not help my nausea.

David and Annie were standing at the bar when I approached to tell them it was midnight. It was time to relieve my brother from his duties as agreed. As I was feeling a bit poorly, I decided that I would go back to the hotel. Annie could stay if she wanted. I waited for a few minutes for their response then turned and walked briskly towards the door. As I approached an invisible energy force, seem to hit me preventing my exit. I felt faint and was about to collapse. Warwick and Raff Ravenscroft, the saxophone player for the band caught me. Raff and his girlfriend guided me out of the door like protectors and we all got into a cab back to the hotel.

Raff had been there the night before at another party. He said that there was a very demonic and hypnotic energy in the place and it was best that I left when I did. Raff was a friend and he knew how sensitive I was. I never heard of, nor consciously experienced anything like this before. Apparently, he grew up aware that there was more to life than what was visible because his parents were Steiner teachers. He was familiar with the story of God and Lucifer. And Demons apparently. I had only seen it in the movies as some fantasy of some writer. What I had learned in catechism held a pale image to this. It felt like I was in a horror movie and I was worried that David would be all right.

We all went to the hotel bar until they were sure I was stable. Stephen had been great and the girls were sound asleep safe from the storm. The next day I was glad when we left the city. I was very disturbed by this experience. One, which I could not share with many. Had this been a hallucination? Perhaps an Acid Flashback? Were Demons real? According to Jungian philosophy, hallucination or not it was my reality. I had to get to the bottom of it. I did not like it. I prayed to take it away. I was a sensitive and a delicate flower struggling to hold love and beauty as my primary focus. It was enough that my mother always worried about the Rock 'n' Roll life I had chosen to live. But this?

The anxiety of the Wall had been enough of a reality to cope with up until then. I was entering a spiritual crisis it seems. Perhaps, upon reflection, it was an awakening for me. So, before we left, I spoke to someone back in the UK who could pass on a message to Mrs. Tweedie. She was the only person I knew at the time to give me a deeper insight about this experience. We were not churchgoers. I had left my faith in Christ behind me. I waited anxiously for a reply when finally I received a message from her saying not to worry that I was protected. She said that I should come to see her when I got home so she could further help me understand that God always protects his children of light. She told me that I was on the right path.

The girls and I traveled back home to England while David continued his American tour. I would join him later in California. As soon as the girls settled in their normal routine and back in school, I went to see Mrs. Tweedie as she requested. She took me into her private room and sat me before her on the bed. Looking at me, her blue eyes filled with compassion, she said, *"Now, dear, tell me what happened."* I shivered from the memory as I related the whole story back to her. She then gave me a protection visualization and said, *"One day you will not need any protection for the Love of God will increase within you and Love will take the place of all your fears."* And she was right.

'KWAN YIN'

2007

'Ethiopia'
"We can Save the World"
Artwork by Ginger Gilmour

CHAPTER 54

LIVE AID
WE CAN FEED THE WORLD

1984

We were staying at the Sunset Marque in Hollywood, California and I invited a dear friend Laurie Scott over for lunch and then to the show. It had been years since we had been together. We had so much to share, lots of children's stories to tell. We met first in the afternoon at the hotel while David was doing his sound check. She was very involved with the Ethiopian Crisis. A crisis? It was the first that I had heard of it because caring for my children kept me focused in another direction. I found the information she revealed very shocking. They needed help! We presented the information to David, who was open to participating in doing a show but in the UK. I wished that I played guitar so I could do more.

Laurie only had a three-week window to organize things and discuss it further with us, as we would be going to Lindos after returning home. The Concert was to be called "One Life, One World" and to be held at Wembley Stadium on the 9–10 of March 1985. She was pushing time but miracles do happen. Jonathan Weston and Henry Newman were her main team. We allowed Laurie the use of our London Home on Maida Ave until they secured offices. Harvey Goldsmith was to be their promoter thanks to our connection. She was operating on a shoe-string budget and worked day and night. Her heart was so motivated to succeed in helping the starving people in Ethiopia. She was inspiring many. Germaine Greer called out to the world saying, "*All they have is dirt! For God sake, we must help them!*" The fervor was building. Her cry for help still rings in my head whenever I read her words.

It was a major task and I was a novice. Laurie worked and organized many events previously for Humanity. She was a trooper. I spoke to Bob Geldof often since the making of the Wall. He said that he would support it. The climate of the day with many stars was of great resistance. Many were suspicious of anything like this at the time. It was hard work inspiring them. Even George Harrison came to David and advised him not to let me get involved. He said, "*I went through a nightmare for nearly nine years with the tax man over the Bangladesh Concert. In the end not many were helped just the lawyers.*" He continued, "*Your heart may be motivated, committed, devoted but getting it done, then facing the process of the tax man and then making sure the money got to the people is a nightmare. Don't do it!*"

I think this cast a cloud over David. I continued, but it felt like a salmon going upstream. I had lost my ballast. Laurie and I met with Bob at Fortnum and Masons and asked if he would give us support getting acts. I created a poster, which Bob said directly as he does, "*That's too pretty.*" We still chatted most days on the phone, as we were friends. There were many other meetings searching for sponsorship. Time was passing and each day 40 people were dying under those white tents in the baking sun. The tide was turning but not in our direction. Both Laurie and Jonathan worked day in and day out, struggling to find the light at the end of the tunnel hoping for a miracle.

In October 1984, images of millions of people starving to death in Ethiopia's famine were broadcast on Michael Buerk's BBC News reports. Bob saw it and was shocked. The images were riveting and went deep. It further motivated him. He had to do something to help. He called Midge Ure hoping to get him on board. They formed Band Aid with the intention of recording a single to raise money. In December, Bob, Midge and many stars got together and recorded "Do They Know it is Christmas?" This started to change the momentum in the minds of many stars. In America USA for Africa recorded, "We Are The World." Despite this, Harvey Goldsmith withdrew from our concert, which was a great disappointment. Later we were to discover why. Bob was called by God to carry forth the mission. None of us knew this at the time and was not the way we thought. We were just carried along by the tide.

However, the suspicions did not stop there even though the record was a success. Band Aid money was still questioned, but despite it, Bob Geldof had the tenacity to badger the stars and the money-men. He played the game and went to Ethiopia with the supplies. He wrestled with the press and succeeded. Bob was described as the "Terrier that wouldn't let go." He announced to the press, "*I am going to do my own F***ing concert.*" So that was it.

Harvey left our ship for another. Looking at the video of the making of Live Aid, I understand more the process he and Harvey went through to make it happen. I did not have that capacity. The wind in my sails could not have gone the distance as they did. I passed the gauntlet within my broken heart to them. Laurie was beyond disappointment when she heard the news. She was heartbroken almost beyond repair.

The times were a changin' in London to add to the tension. London was all a rage with fighting. Violence was everywhere in England. The music scene was difficult too. Everyone thought Bob was making money off the idea of a Live International Concert. Many thought the idea was just another way to fame, and they were going to be used. They thought the money would be mis-allocated into Bob's pockets instead of the starving populations, suspicion was rampant. We had the same difficulty. HELLO? Why is it so difficult? Why not? These are starving people. Why doesn't your heart say, "YES?" We were little guys with heart. Bob had a mouth.

To make it worse, he was considered a foul mouth, fading pop star in dirty clothes and unwashed hair. They shouted, *"Why should we listen to him? Why should we do it? What a bizarre idea!"* Most were frightened it might flop and tarnish their image, (So many egos). Were they that fragile? Nevertheless, Bob pushed and pushed and pushed. I wonder how many times he said the F*** word. George was right; it could have been a nightmare for us. We didn't swear.

There was a moment that I exploded months later. A fiery beast arose when I read in our daily papers that Bob was considering pulling out. He was considering pulling the plug. With what I know now, I do understand, but then rage took control and I learned to swear. I called him. *"Bob, you took the horn away from our concert for a larger one behind my back. I cannot deny it, it was very hard not to feel hurt and ever consider speaking to you again. It was challenging to find understanding, compassion and then to support you. But if you do not do Live Aid now, it would be absolutely tragic and a sin! YOU MUST DO IT!"*

As time has passed, I have come to so admire him. I have joined the flocks that call him Saint Bob—Even if he resists the term. His candor makes me smile. His tenacity I admire. During that time, He became the world's champion. No longer just a rock star disappearing from view that swore on stage. No longer was he some guy in a film depicting an addict in a rock band's movie about a wall. He was a modern day hero. His soul was doing what he was born to do. Live Aid rocked the world into action, at least for a while. What a mantle he now carries. What responsibility of power does he wield?

13 July 1985 has gone down in history as the day that music changed the world. Curiously, but not so curiously, in the end everyone tried to get a spot in the show, the phones were ringing into the night. Bob, Midge and Harvey including many others were on tenderhooks until the very end. They had the acts. What about the stage? Nevertheless, they did it! The world had 16 hours of music that brought tears of Joy to many. I watched from home, as I was pregnant with our fourth child. It would be too hot and the day would be too long for me. In addition, we were moving house. In the end, David went and played with Brian Ferry and returned home with many stories.

The story of Live Aid will always live on in my heart with gratefulness. It was a vast learning curve of the need to help humanity and opened my desire to serve. But it left me asking how may I serve more? My answer to that question would come as the years passed. Honestly, I could not have come close to what the boys; Bob, Midge, Harvey and their team, achieved to create Live Aid. Therefore, I do hope somewhere; somehow, our efforts did help to make it so.

I still wonder about the follow up and the current need of the people. They are still starving and so many others too around the world. There is such a hill to climb for mankind to "Feed the World." I wonder when it will change. While writing this I found an old Facebook message to me from Laurie's daughter, Erin, who I have watched growing up since our Live Aid adventure. She wrote:

> "I was at the convenience store yesterday, and this little boy was trying to buy a sandwich with about 90 cents and the lady kept telling him he didn't have enough money. His face looked so sad, hungry and about 8 years old. I of course paid for his sandwich and he was so grateful. It breaks my heart to see a

hungry child, while my own nephew has thousands of dollars in a bank account to spend on violent video games and paintball battles. How can we fight this hunger problem? How can we fight against poverty? One mouth at a time I suppose."

...That is the question.

'TORCH OF LIGHT'

2010

David and Matthew

CHAPTER 55

MATTHEW GILMOUR BORN

1985

Within a few months of knowing Mrs. Tweedie, a Peace Conference in Amsterdam requested her to be one of the speakers. Many of her followers planned on going. David was on tour and I asked if he minded me going off for a few days with them. The children would be fine as we had a wonderful nanny whom I trusted implicitly. Her heart was gold and had been with us for a while. She was Annie Rowland. Bless her. Our hearts were one when it came to loving the children.

Therefore, I went off to Amsterdam with the group. We stayed in a B&B and I shared a room with Miriam Freedman. It was quite Spartan and the toilet emitted the most awful smell. Luckily, we weren't there for most of the day, and in the evening we had to open the window to be able to sleep. When we returned before going to bed, I washed my knickers and put them on the radiator to dry for the morning. Miriam and I laugh to this day, of how she had so expected the little rich girl would find this environment difficult. She was amazed how I just got on with it. In fact, it was a lot of the others who complained.

Besides going to the talks, we went to many art museums. A lot of Mrs. Tweedie's group were artists and I learned so much from them as time went on. During that trip, something was going on inside my heart for I kept feeling such Joy and Peace. Yet, I kept feeling such sadness in front of a few paintings. When we stood before Rembrandt's painting the *Night Watchman*, I burst into tears. Then at the Van Gogh Museum, it happened again before the famous painting of *Gauguin's Chair*. I found this quite strange for I was sobbing uncontrollably! This was not like me to do such a thing. And why? So I asked Marie Lancaster who was standing next to me why I should be feeling like this. She said, *"You probably are sensing the deep anguish of Van Gogh when he painted it. Being in Mrs. Tweedie's energy tends to open our hearts."*

We always had lunch in the cafeteria where the conference took place. I was in the queue and filling my tray with an array of delightful looking food when someone from the group came up to me. He said, "*Mrs. Tweedie wants to see you.*" Not knowing what to do under these circumstances, I asked him, "*Ummm, do I eat first, take my food with me or just go?*" He replied, "*Just go. She is waiting for you downstairs.*" So I put down my tray and followed him. She was sitting in the corner wearing black, which she did when she was on duty. I came close. She said, *"Sit down dear."* Nervously I did. *"Ginger I need to tell you that you are carrying a King inside you. It is a boy."* I blinked and started to review when my period was due. *"Don't worry all will be well. He is a lovely soul."* Well, if that wasn't a show-stopper. Obviously, it was time to get a pregnancy test done. And give up on thinking the coil was a good contraceptive for David and I. God had other plans. Clearly, this child was destined to be born.

Therefore, when I returned home, I did the test and sure enough Mrs. Tweedie was right. David was home and when I told him, he went quiet. I panicked silently. I knew he was under great stress, but the degree of which I had no idea. He held a lot to himself as of late, but I could feel an undercurrent of tension. The whole Pink Floyd financial pressure was paramount in his mind, to what extent would not manifest until a while later.

Several weeks later, David came home and asked if I would mind moving house. He had found one he fancied and was less expensive to run. It was Monksbridge in Sunbury-on-Thames. So we began the process. We were going in two different directions and perhaps this could put us back on track. Since my difficulty in Clare's pregnancy, it had become necessary to lead less of a Rock 'n' Roll life. David had sought refuge in the friendship of Mick Ralphs who lived nearby. So I agreed. We would move.

The task to redecorate our next home, yet again, was given to our dear friend Warwick McCreddie. I was really pregnant so we stayed in our London house on Maida Avenue. It suited us both to be in town. David was close to management as much started to happen in the continuing Pink Floyd Saga. I would be close to Dr. Sharma in the event I needed medical attention. Plus, I could meditate every weekday with Mrs. Tweedie.

I was focusing on my pregnancy and with kids. With each one, I developed my vision further of how special the environment was for a child when it was their moment to enter the world. This time I met Leboyer. Mrs. Tweedie had us all go to a lecture he was giving in London. His vision had progressed beyond a baby being born into water. He had spent time in India with mothers who used vowels in their pregnancy and delivery. Leboyer then returned to Europe and the UK to encourage western mothers to do the same. His lecture that evening really inspired me.

We contacted each other and he referred me to a midwife who had worked and studied with him, and she lived in London. Her name was Gwen. Her surname has left my memory. We met regularly and practiced the vowels "A" (Ah) and "O" (Oh). And since I had the last two births at home this would be no problem to do again. The National Health System would agree. Since my first pregnancy, Spiritual Midwifery inspired me. My ultimate dream was to give birth on the floor. So this would be the one as I had no other physical complications and Gwen was on the same page.

I meditated each day and sang to my baby growing inside. I continued going to Cecil's classes while I still could. One day while we were working with color in the summer, Cecil came up to me and said, "*Did you know your baby is wearing a crown?*" Again, a sign from above as to what the baby's nature was. Another indication surfaced when I was driving to London from our old house to the new one. I had experiences of my baby radiating a meditative energy. I was on the motorway driving 70 miles per hour when I had to do some serious talking to him. Normally my meditative energy came from the crown or the heart center. This time it was coming from my tummy and it was so powerful. I nearly had to stop.

Meditation is not normally something one did while driving on the motorway. Fortunately, I managed to get it under control. When we eventually moved into London, and as I got larger, someone from Mrs. Tweedie's group would pick me up in their car. It meant a lot that I could get there and be in her energy. I wanted our child to grow in Peace. I was too big to drive at that stage. In fact, it was a daily feat to climb the stairs of our London home in my last few weeks. I did have to laugh as I waddled around the house and struggled up the long flight of stairs. I could have done with a chair lift. Towards the end, I had to plan my day for which room I would stay in. I read a lot.

On 24 October 1985, I went into labor in the late evening. And on the 25th, Matthew Jon Gilmour came into the world. We had placed a mattress on the floor at the bottom of our bed. He came quickly. And the vowels were incredible! Gwen did not have to ask me, "Are you in pain? Are you having contractions?" For when I was having them, I would sound either the "Ah" or the "Oh." She would know the length and the frequency. AND she would know if I was not in control for another vowel would appear, "EEEEE." I would go into shallow breathing. It was important to breathe into my womb with an open "Ah" for it kept the passageway open for the baby to come easier. An "EEEE" meant I was tense. Whenever this happened, Gwen would sound the vowels from a peaceful place to re-align me. It was amazing! Such group work.

However, all was not to finish as we had dreamt. Matthew slid onto the mattress radiant as a bright light. I was on all fours. He was still on the umbilical cord so there was no need for him to breathe yet. But Gwen panicked and gave him oxygen before she dealt with the cord. She wanted to be sure that he was breathing. She shared a story with me after Matthew was ok. Apparently, she had lost her last delivery at that point when the baby was still attached to the cord. I hope Matthew's delivery changed all that for her.

I know she played it safe, out of care. But poor Matthew screamed and whimpered for nearly three hours. I held him and spoke to him softly that all would be well. We love you deeply. I know it burns. I am truly sorry. Eventually he fed on my breast and slept for ages. We all slept together David, the baby and I. We slept together for months as we had with our other babies. I stayed at home for nearly a month since I had come to realize that this was as important for me as for the baby. I wanted us to bond together before entering the outside world. No loud noise for us this time and no going out into the shops until we were ready.

Each pregnancy was different and I learned so much, especially about myself. I often wondered why it was that when one became more a master in creating sacred moments in childbirth that one could no longer go on having babies. Nevertheless, this too was to change for the opportunity arose several times to work with couples throughout their pregnancy in the years to follow.

It was special to work with the Dad and Mom consciously. They would lie together. The father would place his hand onto her tummy and together they would send love to their wee one. Many have given me the chance to serve in this way so I can pass on my knowledge. Christa and Paul, who we knew from Greece were the first. I was with them all the way through the birth of Selena in the Rhodes hospital and after. David and Diana in San Francisco were the next couple to share this sacred moment. They were in Mrs. Tweedie's group and we would meet regularly when they were over. I feel honored to have been allowed to enter and be so close with them during the sacred moment when their child entered the world.

The day came to decide upon a name for the baby. David and I always had a list of names that we agreed upon, but Alice had it in her mind that Matthew had to be a John. Olivia Harrison called one day and Alice answered. David was not home, and Olivia respected the need for quiet time for mom and baby. So she asked Alice what we had chosen to name our baby. Alice said, "*John.*"

A while later, the Harrison's sent us a gift to honor his birth with an engraved silver egg cup and spoon. It said, John Gilmour. *OOPS*. Alice was not too happy when we said he was to be named Matthew. She was so sad that we came up with a solution. We called him Matthew Jon Gilmour. They call him Matt now. They are all close and he towers over them being 6ft 3" tall. He loves putting his elbow gleefully on their shoulders with a smirk.

Many months had passed, when Mrs. Tweedie offered to give Matthew a Sufi Baby Blessing. It was rare for her to do this. I felt it was a gift from Heaven for him to have her blessing. Many people came and crowded into her small living room. They brought an abundance of sweets and flowers. The girls and Annie stood around in a circle as Mrs. Tweedie did the ceremony. As I recall Matthew cried for a bit, then went quiet. I suppose the energy was stronger than what he was used to. There was something special about him because everywhere we went people would stop to gaze at him. If he was in the pram, time and time again people would walk pass and return to look. I have always felt that he has a destiny of which would bring great responsibility.

'Affair of the Heart'

CHAPTER 56

AFFAIR OF THE HEART
1ST EXHIBITION LONDON

1986

We had finally moved into Monksbridge and I was in a highly creative painting cycle upstairs in our little den, which connected to our ensuite bathroom and bedroom. Everywhere I had large canvases leaning against the bookshelves, the fireplace, the desk, the window, the floor. I would go from one to the other as the impulse came to me. Plus, it was convenient to paint in there for the girls could be splashing in our bath getting ready for bed while I would draw or paint in the connecting room.

I remember once Sara, who was still crawling, went into that room while I was tending to Alice and Clare. Bath time was noisy and rather wet sometimes, but fun. Anyway, Sara was a bit quiet, which was her nature, when I noticed she was gone. I thought I had better check on her so I followed the sound of her gurgles. There she was sitting on top of one of my oil paintings, which was on the floor. Yikkees! I had been working on it earlier so the oil paint was still wet, I might add. So back into the bath she went. I had my task cut out for me, covering up her fingerprints and picking out the hairs because one of our cats decided to join her in the fun. Dear, Dear, the life of a mother who is an artist.

David was working downstairs in our lower sitting room most days writing lyrics for his next album, *Momentary Lapse of Reason* with his co-writer. One afternoon, I returned home very excited. I had news of my first exhibition offer at *Themes & Variations* in Nottinghill Gate, London. Julianna, a truly wonderful friend from Lindos, was the innovative and creative owner. Her shop supported the artistry of many established and beginning artists. That afternoon, we had met for lunch, to share stories about our growing children and creativity. I had one of my paintings with me that I just collected from the framers. She loved it and suggested that I have my first exhibition at her gallery. Gosh! That was an unexpected gift from the Universe.

David's co-writer was curious as to what I might exhibit, as he didn't know that I painted. I offered that he could come upstairs later when he had a break to see what I was working on. After dinner, he climbed the stairs up to the den to have a look. Upon entering, he began to get very emotional and nothing but critical words came forth from his mouth as he swirled around from one painting to another. I was rather taken back with the force of his descriptions. *"That one is like cats piss."* It was a woman with raised hands covered in white light rays on a yellow ochre background. *"And that one you should be cut up with a knife!"* It was a man in a lovers embrace with a woman floating in the water. My eyes blinked in disbelief as the shock penetrated my heart.

I had to sit down on our daybed while he continued to assault my artwork. What happened next was equally surprising. He sat next to me and said, *"Let me out of here!"* Again, I looked at him in disbelief. *"Excuse me, but the door is not locked. You are free to leave at any moment as free as you were when you entered."* He stood up to leave but then sat down again. I asked, *"Why did you say all those things? Why are you so upset?"* He looked at me through his anxiety and said, *"You don't really want to know!"* I waited. He continued to tell me of his broken relationship. Then he left me stunned sitting on the bed when he scurried out of the room like a man carrying the weight of the world on his shoulders.

I had to get up early for the children the next day. Befuddled, I had a bath and went to bed. In the morning, I always walked from our bedroom quietly through the connecting bathroom through the den so as not to wake David. And there He was asleep on the daybed amongst the paintings. Well, if that wasn't instant karma. Poor dear.

When I returned from the school run, he was sitting rather forlorn at our kitchen table reading Mrs. Tweedie's book *The Daughters of Fire*. He must have brought it down from the den. He looked at me from his cup of coffee and sheepishly said, "*Ginger, I am so sorry for my behavior last night. Can you forgive me? Also, may I borrow your book, by Mrs. Tweedie? I am lost and need guidance.*"

That afternoon I had my weekly class with Cecil Collins in life drawing. I must have looked rather low, as he approached me and asked if I was all right. I told him the story of the night before. He listened then said to me, "*When is your exhibition? For if you are getting such reactions, your work is touching Hearts with the Truth. I with Elizabeth will come to support you.*" Needless to say, I was honored by his words and to think that both of them would be coming was extraordinary.

I continued to finish my paintings with anticipation of how well received they will be. I decided to call it *An Affair of the Heart* and it certainly was turning out to be that way. I had one painting, which was of a girl releasing a dove to the light from her hands in reds, pinks, yellows and whites. It was finished and it was resting on the mantelpiece in the den. One day I walked into the room to find Alice looking at it sitting on the floor. She looked up at me, her blue eyes shining like pools of crystal water, "*Mommy, does an exhibition mean that your pictures will be going away?*"

I sat on the floor next to her sitting her onto my lap. I said, "*Alice, Your Daddy and I and all your family love you so, but not all people in the world are as fortunate. God gave your mommy a special gift and that was to be able to paint his Love for all his children. These paintings are for them. They are to give them Love. So I have to let them go. If I don't, my gift may be taken away and given to someone else for it would be selfish to keep them all."* She cried and pointed up to the *Child and the Dove*, "Will that painting have to go? I really love it." Apparently, she came after school each day and sat in the room looking at it. Holding her close, I said, *"Maybe, but if it does, I can paint another one for you."*

The day arrived and I had over 32 pieces of artwork, including life drawings from Cecil Classes. The gallery was full and we had gentle music playing all afternoon. As each person came, my heart got fuller and fuller, especially when Cecil and Elizabeth arrived. They really came! It is amazing how much it affected me to be together with everyone. I found that as each entered I just loved them all.

Such an affirmation of heart filled the room. The art, the people and the music were One. I really wanted to keep the watercolor of the *Resurrection* for me, but I decided instead to put a red dot on the *Child and the Dove*, for Alice. As it turned out the *Resurrection* didn't sell. I got to have it I guess for my gesture of kindness for my girl. The story had a happy ending for Alice was very happy when she realized that the red dot on *Child and the Dove* meant it was hers.

'GARDEN of BEAUTY'

2009

Feeding the Birds
Lake Ontario, Toronto, Canada

CHAPTER 57

MOMENTARY LAPSE OF REASON

1985–1989

Day after day, the sting got stronger. Accusations came from all directions. The battle for the name went on and on. I remember the moment David further closed his heart, and rage took its place. He tried to contain it, isolating me from the process. However, the Wall of protection and readiness for battle came between us as well. I remember thinking, if this is what it takes then go for it! His integrity, his rights, his principles were at stake. I silently stood beside him before the wall. A battle cry went out. "Pink Floyd" is ALIVE! His mind left Gilmourland, as his focus changed, directed toward the attacks. He was determined not to lose. Nick joined him and so did Rick.

They questioned, *"Can we do it?"* The nerves were high. The gauntlet, mainly held by David, as the creation of the next album developed. The fire inside had grown dim, but rose again from his anger within. In a creative process, David was by his nature a person who sought to work together with everyone involved. Even to compromise beyond being visible to get the album done. However, if injured and walked over he stands immovably stubborn. In this instance, the pain was intense and I watched each of the band members rage in theirs. David hurt, Nick hurt, Roger hurt, Rick was no longer there and Steve held the reins tightly. The press had a field day as their fans teetered in their opinions.

I watched and continued to hold the routine at home with the kids. My heart left alone in the task. His alienation, greeted with Love and support, as I knew this was bigger than we were. He stood for equality, respect and justice. The voice of Justice would soon be heard and clear the way. Days in court pursued them—Solicitors after Solicitors—In the end they won. It did not tear down the inner wall because there was more to carry, as we went into our future. Roger screamed, *"They are a spent force!"* *"No way!"* they shouted to the world. Determined, they went forth holding the vision.

The *Pink Floyd* name was theirs. However, despite winning the lawsuit, the record company still stood on pins and needles. *"Which one's Pink?"* In that climate, finding a promoter that would take a risk was a challenge. Was Pink Floyd just a shadow of what went before? Roger's voice went far heralding his bitter attacks that he was the one, *"They won't do it!"* That was just the thing needed to strengthen David and Nick's resolve. They found one in Canada.

I stood within this force on high alert and concerned. Little did I know that David had mortgaged our home and Nick his Ferrari to finance the venture. I sensed something extra that was worrying in my heart within the tension. We, our family security, were on the tightrope as well. Millions were needed. I wish he had shared it with me. He would have known how much I supported him all the way. No wonder David grew more withdrawn from me. Our eyes stopped meeting. I kept looking. He was holding more than tension. He was holding a secret.

Then one day Steve O'Rourke took me out for dinner, alone, in our little quaint restaurant down the road. From behind his glasses, his jaw terse, he delivered the message that the band would have to do another tax exile. I stared through him, as I remembered David's words after the last one, *"Never again."* However, Again had just arrived and Steve was instructed to tell me. I wondered to myself,

"Would you also be instructed to tell me if David wanted a divorce?" I felt something was changing between us. Perhaps I was now the writing on the wall? All I could say was "*Oh, When?*"

My heart ached in quiet desperation. Was I becoming more English? I continued yearning for our love to return. Each night as I held the children in my arms, tears would often escape revealing the truth of my inner dilemma. The emotion arose within me in the night. "Help," I pleaded with the God above. I went and stayed for a few days with a girlfriend, Mona Wirtz. Often I sought refuge in our friendship and I slept on her living room couch. Occasionally my eyes would open to the smell of a hot cup of Chamomile tea next to my bed. In my delirium, I saw that if the tension did not go away, if I could not release what had gathered, I was heading for illness big time. I returned home determined to find a way.

Then God sent me a truly wonderful elder woman who I believe was an angel. Her name was Lily Cornford. A friend had given me her number and told me that I should go to see her. She had the gift to heal one's heart. She lived in Willesden in a basement flat where she had a clinic and on Saturdays gave free treatments for children. As I entered, a passageway led to the living room, which was the waiting room. People and children were waiting their turn to see her. There were two modest rooms to the side formerly used as bedrooms. In one of the rooms, she was waiting for me in the dim light, sitting next to a narrow cushioned table in the center of the room. A spare chair was near her. As I approached, her gentle voice guided me and with a gesture of her hand said, "*Sit child. Why have you come?*" The tranquility and love in the room released my pressure valve. Tears rushed down my face. She handed me a tissue and waited until I calmed down.

Lily was like my Nan, gray haired, bonnie and full of heart. Her eyes filled me with loving kindness from the start. I told her my story. She listened for what seemed an eternity as my life unraveled before her. Leaning on the edge of the table, she asked, *"What drugs have you taken, dear?"* I replied proudly, *"Lily, I haven't taken any in over twelve years! Not even an aspirin." "Well, dear, you still have them in your aura. But don't worry, you have come to the right place!"* Tapping on the table, she said, *"Come dear, lie down."*

I came to know and practice her form of therapy years later. It works with the energy of Love and Color. Its main intention was to guide the person to find his or her own healer within. During my treatment, I traveled to such a place of inner calm that a new journey of health began. It was to be the first of many, which aided in the feeling of being loved, including the children.

Back in Gilmourland, preparations continued forward to travel again after our summer in Lindos. We were to start in Toronto, Canada. The band would be rehearsing for four weeks in a bonded warehouse at Lester Pearson International Airport. They had created a huge spectacle A la-Floyd, but a lot had changed technically since they last had been on the road. Rehearsals were imperative. Timing was imperative. Instead of a handful of technicians, there were 200. I lost track of all their names as they came and went. Faces would begin to be familiar and then disappear.

There were three separate stages that required maneuvering across continents in the year to come. The technical side was more complicated than ever before. The mixing area looked like a NASA base control. Before, when I sat there it was so much tinier. Now, I felt as if I was in a space ship listening to "Ground Control." In addition, the loading of the trucks had become a science. What a task it was to load and unload the trucks, it was larger than the *Animals* Tour! Trucks to take away. Trucks to unload in relay.

I remember how small our little ones were when they stood before the eighty-foot high stage in the echo of the warehouse. Their little blonde heads leaning backwards as they looked for their Dad. It was HUGE! A metal cage one hundred and sixty feet long and ninety-feet deep was created almost the size of a Boeing 727. The warehouse was a perfect place to rehearse for the tour. It was private, secure with lots of space to play and build.

Eventually word got out. Small groups of people passing by would stop and listen. On the night of the full run-through, they had an audience. It was a great private gig as it was greeted by the evening breeze and the color of dark blue. From a distance, the light show seeped out of the cracks of the warehouse making it look like something out of *ET* or *Batteries Not Included*. The rumble of the airplanes landing added to the sound effects.

We were renting a wonderful home on Lake Ontario. Each evening the children and I would walk to the edge, climb down to the jetty with bread and feed the birds. The lake spread out before us for miles empty. The blues and pinks of the approaching sunset filled the sky. It was quietly breathtaking. The girls were excited, waiting for the moment to arrive each evening. Matthew was a babe in arms, a toddler. "*Mommy, Mommy, where are the birds?*" "*Just wait they will come. Start with little pieces and drop them into the water.*" One by one from out of the blue, birds would start to fly towards us. So many, that on some days, we did not have enough bread.

There was a park nearby where I would take Matthew in his stroller when it was sunny. It was a special time for us and the park was full of Canadian Geese. They had not left yet for the winter. Wherever we turned, we had to walk amongst them and they seemed quite at home with humans. They are so majestic, very similar to swans. Straight out of a storybook. I had never seen them before except in a V formation in the sky. Matthew seemed to have a special rapport with them as they often came close and hung around. We had no food for them. They just came to us. I had heard that the males could be aggressive, but they never were. Often they spread their 5ft wings and took off in flight. Matthew would giggle and point to the sky in wonder.

Other animals that hung out in the park were black squirrels. Their fur was the color of black mink. The blackness was so deep with tinges of midnight. I never knew they existed until we came to Toronto. They ran, they played, they chattered. Standing adorably on their hind paws, sometimes with their front paws held in front of their bellies like small furry beggars.

They were easily won over with a couple of peanuts. Or was it us that were won over easily with a couple of peanuts? There were plenty of trees for them to have as their domain as we walked below with our children. I wondered why Black? So I looked it up. It seems they are much stronger and survive in the cold winters over the gray squirrel. One advantage was that their color keeps them warm. Interesting.

One day it was raining, droplets with infused sunlight upon the window caught my eye as my reflection was on the inside. I bought some oils and a canvas and decided to paint that image. I was not to finish it for years, as I wanted to learn how to paint a raindrop. Wherever I saw raindrops on the window or in a painting, I studied them. It was a passion for years. I realize now I was seeking to paint my tears of that period. Tears of lost love. The Cry of the Heart longing for it to return.

***

In the late 90s, I was asked to an exhibit in Los Angeles for the Whole Life Exposition. David and I had already separated and the children and I were living in Brockhurst. I reviewed all my unfinished artwork when I finally decided to finish it. I called it *Reflections*. Brockhurst had a separate cottage that I converted into a painting studio upstairs and a guest cottage, which Emo lived in for years. We had classes there that Cecil inspired since I found that it served to keep my creativity flowing. So the day had come to finish painting my tears. I placed *Reflections* on the easel with a view of the garden and began to paint.

To my surprise, instead of painting raindrops, I wound up painting droplets of sunshine. There I was in my studio with my unfinished canvas before me. I was holding a recent Polaroid of me in one hand and the brush in the other. I tuned into my creative space, working in harmony with my inner self, the photo and the artwork before me. I was in another reality held in an altered state seeking to be one with the painting. The paint on my brush seemed to be droplets of golden light. I blinked. I took another color. Again, droplets of golden light appeared onto the canvas. The painting, my heart and the photo had become One. Moreover, what was revealed to me in that moment was that I no longer had inner sorrow. I was full of Joy. The raindrops no longer needed to be painted for the tears had gone. I was painting Joy. Across the room there sat the man who guided me to Love again.

'Momentary Lapse of Reason'
Harmony out of Chaos
NYC 1987

CHAPTER 58

HARMONY OUT OF CHAOS
NYC

5–7 OCTOBER 1987

The Floyd were playing Madison Square Garden over three consecutive days. *Momentary Lapse of Reason* had been on the road and it was the first concert in the city without Roger. The gigs before proved that the Band was still in business. "The Floyd is still ALIVE" was the word on the street and the headlines throughout the press. Chinese whispers spread from state to state. The magic was still there. They had succeeded, but there was still work to do to rebuild the walls.

Before we left England, Mrs. Tweedie had asked me if I could take the draft of her book to Dr. Werner Engel, the president of the New York's Jungian Society. He was to write the foreword and I would be there to insure he got it. Once we settled, I called him, a deep Germanic voice answered, *"Yes? Engel here."* My shyness kicked in with the realization that I was about to speak to someone who was a highly regarded Jungian. I found my voice and told him why I was calling. We arranged to meet the following morning at 11:00 a.m.

He had an apartment very close to where John Lennon had lived. I rang the bell and was let in by a woman who ushered me to sit in one of the multiple chairs in the long corridor. The walls were lined with certificates, framed pictures, bookshelves filled with books, and tables. I waited patiently until he finally came. His deportment was gentle and gracious as he invited me to come into the next room from whence he came.

The room was like entering into a Victorian film set. Books piled high on every table, aspidistra on a pedestal in the corner, dim light entering the room through the lace curtains. He offered me to sit in a leather chair next to his desk that was covered with piles of papers. He pushed them aside, looking for pen and paper. I handed him the manuscript. Looking through his eye glass he said, *"Well Ginger, what brings you to New York?"* His demeanor was so clear and full of genuine interest. A quality I found easy to trust. His compassion opened my heart. It felt as if he was speaking directly to my soul. I lost all perception of the time as we chatted and had tea.

At one point he asked, *"Ginger, I am very interested in how Rock 'n'Roll music affects the psyche. I was wondering if there was any way you could help me in my research?"* With a rather girlish grin cocking my head, I said, *"I think that would be possible Dr. Engel. When are you available?"* We arranged for this to happen a few days later, but in the meantime, he invited me to come again the next day for he said that he would like to talk to me more about Mrs. Tweedie's book.

I went to lunch at Schwartz Deli. Famous for their Reuben sandwiches and other yummy things. I was now a vegetarian but still loved sauerkraut. I was passionate for Reubens before, so I fancied a vegetarian one if possible. As I entered the deli, it was packed. I waited in line for my turn to come. The energy in the room was very New York; People in a hurry, Wonderful food, the clatter of plates and the smell of coffee.

I have found many New Yorkers of the male gender in service love to have a flirt with a pretty girl. And so it was that day with me. In a very New York Jewish accent one said, *"And what can I do for you today, honey?"* I gulped as I asked with a smile, *"Well could I* have a Reuben without the corn beef?" He nearly choked. Then shouted across to another guy behind the counter, *"Hey Mac, this lady wants A REUBEN WITHOUT CORNBEEF! Can we do that?"* A voice came back with a very affirmative, *"NO."*

I could not believe it. My waiter stood behind the counter in his white apron and hat, hands on his hips, just waiting for my response. Ok, I thought to myself. *"Sir, would it be possible then to have a sandwich with Swiss cheese, sauerkraut, mustard, dressing and on dark rye? With a pickle and an ice tea?"* He said, *"Sure lady, we can do that!"* That was something right out of the film, *Easy Rider* when Jack Nicholson was ordering his breakfast.

When I visited Dr. Engel the next day, I was in a state of vulnerability, which he noticed. He directed our conversation without commenting directly. He was a master of Heart. We talked about my sensitivity and being around a Rock 'n' Roll environment. He then asked me, "*Ginger when you were sitting in the hallway, did you notice my certificates?"* "No, I didn't Dr. Engel. I was more interested in your books, Why?" He said, *"Well, I am a marriage counselor and if you ever need one I am here for you."* I responded with difficulty gulping, *"Dr. Engel that is so kind of you. But I don't think I need one and I hope I never will."*

The following day we organized a limousine to pick him up early, at his request for he wanted to see everything. I met him as his car arrived with all his passes. I gave him the grand tour for we had enough time. He questioned everyone about the technical aspects and then more psychological ones regarding life on the road. I took him to his seat as the audience was coming in. I asked if he would like earplugs but he said, *"No. I want to experience the whole show."* He was eighty-six. Afterwards I took him backstage to meet the band. While having a drink and a nibble, he said to me, *"Ginger I do not know if you will agree with me, but the place where you and I touch through meditation, is the same place your husband's group reaches while transforming Chaos into Beauty."*

    His words captured so much. Over the years, this always touched my heart. *The flavor of Beauty that remained after all the pain.* I had come to realize that the task of Life was to transform Chaos into Beauty. This is what our love meant to me. Despite the challenges, we have always allowed Beauty to Win. This is what, even today, I feel, David's emphasis on the importance of what the underlying music spoke was essential. It sought to uplift not to drag down, to break-through not to break-down.

    It was the music's transforming quality of the "Darkness," which spoke to us all. It reached beyond the words to our hearts in the notes they played. It silently, in its Beauty gave us Hope in a troubled world. I have said, "Thank You," so many times upon reflection, for the inspiration that gave me courage to create Beauty at all costs. Losing that quality brings our demise. This I gained without knowing about it. It was a seed planted that would grow to flower later.

'GOLDEN MESSENGER'

2010

Kalu Rinpoche prays
for our family

Bella Franzoni brought him our photo

CHAPTER 59

A FRIENDLY MONSTER IN THE HOUSE

1986–1987

I returned to England after the NYC gig. Things had started to get difficult, as the tensions and tremors were filtering over into our home life. I was getting worried. Dr. Engel very kindly offered to give me sessions over the phone. I was having many disturbing dreams, which as he was a Jungian, he helped me to understand. He often said to me, "*Ginger, you are Breaking-through not Breaking-down.*" With his counsel, I have come to realize that all experiences are opportunities to grow and touch our soul purpose. With this perspective, I was no longer a victim carried along in the drama of life. I found that there was a higher intention. And eventually I was to know that God was a God of love and prosperity, not a God of wrath which was man made. But I was still new to these ideas as a living truth.

I was discovering that depending on how I dealt with my thoughts, my frustrations, my fears would determine what came next. That my words commanded my life. By contemplating the thought about my dreams, being a *Breaking-through* and not a *Breaking-down* shifted a lot. I saw my perception change from darkness to light in regards to almost everything. He said that I was who I was because of the words I spoke each day.

New possibilities were emerging. I saw how important it was that in times of trouble how my words could shift the results.

Therefore, I started with little things. I noticed that each time people greeted we would tell our problems. We passed on our fears and our woes. I decided to exchange the good times first and listen if needed in order to help. I discovered with each time I shared my difficulties I would go down. A cloud would come over our heads. Our lights would dim. Each time I shared my happiness I would rise above the storm and leave a sparkle behind. I had to find a way to uplift the situation and yet honor each others challenging moments. It was a pattern that I was trying to transform.

David was still on tour, so each evening as the sun set I would sit in our bedroom by the tall windows in our rocking chair overlooking the River Thames meditating. I visualized his success that the world would receive the Beauty of what they all had stood for within that album, within their hearts, within our lives. Mrs. Tweedie also had the group do this each day in her home. We sprinkled them with God's Love and protection.

I felt close from afar. My love had a purpose. They did more gigs on this tour than they had in years, back to back and it was a success. The magic, the miracle of their stance was with them. I have found that each time one stands for a higher purpose, each time one stands and not die we are rewarded. I had never experienced it to be so true as on that tour.

During this time waiting for our family life to be returned, I went to Lily for healing. I took the children as well. In the first session with Sara, Lily was sitting at the top of the table with her elder loving hands gently placed upon Sara's head. Lily softly asked her after a few moments, *"Sara, do you see fairies?"* Sara nodded "yes" keeping her eyes closed. Lily's Love seemed to fill the room as she continued to ask, *"Not everyone sees Fairies, do they?"* Sara shook her head as if to say "no". *"Well, I see fairies Sara,"* Lily said to her. Sara was quiet, then said, *"OH?"* That was where we left it. Later that month, Lily gave a lecture on Fairies and all their colors.

She told how they did the work of the Lord maintaining life until humans really did their duty as caretakers.

One by one all the children came down with Chicken Pox. One by one, they slept in my bedroom on the couch in the dark. I had to draw the curtains for they were sensitive to the sunlight. It was a long month. During that time, I told Sara about Lily's fairy lecture. How each fairy had a different color and purpose. To my surprise, she knew and told me about their color and the job God had given to them. My heart was filled with a smile and a tear.

I was not the only one having nightmares during this time. Alice was having lots of them. Some evenings I would find her running down the hallway screaming, *"NO! NO!"* I would catch her and hold her in my arms as her screams changed to sobs. Over and over every night we had this experience for weeks. I spoke with Margaret, a psychiatrist who was a dear friend of Mrs. Tweedie's. She worked with the group on such matters. She said to continue doing what I was doing and at some point Alice would tell me what the dream was about. One day she did. She said that a monster was coming after her who was really scary.

I had been reading a book about a South American tribe who shared their dreams each morning. If a child had nightmares that a lion was coming to eat him, the tribe would advise that the next time he must face the tiger. That he must try to make friends with the tiger. So this is what I encouraged Alice to do. *"Alice you must try to make friends with him."* She said, *"Oh, No. I can't do that. I can't face the monster. I can't be his friend."* So a few more days passed and the monster continued to come.

She continued to be found in different parts of the house screaming and panicking. I decided that she should sleep in our bedroom on the couch. One night at bedtime, I suggested that perhaps she should tell the monster that your mom wants to talk to him if he doesn't want to be friends. The next morning she awoke with a smile, bouncing onto the bed. With a sparkle in her eye, she said, *"It worked Mommy! I told him that I wanted to be his friend!"* *"Really Alice! That is wonderful! What did he say?"* *"He started to cry and said that no one had ever wanted to be his friend!"* she said proudly. Needless to say, I was glad that was over. Now we had a friendly monster in the house.

'SISTERS'

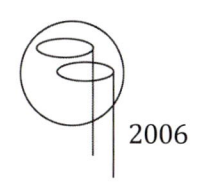

2006

Skiing in Zermatt, Switzerland

Ski instructor, Genevieve

CHAPTER 60

DR. GERHARD ADLER

There came a moment that my process was getting deeper and more of a challenge. Dr. Werner Engel felt it would be best to have contact with someone in England. I was awakening to the adventure of my soul quest beyond the daily challenges of my personality fears and desires. A tsunami was approaching and at the same time, a fire was beginning to glow which he recognized and valued. He saw how fragile and delicate my flame was and did not want it to go out or be swallowed by the storm. One day he said, *"Ginger I want you to call my dear friend Gerhard Adler and tell him Engel has sent you."*

    Goodness! My nerves rose at the thought. My shyness kicked in as I began to dial his number. He answered, *"Hello, Gerhard here."* Heat surged throughout my body as I searched for words. Clearing my throat, I said *"Hello, Dr. Adler. Dr. Engel said I should call you and that I should come to you for analysis." "He did, did he?"* and paused in thought. Time seemed to go on forever as I waited for him to speak. *"Well,"* he paused again. *"Can you come tomorrow morning at 7:30 a.m.?"* I said, *"Yes, Thank you, Can you give me the address?"*

    The whole day after my call was spent wondering what was about to happen tomorrow. Dr. Adler was the top in Jungian Analysis and trained by the master himself. Was this a blessing, which would ease my problems at home and in my heart? I hoped it would. I had to get up early to get from where we lived to him at 7:30 a.m. He lived in Hampstead and worked from there. The drive across London was full of thoughts about me turning around each time I had to stop to look at my A-Z for directions. Finally, I found myself parked before his house. I made it and on time.

It was raining, but I chose to leave my umbrella in the car. I walked up the stairs to the front door and rang the bell. I waited shivering from anticipation. By the time he came to the door, I was drenched. He let me in with a warm welcome similar to Dr. Engel. I began to feel safe. Leading me to his downstairs room in the back of the house, we passed through his living room. The decor reminded me of the austerity of the fifties with upright furniture to sit on with scattered pillows in different muted colors.

I entered his room, which was full of books and comfortable typically English chairs. The morning sunlight began to brighten the room as he gestured for me to sit down. He held the silence for a while as my heartbeat slowed playing with my wristwatch. He always began with silence as though he was tuning into something beyond my normal reality. I wondered if I should say something, but I was too shy.

Again, I began to have a feeling of timelessness as I had done with Dr. Werner Engel in New York. We spoke for an hour, but I do not remember what stories I shared, only the stillness of his listening. I was graced to have had six sessions with him. One morning, Mrs. Adler answered the door. She said that Gerhard had passed over in the night. As I stood at her door in the early morning chill, she continued to speak to me. She added that they had discussed which of his clients she might take over from him before he died. And if I was willing, we could start in the New Year once all the formalities were completed. She asked if she could have a few weeks to re-orientate.

***

As I was writing of the moment when I first met Dr. Adler, I had forgotten what he looked like. I was also struggling with the time sequence between meeting Dr. Werner Engel in NYC and Dr. Adler passing over. Therefore, I took some time to ponder. I found a documentary called *The Matter of the Heart*, about Carl Jung in which he was to appear. I made a cup of tea, sat on my couch and watched it. Unexpectedly, I discovered the answer to a question concerning the shadow, which had plagued me ever since becoming aware of Jung and the Collective Unconscious, including the Anima and Animus.

I had watched this years ago, when it first came out in 1986 but I never understood its message. They say that sometimes one has to hear something seven times or more before it goes in. And each time a little bit of Light in the message takes away a bit of the Shadow of unknowing. I was now inspired to understand more. I always placed a shield between me and the shadow, as I thought it was the darkness of evil. I wanted only to focus on Love, Light and Beauty. I choose this as our world is so familiar with war, crime, fear, negativity. I felt strongly that Humanity is on the brink of forgetting our essence of Divinity and what was sacred.

In the documentary, I discovered the shadow was a folder in me marked "Do not enter—House of broken dreams." It manipulated me from deep within. I was a puppet controlled in the darkness. I had locked away what was too painful to deal with for I was in survival mode. "Maybe later I will look at it," I told myself. Fortunately, that time has come for I see I was its victim. It played with me. I was not free. Even images of Love put away played with me. I look into my shadow now because it is filling with Light.

***

After I left Mrs. Adler, I drove home stunned by how life could change on a dime. I was still in a Jungian process so I agreed to see her in the New Year as I stood at her doorstep. Not knowing whether it was a good decision or not I was learning to trust what lay before me. I was learning to trust my heart guidance. I was noticing there were often two voices, which gave opinions in my head as to what I should do, what choices I should make. Each had a different quality. As time went by, I grew more familiar with them knowing why I should listen to one and not the other.

One seemed to be a Call, a Message from my Soul. I was not favoring it being a message from God at the time as I do now. I could accept it coming from the Angels. It had a warmth and a feeling of Love guiding me. Something I could trust. The other one made me a bit hyper, anxious and on edge. It felt like I was pushing a stone uphill. I did not always go with the one that called me from my soul daring me to live what it suggested.

I must admit I hit the brick wall more often listening to the other one, which made it a tough way of learning. Why I chose being anxious was a mystery. Maybe it had something to do with the Shadow? Maybe it had something to do with my childhood. I did try ever so hard to be accepted by my peers, my husband and my family. My self churned inside as I tried to find a balance. I did think differently than the norm, at least in the Rock 'n' Roll of the day, which didn't help.

***

Anyway, Christmas was upon us and David would return around 15 December, so time passed by with lots of festivities in our family custom. I had 1000 Christmas cards to sign and send. It was something I loved to do each year. With my new understanding of how words could carry love and joy, I did so with each signature and stamp. I called upon the Spirit of Christmas as each card went into their respective envelopes.

David and I wrapped presents upon presents in our telly room. As we were working away, our Lady dog sat under the piano playing with some ribbon. Sometimes she would rush into the moving wrapping paper, sliding into the middle of what we were doing. We did this in the night after all the kids were safely tucked in bed.

David took a phone call while sitting on the floor amongst the wrapping paper. I was busy with the smaller ones when he resumed wrapping after the call. With each pile of finished presents, we would put them under the tree. We suddenly burst into uncontrollable laughter when we noticed that David had wrapped a present with the phone cable running through the wrapping! He had to start all over because it was a very large one. No worries.

The holidays were spent having large dinners either at our home or at his Mom and Dad's. Boxing Day was usually with friends. That year we went to Zermatt to ski and have New Year's Eve with the Lords and the Paices (Deep Purple), which had become an annual event. The children were amazing skiers, especially Clare, fearless and so close to the ground that her aerodynamics were to her advantage. She looked like something out of *Star Wars* as she whizzed down the hill, leaving me in her wake.

Once I remember she went in a different direction back to the main street than us. And as we came into town, there she was just to my right flying in the air happily. She hadn't realized that the path she had chosen ended with a drop into the high street. She was fine, but her acrobatic stunt took us back a bit.

I just loved Zermatt with the horse drawn sleighs, the fur blankets and the tinkles of the bells as we drove along. It was something out of Dr. Zhivago. Everyone was dressed in bright colors reflected in the snow. The "Shush Shush" as we walked down the street in our skies and crisp air upon our faces was sorely missed when we returned home. I always returned feeling so healthy. What they say about mountain air is true, especially the hot cocoa and fondues of Switzerland.

It wasn't long before David was due to go back out on tour. Australia this time. I was to meet up with him for the Japan tour with Matthew. In the meantime, I hired another nanny; one to travel with me and one to stay at home, as the girls were in school and could not come. I continued my weekly classes with Cecil and analysis with Mrs. Adler.

WELCOME HOME DAVID

Lily Cornford & Ginger
1987

CHAPTER 61

WORKING WITH LILY

I began a course in Mental Color Therapy with Lily. Vickie Lord and Jackie Paice, twin sisters and wives of two members of Deep Purple did as well. We had become friends when we lived in Hook End and for years spent our skiing holidays together. Another girlfriend, Jill Robson made it a foursome who I had met through Astrid Rush after Sara's birth.

Lily and her co-worker, Ronald Leach, and co-founder of this form of therapy would sit in their white coats at either end of a table in the front window. They took turns reading from the papers that they had handed out to us. We would be in front of them listening and taking notes once a week for months. We not only learned the structure of the body, but also the healing power of color plus the energy systems similar to acupuncture.

Most of the therapy focused around the therapeutic qualities of color mixed with Love. Pink was Lily's favorite color and she teased Ron often about not forgetting to put in a bit of pink. We learned to visualize color instead of using physical colors as it is in many other therapies. She felt certain that our minds and hearts were our best tools.

The children loved her. She was our Nan in many ways. Lily use to say that if she were a Fairy Godmother the one quality she would bestow upon a child would be to have a sense of humor. Laughter and Joy were the key to Happiness and opened our hearts to receive God's Love. To me she was an Angel amongst us. She often would say that she knew they were there, but was never graced to see one.

So we began to work in the clinic with her as time progressed in our training. I learned a lot in those days about humanity and myself. We had many that were deformed and it was a challenge at first not to judge and withdraw. I saw a lot of the sadness and sorrow many carried. Looking back, I wish I had more of an understanding of Christ's Love. I could have helped them more. However, Lily worked closely with his energy believing that our hearts would open for our intention was pure. He was always there.

On Saturdays, we offered a free children's clinic. They were special even within their difficulties. I have always had a soft spot for the wee ones so I felt at home with them. The moms and dads came baring their sorrow holding their precious treasures looking for hope as they passed them over to us. Lily went from one family after another with her Love. There were toys and books in the corner for the older children while they waited for their turn.

I remember one child suffered from severe allergies to many foods especially sweets. She was so in distress about this for the children at school would tease her and wave their Mars bar in front of her face. Lily said to her, *"Don't mind them dear. They do not realize what poison they are eating. It is not their fault. Just pray for them. You must realize how wise your body is compared to theirs. It speaks to you. Your reactions are just because it knows that it is poison."*

I worked more and more together with Lily. We worked in pairs. It was interesting that many of the patients directed to me involved casualties of drug addiction and wild living. I found myself understanding their problems. Often I realized it was an opportunity for me to reflect back upon my own choices and challenges. They would arrive in taxis boasting in the waiting room about how much they spent getting high.

Lily finally decided it was necessary to start charging. They needed to put a price on their health otherwise, they would continue making the wrong decisions. Inspiring respect for others and oneself was her intention. Sadly, our world works with money in the way that it does only by putting a value on something if it has a price. She decided to use it as a tool, but minimally. She said, *"Miracles can happen when we shift our perspective and take responsibility for our choices instead of abusing one's own health. Money can serve to heal."*

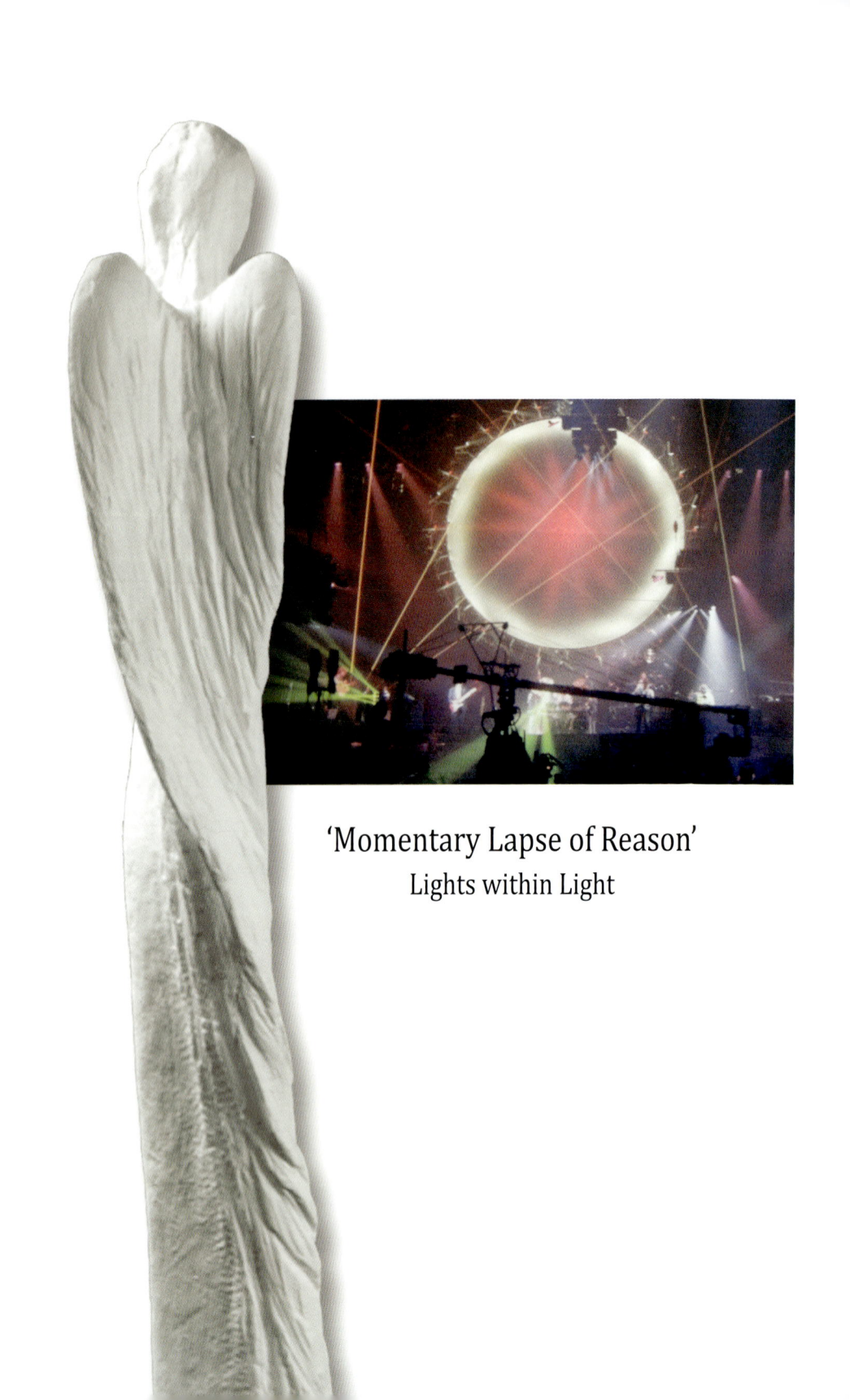

'Momentary Lapse of Reason'
Lights within Light

CHAPTER 62

WEMBLEY CONCERT

AUGUST 1988

The band toured throughout Europe and were home the first few weeks in August, before going back to America on the Northern leg of the *Momentary Lapse of Reason* tour. They had two gigs scheduled on Friday the 5th and Saturday, August 6th at Wembley Stadium. As I recall Sue Turner, our secretary, and I had our work cut out for us, managing over 1000 tickets just for our friends and family, not to mention back stage passes. On top of which, Mrs. Tweedie was interested in coming. This phase of touring with the Floyd was not only the congregation of family, film stars and known musicians as before, but also philosophers and spiritual leaders of the times.

The elements requiring Mrs. Tweedie to arrive at Wembley Stadium, amongst over 90,000 fans, seated within the volume of the sound, was quite a task. Two friends, Andy Robson and another man, (sadly, I have forgotten his name) worked as security for the Guru Maraji Ji and came on board. Many of our friends were his followers, which we had met through Olivia Harrison when we lived at Hook End. Not only did they serve him in that capacity, but in a more creative way, decking the halls with Beauty for his events.

On one afternoon, I organized them coming to the stadium to plan the logistics of getting her in with the greatest amount of care and safety. Watching their efficiency as they walked around felt as if they previously worked for the president. We asked Robbie Williams, production director, what would be the best way and time for her limousine to arrive into the stadium. In addition, which seat would be best for her, which was not in front of the main speakers.

Our Mrs. "T" team was set-up with long distance walkie-talkies, backstage, and car passes as well as authorization for preferential treatment by the road crew anywhere. The night arrived and they were ready with a plan. One would be her guardian in the limo while the other was waiting at the stadium. She awaited pick up with her companions, Mona Wirtz and Luetz, who were dear friends of mine. While en route, each guardian kept in touch regarding traffic and the arrival of the audience. She traveled through the private passageways, as much as possible, to her seat. In addition, Sue and I made sure that many of the group who came to her for meditation and counsel would be sitting around her.

The seating plan was always one of balancing who sat next to whom. The mixture of many groups of people, estranged and friendly, and cultures was a test and yet harmony seemed always to be there in their differences. Art had a way of doing that especially in my experiences with the Floyd. Or perhaps it was our mutual philosophy of care for the ones we loved and respected. The gig went very smoothly and Mrs. Tweedie found it an interesting experience. She like Dr. Engel wanted to know what influenced the younger generation's psyche, first hand. She even went so far one year, as to take an acid trip with Timothy Leary in California.

After such a large organizational feat, I had always felt it was important to honor my closest staff for working beyond the call of duty. In this case, it was Sue Turner. Burning the midnight oil upstairs in our little office at EMKA, the Floyd's offices, was often where she could be found. This year I wanted to do something extraordinary for her. I pondered it for a few days. The touring pace continued onto Manchester and Dublin. She had been on duty each day with little rest often.

I stayed home with the children. Then it came to me. I will send her a dozen roses every hour throughout the day starting at 9:00 a.m. until 5:00 p.m. Her day usually finished between 5:30–6:00 p.m. After the fourth delivery, Sue was pleading with the driver, *"Please tell me is there anymore coming?"* He said filling her arms with the next bunch of flowers, *"No idea luv."* I asked the florist to keep it a secret. When the day drew to a close, Sue went home in a London black cab full of roses smiling.

"Daddy too loud"
Moss Garden
Saiho-Ji Temple
Japan

CHAPTER 63

DADDY TOO LOUD
JAPAN

1988

David had been away for two months touring in Australia and New Zealand. I was to join him in Japan with Matthew who was just about three. The girls had to stay back in the UK as they were still in school. English schools were getting less sympathetic about us taking them out on tour or other exotic places except on holidays. I loved watching David together with Matthew. They were like carbon copies, little and big. They were mates. David always wore a brown leather-flying jacket and so did Matthew for I had found a child version in one of the London markets.

Some of the first concerts were to be in Tokyo. Matthew was always attracted to David when he sat at home or back stage or in the hotel playing the guitar. He would teeter on the edge where David was sitting listening, fascinated. The day came when I said that we would go to the concert and hear Daddy playing on stage. We went together for the rehearsal including our nanny, Rebecca, intending to stay through the evening concert. I took Matthew out to the mixing desk to let him get around in freedom. He loved running around the empty seats. The auditoriums were like being in a huge playground, except for the wires. Thank God, the wires were taped down. All the roadies loved our kids. They were big brothers and the kids had a very large family.

The rehearsal was about to begin so I walked over to where Matthew was playing. *"Matthew, Daddy is going to play now. We must go and be at the mixer."* I held him jumping about with childlike enthusiasm in my arms as we wandered over to where we could stand. For a moment, his eyes were at attention looking everywhere at what seemed like the Star Ship Enterprise. He was fascinated with all the little lights on the mixers and men with headsets calling cues. He always observed the little things.

Sounds of roadies clattered as the band entered onto the stage. David picked up his guitar as the rest of the band took their places. With the first note that loudly traveled around the empty auditorium, Matthew screamed, "*DADDY LOUD! DADDY LOUD!*" His shouting continued as I hurriedly took him down the aisles to the safety of the backstage. The music got louder as we sought refuge. The band went into full swing. The auditorium was pulsating with the volume. His little hands clung to his ears as he continued to shout, *"DADDY LOUD! DADDY LOUD!"*

My pace got faster all the while wishing I had ear protectors for my child. It was not quite, what I had expected. The other children had seemed ok in the past. Matthew was a sensitive child to loud sounds at home, I should have thought ahead. All was good throughout the rest of the day. He played backstage eating the meal I had packed for his dinner and the snacks, I might add, provided for the band. He played with many who thought he was cute. Eventually, he fell asleep on the comfy couch in the dressing room until it was over when we could take him back to the hotel. Another day on the road with children had drawn to a close.

Since our last tour of Japan in 1972, a lot had evolved in me spiritually. I had become familiar with the teachings of Buddha and many other Eastern philosophies. I now meditated, was a vegetarian, abstained from any drugs and alcohol. I Loved Japanese food and their *Art of Living*. I adored Gardening and Bonsais. I

Loved life so much, so that I was inspired to live a life more based upon Beauty, Goodness and Truth; the Truth of what we truly are as Human Beings. So to return to the place where these principles went back for centuries again, was a gift. I had a long list of gardens and temples I wanted to see with *eyes wide open*. I was more aware and valued the deep essence of their creations and intentions based upon their philosophy.

In the early history of Japanese Gardens, the inspiration came from China, but over time, they developed their own principles and aesthetics. Primarily there are three types: Paradise gardens, Promenade Gardens and Temple Gardens. At the heart of these gardens lies the basic principle that they are a work of art. Often they are an experience with the Beauty of Nature in miniature within limitation. They did not seek to copy, but to inspire. The Japanese always had a spiritual connection with their land and the spirits that are one with nature. Their gardens are different from the Western flower gardens; their creations are in a spiritual and philosophical intention rather than just for its visual Beauty.

Entering their gardens takes you on a journey most often in the quiet that lies within each of us. They are gardens meant for meditation, contemplation and a place where it is safe to invite their Gods and Nature Spirits to visit with us. Every garden incorporated symbols or a task for monks to develop their innate abilities to discover their soul or anyone who had the eyes to see. Each had a different intention for the viewer that would open the door to the highest. Mostly designed along the principles of Feng Sui, which is an ancient Chinese theory of space and energy.

There are various types of Temple Gardens. One that caught my interest the most was the famous "Moss Garden" in Kyoto. Our promoter's secretary told me that it was both a historical landmark and a "special place of most scenic beauty" in Japan. I really wanted to go so she looked into it further. Apparently, since 1977 visitors were limited and had to apply by return postcard for an appointment. They wanted to reduce the damage caused by too many visitors.

It was more difficult for International visitors since we had to allow seven days prior to a requested visit for the return postcard. As I did not know this garden even existed before leaving England, I could not have done that in time. If we applied now seven days would be after we left Japan. Fortunately, our promoter had connections. I was so grateful. There was only one opening for visitors per day so we creatively had to plan our visit around this. David could not come because of his gigs, so our days were numbered. Thank goodness, our promoter was able to provide an interpreter and car.

Since the inception of the "Moss Gardens" otherwise named Saihō-ji, there have been several Tea Houses and Temples built on the very old sacred site. They either caught fire, were destroyed by floods or fell into disrepair over the centuries. In 1336, the famous Japanese gardener Musō Soseki came forth to help revive Saihō-ji as a Zen temple. He changed the emphasis to reflect more of a Zen meditation, which the Renzai adherents continue to observe today. Musō received credit for the relationship and the placement of the stones, which are extremely special.[1] [2]

The moss garden of today was not Musō's original design. Originally, most of the garden was made of pure white sand raked in different designs to symbolize the Lakes of the Gods. However, nature intervened and it rained and rained. Then there was a flood. What was originally white sand succumbed to water, then ended with moss. Due to the additional fact that the resident monks did not have sufficient funds to restore or to maintain the sand art, the moss continued to grow. By some mysterious coincidence, it seems many different forms of moss appeared. Today the garden has recognized 120 different types of moss. I must say, "The green is a sight to behold!"

Saihō-ji has several gardens and Tea Houses. The *Moss Garden* is located in the eastern part of the Temple grounds and under a grove of pine and maple trees with some bamboo. Before entering, the garden visitors must participate in several rituals. These include zazen (sitting meditation), hand copying sutras (shakyō) and chanting sutras. One is then asked to write down one's wish, name and address. The monks keep all the sutras in the pagoda and continue to pray for all who have come and meditated.

When we arrived, we were guided to one of the Temple Tea Houses. We walked up a few wooden steps and they requested us to take off our shoes before entering. At the entrance was a large bowl full of wooden sticks with letters upon them and candles burning. Incense filled the air as we entered. We followed the other visitors to another room to the left. It was quite large and rectangular in size. The windows allowed a view of the gardens outside. There were many low-lying tables of pale pine and pillows for one to sit. The floor was covered with a bamboo mat and on each table, sat a small bowl of ink with a Japanese brush beside it. In addition, there was one of those sticks the shape resembling a popsicle stick but a bit wider.

Everyone sat in quiet, waiting. And as we did, I felt a very strong meditative energy start to take me over. I found it hard to keep my eyes open and surrendered to its soothing power. It got stronger and stronger centered on the entrance as though a being of great purity was approaching the Temple. I was used to this happening with Mrs. Tweedie so it was not new to me. I felt blessed and went into the moment. Bliss slowly warmed my body and so did inner peace. A monk entered the room and took us through a Kensai Zen chant and meditation. Most listened for we were foreigners, but the power of the sounds penetrated and took me deeper into peace.

When he finished an interpreter told us to write a wish and our names and address on the wooden stick. I pondered what to write. What was my deepest wish? I wished for Love and Peace to always be with my family. As we finished, we were told to place our sticks in the large bowl that I noticed when we first came in at the front entrance. At that point, we were invited to enter through the Gate of the Moss Garden. I was already in a very fine place, but the bliss went deeper as I entered the Beauty of the Green, lit by the filtered sunrays through the trees. The air was fresh and smelled of earth and leaves. The sound of water trickled around each corner from the miniature waterfalls. Stillness hung in the air.

The garden is arranged as a circular promenade centered around what they call the Golden Pond. It is in the shape of a heart. The Beauty was beyond words on all levels of my being. The subtle symbolism and the energy of the garden healed many of the tensions I had brought with me. There were no flowers, just green. The intention was not to have distractions that took you away from the meditative experience.

In Mental Color Therapy, which I was practicing back in the UK, green was the ultimate healing color of nature. That day, I had it first hand and deeper as an experience than ever before. What was interesting to me was that I had always had trouble visualizing Spring Green. Lily said, "*Do as if...it will come.*" So from that day forward in the Moss Garden I could visualize Spring Green. I knew its deeper essence.

In a different part of the garden there was a triple pagoda where many of the sutras, of the Renzai Zen teachings are kept. Historically, this form of meditation and principles to live by was popular in Japan amongst the Samari, the warrior-class. Zen Buddhism spread among the samurai in the 13th century and helped to shape their standards of conduct, particularly overcoming fear of death and killing.

It is accurate that (Zen) practices awaken oneself to the already realized Koan through Zazen. A Koan is a paradoxical anecdote or riddle without a solution, used in Zen Buddhism to demonstrate the inadequacy of logical reasoning and provoke enlightenment. In Rinzai Zen practice, a Koan is examined while sitting in order to deepen insight. The placement of the Rocks in the gardens also was a Koan. A puzzle to be worked out, to break the mind from holding on and let go, very similar to the ancient Zen paintings.

On that day, I experienced just a glimpse of this—but the peace has remained in my memory. It is recommended that if you wish to visit this garden the most famous times are either during the East Asian rainy season (in Kyoto, early June to mid-July), when the rains make the moss particularly lush, or in late autumn, when the turning leaves contrast with the moss. And make sure that you send the postcard in plenty of time unless you have a promoter that will sort it out for you.

Pip & Emo

CHAPTER 64

PIP AND EMO

1989

As I stand before the mirror of my past, memories reappear again of people who I knew along the way. There were two of David's childhood friends from Cambridge that stood out. Emo and Pip. Emo was living in our flat across the way when we were in Monksbridge. He entered the kitchen one morning to tell us that Pip had died in Cambridge on the 14 October 1989. He had returned to heroin and fell in a fight. We heard, he had actually died of head injuries from the fall. On that morning, we all sat in silence, in thought, digesting the news. It was another moment of meeting the cycle of death.

Pip's Mom was so deep in mourning that Emo, David and I carried her emotionally for nearly three years. She often came down from Cambridge and stayed with us. Annette and Piers, who were visiting from Denmark, came along with Emo to escort her to the *Momentary Lapse of Reason* concert at the Isle of Dogs. David arranged for a limo to pick them up, which touched her heart with awe and wonder. I went in another car with other friends. She felt that she had witnessed another part of her son's world never revealed to her until that night. She felt she had touched heaven where Pip now was in Peace. He had been such a troubled soul and yet always wore a smile. That night she shed tears of relief to know her boy had been so loved.

***

Recently, I spoke with Emo to understand the history of how Emo, Pip and David had become so close. David being from a well-educated family, went to the Perse school in Cambridge and they were from across the bridge. Emo was born on Queen Street and lived with his Mom. Pip lived in Long Stanton in a caravan next to his father who also lived in a caravan. They were 15 at the time when life started to bring them all together.

Emo worked in the coal yard at Vinters on Hills Rd across the bridge from the Perse. Every Saturday for two years Emo rode the same bus from work at midday as David did to get home for he had lessons on Saturday mornings. Emo drove the pick-up truck full of coal and was always black, which was so the way workers in the coal industry looked throughout English history. He looked straight out of *Oliver* until he showered and got into his Carnaby glad rags. Emo says it took David a while to put the two people together, the black one and the Mod.

It wasn't until they were 17 that they would actually meet in town at the Mill pub where one could hire punts to go on the River Cam. Storm Thorgerson, Peter Gilmour and David were sitting on the wall having a chat. Emo approached sitting next to him saying, "*Hello David.*" He responded, "*Hello, Emo.*" Somehow, David knew his name. From that moment on, they were inseparable.

At the time, Cambridge was full of Mods and Carnaby fashions were all the rage. Emo earned £10 per week, which was a lot, and had no problem filling his closet with incredible clothes like his favorite black leopard skin coat. He wore it everywhere. Everyone hung out at the Rex Theatre and the Jazz Club. The sound of Muddy Waters, Roland Kurt, and the Rolling Stones played as everyone gathered together on the weekends.

Emo was friends with Sid Barratt initially. Their early childhood was so similar. They both lost their fathers and were raised by their mothers in difficult financial circumstances on the edge of town. Emo says that they had more in common than that as they were both sensitive souls and very theatrical. They goofed off a lot around town in their fancy clothes and in the park. They stood out amongst the crowd. Often loudly.

One afternoon they spotted Pip in the distance looking like a wandering Wallaby, long curly locks of auburn hair dancing about under the trees. He too was an eccentric character adding color to the scene. What a time the sixties were. It was a time to express one's nature despite the limitations of being illiterate and poor. As time went on, they got closer. They gravitated towards each other like brothers of spirit.

On one evening, Sid, Pip and Emo were hanging out at the "Criterion" together, which was a beatnik place for Hippy People to hang. Everyone was there. Twenty-five friends, a collection of unique people, David, Storm, David Gale, David Henderson, Nigel and Jenny Gordon to name a few. That evening Emo introduced Sid to Mick Rock, a Pop Photographer from the States, who helped Sid along his career to fame. Mick was later to take the photos for Sid's album *Madcap Laugh*.

One evening Emo went to David's house to hang out while his parents were out to some function. They were in the kitchen frolicking rather loudly when they returned. At first his parents were alarmed for when Emo smiled with a rather uncomfortable garish and whimsical snicker, he didn't have his two front teeth. He looked like a street urchin in their eyes. They exclaimed, "*What's going on?*" whereupon Emo sensed that it would be a good idea to leave.

Doug and Sylvia continued to question David with a tone of disgust, "Why do you bring such riff raff home?" Eventually they would discover Emo's heart qualities. He was a street fighter who protected the neighborhood girls and friends from bullies. He was the front line of protection with angel wings. He took the beating for them, as he was fearless.

Pip, David and Emo became a dynamic trio around town. They were buddies. Unfortunately, Pip became a heroin addict. He had read the books *Naked Lunch* and *On the Road* by William Burrows, which inspired him to think heroin would change his poor struggling life to bliss. He hung out with a few beatniks in town who were addicts and lost his way. Emo at that point looked after him for years trying to steer him in a more healthy direction. Finally, David paid for him to go to a rehabilitation center in Greece in 1971. By which point he had ruined his left arm from shooting up.

The story doesn't end there. At the airport, he was searched. Guess what? He was carrying heroin and got busted. He spent two years in a Greek jail from 1971–1973. No drugs, no friends, couldn't understand the language, it was just in prison and cold turkey. Well it did help him to kick the habit. He began re-educating himself. He read 2–3 books each week and learned Greek fluently. When he returned Emo also had changed. He had a broken heart, was a drunk and on drugs. Pip was so clean when he returned and the tide had changed. He took care of Emo until six months later when he joined the party again.

Eventually Emo would meet Master Charan Singh in 1975. The experience was to heal Emo's heart. Nigel Gordon was filming a documentary called the "Sat Guru" and Emo had to assist the cameraman. As a result, Emo spent a lot of time near his Master. He was restored, clean and devoted. After which Emo became Pip's caretaker again until he moved to London. What a pair they were. We didn't have to hire clowns for Alice's birthday parties. They were so wonderful and silly. The kids loved them, except for one little girl that cried throughout the party each time they came near.

***

David went to France in 1966–68 with Willie Wilson and Rick Wills. They were gigging together but not as Jokers Wild, but as the Flowers. Emo moved to London to Calvedon Rd in 1967. Pip stayed in Cambridge. David returned to London in 1968 and moved in with Emo. They both got jobs working for Ossie Clark at Quorum in Chelsea. David drove the van and Emo put on the studs on the leather Jackets. They met so many colorful people. London was alive.

Emo was close with Sid during his time in London. Their friendship carried over from Cambridge. LSD was the drug of choice, but it was pure. Emo said that after the Floyd American tour in 1968, Sid returned in a very bad way. It is said that he had gone to a party in the States and was given some really bad acid. The trip was one of Sid's worse nightmares from which he would never recover. His deepest fears came out and as a result he became really mentally strung out and ill.

Sid was interested in the teachings of R.D. Laing, a Scottish psychiatrist, who wrote extensively on mental illness. His main premise that influenced Sid was *"Break on Through to the Other Side."* Sid did try. Storm, Dave, Gale, Nigel, and Ponji arranged for Sid to have one on one sessions with R.D. Laing. He only had two sessions because it was too challenging. He continued taking LSD. Instead of breaking through to the other side, he went into a black hole.

One could still have conversations with him at times. Other times it was impossible. He was gone. He often wandered through the streets of Chelsea and Kensington where everyone lived and hung out. It got worse and worse. He couldn't play anymore. He would often just stand on the edge of the stage and stare at the audience. The band tried to hold him together and kept bringing him to gigs. Eventually, Emo says it got too painful for him to watch. He stopped going to the gigs.

David and Emo were living in a new flat in Warwick Square Mews when Roger Waters called to speak with David. They knew each other from Cambridge. Emo was sitting on the bed when David came into the room after the call and said, "The Floyd have asked me to play in the band!" "Wow! Then you don't have to drive a van anymore!" Emo exclaimed rather excitedly. They jumped around the room together like two maniacs. When they both came back to sanity, David casually said, "But Roger said I had to dress like a pop star. What should I do?" Emo responded, "Well dress like a pop star!" "Well how do I do that?" David wondered. Emo suggested, "We can go to Ossie Clark. He has the clothes that pop stars wear." David rolled his eyes in thought, suddenly realizing that he had been delivering the clothes all the time.

So they both went together. Ossie dressed David in a black ruffled shirt and brown skintight velvet trousers. David had maroon Gohill boots already, which really went with the outfit. He did look rather camp and played it up a bit in the shop after hours. Being not quite his style, David was slightly embarrassed for he was more at home in blue jeans, but he transcended it. Getting the job was a gift he had desired. The rest is history.

***

Emo remembers the day that David returned from America, in 1971, and brought me with him to the flat in Warwick Way. I was so shy and innocent. He said David was really proud and showed me off. I had no idea. He said it was evident how much we were in love. We were always kissing and holding hands. To Emo, the beauty of David's face could launch a thousand ships and he found the same in mine. He could tell we were a match made in heaven.

Personally, I remember feeling I had walked into the movie *Blow Up*. It was a movie depicting the swinging life in London, inspired by the real life of a London photographer, David Bailey. My life was to become just that and I loved it. Well, part of it. I really missed home. Fortunately, many friendships were born and lasted a lifetime of challenges, laughter and tears. Emo and Pip are just a few.

***

One of my favorite stories with them was when we asked them to babysit Alice for the night. She was just two, sweet and had blonde pigtails. Pip and Emo were staying the weekend, and Steve and Jenny Marriott had asked us to come over for dinner. At first, the evening consisted of chasing her around the living room giggling. Then Emo played Magic Carpet Ride with her. Pip was in hysterics watching them as they slid down the stairs. Alice sitting on Emo's lap, securely in his arms. Over and over they played Magic Carpet ride sliding into the divan when they hit the floor. Alice getting up, excited waving her arms squealing, "Again, Again, Carpet me, Carpet me!"

Eventually, Emo wanted to stop for she was getting rather over excited. He told her, "Alice, we have to stop now," when she burst into tears. He didn't know what to do next as she sobbed uncontrollably in his arms. Suddenly, he was inspired with a fun solution. "*Ahh*, Alice let's play Magic Box," while he gave instructions to Pip. "Pip, get the dust bin!" "Dustbin?" "Yes, the dustbin, quick!" Pip had to go out into the scullery to get it. Next Emo said, "Pip, get a bin bag!" "A bin Bag?" "Yes you idiot, a bin bag quick! Put it in it! We have to make a magic box!" "A Magic Box?" "YES! A MAGIC BOX!"

Alice was still whimpering as she watched the show from Emo's arms. Finally, it was ready. He said, "Alice, we didn't have a real Magic Box so we made one for you." As he was explaining the plan to her, he was doing it. "The idea is, I will dip you into the MAGIC DIP BOX and I will lift you up HIGH FLY SKY WEE!" Her eyes filled with delight as her tears turned into laughter once again. So for the next few hours, apparently, this went on. Alice squealing, "Magic dip me! Dip me, Dip me! Fly me!" Needless to say, Pip was in hysterics rolling on the floor holding his heart pleading, "STOP, STOP, PLEASE."

We returned to be greeted with a happy child. Still awake and standing in the dustbin grinning. Goodness. The boys did look rather guilty, tired and VERY Happy we were home. The End until the next adventure.

'SERENITY'

2009

Michael Benner & Doreen Key

CHAPTER 65

A MAGICAL TEA PARTY

1989

It was May and the spring flowers were everywhere. Hayley Mills, a dear friend of mine was filming the Disney drama representation of the children's historical novel *Back Home*. She was at home and invited Alice and I over for a barbecue. It was a moment to enjoy the sunshine and the roses in her garden. Plus, she wanted us to meet some of her friends and cast. David was rehearsing and the other children, except for Alice, were with friends.

Hayley had been my favorite childhood actress ever since *Parent Trap* in 1961. It was an archetypal story that hit home and influenced my life greatly as a teenager. It was a touching story of identical twins separated when their parents divorced and then meeting for the first time, not knowing that each other existed.

Now life brought us together. I just loved knowing Hayley. We got on so well. I felt she was my sister in heart. We were almost neighbors. Actually, we lived a few villages apart from each other, but that didn't hinder our growing friendship. In England, that meant we were still neighbors, so long as it wasn't too far to drive. In the past, it would have been by horse, borrowing a cup of sugar or coming for Tea might not have been so easy. But by car, it was a short drive. I could still borrow the cup of sugar before my tea cooled.

On the afternoon of the barbecue, we strolled amongst the flowers of her very English home, Whitehorse Yard, as she introduced Alice and me to her cast of friends. It was a very English affair at her home, soft furnishings and colors reflected the gentleness and joy of her heart. On this day, the meeting of Doreen Key, Hayley, her daughter and later Michael Benner, her husband, was to mark the beginning of several new friendships, which helped support me through many of life's challenges to come.

Hayley was playing the lead role in *Back Home*. Her role was Peggy, the mother, of a 12–year-old girl named Rusty, who during World War II, was evacuated from England and sent to America. When Rusty returns home after the war, Peggy must help her now very American daughter adjust to life in post-war England.

Watching the film, I discovered that during the war, many children in England were evacuated into the countryside for safety from the bombs. Apparently, some children ended up in America. A fact, which not many are aware of to this day. The displacement was difficult to adjust to for many young and old because they were estranged from their family in a world far from home.

The actress who played Rusty was a different Hayley, Hayley Carr. Her mother, Doreen Key, accompanied her because it is required for child actors to be with an adult when on set. In this case, it was her mom. At our first introduction, I knew that I found another kindred spirit of heart. Another sister here across the waters, English, but lived in California. We three giggled the whole afternoon and have continued to be BFF ever since. At the end of the afternoon, I invited them to come over to Monksbridge for a swim. We had an indoor swimming pool just off the kitchen side of the house. I thought it would make them feel at home having been away from California for a while.

As it turned out, Alice and younger Hayley went for a swim, while Adult Hayley, Doreen and I had a "Mad Hatter's Magical Tea

Party," out in the garden. To this day, Doreen still remembers my Alice in Wonderland teapot and little cups and our time together by the Thames as the boats went past on their travels. The English love to motor down the river on a balmy afternoon. Hayley said that as a child, she and her dad often cruised by Monksbridge on a summer's day and wondered who lived there.

Doreen's long-term companion, Michael Benner, was coming to the UK for a visit so I was graced to meet him as well. He had offered to give a meditation class for the crew so I suggested that they do it at our house. David was home, but had a meeting with representatives of the initiative ARC. We held the class in our piano room, which had room for many. The day was special as Michael guided us into our Inner Place of Being, where Eternal Tranquility lies. I will never forget our "Lady" dog sitting by the garden door scratching at the windowpane wanting to be with us too. Eventually she just laid down against the door and went to sleep happily.

They returned to California after the filming finished and we would not meet again until 1994 when Doreen returned to the UK with her dear friend Genevieve. They were visiting Princess Helena Montafian in Hampstead, when somehow my name came up in conversation. They both joyfully exclaimed in unison, "Oh my God, I know her!" Princess Helena asked Doreen, "Shall we call her?" I was home and was so pleased to hear from Doreen that I forgot about my dinner party in the other room (Oh dear). Doreen was flattered that I chose to speak with her so long. How could I not? She was one of my sisters from across the ocean. My guests did understand.

I invited them both to Brockhurst, since I had moved from Monksbridge by then. I am glad to say that from then on our friendship burned brightly. As I came to L.A. often, I stayed with Doreen and Michael for their home became my home. I grew very fond of those times and enjoyed listening to Michael on his radio shows. He was a DJ for KPFK Los Angeles, which is one of the only remaining non-commercial public supported radio stations left in the States. Jackson Brown said, "Your programs have always been a source of inspiration for me. I'm always amazed by how much focus and clarity and renewal comes from just a few minutes of what you have to say." I felt the same way about Michael's show. In addition, his voice could calm a lion to sleep.

"Inner Vision," is what he named his show. He interviewed many well-known people from Timothy Leary to Martin Sheen, Fred Alan Wolf, Richard Bach, Marilyn Ferguson, Andrew Harvey, Laura Huxley; from Philosophy to the Spiritual to Rock 'n' Roll then back again. The list is long and so is his accumulated wisdom. He even invited me to be on his show twice, which is on my website if you care to listen to it. I must admit I was a bit shy, but Michael's guiding presence put me at ease, his Chuckle helped.

Today his latest Humanitarian adventure is teaching Self-Awareness and Emotional Intelligence. To guess whom? He is teaching at the Orange County Sheriff's Academy. Would you believe it? I hope you do because it is fantastic! Wow! Peace on the streets! I have to speak more of him, for he served twelve years as disaster chairman for the Glendale Red Cross and did so many other acts of service for us all. He is one of the unspoken heroes of our time hidden behind humility and a tender caring heart.

Doreen has often shared the story of how she fell in love with Michael one afternoon as she was driving along the road in L.A. and heard Michael's voice on the radio. She was so touched by his wisdom that she just had to meet him! Their love story is another one that warms my heart, especially observing their closeness that continues on to this day. In April 1995, they married. As the announcement of their wedding became public, Marie Hall, the wife of Manly P. Hall, philosopher and mystic, offered them to have their reception in her L.A. Home Garden. Doreen had gotten very close to Marie Hall after Manley had passed and took care of her for over twelve years. I was in L.A. at the time and I offered to have One Hand Clapping perform at the reception. It was a Buddhist Tibetan Bell ensemble, by a dear friend Yogi John Franzoni, who we had known since recording of the *Wall* in L.A.

Like Michael, Doreen takes a serious interest in the evolution of Humanity towards Peace. She hosted a radio series for KPFK called "Profiles in Peace," where she interviewed fourteen leading activists of the twentieth-first Century. From Gore Vidal, Ray McGovern, Andrew Harvey to William Rodriguez. They are still available to listen to on www.profilesinpeace.com. The one that moved me the most was William Rodriguez. He was the keeper of the keys for the twin towers. His story is so moving and tragic but on the day of 9/11 he was brought back to God.

The buildings were falling. There was no way to save anyone else. He had been up and down the stairs repeatedly as the sheets of glass fell around him. People were diving out of the windows above crashing to the ground. The smoke blinded his way and hindered the work of the N.Y.P.D. When it was obvious he could no longer be of service opening the doors, helping many to evacuate, he sought refuge under a fire truck until the deluge ended. What seemed like an eternity, it finally stopped. As he emerged from the ashes, IT happened. A gift from God.

Just at the moment he left his place of safety, crawling in the rubble as the sirens echoed in the distance, the tires on the fire truck exploded. Just a few more minutes he would have been flattened under its 80,000 pounds of metal. He knew it was an act of God. It touched his heart deeply as a revelation. He said, "I returned to God again that day."

Gilmour Family
Clare, Matthew, Alice & Sara
with Mum

CHAPTER 66

WAITING IN GREECE

David was still on the *Momentary Lapse of Reason* Tour so I took all of the children to Lindos. We decided to stay at our home in Pefkas to be more with nature. Each evening we would come back from the beach, shower and watch the sunset. The Eucalyptus and Pine trees would impart their fragrance as the evening Cicadas sang, announcing the approaching night. We loved our miniature Italian Rhodian Villa, built in the twenties, with its pink bougainvillea's set against its ochre walls.

Many years ago, we used to pass-by with the boat on the way to our special places to snorkel along the coast. It had a magical mystique hidden behind the pine trees that framed its golden structure. There were plenty of stories amongst the villagers as to why no one lived there. Then one day, Andoni Mingos who worked with us in the restoration of our Lindos villa approached us. He was Major by this point, I think.

Apparently, the villa was for sale and he was wondering if we wanted to buy it. The family that owned it also owned many other properties of historical value on Rhodes including this one. They had a huge tax profile to pay and had to sell something. The family was scattered all over the world and had to come from far and wide to discuss this. They decided to let go of Pefkas, which is when Andoni approached us.

The purchase took a little bit of negotiating, but we eventually became the new owners. I will never forget the day we got the keys and opened the creaking green Italian doors. It was dark and the smell of mildew was present. We entered the main corridor, which went from one end to the other revealing a wonderful view of the sea when we opened the other door. This corridor was not large and we had to walk around a table that we could barely see until the light of the day entered.

Our mouths dropped as we saw that the table was still set for breakfast and the newspaper open. It was spooky for we could feel that they had just up and left, locked the door never to return. One of the stories was that the family had definitely left the island long ago during the war. The house held the story silently until we entered that day.

I loved how it was set amongst a vineyard needing loving care with a desolate walk to a cliff edge overlooking a barren beach. We were alone except for the scorpions and the cicadas. The floors were magnificent mosaics straight from Italy. The main corridor we converted to a sitting room with traditional wooden day beds. The two rooms either side became bedrooms on one side and the other two we made into an open plan kitchen and dining room.

I stenciled every room with traditional Greece designs and one Art Nouveaux as the furniture we inherited was from that period. We made terraces of Kouklakis and placed terracotta pots with Oleander and grape vines to cover our new terrace to create shelter from the baking sun. The little cottage on the edge of the property was our nanny's delight. Little kittens hid in the drainpipes that the children always wanted to keep. Basically, we loved it!

Often we would all go into Lindos for dinner at Mavrikos, the main family restaurant in the square. The children would run up to the kitchen to give both Michaelis and Dimitri their traditional hug.

I would ask to see what fish was fresh for the others as I was still a vegetarian. We shared dinnertime with many of the local Italians who also had villas in the village. Each of us had our own long table under the fans, speaking in our mother tongue. We were growing old together as we watched our children, summer after summer, becoming adults, eventually going to the discotheques as their parents had.

Tourism and air conditioning were taking over but the memories were still reflected in the white walls around every corner. We now had mobile phones instead of going to Yani-ring ring near the square. Socrates Bar had moved again, but this time to the villa where David and I had had our honeymoon. Lindos even had a Spa where we could have a massage instead of within the walls of our own courtyard by a traveling good-natured masseuse.

The temperature each summer was getting hotter or perhaps it was me. I found myself sitting in the shade of the trees or under the umbrellas that filled our once vacant beaches, instead of sunbathing. I watched from the beach restaurant owned by Papa George, as the kids played in the water. At sunset, the beach returned to stillness. The sun burnt tourists returned to their rooms to shower leaving us alone to savor its peace.

***

In later years to come, before going back to the villa Annette, my dearest friend from Denmark, and I would enjoy a George Special (a coffee and ice cream smoothie). George would often be playing backgammon with Socrates. Sitting there became a ritual, despite things had changed. We sat taking in the last remaining sun as her children, my baby dolphins played in the water. The jetty was gone from our favorite boat beach. There were more restaurants, cafes and tourist shops. George's hardly noticeable but still there. In addition, many more Yianni-speed boats and banana rides were rushing about the bay. We had to be very cautious swimming and diving, keeping an ear for the buzz sounds of the approaching speedboats.

One evening, when the children and I decided to stay at home in Pefkas, we received a very worrying phone call. It was a very dirty, threatening phone call. I was shocked and concerned. We were alone without any male support. I called Peter Long who took care of our houses. He came over in a shot and even slept on our couch for days until we were certain that it had stopped. He was a wonderful support to us, especially when David was away. I could count on him. Years later, as Matthew grew older, he often took him and his friends to the local miniature racecar track. A substitute Uncle he was.

That summer, we waited for David to return and have our family united again. I was breast-feeding Matthew, which kept me occupied. Linda Hewitt and her daughter, Phoebe, came out for a few weeks, bringing extra sunshine to our group and an elegant flair of fabrics as they walked down the beach in their sarongs. Phoebe was one of Alice's best friends and Linda was one of mine. The days were filled with friendship as the summer went by.

'EARTH-SONG of WOMAN'

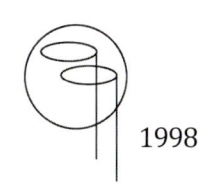

1998

Jill Robson

'A moment of healing'

CHAPTER 67

JILL'S ACCIDENT
A MOMENT OF HEALING

We had invited Jill Robson and her two children, Angela and Myles to stay in our Lindos house while we were in Pefkas. Andy, her husband, was busy in the UK and could not come. We were good friends and spent a lot of time together in England. Jill studied with Lily at the same time as Vicky, Jackie and I. In the first bloom of our friendship, Myles had a crush on Clare when she was five. I will always remember their early romance.

Clare with a temperature was lying on the kitchen bench and Myles sitting next to her on a chair wiping her forehead with a damp cloth. *Ahh*, the innocence of two young hearts that fades into friendship later. Angela and Alice were close friends and eventually shared a room in boarding school. Later after they left home, they shared a flat together. Angela is now an actress and married in NYC. Her stage name is Angela Dee and she seems to be doing well.

David and I had bought a share in a sailing boat called the "Viking Girl." Part of the agreement was that for several weeks a year, we could schedule adventures around the Mediterranean. This year David was away so I organized brief trips just off the coast of Rhodos. We boarded in Lindos for our first excursion. We stayed over night cruising along the coast from beach to beach. The kids doubled up in the bunks and some slept on the deck for the weather was so warm. They played under the water like little Dolphins free of gravity. One with nature and the sea.

The day was falling beneath the golden sun on the horizon. We had to return. The water was flat as glass as we entered the bay using our engines for the wind was no longer. A day out on the water away from the clamor of the daily tourism always brought Peace to our hearts as we walked back up the hill home.

The next day "Viking Girl' called to say that they were doing a photo shoot and offered for us to join. I had told Jill it was an awesome experience to be out, way out to sea and she should go. I said that I would keep an eye on the kids, so she could have a 'Mum, Time Out." After having four children, I knew the value of those moments. At the end of the day, Angela and Myles returned to our Lindos house where they were staying until Jill returned. Linda, the girls and I returned to Pefkas to be with Matthew as I was still breastfeeding him at bedtime. We would shower and meet later at Mavrikos.

Then came the call, Linda answered to be told that Jill was in the hospital. The taxi had had an accident on her way home. I called Pavlos (Paul) to be my interpreter for he lived in Pefkas. We were very close since helping him and Christa with the birth of their daughter, Selena. We drove like the wind into Rhodes to the hospital. We had had many experiences there over the years and it was not a place to be alone without a guardian. I will never forget the time Robert Plant and family had an accident on their way to stay with Phil May (Pretty Things). The trauma they endured until the English paramedics arrived from London is quite the story and a very learning experience for us all.

When I arrived, she was there in the corridor still in her bikini covered with dirt and dried blood. The sight of what I saw took me back. She was the color of deep purple, green and brown. There was not a patch of normal peach skin. Her eyes were like black pools pleading for help. I was in my early stages as a therapist and I was not sure how the Greek hospital would respond to me doing our healing procedure visibly. I had insurance to do work in public, but even so I worked silently, grateful that most of our therapy comprised of visualizing color and Love. I worked first by gently sweeping her aura as though I was sweeping away the flies, looking side to side for suspicious eyes, noticing all the while, the splatters of blood on the green walls from the dead mosquitos. My heart was pumping to work with the state of her condition and the limitation of my abilities. I prayed for her to live for her life force was just a whisper. I worked, asking for guidance, into the night holding her hand standing there in the corridor.

***

Recently, Jill shared her side of the story with me. She had boarded "Viking Girl" in Lindos looking forward to having a day out on the sea. She did not realize that they would not return to Lindos. Nor did I. Getting off in Rhodes harbor was quite daunting as she wasn't properly dressed. Only wearing her swimsuit and sarong, she walked along the harbor looking for a taxi. She had great difficulty finding one so she walked and walked until she reached the main shopping center in town. Rhodes is a bustling town full of tourists where she then found a long queue of taxis waiting under the trees near the market place. However, taxi after taxi refused to take her. She felt so vulnerable in a foreign culture not knowing the language or their customs, wearing a bikini on the main street. Finally, she found a taxi that would take her back to Lindos. All the while she felt unsafe. The driver gave off a rather untrustworthy presence, so much so, that she called upon her guardian angels and guides to protect her. She huddled up as small as she could behind the driver on the back seat so she was out of range of his eyesight. As they drove out of the city, she found comfort watching the sunset. Her time out on the sea had filled her heart with such appreciation for being alive that her fear dissolved for the moment, its fragrance of Beauty sustained her.

Suddenly, there was a loud bang and the force of a crushing impact. An oncoming car pulled out in front of a tractor into their lane and they collided head on. Car against car. The taxi was hurdled into the air. It rolled and rolled and rolled into the field. Grasping onto anything she could while being thrown from side to side and she screamed, "NO! I am not ready to DIE!" Then it stopped. Until she started to move, she was not sure if she had a body or not, if she was still alive or if she was on her way to Heaven. Still conscious she knew she had to get out in case the taxi caught on fire. She looked around for the driver. He was not there.

According to her recollection, the passenger side window was open and she could barely squeeze out to safety. She crawled until she reached the side of the road, sat there in a heap waiting for her Rescue. She was still alive. At last, a car stopped and a most wonderful family came to save her. Within her delirium, she remembered my mobile number, which is how I came to know she had been in an accident. Otherwise, she was an unidentified tourist with no means of proof of who she was. Jill said it was an almighty relief when I arrived. She could surrender knowing that her guardians were close. Pavlos was my ally in getting us through any barriers of communication and red tape.

The night was long and shared with the driver's family. His life was held in suspension upon the operating table beyond the grey doors. We waited together, with the sound of their crying and the clicks of their worry beads adding to the tension within the stillness of the corridor. Finally, the staff moved Jill to the ward where she would remain for days. They laid her in bed with sheets still covered with blood of the patient before. I had seen this before. I knew how to muster up the will to get clean sheets from the staff with Pavlos translating.

I insisted on a bowl of water, towels and soap in order to clean the mud from her bruised body. To this day Jill says, "OH MY GOODNESS. It felt *sooo goood*!" She goes on to say, "It was such a gift to have you next to me during those very vulnerable hours and I know you were working your magic too. Thank you Ginger, we had an experience together that not many folks share."

Andy, her husband, did come to get Jill. It is not any easy task getting a patient home to the UK. We have known many who have attempted to do this in the past. Her journey home was like a sketch from Monty Python as she puts it. She was on a stretcher, secure she thought, until she started to slide off while being carried up the stairs. She giggles now reliving the story.

Fortunately, Jill did live to tell the story of a moment that changed her life. It changed mine too. Arriving back in England, she still wasn't sure if she was dead or alive. She wasn't sure whether she was really interacting with others, her reality was obscured. There seemed to be a time lapse. After several healing therapies, she discovered of how "Oh my God, I am dead," had been planted deep within her subconscious from the horrific shock. So for many months she unknowingly believed she was dead. I think, if Lily had still been alive, she would have told Jill to get back into her body.

Twenty-five years have passed and Jill's story does have a happy ending. She went on to study and practice Psychotherapy and lives in the States pursuing her soul service of helping others. Our friendship has rekindled and we have come full circle, reunited on the Bright Side of Moon, sharing more stories to come.

***

David eventually arrived and we were all happy to have him back with us. He looked tired. The stress was showing, having taken on the main responsibility of the band on this last phase. He would stay out late. To some extent, I knew that this would be the case. Coming home off a tour of gigs and late nights does not make it easy to step back into home life. But my heart really yearned for him to be back. It yearned for the David I loved.

One night David had gone into town and I would meet him after I put the children to bed. A knock came at the front door. It was Sue Turner our previous nanny, now secretary. It was nightfall and she flew in with some urgent papers for David to sign. She left as suddenly as she arrived to catch David in town. At the time, I was in the dark. But for sure, it had something to do with work. Later I was to discover that it pertained to the Record Company wanting another album. She brought the contract to sign. Our life, still being determined by the needs of owning the Pink Floyd name, and (I believe) our not so sure financial situation.

The next morning while we were having tea on the veranda, with Matthew sitting on his lap, David told us that he needed more time to unwind. He therefore would not be coming back to the UK with us. The children had to start school so there was no way for us to extend our stay. He had promised that we would start to have more time together, but he really needed to have some time out. I could sense that there was more weighing on his mind. His silent repose was his pattern even though words of concern showed in his eyes. I had learned to wait, to get on with daily matters and keep praying for the best.

'AERIEL'

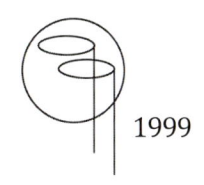

1999

David leaves the family

CHAPTER 68

DAVID LEAVES THE FAMILY

David returned home, but instead of fulfilling his promise to be with us, he had to go back into the studio. He would work late into the night. Our home life filled with broken promises to have dinner with us time and time again. I asked him if he were to be late, please just call and tell me. He said, "Yes" but didn't. He promised to take the children to school, but couldn't get up. I covered for him with more stories. They listened with a pout. He was not there. What had once been Roger's story was now ours. There was no one home in his being. It seeped in and suddenly there it was. I had no idea which way to turn. The coldness went deep. Caught in the briar sang in my heart. Stuck between the thorns. What happened to the Joy, the Love?

Not knowing when David would arrive home—repeated itself again and again. I had no idea what to expect next. This was not the David I knew. When on another night he did not come home at all, I could not sleep as the hours went by and no word. He was not at the studio. He had already left. I called Steve O'Rourke. He had no idea where he was. I called Melissa, she laughed. I was hurt by her jovial light hearted response, "That's Rock 'n' Roll." I said, "Melissa! I am worried. It is 4:30 a.m. in the morning and he is not home. He has not called AND the other night the police picked him up for drunken driving! It could be serious this time!"

I was fraught with worry. In the morning the children asked, "Where is Daddy?" I lied and said that he had to work late at the studio. After the school run, I called the studio. Phil Taylor was there and said that they expected David around 11:00 a.m. Something inside me broke. No more stories. No more lies. No more waiting. I exploded. So I packed a suitcase and drove to the studio. He was there. "Where have you been?" I shouted, holding my tears. No answer. Our eyes stared into the space between us. He was Comfortably Numb. The song had become the man. "You promised! I cannot cover you anymore with the children. I need YOU!" I dropped the suitcase before him and said, "Come back when you are ready to be with US!" He never came back.

We did have a chat with the children about the state of affairs weeks later, but they continued to hope he would come back. Months went by when he sent Jerome with some separation papers for me to sign. From time to time David did come to see the children and get more belongings. One day when he came, I was writing at our desk upstairs. The door was open. I could feel him standing there held in silent desperation, watching, searching for something to say. I did not turn to draw out his thoughts as I did in the past. I waited, but he left. I really don't remember much of that period. My mind was empty. My heart hurt. It is all a blur. One thing for sure, I was amazed how much room in my mind was a vacant space, once filled with thinking every day as a wife and mother.

Our house, Monksbridge, overlooked the River Thames. We had a huge chitalpa tree with a wooden swing. In those days, I would swing in quiet reflection while the children were at school. Sometimes I would wander and sit by the river. There was a little island with a bridge, which led to another part of the garden closer to the river. It is said that King Edward and Lady Simpson used to stay at Monksbridge. In fact, they gifted the property with a Teddy bear shaped topiary tree as a present, which someone planted on the island. Most days I would go over the bridge and sit. I would watch the leaves pass by in the current moving downstream.

One day when I was sitting there with such remorse, I was not sure whether there was any life for me after David Gilmour. I contemplated ending it. I saw through my grief, the place where I was free. I had seen this place before as a teenager. I just had to let go. Just jump. The current would do the rest. But just when it was almost a reality, I heard the laughter of my children in the garden. They were home from school. I went into automatic pilot and picked up my battered body, for that is what it felt like. Crossing the bridge, I entered into my future as a single mother with four lovely children. Little did they know that they saved their Mom that day with the sound of their Joy.

I shared my story and thoughts with Dr. Barot, who had become our homeopath after the passing over of Dr. Sharma. He gave me a bottle of remedies and said, "If you find yourself in that situation again, take two of these pills and wait ten minutes before jumping, if you can." I never used them. The children were my panacea. Mothering was my strength. Their laughter helped me to remember how to laugh for my Joy was clogged up. I have since discovered the healing power of Joy and Laughter. It's a gift from God. I now know, from my own experience, that Laughter breaks down the walls of sadness. It strengthens our immune system, clears the brain, reduces our blood pressure, but most of all it brings healing. Since, I try very consciously not to let my laughter get rusty. Giggles keep me going.

Sir John Tavener

CHAPTER 69

SIR JOHN TAVENER PASSES OVER

12 NOVEMBER 2013

A great composer, a great spiritual leader passes over. Sir John Tavener died on 12 November 2013.[1] His passing over changed my energetics of life on a very deep level. My heart grieved and yet I knew he was with the Angels. I felt the doorway of where he was. I had known him for many years and his music still holds a special place in my heart. His vision and his path inspired me along my journey.

I remember the first evening we met. Cecil and Elizabeth had invited us both for dinner at their home in Paulton Square, London. It was long before he became World famous on a grand scale. I had never heard of him until that night. We all shared our individual stories. Then towards the end of the evening, Cecil commented to me, "Ginger, I think you have been surrounded by Angels all your life to have survived and still have your wings!" He chuckled in his very Cecil way.

It would be years before we were to meet again; it was after David and I had separated. I was organizing a charity concert for Lily at Westminster Central Hall called *Christmas Carol Fantasy*. I asked him if we could use one of his songs. John was very moved that Lily had dedicated her life for humanity with so much love. So instead, he composed a song and even played the huge organ on the night. His song, titled "Today the Virgin," was sung by the

Allegri Singers and conducted by Louis Halsey. At the time, the song was held in the memories of my videos, waiting. Chester Music (John's Publisher) recently said it has now been recorded commercially and sung by the US male voice choir Chanticleer.

In the spring, John and his wife Maryanna came for lunch once at my home in East Grinstead. We ate out on the terrace under our big umbrellas beneath the magnolia. John went for a walk in my garden after, while waiting for our coffee. I had a wonderful Japanese style waterfall around a pond covered with large rhododendrons of many colors, designed in the Victorian Era when the rich and famous brought back plants from around the world. It was a period of English History, which valued the Beauty of the gardens.

Before he returned, Maryanna shared with me how unwell he was but his creativity kept him alive. John was not well, for he suffered from a hereditary condition, Marfan syndrome that causes heart defects. His life was always in balance between pain and the angels. She insisted that I should come and visit them, which I never got the opportunity to do. We spoke on the phone periodically and shared visions of a spiritual and creative nature. He oscillated between bliss and suffering in the world at large. He had found refuge in the teachings of the Russian Orthodox religion. Which from my limited understanding supported creativity as a path to God.

Lily had once given him a treatment and said, "John you are so in heaven that you need to come down to earth occasionally." I think having Maryanna and his three children served him to do just that. I do know they had a great love, love for each other and their common interest, music. He had just composed a new love song for her that was performed at the Southwark Cathedral in London the Friday after he passed. He meant to be there.

Over the years, I kept in touch by going to his concerts. Chester Music regularly sent me his schedule of performances. He had the most incredible ability to lengthen the sound of a stanza without technology like the one Floyd did with their *Sound in the Round.* The Tallis Scholars worked often with him (as did other choirs) who specialized in sacred and secular music under the direction of Peter Phillips. Often the music would start on one side of the stage and then travel to the other still moving without a breath.

John was deeply spiritual. His music seemed to be born from the Heavens. I often asked him to request the audience not to clap at the end of the performances, for unknowingly, they scared the invocation of the angelic beings away. His music transcended the noise of the street and within our hearts. My wish was that we should just sit there in silence and allow the beauty of the evening to drift deeper into our being. To all walk into the night carrying not the sound of the clapping but our union. Sadly, that is not in our culture to understand or value, yet.

There was one summer when David and I were in Lindos. I was feeling isolated from everyone and vulnerable. The gossip and judgmental attitudes placed an uneasy distance within our friendships. I was never one to feel comfortable about name calling and segregation into packs like wolves. Though wolves have more integrity. I sat on the beach with headphones playing "Ikon of Light" over and over again. I listened to John's song of the celestial choir all day while the tourists frolicked in the sea. It was my salvation from the maddening crowd that year.

I was secretly somewhere else, safe from the brewing storm. Screaming and loud noise were becoming a problem as I went deeper into the "Silence that Sounds." It seems to be the nature, part of that process, until one is established and united with your spiritual purpose on Earth. I am glad it is lessening. Just in time for Matthew to be on stage playing his own compositions and guitar!

One of my most memorable concerts was when John, the Tallis Scholars and Sting worked together in 1998 at the National Gallery in London. I escorted Elizabeth as Cecil had passed over many years before. We had become good friends by now. Cecil said that Elizabeth was his muse and so did John. This concert at the National Gallery was an experiment, where many forms of art would come together to touch and uplift us all. The paintings, the music, the poetry with the architecture would demonstrate the power of art to bring the sacred to Humanity.

The National Gallery was a series of rooms with very, very tall ceilings. The walls, lined with paintings from the Dutch Masters. We sat in the third gallery from the front where the stage was. During the evening, singers would appear in different parts of the hall. Some were behind us. Others were in a room behind the stage, as well as on stage. Coupled with the signature of John's work, his extending of the sound, enhanced the experience that went deeper and deeper as the vision unfolded.

Sting read the text, which empowered the body of the music. We were teleported into heaven and the Angels joined in the choir. My eyes drifted from one painting to the next. The colors, enhanced with each note. The prose accentuated with the sound of Sting's voice. So distinctive to me, having watched many interviews on telly over the years. Elizabeth would smile from time to time. I felt honored to be sharing this event with her.

Just when we thought the evening had drawn to an end, John spoke to us. He looked at Sting and said that they had a surprise for him. During rehearsals, they realized that he was more than a rock star with a guitar. That he, also, had been classically trained. So they conspired and had "Fields of Gold" transcribed, to sing it on this night. My mouth dropped, amazed for that is one of my favorite songs by Sting. There he stood, flushed deep within his heart when they began to sing. The audience held in the unexpected beauty of the moment as they sang together for the encore. I know the lyrics by heart. What happened to me transformed all those years of Rock 'n' Roll. They became sacred.

***

Then the world stood still again. The "Heart" of the World had died. Princess Diana left the world to make her final journey to the Divine. On 6 September 1997, her funeral was held in Westminster Abbey, London. Three million people gathered, held in their common grief and loss. Two Hundred nations watched as the Dean commended Diana's soul to enter the Kingdom of Heaven,

> *"Where grief and misery are banished,*
> *and*
> *Light and Joy evermore abide."*

The Welsh Guards shouldered the coffin, led by the ivory cross, as they marched down the nave, to the deeply moving "Song for Athene," composed by John Tavener. The Orthodox Funeral Service moved ceremoniously. Heads were bowed, row after row. Tears fell upon the floor as she passed by. The Lilies on the top of the coffin spread their scent and beauty as the procession went slowly forward. Bobbing gracefully with each step holding the space for us to grieve as the lyrics and the choir's angelic voices filled the Abbey.[2]

Many others and I watched motionless in front of our tellies at home. Breathless as the song touched our hearts with the reality. She is gone. For one minute, the nation honored her with Silence. For one minute, the world honored her with silence. The "Heart" of "Hearts" had passed on. Now John has joined her.

Talking with Animals
Samantha & Stan Khury

CHAPTER 70

TALKING WITH ANIMALS

1992

Lily was asked to speak at a conference in Phoenix, Arizona. The focus was to be on the Multi-Faith and Inter-Dimensional aspects of Life. I decided to go with her again on her journey to the States. Vicky Lord, wife of Jon Lord of Deep Purple, would be traveling with us. Vicky, her sister, Jackie Paice, and I often went on adventures with Lily together around the world. It was quite a vision; Lily, everyone's grandmother, walking along joyfully through the airports with three Rock 'n' Roll wives, blonde, radiant, and assured. Being on the road, we found so familiar. This time it was on a quest to help humanity.

At the conference, we met Samantha and Stan Khury who worked with animals. Samantha had a particular technique, which really inspired me to learn more. After her talk, I realized that I wasn't far away from doing her technique. Her therapy developed a doorway, a silent language, a common connection with the animal Kingdom, the place where all creation is one. She communicated with animals through visualizing pictures. In fact, before humans started to use the spoken language, we also communicated through pictures, inner pictures.

Between the lectures and in the evenings, we spent many hours together, deepening our understanding of this process. She shared many stories to exemplify how she successfully solved many issues between animal and man. One of my favorites was a woman in Boston, having trouble with her cat. It was not using its cat litter box and was leaving little piles all over the living room. When Samantha visited her, she recalls entering a Victorian style home; it was as if she was walking into an old movie with the anticipation of being greeted by Humphrey Bogart in the next room. The entrance hall was huge and grand with marble floors and a crystal chandelier. Everything was covered with white cloths: the chairs, the tables, and the paintings on the wall. There was a feeling of the past and the present was asleep.

    The woman, her name I have forgotten, came out from a room on the side of the hall into which she led Samantha. Her precious cat took to Sam's lap as they discussed the current problem and sipped on tea. The next step was to be alone with the cat, whose name I have also since forgotten. Let's call her Honey. Sam and Honey wandered into another room next door to be private. This room also seemed to hold the past; days gone by, for the same white cloths covered the furniture.

    Samantha held Honey in her lap and gently stroked her long fur. In this process, she begins to calm her own inner world first. Animals are very aware of our state of being, whether nervous or calm. She then filled her heart with Love but not overpowering. The next step is to create pictures or a movie. Sam pictured Honey making a mess on the floor. She pictured her mistress not being very happy. She then pictured Honey going in her cat litter box with her mistress being happier. She waited patiently for pictures to come back.

    What she saw was the house full of lights and flowers. There was a party and many were there. Honey's mistress was walking down the stairs in a beautiful dress, radiant, full of joy. Then Sam received additional pictures, consistent of the house closing down. The curtains drawn, holding back the sunlight. Her mistress withdrew and hid in her room. On some occasions, she would sit in the sitting room in a slump. It was the only room, which allowed some sunlight.

The next pictures showed Honey not using the cat litter box, stomping about indignant. The movie went on. Animated at last, angrily, Honey's mistress would get up from her chair. Samantha went back into the sitting room and shared the story. She asked if it made any sense. The woman burst into tears. The evening of the party was the night before her wedding. Her fiancé had a fatal car crash on the way. Her world went dead. Her heart's joy was stolen as she went into shock. The house shut down. No one was to visit. The woman and Honey sat in the shadows of what went before.

Samantha and the woman both concluded that Honey was most likely worried. However, the secret to change Honey's behavior is to have her mistress come alive and act as she did before Honey quit using the cat litter box. It worked. Six months later Samantha received a Polaroid of Honey sitting on her mistress's lap very happy. The room filled with flowers and the cloths removed from the furniture. Honey was using the cat litter again and her mistress had returned to the land of the living.

My second most favorite story took Samantha to a ranch in Virginia that bred thoroughbred race horses. They had a two-year-old filly that was not eating and were very concerned. The horse was in its stable when Samantha approached her. She began her pictures. She visualized a series of images that told the story of the horse not eating and her owners being worried. She waited. Images like a movie came back. She saw the horse happy, running freely in the field. The next image came as a dark stable, no room to run free. Then the filly was forced to run on a hard track pulling a trap. She was not happy with her life and did not want to eat. She did not see why she had to anymore.

Samantha related the story to her owners. She suggested that perhaps there could be a compromise. Maybe they could make a deal, allowing her to run free again for some of the time. Instead of being on such an extreme training schedule, they should slowly introduce her to a different future. They agreed to try it, hoping that it would get her to eat. They did not want to lose one of their valued breeding horses. But how would they know?

Samantha returned to the horse and relayed images of the deal. She showed images of how one day she would fly like the wind. Other days she had to be trained which meant pulling the trap. Her owners agreed to let her into the field each day, but she had to eat. The only way for them to know that the horse agreed to the deal would be if she ate some food. So Samantha thought of images, of her eating from Sam's hand in front of them on cue. It was successful and the horse and its owner lived happily ever after as far as Samantha was aware.

Over the years, Samantha, Stan and I have met up often. It has been many years since our last meeting and she was involved with a very huge challenge. Apparently, the bears in a particular Alaskan town were giving some problems to the community. Of course, it was the bears being the problem, not the fact that the humans built their homes across their normal migratory path to the river when the salmon were in season. The first year, the bears passed by the smells of the barbecues and the trash. The next year, they took to raiding the bins on their way to catch their next meal of salmon. (It was easier.) Then the problem got worse when the bears took to entering the houses, following the smell of the sausages frying in the pan. *Guess who is coming to dinner?*

The community was ready to get their rifles and shoot all bears that violated the safety of the town. It was THEIR TOWN, not the bears, despite their building on the path to the river. The Forestry Department called in Samantha to help because they feared for the survival of the bears. The plan was to catch one of the bears and have her speak to them about a compromise.

Somehow, Sam was to communicate that humans could be rather narrow-minded sometimes. She offered a proposal of how the bears might be the wiser and work with the humans. The Forestry commission offered that they would guarantee a safe new route to the river through the forest. This new route would prevent the humans from shooting them if they agreed.

Samantha was nervous since it was the most complicated project yet. They were to put a tracking device on the bear and wait until the next season. Time has passed and I can not say what happened for my own life became very focused on other matters. I do know she does have a website. I shall attempt to make contact again. It is interesting how life's cycles can go in and out of relationships from before and then start again. After being in Arizona with her, I returned home and told the children of my discoveries.

We had acquired a new puppy named Joe. He was another white Alsatian, cuddly and innocent. His paws were big and his left ear flopped. He was in the habit of taking the kids shoes and hiding them. We panicked often that he would destroy them in his teething fever. It was Sunday evening and we were washing the dishes, when Clare came in crying that she couldn't find her other new shoe for school.

I turned and looked at Joe. He was sitting there looking up at us as though he was watching a tennis match. I knelt down to him and began to do Samantha's technique with a Ginger twist. I went inwards and made myself a pool of calm. I added the color of blue. Then I filled my heart with Love and added pink. I then made a movie of Clare missing her shoe. I had him be the hero, coming back in the room with the shoe making Clare and me happy. He kept nodding at me with his big brown eyes, licking me from time to time. Nothing happened.

Oh well, it didn't work this time, shrugging my shoulders as the thought ran through my mind, "I am a novice, back to the drawing board." The girls finished the dishes and I went over to the studio. About an hour later, they came running over shouting with glee that Joe had brought the shoe into the kitchen. "It worked Mummy! It worked! AND he didn't chew it!" My abilities increased with time and Samantha's advice for when we left the animals at home worked beyond words, literally.

She said to visualize yourself walking out the door showing the time, where the sun or moon was in the sky. Visualize the passage of the sun and the moon as many days as you are to be gone. At the end of the story, show them getting a reward the moment you are to walk back in the door. Also, if you are away for some time, show them who will be coming in to feed them. If you have a cat and a dog give them both something to do. For instance, the dog checks the doors and the cat can check the windows. They both check on each other. It is important for you to give them something to do so they don't get bored. Speaking to them in their language in this way helps them not to worry. They know they are safe and when you will return.

My final story to share about Samantha is so precious. I went to their home in California to discover that it is a sanctuary for birds especially the ill and abused. They had a conservatory where the birds were free to fly and even go into the house.

What was very special and sweet is that Samantha had a little bird, a little robin, with whom she would travel around the world on her lecture tours. What was amazing and sweet was that he did not travel with her in a cage. Unbelievable as it might seem, he traveled in her pocket. Samantha said she would silently whisper to him within her thoughts to be quiet and stay still. Even on the plane, even all the way to London, little RJ (the name she called him) would be in her pocket, unbeknownst to the stewardess and all of her fellow passengers. The story brings a smile to my face each time I remember it.

These stories I share with you still touch me deeply with hope. They confirm to me that Humanity's hearts are pure. The love in both Stan and Sam's hearts filled the room wherever they went. Their eyes shone with the golden light of Goodness. I feel so honored to have shared time together. I learned so much. For me, we are together any time I see the birds in the sky and hold a cat or look into the eyes of a dog or a horse. Bless you, wherever you are today.

'Dolphina' in Bilsham Studio

Artwork by Ginger Gilmour

CHAPTER 71

A DOLPHIN EXPERIENCE
SAN DIEGO

1988

What seems like many years ago, a voice spoke to me in a dream that said, *"You must meet the Dalai Lama!"* It was a very powerful directive, which left me wondering, *"How?"* It wasn't long before my question was answered. With the morning post, I received an invitation to a luncheon where I would meet the Dalai Lama and by chance, Horace Dobbs, the founder of International Dolphin Watch. This meeting inspired the beginning of a process, which led me to seek the "Magic of the Dolphins" a few years later.

Before this experience of meeting with dolphins was to occur, a deep friendship developed between Horace, my four children and me. We looked forward to receiving each new book he published about dolphins, which he very kindly sent to us. The reading of his adventures at bedtime took us all on journeys into this magical world for some time, while the dream of swimming with a dolphin was building in our hearts.

I was working part time with Lily at the clinic and she needed a companion to go with her to San Diego for a conference. David and I were living separately. So I volunteered. It was a three-day lecture and workshop with some time off to sightsee. Everyone called her "grandmother" and I could understand why as the days passed. The conference primarily focused on inspiring us to take responsibility for our actions, feelings and thoughts to restore Peace on Earth as caretakers.

Lily brought in the aspect of healing through color and love. I made sure she had her food and drinks because it was not easy for her to walk. In between lectures, we saw patients. We worked together as a team. Everyone thought she had the healing energy of the Angels. She also had a heart of gold. Her wisdom and love inspired everyone. It was during this time in San Diego when I met a woman named Elizabeth Fortune, a facilitator of Dolphin Swims. I remembered the healing power of dolphins and spoke to Elizabeth seeking her advice.

As it turned out, Elizabeth worked out of the Bahamas during the winter months and I was planning to visit my mother in Florida with the children at Christmas. The coincidence was a major indication for me to book a "Dolphin Experience" with her pronto! In the remaining days of the seminar, our mornings were free, so Elizabeth suggested I should take this opportunity to begin my relationship with the dolphins at the San Diego Sea World.

On the first day, we went to one of the outdoor feeding pools, which had the female dolphins and was open to the public. Lily came with us and sat on a bench nearby, as she could not stand for long. She loved to be in the gentle sunshine of California and the scent of the flowers. Elizabeth led me to the edge of the pool where the dolphins were. As they swam by, one of the females studied me with one eye as she passed. Each time as she circled, coming closer, Elizabeth would introduce me to her by name. It seemed to me that she was listening and checking me out. After a while, the dolphin slowed down and nearly stopped on the ledge by the wall where we were standing. At this point Elizabeth encouraged me to touch her. The sensation was like touching warm wet silk. The moment passed as she swam away, but then she would return.

A special moment occurred next. On her next circle, she stopped right in front of me. My stroking hand came to rest at a point on her side, allowing a deeper moment of contact. And as we did so, my hand seemed to activate with healing energy and was healing something within her body. Time stood still as the heat of my hand increased. The dolphin just stayed and stayed. Eventually, a passing stranger interrupted the silence and she swam away.

To this day, I still feel the moment of having received the honor to have a mammal allow me to heal her. For I was a novice in training at the time and this experience of trust went deep into my heart empowering my self-confidence. Its essence left me with the feeling that I had graduated into another dimension of Life's Great Healing Adventure.

On the second day, Elizabeth left me alone beside the pool and as I watched these majestic beings alone in the sunshine, I decided to do my healing harmonics. I closed my eyes and as my harmonic sounds drifted over the pool, the air once again grew still. After a while as I was held within a meditative state, a gentle sound, a calling, was entering my sound. I opened my eyes to see and there before me were three baby dolphins, heads upright out of the water joyfully making a sound in a similar tone as my harmonics.

I stopped in amazement, astonished, feeling blessed, but had to continue for they made a crackling sound, giving me the impression they were saying, "Please don't stop! More!" So I continued. Each time they would close their eyes and start to swoon,—swirling in graceful movements before me—always keeping their throats facing me and out of the water. This went on for some time, me singing harmonics and them swooning. Each time I stopped to have a breather, they would request for more. "Cackle, Cackle," they would sound while nodding their little heads, their eyes filled with delight. It was such a precious moment. It was as though we were communicating without words and I was entering into the world of the dolphin. As one can imagine this again was deeply moving for me, but there was an experience even greater to happen the next day.

On the third day, Elizabeth took me to a third pool where they fed the male dolphins. At the time I could not imagine anything greater than the peace and affirmations, I had already received. I was just happy to be there. Sea World had become something beyond what I had experienced in the past. The males had a very different energy than the females and the babies. They were very much to themselves at first. They kept their distance and circled round and round watching me. Their bodies were larger and full of power.

As I watched and observed, I began to feel an energy in my heart encouraging me to open and receive their love. It went beyond infinity. It was then that one male came closer and kept looking at me as he circled the pool. My heart became warmer as his energy penetrated deeper. Tears fell from my eyes. It seemed that old wounds were dissolving. All my life I had spent silently wanting and dreaming of deep love.

I wished for my "knight in shining armor" to appear—to love and be loved deeply without fear of surrender, dissolving, and yet still have the strength of our own identities. That dream had disappeared within the tensions of our separation. Then it happened. My heart filled with such a feeling of Joy and Love that I had to pinch myself to see if I was dreaming. The dream was fulfilled, but deeper. Goodness, I was having an experience with a dolphin like in Horace's books!

An inner voice beckoned me to give more, to open my heart further, to receive more. It was OK. I was safe to let go, to what was the Love in my heart given to me from God. The Divine gift we all have, that I held a secret most often, out of respect for it takes two to go there. I thought, this male dolphin encouraged me to Let go. I would not hurt him with the full Love of my heart.

In my training, I had learned to respect the different levels of others. Humans do have boundaries, but not true with the dolphins. To have my love accepted without the dimmer switch was quite a relief. This was an experience into Infinite Love. (One that I shall cherish for the rest of my life.) At the time, I remembered saying to myself "Wow! Everyone should have one of these."

I returned to daily life with my human companions, holding a memory that gave me the strength to go on. Of course, in the days and years that have followed a question often arose, "We cannot all swim with the dolphins. We must also protect these wonderful creatures from harm. So in modern times, we must find another way to find "infinite love?"

And it was while in my studio, it became clear that each time I began my work, the doorway opened to that timeless moment. Creativity was a key. Many say to me, "Oh, I am not an artist." However, I have discovered that what I experienced with the dolphin is the creative force of life itself. It is that doorway, which opens when one sees a sunset, the blossom of the cherry tree, a newborn lamb. Most of all, it is Beauty that takes us there. Precious and sacred, Beauty touches the heart and guides our way.

I have come to realize the dolphin has shown me the way to my own inner beauty and once the path is there, it doesn't go away, unless I choose to close the door. They showed me the way to touch the God within Me. As an Artist, I am now on a quest through my art to create doorways to the Beauty within, to inspire others to seek the "Art of Living" through Beauty. And always remember to bathe in its essence...to Beautify, Beautify, Beautify!

We are the co-creators of our world, if only we realized how much we have the power to create Heaven on Earth and it lies within our Hearts. To me the dolphins are special beings, who, by their nature are here to help us to find our true self and perhaps by their example we can learn to live together in Peace. Hence, in 2001, my sculpture of *Dolphina-the Spirit of Peace* came into being. She now lives in the garden of the Humber Bridge Country Hotel, formerly the Reeds Hotel. *Dolphina* has survived severe flooding, gales and rain, plus more that nature and man could have flung at the hotel. Many will be able to return to the healing presence of the Hotel once restored to its new face of Beauty, hopefully in the Spring of 2015. *Dolphina* awaits.

'ANGEL on the THRESHOLD'

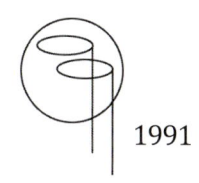

1991

'House of Broken Dreams'
Kauai, Hawaii
1989

CHAPTER 72

HOUSE OF BROKEN DREAMS

1989

As I write each morning, the chapters between the threads of our marriage get longer and longer, thinner and thinner; I enter into those moments when our dreams are being broken. I have to face the emerging sorrow of the chasm that was building between us. I struggle to face the computer, to touch the keys. I ask God, to please, give me the strength to transform what is still held inside. I pray for help, so that Joy will return and the Peace of "*Who I Truly AM*" will be restored to me. My answer came in the morning affirmation from Joel Osteen:

> "When you pass through the waters,
> I will be with you,
> And when you pass through the rivers,
> They will not sweep over you."

Thus, I began to write again for He was with me parting the seas of the unknown. Doing this would reveal what was best for my life. So I took a deep breath and continued. I have been courageous before and took steps to trust my future led by His grace. I shall do it again.

We, (David and I), were living in separate houses, separate lives joined only by our children and a piece of paper affirming, *"until death do us part."* Could we go on? We decided to meet in Kauai for a try. We never really discussed our intention; we were not really discussing much on deeper levels for years, nor did we allow our hearts to be open as before. The mask had become our relationship. False smiles, without the sparkle in our eyes, hiding the struggle, still doing the dishes and taking out the trash. The Wall was being built with each day. What do we do? What can we do silently? Is it over?

The children and I traveled separately for David was touring somewhere in the world. We also invited one of Alice's dearest friends, Phoebe, to come with us. I do not know if you have ever done that trip to Hawaii from England, but it is LONG especially with five children of varying ages. First, we were to fly to Los Angeles then to Oahu and then take a small plane to Kauai, never knowing that Phoebe was terrified of flying. It was to be revealed on the way mid-flight to Los Angeles.

Thank God, our kids were troupers when it came to flying. I had never experienced the level of fear that Phoebe went through during each flight. I was amazed she even got onto each plane as the trip went on from LA to Hawaii. I tried everything homeopathically I had with me. Arg Nit, alternating with Aconite and I visualized all the colors I knew to bring calm. I was on duty for the whole journey holding her, stroking her forehead, speaking words of calm. Alice tried to keep her distracted with games as the rest of the plane watched their movies.

I have made that journey from London to Los Angeles holding a baby, walking up and down the aisles, bouncing her to keep her from disturbing others. It was ten long hours, but this was more difficult. I didn't know Phoebe's deepest patterns of how she worked when in extreme fear. I didn't know she was afraid of flying as I said before! I was learning fast. The tension and concern was huge. During the layover in L.A, she returned to her bubbly self as though nothing had happened. We all discussed the way forward if there was one.

She promised to try to work with it, but as soon as we were air born again, snap, the uncontrollable fear arose. By the time we had to take the little plane to Kauai, I was frazzled, desperate, beyond having the strength to be compassionate. When she started again, I took a different course of action. I demanded that she pulled herself together! For God's sake, she was thirteen! "Phoebe, I am sorry but enough is enough!" Thankfully, she did it. It worked, but I felt guilty for demand was not in my program.

As soon as our feet touched the ground of Kauai and we knew our journey was over, the bliss of the flowers and the Aloha spirit of the island once again took me over. We had rented a most wonderful home. Well, it was more than a home it was the historic plantation estate of Albert Spencer Wilcox, Keolani, which had stood for over a hundred years. In Europe, this was young, but in Hawaii, it was ancient when you consider the weather it has probably endured. Its beauty soothed our weary hearts as we sat on the veranda looking over the lawn past the coconut trees to the blue of the ocean.

When David arrived, the children rejoiced and ran into his arms, *"Daddy, Daddy!"* He smiled stooping down to hold them, looking up at me, his eyes distant, questioning, unsure. We slept in different bedrooms joined by a glass partition. And our days went on, "as if" we were a family. The children played happily as though the dream was still playing, rejoicing in the presence of their Mom and Dad together.

There were horses in the stables and they often rode bareback in the waves. They had races on the lawn in the two jeeps. David allowed them to have the freedom to drive on our private property. There was plenty of space for them to learn. One was red and one was black. Alice and Phoebe were the drivers with Clare and Sara their individual passengers. There were two rows of coconut trees, which formed their racetrack. The game was to see who could collect the greatest amount of coconuts in the shortest amount of time. Until one day, looking through the window, David noticed they were getting reckless and stopped it.

We made new friends and were truly happy that Suzanne and Graham Nash were staying on the island as well. Graham must have been an early riser. Each morning as we walked out onto the veranda by the kitchen with our tea, there was a basket laden with fresh papayas from them. I discovered many years later that David always answered the phone saying, "*House of Broken Dreams.*" I am glad I had not heard him saying that, as it would have upset me deeply because I was still trying to glue the dream together. At some point, Graham asked if he could use the line for a new song. As years go by, I still weep each time I hear it. So beautiful, but so sad.

We had several dinner parties where we invited many of the locals. I remember the first time I met Marguerite Gaffney who became one of my best friends and is still to this day. She was radiant, full of beauty, heart and laughter. We had so much in common. Our paths were leading us along a similar journey, from Rock 'n' Roll to Hawaii to Spirituality. Her first husband, who was a promoter, died of natural causes. Apparently, she knew of me from afar, for she was there at the gig when the Floyd played in Philadelphia. Small world. Evenings passed sharing thoughts and building our friendship.

She shared with me the educational theory of Rudolf Steiner, inspiring me to look into its principles further. All three of her children were going to the school in California. She was very involved with creating the events for the school, as she was more than a mum. She was an artist, a visionary. I am grateful for that moment when we met since she has been a great support for my heart along the way.

Hayley Mills arrived with her two sons, Crispin and Ace. We had become close friends when we lived in Monksbridge and as they were in Los Angeles we invited them to visit. It was a special time. Her laughter fills my memory, thinking of her as I write this chapter. We played tourist, which comprised of fruit smoothies at the huts along our drives and watching rainbows. Drinking fresh coconut water with a straw from the coconut was an awesome delight. It was light relief to have them with us. We often went for dinner at our favorite restaurant called the "Dolphin."

One night I had a dream experience, a teaching dream with Mrs. Tweedie. I sat with her in her London room, on her divan in her living room. She spoke and spoke. I did not remember anything the next morning except that when she finished she said, "Well then, I have told you everything you need to know. You do not need to come to see me anymore." I pondered that for days. Was that true? She often spoke of teaching dreams. Was that cycle over, her guidance? I waited for six months when I returned before going to see her. She ignored me as though I did not exist. So I left not forcing it. I was never to see her again. I had to find my next step alone, it seemed.

Looking within

CHAPTER 73

MRS. HELLA ADLER
JUNGIAN ANALYSIS CONTINUES

1989

The New Year had begun and so did the continuation of my Jungian analysis with Hella Adler in Burgess Hill, now that Dr. Adler had passed over. She had completed her religious observance to the Judaic tradition that they both shared, in these matters. She was ready for us to begin. Her consulting room was upstairs full of sunshine. As one entered, she would be sitting in a large comfy chair right there before you, her knees covered with a blanket and a gentle smile of welcome. Like Gerhard, I felt at ease in her presence. I often sat either on the couch, where there was a sheet of newspaper to put one's feet, or on a therapeutic rocking stool placed nearby.

Mrs. Adler's theoretical position was broadly similar to her husband's; both were disciples of Carl Jung's theories of analysis. She was more interested in the effects of childhood and infancy in the development of the maturing adult. In particular, she was interested in the body-mind split and how this influenced certain illnesses such as cancer. However, they both placed emphasis upon the importance of dream analysis, which included attention to transference and countertransference dynamics. This was more important to them than technique because it leads to a better understanding of the ego-self relationship, and thereby healing of neurotic wounds.

Working with her gave me hope that I could go further along my inner journey that my soul longed for and that she would be my companion along the way. I came to her with a dream one day. I was in a fighting ring with David. The ring was in a mist and I was on the floor as he was kicking me in my stomach repeatedly. A voice spoke from within the mist, "Ginger, Get up and leave! Do not accept the fight and be a victim." I did not take its advice and David continued to kick me. Finally, a great being of light came into the ring, picked me up and carried me away. Its last words carried forth majestically as we left, "ENOUGH of this!"

Mrs. Adler listened until I finished and then suggested for me to tell David the dream. "Do not discuss it, just share it as a strange dream in the night" she insisted. I followed her advice. What is interesting was that throughout most of our later years of marriage, each time we had the slightest difficulty, I would feel as though I was kicked in my stomach. Our communication was most often shared silently, in our telepathic bond for that was our way. Both of us stayed away from verbal confrontation, which became both our strength and our weakness. After sharing the dream, my stomach aches disappeared.

I started to realize just how much the Self is the dynamic, regulating and integrating principle in one's life. I came to realize how much my healing was dependent on self-realization. Mrs. Adler often would say how vital the role of the individual is as a participant in the development of one's people and our culture. Jung said that the relationship with the Self is at one and at the same time a relationship with one's fellow man. Herman Melville wrote a long time ago, "A thousand fibers connect us to our fellow man."

Therefore, it seemed that my analysis and my work with Lily was taking me on a journey towards self-realization and touching the energetic space that linked me with Humanity. It was giving me tools that would develop that innate aspect asleep within myself. It did require me to allow myself to be honest about my projections and withdrawing them. It was hard work to become aware, to admit, to withdraw and then to allow a new self to be born. This process was so inspiring for I could feel what once was a divided psyche was healing, becoming whole. One day, the penny dropped, I would also be contributing to the *fragmented collective psyche.* The effort was worth it, I told myself, as the mud started to clear.

I was becoming aware of how to observe what the Jungians refer to as the numinosities in ordinary daily life. Numinous referring either to a quality belonging to a visible object or the influence of an invisible presence that causes a peculiar alteration of consciousness. Some may call it the hints from God. Sometimes, delivered straight to your door, sometimes revealed during analysis or any other time when one is in a heightened state of awareness. Carl Jung wrote in a letter in 1945, *"The approach to the numinous is the real therapy, not, the treatment of neuroses."* This fundamental attitude leads one into a strong subjective experience of the objective psyche.

Mrs. Adler often worked with me through creative drawing with my imagination. The most revealing one, was an individual slumped on the floor in the shadow against a wall. She was held confined in a small room with no door. High up on the wall out of reach was a tiny window with a most beautiful view of the countryside. The Sun was shining and the field was full of red poppies. Interestingly, the shape of the individual slumped on the floor was pink, faceless, and looked like the Floyd's PINK from Gerald Scarfe's drawings for the *Wall* film. So I wonder, even today, who was I really drawing or what part Pink had become me at the time.

At some point, Mrs. Adler suggested for David and I to have a joint session. She asked him what he felt was the difficulty in our relationship. He responded that it was Mrs. Tweedie. She asked why he felt that way. He said, "She is power mad and controlled her followers." She furthered by asking him, "Do you think that Ginger is under her power?" He said, "No." She asked in response, "David have you ever considered that both Mrs. Tweedie and Cecil Collins were giving her a more positive mother and father presence to heal her childhood experiences?" He was silent. We left Burgess Hill that day in separate cars, separate houses, separate lives.

Further, into my analysis, I mentioned to Mrs. Adler that there seemed to be something controlling my behavior, beyond my conscious awareness. I felt that I was a puppet to some unseen program. She recommended that I should make an appointment with a visiting psychologist called Dr. Rossi from the Erickson Institute. He specialized in a form of Hypnotherapy, which enabled one to go deeper into the subconscious but consciously. He was arriving soon to share his insights with 40 of the Jungians in London as well as giving individual sessions. His appointment book was full, but Mrs. Adler suggested that I be his guinea pig during his talk with all the psychologists on the Saturday. I agreed and waited for the day.

Saturday arrived and I set off from our house in Sunbury-on-Thames across London to the hall where they were meeting in North London. I was familiar with the area, but on the day, I couldn't find it. It was long before GPS and despite the A-Z I found myself just going around and around in circles. I was getting a bit worried since it was a bit close to the time I needed to be there. I did not want to be late. I have often found that when some deep awakening is about to happen to me, my mind freezes. So I pulled over and spoke to my mind and heart, "What I am about to face is good for our future happiness. Could you two work together with me? Please."

It worked. The energy cleared and I found my way. The inner doorway to my GPS opened and I was not late. In fact, I was only a block away. I walked up the stairs to where they all were gathered. Mrs. Adler and Dr. Rossi were waiting and motioned for me to sit in a chair at the front of the room. I was nervous as I looked at the 40 individuals sitting before me. I understood that this form of hypnotherapy did not reprogram me like hypnosis did. It just opened folders of memory only with my approval.

Dr. Rossi's voice was soothing as he took me into the journey. There was a mist that appeared. He asked if I was ok with how I felt. He asked this with each phase, each image that appeared. The first image that emerged from within the mist was me, toddling along a very busy city road. All I saw were shoes, legs and wheels of the cars in the street as I wobbled along. I was probably three years old. Dr. Rossi asked me to go back into the mist, inquiring if I was ok with the images and if I wanted to share what I had seen. I said, "Yes" so I shared this with all who were in the room. He asked, "Shall we continue?" I said, "Yes."

I was in the mist again—an image emerged of a man picking me up off the street. He carried me up stairs into an apartment building. He opened the door of a flat. He started to kiss me and stroke my head. I was crying and crying and wouldn't stop. Dr. Rossi could feel my tension rising and asked me to return to the mist. The image faded. The process was repeated again... "Ginger are you ok?" "Yes" "Do you want to continue?" "Yes." From the mist, I was back in the flat crying. The man was still holding me, stroking me. His face got worried and tense when he dropped me onto the floor. He ran towards the door and as he did, he kicked me in the stomach.

I got to my feet and went towards the open door. A woman had heard my cries from the flat below and was climbing the stairs towards me. She picked me up and took me to the police station.

The hypnotherapy session was finished and I shared the last images of the story. What was interesting is that all through my childhood, my family often told the story, laughingly, about how once when I was little, they had to come and fetch me from a police station in Philadelphia. They had no idea how I got there.

Back in analysis, Mrs. Adler and I discussed my experience on the weekend. I saw within that story why I always froze when confronted with an argument. That experience happened before I could speak, making it impossible for me to defend or express myself any other way but to cry. I *froze into hopelessness* not able to escape. This was my inner private way all my life. I was a shy and silent person. Observant and always fearful of being hurt, needing to be protected. So many insights were revealed to me that one afternoon. I could understand further, why my stomach ached each time life proved difficult. I was back there. A new future laid before me.

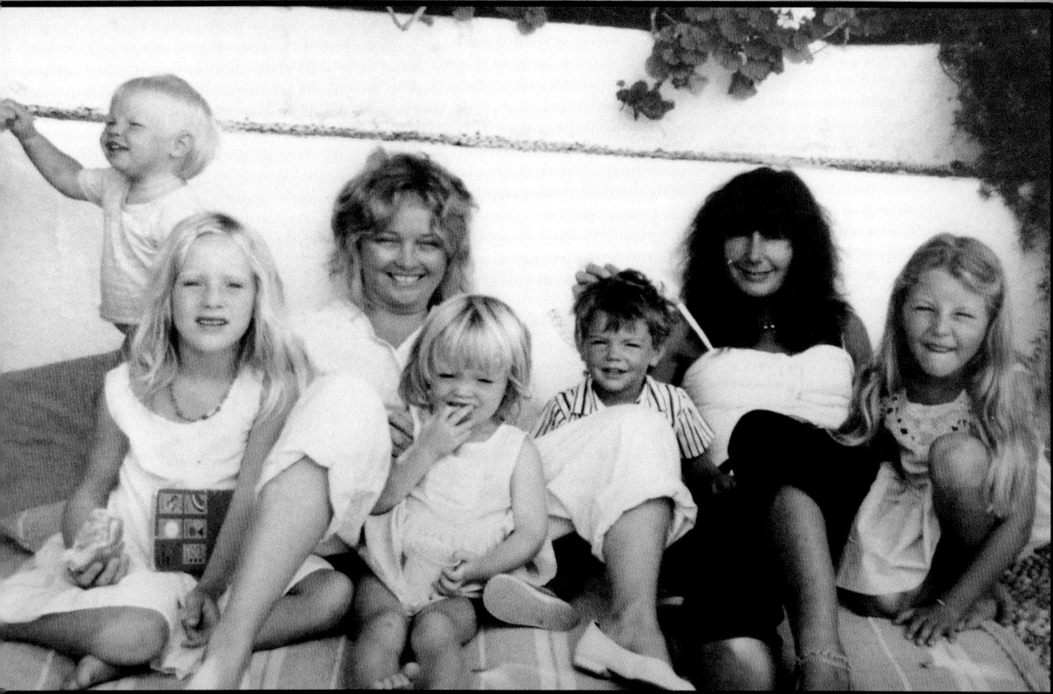

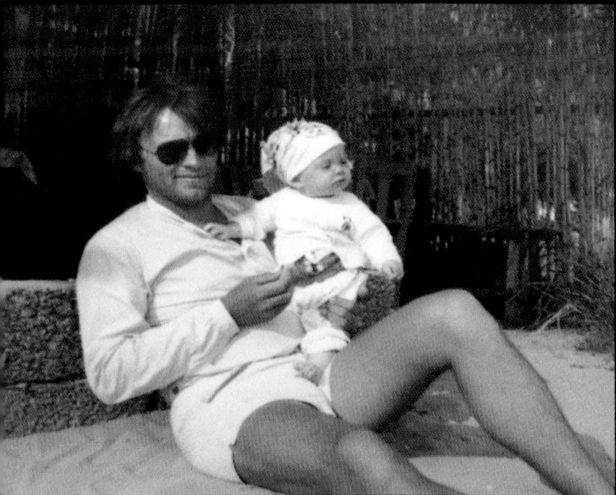

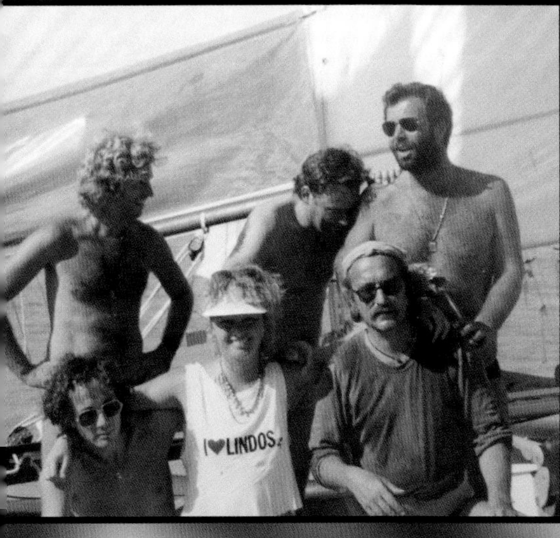
I ♥ LINDOS

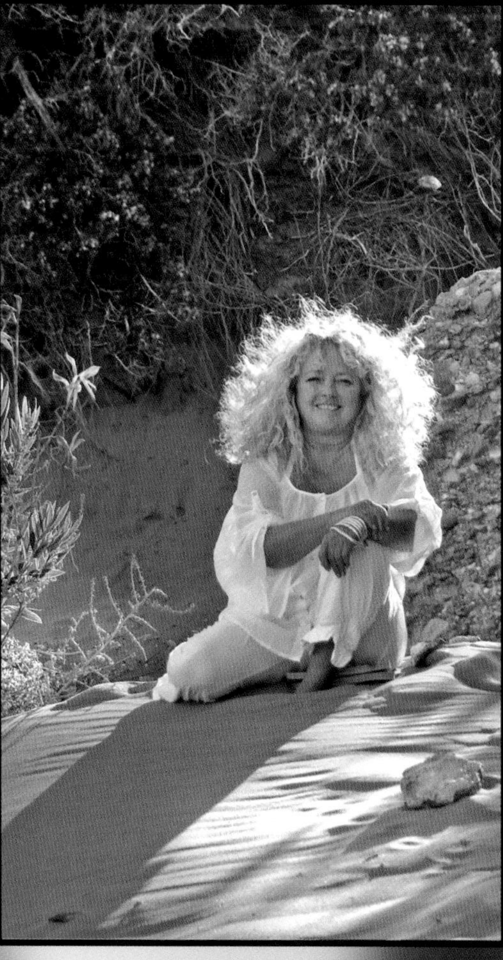

Together

Ginger with Graham & Susan Nash

CHAPTER 74

TOGETHER WE SAVE THE WORLD
CHICAGO

1968

Last night I had been re-reading the chapter of when we had returned to Kauai, seeking to add the one about my analysis with Mrs. Adler. I found myself listening again to the "House of Broken Dreams" on YouTube. A lump and a tear filled my heart as I listened to the lyrics again after so many years. Graham so captured the feeling of our circumstances that summer between David and I. We were "painfully trying," our eyes missing each other.

The brilliance of its simplicity and the depth of the lyrics moved me. As it played inside my head, the memory transported me back in time. Each line, each picture, reminded me of what had torn us apart, the heartache, the pain behind the laughter, hoping that it would go away. I reached out to the place where love was once shared deeply. Now separate hearts. I try to sleep. My mind awakened resistant to slumber.

Ahh, a cup of Chamomile tea, that will help. Sitting on the settee, turning on the telly, seeking another thought, a distraction, there he was. Graham Nash. Synchronicity had followed me. The interviewer asked about his life and his philosophy of how to write songs. I was captivated. I discovered another side of him. Crosby, Stills, Nash & Young, filled my life in the sixties. It was the voice of the times. Their sound was our culture. Their melodies were me.

Watching Graham speak last night, I appreciated more of their contribution they had given to the World. Thoughts I had gone to sleep with, re-awakened in the night.

I never realized how much of a storyteller he was. He said to be honest when you write. Be real. Don't make it up. Tell the truth of what you feel. He shared many stories that I had never heard sitting on the veranda after dinner in Kauai. He spoke of the making of "Chicago," which took me back to 1968 as he sang the song. There I was sitting in front of the telly in Ann Arbor, glued to the images of many policemen dragging protesters down the street. Gas bombs filling the air with smoke as the world watched. Then the broadcast stopped. Blackout. The cameraman was assaulted. A voice, a forewarning, "The World is watching!" The last image was the policeman hitting the camera with a club. The moment was gone.

I was stunned. In the morning when I looked for what had happened, scrolling from station to station, it was all denied, trivialized. "But we saw it!" I screamed at the telly. I was nineteen. I knew then that America had changed, but was not the one of Abe Lincoln. I was no longer part of what it was becoming. Destiny was calling. The Spirit of Liberty for All—Imprisoned in a lie. Hope was leaving our hearts covered in a mist of deception. And we were falling for it as we held our dreams pinned to the walls. It was so subtle, a slow indoctrination of our minds despite we had seen it happen. Aldous Huxley was right. *A Brave New World* was becoming a reality.

It was the 1968 Democratic National Convention. JFK, Martin Luther King and Bobby Kennedy were dead. It was a year of violence, political turbulence, and civil unrest. Riots broke out across the nation. The National Mobilization Committee to End the War in Vietnam and the Youth International Party (Yippies) had already been planning a youth festival in Chicago to coincide with the convention. They had asked Crosby, Stills, Nash and Young to play. They couldn't. However, they spoke as the voice of the sixties. They encouraged us to change the World in the song "Chicago." And We tried. And still do.

Mayor Daley had other ideas as the 10,000 demonstrators gathered in Grant Park, Chicago. At 3:30 p.m. on the 28 August, a boy was taking down the American flag at a legal demonstration when the police barged in. They beat him and started fighting with the protesters. All hell broke out. Rocks and food were thrown as their only means of defense as they fought for their rights to speak. The crowd shouted as they were being beaten, "WE WON'T GO! COPS ARE PIGS!" That didn't help. They fought and fought, helmets, clubs and fists each determined to win.

The head of the SDS (Students for a Democratic Society) shouted, "Scatter throughout the city. If there is going to be tear gas everyone should know!" As a result, 23,000 police and National Guardsmen took further action under the orders of Mayor Daley. So much tear gas filled the air that it reached the Hilton, where the convention was in process. Fighting was everywhere.

Then it happened—right in front of the convention center. For seventeen minutes on national television images were ingrained into our minds forever, if you were a witness. Images that would remember the day the police rioted uncontrollably in Chicago. Do you REMEMBER? But it was not only outside. It was inside. Security guards hauled out a delegate from Georgia. Was he a delegate or not? CBS correspondent, Dan Rather, who was reporting, wearing his headset, went after them. The man was stopped, roughed up, punched in the stomach and the nation heard his demands to the guards, "Don't push me! Take your hands off me unless you plan to arrest me!"

They backed off as CBS News anchor Walter Cronkite turned his attention to the matter. Rather and Cronkite were amazed. [1]

What was happening outside was now happening inside. And it wasn't the anti-war demonstrators only. Someone was playing a game of Power. Connecticut Senator Abraham Ribicoff spoke out about the violence outside the convention hall by saying, "With George McGovern, we wouldn't have Gestapo tactics on the streets of Chicago!"[1] Daley was not happy and there are conflicting reports about his derogatory comments referring to Ribicoff, as being a Jew and to go home!

There was an investigation committee after, which seems to take the blame away from the Mayor. It was a release of pent up emotions, they said, that got out of hand. After 48 hours of rioting, Chicago was a path of destruction and chaos of fires, looting and damaged buildings. With the streets closed to traffic, they placed the city under curfew. Bulldozers had to come in and move away the rubble, with embers still smoldering. Where once stood homes, vacant lots now appeared. Hunger set in as a food shortage settled in the aftermath.[2]

Daley issued an order giving the police authority, "Shoot to kill any arsonist or anyone with a Molotov cocktail in his hand…and…to shoot to maim or cripple anyone looting any stores in our city." Martial Law became the name of the game and 135,000 Americans agreed that Daley's actions were correct and appropriate under the circumstances.[2]

And the chorus of "Chicago," by Crosby, Stills and Nash [3] still plays in my head over and over to change the World. Can we? Yes, WE CAN! It was 3:00 a.m. I went back to bed and drifted back to sleep. As I lay there, comforted by my duvet, the songs faded from my mind, leaving me to dream another dream. I was back in 2014 remembering.

'GOD'S WARRIOR'

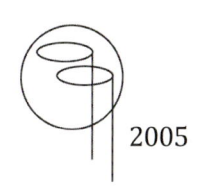

2005

The Floyd are Alive!

CHAPTER 75

ISLE OF DOGS CONCERT

JULY 1989

The *Momentary Lapse of Reason* tour had returned from Paris to play for six nights at the London Arena in the Isle of Dogs, London. The children were going and suggested that I should as well. I tried to resist their pleas for the pain was too close. Alice, bless her heart said that I MUST and went about organizing my tickets. She had difficulty and was embarrassed to tell me that the only tickets I could have were in the bleachers, not with them. Emo and Pip's Mom had tickets somewhere else and a different limo. I decided to brave the storm to honor Alice's efforts.

And a storm it turned out to be, but more for the audience. For some bizarre reason, the London authorities requested the fans to enter the arena in single file. The Floyd were known to be punctual, but this night it was broken. It couldn't be. What should have been a 7:30 p.m. start became an 8:10 p.m. start. To make matters worse, the beginning of the show was further broken as many entered late. The laser beams cutting across their vision and smoke from above made it more difficult as they clambered for their seats. It was such a commotion. Balancing their drinks and food, many already seated had to stand while others settled. It created quite an unexpected disturbance as we tried to be held by the music.

The problem that helped create this clamor lay in the fact that once inside the first doors, there was a special offer:

> *'Special offer,*
> *5oz hamburger, relish and Lager*
> *£3.'*

The Brits love their lager at a concert. I always found this to be in sharp contrast to other countries, the allowing of alcohol at a show. Consequently, there were long queues of fans, already late, buying hamburgers, lagers and T-shirts. And I was amongst them, not buying, but just getting in along with the other ticket holders. I had rented a limousine and Hank was our driver. Jill and Andy Robson and friend came with me. It was a bizarre beginning as our limo left us out in front of the arena. Hank would wait until it was all over in the main parking lot. He said, "Call me when you want to leave."

Our seats were on the side bleachers as Alice said they would be. My breathing was a bit short as my anxiety built waiting for some fear to go away, some embarrassment to fade. There were sounds of an airplane going overhead that got the audience shouting and excited, but it was not part of the show. It was a plane going to land at Heathrow Airport. Good timing it fit right in. Memories of the American *Animals* tour returned. The show began. David enters on the stage and gave a run-down of what to expect.

My heart stopped as I sat far away in the shadow. Song after song played. The fear changed to an inner smile because I was listening to part of my life story. I heard the Joy and the Love that had been there. Each song another memory returned. Where I thought hearing the music would stir the wound, it didn't. I was filled with gratitude for my life instead. I no longer had to run away when I heard the songs playing in the shops or restaurants. I was happy to be me. That evening helped to wash and temper the pain.

Sue Turner had secretly arranged backstage passes for me and my guests for the party. I was not sure whether to go or not. I would see on the night. I wish that I had chosen not to go because the Joy was about to change despite feeling safe with my guardians. I had to go to the ladies room and left Jill, Andy and friend at the bar. I was still in the cubicle when two women came into the room. They were washing their hands, chatting, sniffing a line of something. One said in a drunken stupor, "Wow, I wouldn't mind getting into Gilmour's pants!" the other woman, whose voice I recognized, said, "No problem. I will introduce you. Get it on!"

    I was so taken back, first, that a close friend, whom I choose not to name, would be so vile. But, Hey, we were separated. He was free bait for the sharks. I waited until they were gone holding back my sorrow. I kept my head low while walking into the flurry of the packed roar of the dancing crowd. Eventually, I found my companions and asked if they minded if we left. "Of Course," Jill said, as she put her arms around me, concealing my flood of tears. We left unseen. I shared my story in the limo and silently rode home held in the love of dear friends. Another chapter was beginning.

Band of Merry Elves
Christmas Carol Fantasy
1989

CHAPTER 76

CHRISTMAS CAROL FANTASY

DECEMBER 1989

I was now working alongside of Lily in her little basement flat in Willesden and had become a Trustee for her charity. It was becoming evident that we were in need of larger premises for many were coming to us for help. Therefore, I came up with the idea to have a concert to raise funds. Miv Watts/Brewer was living with me at the time and she came on board as co-producer. Nigel Gordon volunteered to be my director and production manager for it was becoming a huge logistic affair. I designed, organized, inspired, and held it together, which was such a learning curve. At times I felt overwhelmed, Lily said, "*Ask the Angels, dear, to send help.*" So I did, often. I can assure you.

It all began because "I love Christmas!" I asked everyone, "Have you ever dreamt that Christmas could be a time full of Joy and Harmony? A time when all your friends and family can come together and share all the love in their hearts and not argue?" I did, and each year I sought to create an environment, in which Joy did happen within my own home. This year it was also to happen on the stage at Westminster Central Hall, London.

Our basement telly room transformed from David's telly room, as we were separated, into our Home Command Center. The computers were big and held their stations like robot pods upon the desk and tables. Unfortunately, we did have a few problems for they would crash from time to time. I think the Angelic force was a bit strong for them or was it the opposition, the gremlins. Consequently, our IT person was invaluable.

Lily had dedicated her life in helping others to find their way back to health with the use of Mental Color Therapy and Love. And PINK, her favorite color! She said, "There is no illness too great or too small. We never refuse anyone." She has treated everything from Aids to Cancer to Alcoholism, Drug Abuse and Hurt Hearts.

Lily formulated the school's guiding color principles, which include training the therapists to be the instruments. The color literally comes through our hands, our throats, our foreheads, our hearts. Where the medical profession changes the chemistry of a body through drugs, we change it through visualizing color, for color is a vibration. We teach our students to go into the parks and gardens and memorize the colors of the flowers: roses, buttercups, daffodils, the trees in the spring.

This project to raise funds was neither too great nor too small for me as I was dedicated to helping Lily and our patients. I decided to create a Christmas Carol Fantasy with angels, fairies and stories with children singing all the favorite songs we knew and loved. The choir would sing several hymns composed by John Tavener. The Prima Ballerina from the London Royal Ballet danced the *Sugar Plum Fairy* surrounded by 32 fairies from our children's school. Simon Ward, the actor, read the Orthodox Service for the Nativity as we began the evening, "*Let Heaven and Earth today prophetically exalt, and let the angels and men spiritually rejoice: for God hath revealed himself in the flesh unto those who were in darkness and sat in the shadow, and hath been born of a Virgin.*"

Throughout the six months it took to plan and execute, each day brought new volunteers to help it into manifestation. I felt I was being guided by something greater than me, the Divine power of our Creator and his team of Angels. Miracles happened each day.

Lily repeatedly said for me to ask God and the Angels for what we needed. I took her advice and spoke to them. One day I asked for a PR person for we desperately needed one.

I was having lunch with a girlfriend, Ruth West, in Chelsea. She brought another friend. We were chatting about the event and its vision and our need. Her friend, Marion Board listened attentively until I had finished. Then she leaned over into the conversation and said, "I can help." With my eyes wide open and filled with amazement and unexpected Joy, I exclaimed, "Really?" "Yes. I can do that for you." She was the PR for the Dalai Lama on his last visit to Britain. PLUS, she had some time off. (Another Miracle of Grace.)

It was hard work, balancing its creation, with single motherhood and running our household, which was expanding with volunteers sleeping everywhere. David was living on Maida Avenue. However, he said he would help organize the "Rock 'n' Roll" section, which we called the "Christmas Carol Fantasy Band" and the "Celestial Orchestra." The band comprised of Paul Young, Vicki Brown, David, Jon Lord (Deep Purple), Mick Ralphs (Bad Company), Rick Wills (Foreigner) and Nicky Claird-Lowes (Dream Academy).

They performed "Happy Christmas-The War is Over" and "Imagine," as two of the last songs. Paul Young made a special appearance. The Celestial Orchestra included Raff Ravenscroft (sax), Jody Linscott (percussion), Jane Lister (harp) and the English Rose Quartet (strings).

"Jingle Bells" played in our office for weeks. The children came in and out singing "Rudolf the Red Nose Reindeer" after school. Miv was super and got a seamstress in Norfolk, Andrea Galer, to make the costumes and Sandra Kamen made our wings for our fairies. In addition, she knew the hair and make-up artist for *Phantom of the Opera*, who came on the night with her hair extensions, make-up and a full team of helpers.

Our thirty-two fairies looked straight out of *Midsummer's Night Dream*. Gosh, they were gorgeous with their long tendrils of hair cascading down touching their wings! Their innocence and purity came alive as they pranced around back stage. Miv did so much more. She was indispensable. We were such a team. We both surrendered our heartache of broken marriages into the Joy of what we were creating for others. We surrendered to its Beauty and Love.

We only had two days to rehearse, which also included the performance, due to limited funds. Nigel Gordon, co-director and producer, and I spent a lot of time at the mixer with our lighting and sound crew, Guy Fowler, Jon Vogel and Mike Lowe. Luke Gray, Barry Knight and his team, whom I knew from the Floyd, took on being my production assistants of our Fantasy, along with Tim Hain, Alan Lee-Dreamy, Daisy Gordon, and Tim Sweeney. Britannia Row Productions provided all the sound and lighting gear. Thank you Robbie Williams!—You are a saint. Langley Iddens who lived at David's floating studio, Astoria, took on the management of each act backstage. He was a trooper.

Westminster Central Hall primarily hosted Classical Music. The stage was open for orchestras with no curtain you could close. So I had to come up with a way to change the scenery and stage props between each act. I didn't want to have them all in black T-shirts. Then one day I had a brainstorm! It came to me while I was watching a Christmas video with the kids. I needed to call on Santa's Little Helpers. "Yep, that is what I needed!" So I enlisted many of my gentleman friends to be Elves. I teased, I whimpered, "Please." They conceded, all Thirteen of them!

There they were, men in tights and pointed hats. The lights would dim and the song "The Hall of the Mountain King," from *Peer Gynt*, would play as they scurried in the dim light of the Christmas trees, across the stage removing the carpets putting in the new props. DoDoDo DoDoDo Doo doo Doo Doo doo Doo doo DoDoDo DoDoDo DoDoDoDoo.

Legs Larry Smith, who I had met at Friar Park through George Harrison, was our Chief Elf. His jovial nature and ability to be a leader of Men in Tights kept our spirits High. I still see his smile as he led them across the stage during rehearsals. Our elves became a gang of jolly helpers. They said it was one of the best nights of their lives once they surrendered. The motley crew were Tony Howard, Jeff Dexter, Alan Lee, Charles Littledale, Greg Gordon, Michael Eccles, Tony Black, David Larcher, Willie Wilson, Nick Griffiths, Andrew Mornan and Phil May.

Half way through the rehearsals, we had a disturbance. The fire alarm went off. "Goodness, what do we do?" turning to Nigel while all stood still. No elves. No Fairies. I was just on my way backstage when the production started again. Later, Langley related the story to me. "I was sitting there at my production desk with my headset on, surrounded by fairies waiting to go on. When I turned around to give them their cue, I was surrounded by lots of firemen!" David and his manager, Steve O'Rourke, happened to be backstage and somehow sorted it out. How, I still have no idea, except there was no fire and the rehearsal went on. Days later, we discovered that it had been a prank. Two crazy girls, actually women, thought it was funny. Gremlins had struck again as they seem to do when something of Love and Light is manifesting. But the show went on.

At the last minute Liz and David Emmanuel, the designers of Lady Diana's wedding dress, asked for a favor. They were just creating a new idea for a television show. "Christmas Carol Fantasy" would be just perfect to film for one of their first shows. I said, "Yes," not realizing that they would need different colors of lighting than what we had planned. In fact, they needed too much light. Simon Courtney-Taylor, our lighting designer, had his work cut out for him. What a hurdle that became to find a compromise.

Two rehearsals and one performance is all we had. How could we resolve this? Usually there is a specific night for filming? We didn't have that as an option. In the end, we did it with the minimal creative disturbance.

The Emmanuels interviewed everyone. Their first port of call was backstage where all the Rock Stars were hanging out. They asked David why he was doing the show. He said with a wry smile, "Well, my wife asked me to do it." Then they pulled me aside in the foyer. I still have the footage and I looked like a shy doe-eyed young girl and definitely not used to interviews. They helped me through it with ease. Liz and David Emmanuel, with an air of confidence and a smile, asked me their questions with my attention divided, holding my composure, still needing to direct the rehearsal, pulled in many directions.

The world inside the road crew's headsets, shouting swear words, was a complete contrast to the sacred sounds of the choirs in the hall. "Come all ye faithful" was blended with "F***, can you get those bloody fairies on stage! Where are they! OMG the harpist is freaking out! Someone tried to move it. What a prima Donna!"

Each act had unexpected problems we had to sort out. The string quartet had a problem. The Harp strings cast shadows of black lines from the lights across their sheet music. The harpist had a problem as the fairies plucked her strings with their wings as they passed by. The prima ballerina from the English National Ballet could not see the stage with the blue lights of the film crew and needed a spot on her. The film crew didn't want the pink one.

Just when I thought everything would go well, we reached the Rock 'n' Roll section. They grumbled, "Why are the amps so far away?" Barry Knight, our stage manager, explained, "We were limited on space and it is a juggling act". Grumbling under their breath as they slung their guitars over their shoulders, Barry teased them, "Come on guys. Don't be little boys. You have been in this spot before." He could speak to them this way, because he knew them all. Throughout the day, Barry did a great job calming the waters with each act, with each ego. He was our diplomat extraordinaire, a natural with a smile and a sense of humor.

So many wonderful people came forward and volunteered. There were artists and set designers, all helping in so many ways. Mona Wirtz covered my back and made sure I drank plenty of water. Mary Komoki and Rosland Titera organized all the graphic design of my drawing of an Angel including the printing of the brochure and posters. Josh Pinto did the printing. Annie Rowland organized the food for the crew served on a huge mirror. Ruth and David Einsenhart made our ten-foot "Tree of Life" for center stage. So much more was gratefully donated: advertising, the typesetting, the props, flowers, two large Christmas trees and the fairy lights. The list goes on and on, creating a union amongst the Hearts of all involved.

The magic of the sacred built as each song progressed. Tamasin Gough's angelic voice touched our hearts with "Once in Royal David's City," as we stood and rejoiced together. *"For he is our childhood's pattern, Day by day like us He grew; And he feeleth for our sadness, and he shareth in our gladness."* The Allegri Singers took us further along into the night as they sang "I saw three ships" and "Away in a Manager" as their voices called out, *"Be near me, Lord Jesus; I ask Thee to stay close by me forever, and love me, I pray."* The procession began after the Sugar Plum Fairy finished her dance. One hundred choir, dressed in ochre robes entered the hall from behind. Their faces lit dimly from the candles they were holding.

"O Come all ye Faithful" brought us to the Christmas Story of the *Happy Prince* narrated by Robert Stephens directed by Simon Gough. Ed Shearmur created the music played by our Celestial Orchestra. The spirit of Christmas traveled from person to person uplifted by the harmonic sounds of the premier of John Tavener's new carol, "Today the Virgin." The Allegri Singers, conducted by Louis Halsey worked together with John, as they have done often in the past. His heart and his love of God spoke through all that he has written. I was honored to share this moment with him, grateful to share several of his compositions with everyone on the night.

Raff Ravenscroft, the famous and wonderful saxophonist, composed and played "The Journey." He came through the mist from above the stage into the blue light on the stage. His hair full of the curls we knew so well, as he swayed in the melody of his music. Simon Ward read the Gospel of St John, Chapter One, Verse 1-14, "*In the beginning was the Word, and the Word was with God, And the Word was God.*"

Tears came to our eyes as John Lord, Deep Purple, played the Song "Lady," written by Andy Robson. Vicky Brown's voice called forth the Guardian Angels of Lily's Heart. She sat in the front row with tears touching her face, blushing and humbled, which was her nature. "*As you sit and watch I can tell you now, your eyes, they sparkle and your hair's like snow. When you laugh, there is magic in the air, and my heart fills up 'Cause I know you care. Hey, Hey lady, lay your hands on me, tell me what it is you can see.*"

The hall filled with a fine mist of smoke drifting over the stage into the audience. The Christmas Carol Fantasy Band and choir entered. Everyone stood holding hands swaying to John Lennon and Yoko Ono's song "Happy Christmas" (War is Over). Paul Young's crystal clear notes, unified in harmony with everyone brought the evening to a close as all the fairies and elves and performers and road crew entered the stage. We stood together in Love, when a surprise Sir Henry Cooper, an English heavyweight Boxer, descended from within the crowd as Father Christmas in satin red shorts, boxing gloves revealed as he joyfully opened his cape.

One by one, the audience together in Christmas spirit left their seats entering the night air, back into the London traffic and decorated trees around Westminster Abbey. All our roadies began clearing and cleaning, restoring Westminster Central Hall ready for its next event. Miv, friends and I went on to the charity dinner in our finery and danced the night away. It was her birthday. A new cycle was beginning for both of us as we brought in the next day celebrating.

END of a Dream
One door closes as
another opens

CHAPTER 77

DIVORCE
FROM A DREAM

1990

Life was draining from my heart. The time had come for us to divorce, to face the Wall between us. Unfathomable tears flowed each day and into the night. I spoke to God for direction; must I soldier on in this emptiness, or do I let go and accept the loss. An Inner Call from my Heart ushered forth. "*Please help me. What do you want me to do?*" I sat at the desk, my head in my hands waiting for insight. Our children played in the garden as I looked at the papers from the lawyer to sign. Was there life after David Gilmour? Friends held me in their hearts comforting me as I faced the pain. How can I do this? The dream was not supposed to end. We had made a commitment until death do us part. The dream was to "Live *Happily Ever After.*"

Lily encouraged me to place a flower by my bed so the first thing I saw every morning was nature's beauty. But, I needed something more. Each day was a task to find a smile as I made the breakfast for the children before school. The heartache was like torture. How I wished for a miracle. I circled and circled in my mind. Panic gripped my heart. It was over. My Love, my Dream. What do we do now?

Versha and Johnny Rae became one of my protectors, my first line of defense. I had helped them over the years and now they came to me. Johnny was a lawyer and offered to represent me.

Without them, I would have faltered underneath the tide of emotion. In England, one needed to have a solicitor specifically for these matters plus a barrister. He found me an angel called Kathryn Peat who later found me my barrister. Together we walked the path to find a reasonable way forward. It was hard. Johnny became my trustee after the settlement. A man I could trust with our hearts.

I decided that Monksbridge was no longer the place I wanted to raise the children. Plus, the memories were too difficult to transform there. So I began to search for another. Miv Watts continued to live with us after the event for Lily as her marriage had dissolved as well. She became a great help. Together we searched the nearby countryside and beyond. We held each other along the journey repairing our broken hearts.

I had many variables to consider besides finding the house. I had to decide on the county, the schools, how far from London, cost of living, etc. My life had gone beyond the stability of buying avocados, packing of school lunches and doing things with a partner, I loved. I had to learn fast how to carry most of the load. Thank God, I had help.

In England, the school system is such that sometimes one has to find a place in a school for your child years ahead. This I found difficult to understand as an American. So not only was it a task to find a suitable and affordable home, but there had to be a school locally that had to have places for the children. When we lived in Hook End, they had gone to a Montessori School called "Dolphin." When we moved, I wished for a Montessori School, but there wasn't one near us when we lived in Monksbridge.

We moved them several times. Honestly, I searched and searched but did not find my heart's desire in our area. They were just not forward thinking or creative enough for me. I strongly felt that a school should draw out what lies innate in a child, not to just develop one's memory for accepted facts of what a society wanted. I wanted them to be in an environment, which encouraged them to really think from their soul purpose. Not much to ask? Seems it was.

One day Miv came home smiling with a paper in her hand. It was a black and white description of a house called Brockhurst in East Grinstead, West Sussex. It was on the market but not opened to be viewed. England had experienced terrible storms and many trees were down on the property, especially around its lake. Even near us at Monksbridge, oak trees had fallen everywhere, especially along the main avenue up to Hampton Court.

It was a very strange time. We had had a drought for years and all the tree roots were shallow looking for water. However, this rain passed over the dried surfaces. The strong hurricane like winds just toppled them over like bowling pins. It felt as though something was missing from nature. A feeling in the air as though Death had covered us with her cloak. All along the road laid these great beings, never to stand again. Traffic slowly inching along as the men cleared them away. It was so sad.

One day Miv and I decided to go on an adventure into West Sussex to, at least, see what we could see of Brockhurst. She was good like that, always fearless, ready to have an adventure. So off we went like two explorers. We drove up the long drive and around the back. No one was home. It was like a fairy castle. I said, 'This is it! I want it!" Miv replied, "Ginge', you must see more houses!" "Miv I don't want to lose it. It is the one! I know it! Besides, there is a Steiner Waldorf school nearby. I checked and they have space for All of the children!"

All the pieces were falling into place. We just had to sell Monksbridge and buy Brockhurst. David did advance me the money so it could go smoothly. He also came and approved of the school. So the next thing to do was redecorate, pack and move. I had my team. Miv helped me with my choices in decorating: from wallpaper, to curtains, to furniture. Warwick carried them out with the help of a project manager.

We did have a few moments deciding whether to do French Provincial, Miv's love, or Art Nouveaux, which I favor. She said, "Ginge' here is a chance to totally start new!" Interesting thought, but to make such a change was too much for me at the time, considering what other changes were occurring. I needed something familiar that I loved and felt like home. Therefore, Art Nouveaux it was and Fortuni fabrics from Venice. (Love, Love, Love.)

During this time, I traveled with Lily to the States for she was speaking at a Seven Rays Conference in New Jersey. There I walked amongst a different group of people far away from Rock 'n' Roll. As I sat in the audience and listened to the speakers, I discovered that there is another type of man and woman in the world. Men who consciously seek to reveal their hearts without fear, but with dignity. Women who had the courage, who dared to stand for equality with compassion as bridges for humanity. The men stood tall in their masculine strength and wisdom, their edges softened by their hearts. The women walked radiant in their shining beauty. Love and Wisdom held hands. I remember thinking that if I am to have another relationship let it be more spiritually conscious.

One morning I was walking together down the corridor with Lily and one of the principal organizers, Marianne Castleleno. As we turned a corner, the door to one of the classrooms was open and I noticed a man deep in thought placing something on the desk. He was tall, wearing black trousers and a black short jacket over a white tailored shirt. His long auburn hair tied back in a short ponytail to keep it from his eyes. I only saw him from the back, but I knew he was elegant, poised, and radiated such tenderness.

As we walked, I listened to Marianne and Lily's conversation. They were discussing who, out of all the presenters, should be on the panel that evening to discuss "Sex in Relationships from an Esoteric point of view." I piped up and said, while pointing back to the classroom, "I think the man back there would be a good choice. Who is he?" They both looked and a little giggle appeared as Lily said, "Oh, yes. That is a good idea. Nico Thelman, he would be perfect amongst all the others." She often referred to him as her grandson. It was an interesting evening listening to and observing different viewpoints from all the speakers.

As I sat there, a warmth arose in my being, a new inspiration for my future. I no longer needed to hide my vision nor my journey of returning to my soul. Like Jonathan Seagull, I had returned home. Here before me were my peers, contemporaries in heart and mind. The aloneness I had felt over the years was morphing into becoming All-one. There were others, who dared to Live and not Exist. The Joy of Relief started to wash away the pain with inspiration. There was life after David Gilmour. I would be ok.

After the discussion, I approached Nico Thelman with a few questions. I did not notice that he was speaking to someone when I approached. We laughed often in years to come of the moment I got through his bodyguards. He remembers how my blonde curls held the light and my eyes sparkled with such enthusiasm. I inquired if he ever came to England as he was from Belgium. He said, "Yes," that he would be speaking in Camberley at the Theosophical Society in a few months. I mentioned that I would be there with Lily as well and left the conversation with "I shall see you there."

The next morning I had to leave early to get to NYC to meet with Dr. Engel. It had been his birthday and I had a small gift for him. Lily and I were having breakfast at our table when I noticed Nico in the queue from a distance. He had a bowl of porridge in his hands, walking towards us. His hands were like fine bone china as he gracefully held his breakfast like a precious treasure. He warmly said good morning to us both, had brief words with Lily, then walked away to sit at another table leaving a whisper of his greeting in our hearts. Something was growing between us. We would meet again, I hoped.

When I returned to the UK, Brockhurst was in full swing. The floorboards were up making way for new electric wires and an internal sound system. Stone floors that Miv had gotten from a derelict monastery in France had arrived. There was a new fitted kitchen and conservatory under construction. A little working through of opinions with all the creative crew stood before me. It was normal.

Brockhurst had a wonderful minstrel gallery. Miv suggested we should use a special painting technique upon the walls, similar to what Leonardo and other Renaissance masters used as a foundation under their frescos. Layer upon layer of gesso was applied in various tones of blood red (in our case), plus ochers and greens in the upper hall. Sanding then revealed a movement of subtle colors. A final layer of wax enhanced the luster.

Throughout the process, we sealed off the hallway trying to keep the dust away from the rest of the house. It was like something out of a science fiction movie. Did we dare to pass? What creature hid within? Each day, for weeks, the specialists Bernie and Bernie, emerged a different color, each time covered from the dust storm they created. Tornadoes of color swirled within their bubble, and unfortunately, into the rest of the house. It did create a problem. Thank God, the end result was worth it. We survived!

We converted the back laundry room into the mess hall as there was an Aga and we could be warm. I made homemade soup for sometimes 25 people. They loved it. As it turned out, I was an extremely creative soup cook and recorded all my recipes. Fresh bread was brought from the bakers each day, English tea and assorted biscuits were on hand as an extra way to further honor my crew. The children roller skated down the length of the house and played in the sand piles in the drive. One had to be a juggler of many aspects on a project like this one. But we did it!

The opening party was a challenge. Warwick was still putting up wallpaper until the final hour and, at the same time, trying to light the fire in the main hall without drying the paste. The last strip was up and in time for him to have a shower and put on his finery. It was a grand party. Dreamy and Tim Hain sang in the studio across the garden while we danced. Alice was supposed to do a trio performance with Miv and Claire Finnie, but she was too shy. Joy filled the air and went on into the early morning.

Many came and blessed our new beginning. Smiling friends and neighbors packed the house. Most of our crew stayed over and one by one fell asleep in various corners on the floor or sofas. I think I got to bed around 4:00 a.m. and slept late. I awoke full of happiness and staggered downstairs ready to clean the aftermath. It was gone. Spic-and-Span. The crew had done it all while I slept then vanished. What a gift!

A new cycle began. The children went to school. Emo stayed in our cottage. The builders were gone. I went to my studio to paint. Jeremy Gale taught Cecil Classes there on Wednesday. In the morning, I went for walks with our Lady dog in the forest below on the dis-used railroad track. Sometimes Twix, our cat, would follow us through the field of grazing sheep. In the summer, the children swam in the pool and on alternate weekends, David would take them to London. Life began to have a rhythm.

'Angel of Compassion'
"Angel voices ever singing"

Artwork by Ginger Gilmour

CHAPTER 78

LIFE AFTER DAVID
THE MOMENT OF RETURN

ANGEL-VOICES ever singing
Round thy throne of Light,
ANGEL-HARPS forever ringing,
Rest not day nor night
Thousands only live to bless thee
And confess thee
Lord of Might.

Thou who art beyond the farthest
Mortal eye can scan,
Can it be that thou regardest'
Songs of sinful man?
Can we know that thou art near us,
And wilt hear us?
Yes, we can.

E. G. Monk 1861 [1]

BRIGHT SIDE OF THE MOON

Before I continue my story of my journey to the "Bright Side of the Moon" further, I felt it important to share an insight I had today. Ever since I was little, there has been a flavor, a fragrance of energy, which has always guided me. Sometimes it has been full of grace, others a warning just before I touched the electric barbed wire fence. Fortunately, despite many challenges along the way, I feel, it mainly has been full of grace for which I am eternally grateful. Step by step, it has come closer and closer, this fragrance. Many methods, many teachings have guided me until this very moment. Today, a new awakening is guiding me. After many years of searching, the cherry is being placed upon the cake.

Around the time that my mother was passing over and other private matters were full on, I had a vision of the Christ coming to me. This was a new experience. I had heard of many, who spoke of the appearance of Christ, but was suspicious. I wanted Truth not illusions. Consequently, I found myself along a different path to God than the religion, in which I had been baptized. My family and I were in Florida during my Mother's last days. I held the torch for many but in my bedroom, I cried. It was a tense time, the depth of which I held to myself, always smiling, consoling, listening to others, responding, guiding. Then one night Christ appeared in my bedroom at the foot of my bed. It was so real, beyond doubt. He spoke to me so softly, full of heart, "*Ginger, I have a message from God for you. He says not to worry that it has to be this way for his Divine plan to work out for you, your children and your family.*"

The next morning I felt differently, full of inner Trust and Joy. Had I found my way back to Christ? The days continued full of things to do and decide. My mother was in her final days with us. While she was still clear, she spoke to me. We were alone. Her voice changed as though speaking from some inner place beyond the room, "Charlie, I need to tell you something. Please sit down. I have a secret I have often wanted to share with you but didn't."

Gosh, I thought to myself what skeleton is about to be revealed to me as I sat on the bed? The story of Stephen having a different father had been enough within our family dynamics many years ago. She continued, "It's been very difficult being your mother." Gulp. The air in the room grew silent and suddenly filled with light, as I waited for the story to continue.

Her black eyes sparkled as she shifted her weight leaning upon her pillows. "Charlie, you are an Angel! A real Angel! And I didn't know how to raise an Angel. There weren't any books to help me. I couldn't tell anybody either. I didn't know why God had given me an Angel to care for as I didn't feel worthy." I was amazed at the story she shared. I reflected upon the moment that Elizabeth Collins stood at the top of her stairs. Her last words to me that day was, "*Ginger, don't forget your Angels*!" Since that day, I painted Angels. I believed in Angels. I spent years, hoping to see an Angel. *But to BE an Angel*?

I sat on the edge of her bed mesmerized as she continued, "I just wanted you to know this and perhaps you would forgive me." "What is there to forgive, Mom?" I asked. A tear dropped from her eye as she said, "I might have been too hard on you trying to protect you. And I could not treat you any different than your brothers and sisters." Her breath went softer, fulfilled from the release, the story told, she could now rest. I drove home in a daze. Those moments in my mother's final hours touched me deeply. My life perspective was changing, adjusting, and reviewing all that I have had as a guiding vision influencing my life.

She passed away in late October 2013. In the last nine months, I have had more visitations from Christ full of warmth and Love. I have come full circle to know what has always been in my heart is Him and God. Many will question this, but the reality for me is the Love building in my heart. The feeling of safety grows with each day. The dream of Love is manifesting beyond all I ever imagined was possible. Where I had many questions, many judgments before, I see now they were man made, pale images keeping me away from this Love, which speaks louder. It always has. Goodness, Truth, Kindness, Beauty, Wisdom were my instinctive qualities that stood within all the storms. I just didn't know the source. Who knows if I am an Angel. What I do know is that I am a human being, born to be of service.

Today, I listened to the Angelic Voices of a Choir at Boxgrove Priory, West Sussex, England. I have returned to church where many kind hearts were waiting to greet me. They sang from the heavens on high, (*Angel Voices*) the hymn at the top of this chapter. Stirring memories within me to share with you and opening the doorway of my heart further. The veils are lifting from what went before. I see more clearly the bright path that has always called me to return to the foot of God. I further understand my soul purpose to serve Humanity. And I dare to say that here, to all of you. In Jesus, I have become to discover another part of Me.

After my mother passed, I returned to England, and I wrote this prose to honor her heart, her life and our last moments:

OUR LAST SMILE

The most intimate and transformative moment of all, was when my own mother's eyes would meet mine for the last time.

Her eyes would look into my very soul and my eyes would meet her there... my smile was the last smile she saw from me, it was the last time she would reach to kiss my face, to touch it tenderly.

The gaze upon which we held, stretched across chasms of time and star studded space, beyond our earthly perceptions, and then... there she was in all her splendor, there I was in all my splendor, there we were as radiant light expansive, free flowing, and in bliss.

I travelled and journeyed upon our Love. From the edges of infinity, I called forth to Remember and thus it came. It flooded into my awareness, rising up from my body and was birthed into my life, taking the form of a timeless body of work revealing the workings of the Soul and the silence that midwives our Consciousness.

Indeed, my life has never been the same.

© Ginger Gilmour

MY FINAL WORDS TO HER

Dearest Mom

As the sun set into the horizon
I pondered the Moment
Our souls came together as One…
You, as my Mother;
I, as your Daughter.

We have traveled many journeys
Together through this Lifetime
And perhaps many before.
Our Hearts touching
In Love & Beauty
Bringing Heaven
To Earth.

I hear the Angels rejoicing
For what we have achieved
Through Life's Challenges
You, as my Guardian
My Protector in the Storm;
I as the Artist
Creator of Beauty & Kindness.

I am eternally grateful
To share the divine pathway
With YOU,
My Mother.

May peace be with you!

© Ginger Gilmour

'SEATED ANGEL'

1998

'Reflection'
"Sunlight of the Heart"
Artwork by Ginger Gilmour

CHAPTER 79

TRANSFORMING ANGER

1992

I received a phone call from Marguerite Gaffney telling me about the Whole Life Expo in Los Angeles. She said that I could place some artwork there, if I wanted. It was a big step for me to venture into the Art world of California, but, yet, I decided to do it. I reviewed which paintings needed finishing so that I had a reasonable body of work. I had a few months to do this and set to work. One of them was to be *Reflections*. The one that I earlier described was like painting "Sunlight" instead of raindrops of tears. To me, it was a joyous experience every time I looked at it. It evoked Love in my heart.

I had taken to putting it in the kitchen on our welsh dresser between the colorful Clarice Cliff plates. One Sunday, David's parents, Doug and Sylvia, came to visit us at Brockhurst. We had a wonderful Sunday feast, which is an English tradition. We always looked forward to these family get togethers. Sylvia and I had gone upstairs with the children leaving Doug reading the Sunday papers in the kitchen. When I returned, he was looking rather remorseful, staring at my painting. I asked him if he was all right when he remarked, "I think you should turn that painting to the wall!" Doug was always rather direct with his words, but it still brought a tear to my heart. It was as though he had no sensitivity to the pain I was feeling in regards to David leaving. Plus, the courage I needed to believe my work would stand with others in L.A.

I waited a few minutes as I regained my composure before asking him, "Why?" He replied, "Because it holds me, possesses me, engulfs me. It beckons me to go deeper into its imagery and at the same time gives me something back that nourishes me. I am insatiable for something I cannot describe. I cannot get enough! Therefore, I would have to turn it around to get away."

That was the most special comment that Doug had ever given to me. He was a man that was very private with his emotions as with most of the British of his generation. At first, I found this quality difficult to understand, but I have come to respect its nature. It is as if—they value the importance of silence—their words having purpose when they speak.

During my granddaughter's last visit to the UK from the States, she asked me, "Nana, why are the English, so quiet?" I told her that every culture has something special and for the English it is "To BE Quiet" and once you get to know them they are your best friends! For me, the air breathes this quiet, even in the city. Sometimes I even feel they float along on their silence.

Sadly, it is changing with the fast pace of modern society. It is leading us away from the silent embrace of nature. This is why I went on the Quest to the *Bright Side*. It has always been with me to seek it in the flowers, the trees, the sea and most of all the Love of our creator. Forgive me, if I say it again…not to forget that we all have a spark of the Divine within us to awaken. It is the key to harmony.

Los Angeles here I come once again, but this time I was the artist. First, I was to stay in Santa Barbara with one of my BFF's Marguerite, who is always a blessing to be with. Her home is always a Sanctuary of Love for my children and me. I met with a poster printing company who she recommended so I could print three posters for the Whole Life event: *Box of Illusions, Earth–A Place Where Angels Learn to Fly* and *Terra Madre.*

Cecil used to say that when reproducing one's artwork the colors are often affected by the tones of the film and equally the energy of the photographer and the printer. He said that one day it would come time for us to reproduce our work. What would be important for us to do was to increase the intensity of the colors to compensate, so I went to the printers with this in mind.

I was a tad nervous to start, but they were masters! Not only did they take notes of every possible aspect in its subtle tones, but they also were the first to print digitally. Such a new and wonderful experience it was. In addition, the man working the color ratios said that printing my images brought him great peace. I felt such a novice. He gave me confidence.

The event finally came and I was prepared with the help of Marguerite and her family. I was sharing a large room with several artists. We sat in chairs just beside one of the doors not noticed. My work was hanging in the left corner of the room while the other artist was to the right. We found it interesting to watch the flow of visitors throughout the day. Some would walk directly to the left as though pulled by a magnet ignoring the other part of the room. Some would do just the opposite. It was such a knee-jerk response that we found it extremely noticeable time and time again. It happened every day for the duration of the Expo. It was something for me to contemplate.

One of the highlights for me was to go to a lecture by Kübler Ross, an American psychiatrist who was a pioneer in near-death studies. Her lecture focused on the five stages of grief in the process of dying. She said that there are five archetypal stages, (known by the acronym DABDA, which are Denial, Anger, Bargaining, Depression and lastly Acceptance). When she got to Anger, a light bulb lit inside my head. She said that anger was one of the primordial emotions that triggered our alert button to awaken and seek protection. She observed these stages in anyone who experienced a life-threatening or life-altering event.

Kübler first developed this model based on her observations of people suffering from terminal illness. She later expanded her theory to apply to any form of catastrophic personal loss such as the death of a loved one, the loss of a job or income, divorce or major rejection, drug addiction, incarceration, the onset of a disease or chronic illness, an infertility diagnosis, as well as many tragedies and disasters (and even minor losses).

Why this affected me so much was, not only, how it applied to my circumstances regarding the changes occurring in my life, but she also brought to our attention that there was a positive and necessary aspect of anger. Out of all the stages anger seemed to touch me the most. Supposedly, anger gave one the strength to confront. I didn't know how. For me, all anger was negative. I had grown up with the angry eyes of my mother and shouting from my father. I put anger in a bag and said, "*NO WAY!*"

Therefore, what Kübler Ross said explains why I didn't know how to defend myself. Her words rested inside my mind and heart for some time, but soon the seeds started to grow. I started to change. I am sure I had a few accidents along the way, some shaky outbursts. And even some tsunamis, as the suppressed force found its freedom and ultimate purpose with wisdom. To this day, the Tsunamis are still revealed, transformed into a summer breeze so as True Peace will remain.

'WOMAN and 2 ANGELS'

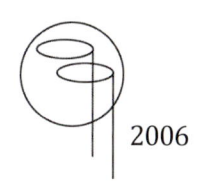

2006

I wonder
What's God's plan?

CHAPTER 80

CAMBERLEY WITH LILY
REFLECTIONS

After returning from the States, my next adventure with Lily was just a few weeks away. The Theosophical Society in Camberley, Surrey, UK had asked her to give a lecture on Mental Color Therapy. I asked her if she could give me an explanation about their philosophy. It was new to me. Lily explained briefly that Theosophy had no dogmas, no doctrines, no rituals and no initiations. At Camberley, the Theosophical Group explored and discussed new ways of understanding science, philosophy and religion that would bring many spiritual beliefs closer together with modern science. She found it was an open podium to present a wide spectrum of ideas.

She said that Theosophy was not a religion. Each person was free to believe and practice whatever he or she chooses with the hope to live a spiritual life, both individually and collectively. There were no prescriptive rules or procedures for doing so, which is why, over the years, Lily spoke at their seminars. I believe She was one of the wise elders and a forerunner in the living of true compassion and love. This philosophy suited my way of being at the time. I see now, it gave me freedom to clear the program and allow a new channel to become that would eventually lead to God.

There were many lectures. I was fascinated and in many ways felt a child with the grownups. A toddler discovering what was in the cupboard that was now unlocked. One lecturer, Dr. Van Buren, spoke on the origins of Acupuncture. He was the founder and president of the International College of Oriental Medicine based in East Grinstead, which was the town where I had just moved to with the children. My ears stood at attention as he told us a story about our soul's journey to Earth.

Within the Oriental philosophy, there is a myth about the days before the soul leaves Heaven. God tells the little one to go into Heaven's pharmacy and choose all the things necessary to make its journey to Earth. The little soul with delight filled its baskets with lots of precious treasures. With each, his little light glowed brighter and brighter as they shone like diamonds with the essence of Heaven. Finally, the moment came to descend the golden stairway to fulfill his task in God's plan. He told the little one that an angel would bring his treasure later. Therefore, in Faith, he began his journey. The only problem was, God did not tell him the delivery date and he forgot to ask!

I have often wondered what was in my basket. What was my soul task and purpose in the plan since listening to that story? Dr. Van Buren also spoke about his clinic, which was down the road from where I now lived in East Grinstead. I was inspired by his lecture so much that over the weekend I made an appointment. My first experience with acupuncture went on weekly for over a year. What transformed for me was amazing. I discovered that there was a little voice inside crying, saying, "*I am soooo VERY tired. Help me, please?*" And it did. I was restored and the little voice went away. I still remember that moment when, what seemed like a miracle, my energy returned to me. I was able to walk forward into my future able to be a single Mom.

Nico Thelman, whom I had met in New Jersey with Lily, was next to give his presentation. He did a demonstration of how connected we all are to each other. He asked me to come up on stage and be his assistant. His presence was very charismatic as he asked me to hold a light bulb while he spoke. I really do not recall much except that at some moment it lit. The audience and I filled with awe and wonder. That is his forte; I was to discover, to reveal the wonder and magic of life beyond all philosophies, religion and science.

Over the course of those days in Camberley, Nico, his group and I grew closer. They were to stay longer in the UK since they wanted to go to Glastonbury. Apparently, they built an octagonal meditation structure in the Ramala Center a few years ago where they stayed, worked and lived. On our journey, they shared many stories of its creation. I asked if I could come with them because the energy of attraction was getting stronger. I wanted to learn more about the stillness and wonder. I felt God was pointing the way. So I invited them to Brockhurst and I would drive us all to Glastonbury.

Annie Rowland, who had returned to be our nanny, prepared dinner for our arrival back home. She cooked a dinner fit for a king and queen. She always did for she was so creative. She was my sous-chef and her food held so much love. It was still daylight, so everyone wandered down to the lake hidden amongst the Rhododendrons, beyond the great lawn, until dinner. Later, throughout the rest of the evening, I put on meditative soothing music as we spoke together.

Our plan was to leave early, so it was early to bed. Annie and I made places for them to sleep. In the morning, Nico shared how they all thought I had monks chanting in my basement all night. OOPS! I had left on the auto-reverse of my sound system—playing a CD of monks chanting. I apologized. All was forgiven, as it did not really disturb their slumber, in fact, it helped. We did have a chuckle, as we ate our muesli, and for many years into the future. I am not sure if I will EVER live down the night the monks chanted.

Miriam's Birthday
With husband Lennie
Driver Hank-extraordinaire
Watts Chapel
Compton, Surrey, UK

CHAPTER 81

WATTS CHAPEL
ANOTHER JOURNEY BEGAN

The children were away with David and I was free to go on the adventure to Glastonbury. I had an English equivalent of a SUV, so there was plenty room for us all to travel comfortably. Key was my navigator sitting next to me in the front seat with the map on her lap. Nico sat way in the back, his tall body curled up so he could fit. He liked moments of being by himself. As we drove along, I shared stories with them about Watts Chapel in Compton, Surrey that was on route. Key was a specialist in Art History and loved Angels but had never heard of it.

Watts Chapel is a Gothic Revival Chapel and Mortuary. It was constructed from 1896 to 1898 with virtually every village resident involved, resulting in creating an interior, which is a magical fusion of art nouveau angels, and Celtic influences. It was the brain storm idea of a local resident artist Mary Fraser-Tytler, the wife of Victorian era painter and sculptor George Frederic Watts. Today there is, also, an Art Gallery containing a large amount of Paintings by the late George Frederic Watts who is known as the Michelangelo of England. His most known is *Hope*, which is of a woman blind-folded sitting on the Earth holding a lyre. My favorite too!

As we walked up the path through the cemetery, towards the chapel, I was transported back to the moment when I organized a surprise birthday experience for one of my dearest friends, Miriam

Freedman several years ago. It was early in the morning on the day of her birthday when I sent Hank from Berryhurst cars in a Rolls Royce to pick her up and her husband, Lennie, who knew about the secret adventure.

Days later Miriam retold the story to me of that day. There was a knock at the door. She wasn't expecting anyone. As she opened the door there stood a very elegant man in a suit. He inquired, "Excuse me, is this the home of Lord and Lady Freedman?" Miriam chuckled with Lennie looking over her shoulder listening. She responded, "Well, there is a Mr. and Mrs. Freedman, who lives here but we are not a Lord or Lady of Royalty!" Hank smiled and said with his deep masculine voice, "Well, you are today, Me Lady! I have been asked to take you out for the day on a birthday adventure. There is your car for the day and I am your Chauffeur."

Miriam was shorter than Hank, and had to look past him to see where he was pointing. She had noticed the car parked across the street and had wondered which one of her neighbors was having a royal visit. She gasped with surprise, wondering who was behind this as Hank asked, "Are you ready?" She nodded looking back at Lennie who also agreed. So the day began as they entered the car. Hank did ask as he put on his hat and started the car, "Me Lady and Lord Freedman, I would be most grateful if you did not try to engage me with questions about where, who, and when, while we are driving. Agreed?" They nodded in agreement and sat back in the comfort of the back seat.

Miriam and Lennie lived near Hendon, which was in North London and close to the motorway. As the car turned onto the M25, Miriam's curiosity rose. Lennie was charming and patient as he pretended he did not know where they were going. They approached Heathrow Airport as the thought entered her mind, "PARIS?" but no that was not where they were going. They passed Gatwick Airport and it came again, "PARIS?" but alas, it was not where she was going. She was confused and yet excited. Miriam loved adventures. This one topped them all.

After about an hour just past Gatwick Airport, Hank pulled over into a car park of a disheveled local pub. It seems there was a cluster of balloons on the door. Miriam looked at Lennie and said, "Have we driven for almost two and a half hours to come to an ordinary pub? There was a better one just around the corner of our home." They got out of the car to stretch their legs while Hank had gone inside. Miriam checked the creases in her dress trying to maintain her composure. When Hank returned thanking them for their patience, for he had needed to go to the gents. In reality, he was phoning me to check if all was ready for their arrival.

I had arranged for their daughter, Alison, and son, Martin, plus many others from Mrs. Tweedie's group and close friends to meet at the chapel. Hank needed to stall for twenty minutes more for not everyone had arrived yet. Walking out to the car he motioned for them, saying, "May you both get back into the car so our journey can continue?" as he revealed a bottle of champagne and two glasses from behind his back. "But first, let's celebrate!"

That brought a heartfelt smile of acceptance to their faces as he opened the bottle with a pop. The bubbles softened Miriam's questioning as Hank reminded her of their initial agreement and praised them for their patience. "You will soon be there," as they drove away into the rising sun. Finally! The car pulled up at a wooden ancient English gate on a little country road amongst the hedgerows. Hank graciously opened the car door for the Lady and Lord in a royal manner. As her foot stepped onto the gravel she exclaimed, "You have brought me to a cemetery?" Just at that moment I appeared taking photographs of her first expressions. She exclaimed, "I knew it! It was you!"

Miriam was still in a daze trying to figure out what was next. Lennie and I escorted her up the path through the cemetery towards the chapel. I told her about the history of how all the villagers had made the bricks and the artwork of the building. She thought it special, but couldn't quite grasp why I had brought her to this place. I guided her further, "You must come inside. It is magnificent!" As we opened the large wooden door, the sunlight blinded us from seeing inside the darkness for the surprise that awaited.

We entered, me holding Miriam's hand, guiding her into the shadows. Her eyes filled with tears as she saw all of her family and friends standing in a circle holding a candle in front of many angels, on the wall just behind them. Soft tones of "HAPPY BIRTHDAY" began as she passed from each person to greet them. Lennie walked close behind his cheeks wet from his tears as well. Joy created temporarily a lump in their hearts. As she stopped before each person, their Love and Gratitude was shared for the day that Miriam was born and walked into their lives.

I had permission for us to have a picnic on the lawn outside the gallery. We laid down a checkered blanket and colored pillows on the grass. The Rolls Royce had a huge trunk for everything needed to create the final touches of the fantasy. More champagne, cheeses, breads, quiches, pickles, cake and candles kept coming forth from the baskets fit for an affair from the book *Alice in Wonderland*. It was not an "Unbirthday Party," but "Hey, it's your Birthday!" The memory lives on in our hearts. We often laugh together, about this Birthday adventure. Miriam always says, "*I knew it was you who organized this! Who else had the imagination and the ability to do such a thing for a friend?*"

'GOLDEN DAWN'

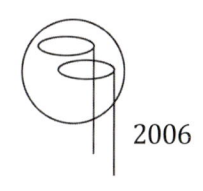

2006

Swimming with Dolphins
Sanctuary Bay, Freeport, Grand Bahamas
1992

CHAPTER 82

SWIMMING WITH DOLPHINS

1992

During the Whole Life Expo, I met up with Elizabeth Fortune again. We shared stories of our lives since our last meeting in San Diego with Lily and the Dolphins. She suggested that I should bring the children to Freeport, in the Grand Bahamas for a "Dolphin Experience." Every December she organized these adventures at the Sanctuary Bay, organized by UNEXSO. Having met and worked together with Horace Dobbs, president of International Dolphin Watch in the UK, I knew the healing powers of Dolphins for the heart and other disharmonies. I decided that she was right and would book a dolphin experience for all of us with her that next December. It would be my Christmas present for the children, Annie (nanny) and myself.

So we waited with great anticipation for the day to come. A week before, Annie, my four children and I were ready for our next adventure. With suitcases packed, backpacks full of things to do during our journey. We climbed into the limousine waiting in the driveway on our morning of departure. As we got onto the plane, the healing already began, for smiles and excitement was filling our hearts. We were happy again.

For years, we had had dreams to swim with dolphins. Every summer in the Mediterranean, we often had close encounters with them, for they would swim alongside our boat as we surfed the waves. They are remarkable creatures. Just their presence brings joy. We often sat on the bow of the boat visualizing for them to come. Calling for them with Love. Each time the children were learning how to speak to the animals with their thoughts. And come they would.

We stayed in a modest hotel complex near the beach. The balmy sea air brought familiar sounds of the steel drums during the early evening. It was nearly Christmas and it was strange to see Santa Claus and Christmas decorations on the palm trees in the local shopping center. AND it was HOT! Hearing "Oh Come all ye Faithful" and "Little Town of Bethlehem" on steel drums was a bit surreal, a bit out of place. Alice found it too much like Disneyland devoid of the local culture. The West had overtaken another island.

She was sixteen and very aware of these things. We had come a few days early so that we could acclimatize to the time change. The children were troupers about this, even knowing not to enter the noonday sun uncovered or without sunblock and hats. Lindos summers had trained them well. Touring had developed less of an expectation of hotel food compared to Mum and Dad's home cookin', if not the Ritz. And the Ritz it was not.

We walked to a boat ferry, which would take us to the lagoon from our hotel, where we would meet Elizabeth each morning. She was highly qualified in facilitating deeper encounters with dolphins. My first proof of this was back in San Diego with her in an earlier chapter. Where, despite they were captive in a limited space, I was graced to have such an unforgettable union with them just leaning over the edge. So I arranged this trip in the hope that it would go beyond anything so far. How wonderful would it be for us to swim with them, to stroke them, to be pulled along and play with them? I wanted especially for the children to have this opportunity. A dream come true.

Our first encounter was with a few Bottlenose dolphins in one of the side pools. We were ready with our wetsuits, flippers and goggles. A local facilitator would attract them with fish before we were to enter. They were HUGE! Apparently, skilled caretakers raised them because they were very human friendly. It was their birth home, but equally, they were set free in the night to be in the deeper waters. They returned to swim with the others and us who came for the "Dolphin Experience," but most probably, they really came for breakfast, lunch, tea and perhaps "Elevenses" (snacks) like the Hobbits in Lord of the Rings.

I just watched our DVD last night of our group swims in the Sanctuary Lagoon. I remember Annie was frightened. I had no idea after all our years in Lindos how much she was frightened of the water. Elizabeth was great in working with individuals with fear, No pressure, only if you want to. Eventually, Annie did go in and touched them with a smile. There is a film so that she doesn't forget the day she transformed the fear and had fun. Despite being a controlled experience, it still was amazing. They are such happy creatures.

One day the kids and Annie returned for lunch to the hotel while I stayed in the quiet waiting for my private session, which was in the afternoon. Everyone had gone, leaving me alone in the silence for a siesta and a bite to eat, I assume. While I sat on the edge of the wooden pier, eyes closed, feeling the sun upon my face, I decided to practice visualizing for the dolphins to appear. I created dream pictures of them swimming towards me. The water was perfectly flat.

Except for the occasional bird diving for fish and the sound of a speedboat in the distance, the lagoon seemed deserted. A meditative energy took me inward when suddenly it was broken by the sound of squawking. I opened my eyes, and to my amazement, there were two baby dolphins smiling, joyfully. Their heads were just above the surface of the water, cackling, as though they were saying, "*Hello, Hello. You called? Here* we are!"

One of the attendants approached me as I sat dazzled upon the long wooden pier that reached out into the sunlit waters. He was tall with native dark skin wearing bright colors and the company jacket and hat. Looking down at me, he said, "Mam, you are free to swim, if you want to be with them," as he pointed at the baby dolphins who were now playing in the distance with their mum. "REALLY? I can swim with them on my own? NOW?" I said, not quite believing what I had heard. He shook his head in affirmation, "Yes Mam. You can. It will be all right. They came to you."

My heart lifted in the truth of the moment as I proceeded to put on my flippers and mask. Entering the water, they returned, and swam beside me guiding me out further into the lagoon. We played, diving together, in and out in a parallel rhythmic motion between each other. Then the mother came to join us. She started to push into me then flip away and dive. Again and again, she repeated this until finally I got the hint. I had to swim more like a dolphin! It worked! We swam. We dove in harmony within the crystal rays of the sun. I was a dolphin!

Part of our Dolphin Experience was to go out to sea and swim with them in their natural habitat. As we went along the coast, the dolphins followed us as the attendant threw silver gifts of fish into their open mouths. We moored in the shallow crystal blue water over the white sand below. We could stand and play together, smiling from ear to ear. Laughter reflected upon the water.

On the way back, Alice remembers getting upset about what one of the attendants said, "Lots of people project different ideas upon the dolphins, but really they are just mammals who are hungry." But that was his opinion, for we knew they were more than hungry mammals, we knew it differently thanks to Horace Dobbs! And my personal experiences.

We were very familiar with how Horace helped many over the years with his Operation Sunshine. He has brought healing to human beings through interaction with dolphins. This initiative and other wonderful activities under his care and inspiration continue to help children and adults, especially those with physical and emotional dis-harmonies. Horace is a forerunner in the world bringing the healing power of the dolphin to mankind.

I did an exhibition with him at the Open University in Milton Keynes, for the 2003 International Dolphin Watch Convention. My sculpture, *Dolphina*, was on the stage while the presenters spoke about their global work and my humanitarian series was in the foyer.

Horace unveiled his new initiative to help heal humanity. His new project was a blow-up dome, which was portable. Inside on the walls projected a virtual reality video of dolphins swimming with background sounds of them communicating, as they do with one another underwater. The Dome could travel from hospital to hospital, school to school, hospice to hospice where the need be. What he discovered in his journey is that the need for healing humanity is great, but at the same time, the dolphins need protection from too many untrained dolphin facilitators.

He has approached governments around the world to form laws, to make sure the dolphins are protected from the fanfare of the non-professionals. He encouraged the forming of legislation so a license would be required that insured a standard code of ethics and understanding for individuals who wanted to give Dolphin Experiences. It had become a fad and the dolphin's protection was a concern.

During our time in the Bahamas, another experience that was available for us was to go scuba diving in deep water. David and I had gotten Paddy Diving Certificates while in Hawaii, but it was a long long time ago. I needed a refresher course and more. My last experience scuba diving with David in Ceylon put the shivers up my back thinking of its memory. Never again was encoded into my mind. Elizabeth said that she and another diver could help me with that if I was willing. We would start in a pool first to get familiar with the equipment and the sensations. We did this for one week until I was confident. Then the day came and we joined others on a boat that would take us out into deeper waters.

Both Elizabeth and the other diver promised that they would stick with me all the time, even hold my hand if necessary. The tanks were heavy as I slowly climbed down the ladder into the waves. My eyes smitten from the salt water of my wet hair, I began putting on my mask. There were many of us in the group and I was in the queue. As I got into the depth of the water, I followed the others into the sunlight rays below. They were swimming along quite fast when I stopped to wait for Elizabeth and my other guardian. They were not there! Fear seized in my stomach. I waited but it grew stronger.

In fact, I felt that there was a shark nearby and images kept appearing in my imagination. The group was disappearing into the distance. I was alone. I was frantic so I turned back as I could still see the bottom of the boat. I had enough control not to bolt to the surface. I didn't want to get the bends. I swallowed my panic as best that I could. Wondering what had happened to them.

I climbed the ladder to discover that my promised guardians were still there. I cried, holding back my anger, "Where were you? You promised!" Apparently, some local official's daughter demanded their attention and was having trouble getting into her gear. Her father was one of their sponsors and she played it. Elizabeth was stuck behind the commotion not able to get down.

I sat on the seat in the front of the boat to gain my composure. My breathing was in panic mode. Elizabeth sat with me trying to calm me down. She tried to encourage me to go down again, to let go of my fear. She promised to stay with me. It didn't work. "Never again" arose in my mind. As I pondered what she said, most of the group were returning from down below. "There was a shark!" they exclaimed. So my intuition was working, sending me a red flag. Actually, the local official's daughter was possibly my savior. Another adventure on the high seas!

'Box of Illusions'
Artwork by Ginger Gilmour

CHAPTER 83

BOX OF ILLUSIONS

After Glastonbury, I began to meet with Nico and his group for spiritual instruction and guidance. They would alternate between England at my home and Antwerp, Belgium, where his center, Thelman Institute, was located. A new doorway was opened into my inner world which would further the contact with my soul purpose. We would sit in the garden, under the oak tree at Brockhurst, studying many spiritual philosophies and concepts of thought. The word consciousness appeared before me to contemplate further. My journey seems to be a series of open windows along the way.

During my time with Lily, I began to understand about the levels of the Human Constitution. The balance of which was of great importance, to living a life of harmony. Our personality vehicle consists of the physical, astral (emotional) and mental realms. Beyond there lies the higher spiritual realms, leading to God Realization. I have found that my path of experiences have been opportunities, to find this balance within me; allowing my heart desires and increased commitment to be of the highest service and help humanity.

As each window opened, Life gave me chances to discover, respond and then transform. Looking back at the physical challenges I had faced during my earlier years, helped me care for my body. Thus building a stronger constitution for the task that was before me, which only God knew what it was. All the emotional challenges and subsequent analysis gave me the tools to be the conductor and participate consciously in my future.

I became able to direct and manifest my soul purpose amongst all the distractions. The whip-tide currents that came before would no longer hold me the victim. Finally, the next phase and most important, was to be the development of my mental and intuitive levels. Once this was complete, the real service would become possible. The way was clear for the deeper work to begin. God was waiting.

The laying of my foundations, I now see, was what guided me to this day so that an inner temple could rise and sparkle. As Dr. Engel often reminded me, "Ginger, you are breaking through, not breaking down!" Lily said, "Ginger there is a light at the end of the tunnel." Joel Osteen says, "We are the children of God. We have Divine DNA." Cecil reminded me, "Below the tyranny and captivity of our images of destruction there still flows the living river of human consciousness that flowers with Beauty, if only we looked." I, too, have joined the many who know that the elements of God's Paradise await us to return to its valley and bathe in its streams of Love. Thus, I am being led along my return to the Bright Side.

With that understanding, I soldiered on. I faced the Walls that had been built, clearing away the rubble as a new temple was being created. I faced the Glamours and False Illusions that I had accepted as the path to Happiness. These realizations crumbled the mask, leaving me vulnerable. It was all part of the process of renewing and alignment.

Often holding on to what the Glamours and Illusions were demanding, while insisting that they were of Virtue, I repeatedly said, (jokingly to allow humor to ease the disturbance), "*My shoes and coats will probably be the last to surrender before*

Enlightenment!" Not realizing that one day my journey would require me to surrender many of my beliefs. Mrs. Tweedie said to me as I sat next to her, "Ginger, one day you will even have to let go of your idea of Love to touch God's."

Really, it wasn't the shoes and coats, but more the attachment to thinking they were me. I thought they were a way to touch the Joy that can fill the heart unmistakably when it comes. I wanted eternal Joy not the Illusion. I would eventually discover, like Dorothy in the *Wizard of Oz*, that it was not the shoes that would take me to OZ. "Really? How?" I silently asked, "WHO AM I? WHAT IS GOD'S ETERNAL LOVE?" On and on these questions returned to me with each new window that opened.

During one of my early visits to Antwerp, I was inspired to create a piece of artwork, later called, *The Box of Illusions*, which contained our Glamours and material desires trapped within the box. The Universe of possibilities limited from ordinary sight. I walked with the group throughout the city; discovering different common images to draw that reflected the concept. I collected objects dropped on the sidewalks. There was a tin of Coke, McDonald chips, postcard of guns and fashion magazines.

As Nico, his group and I, strolled through the public places of art, wonderful clouds followed above adding to the beauty of the afternoon sunshine. They were placed within my painting as a reminder to look up. Everywhere birds would come and sit at our feet and I will never forget how they followed us under the trees. The breath of God was with us as we walked in the silence of the afternoon. The only sound was our laughter. Another window opened. The path was clear ahead in its Wondrous Beauty.

NEW BEGINNING

Looking Out, Looking In

As I wander through the mist of Illusion

Seeking to hear once again

The choir of Angels

Lost it seems within the Glamour

The Sound of Healing Silence

Has disappeared within the noise

Of the passing traffic in the streets

People scurrying anxiously

Amongst

The idle chatter

Full of fear and anxieties

Chaos seeps in through the Walls.

Where has the Wonder gone? The Stillness? Me?

A new Cycle? A new Beginning?

Where? When? How?

Then a Voice

Penetrates the darkness,

"JUST STOP"
"BE"

I was Back

© Ginger Gilmour

'DOORWAY to BEAUTY'

2008

'Heavenly Angel'
Sanctuary for the Spirit
Old Bilsham Farmhouse
West Sussex, UK
Artwork by Ginger Gilmour

CHAPTER 84

SANCTUARY FOR THE SPIRIT

2000

Most of the children were in boarding school except for Matthew and I no longer needed a home where children could roller skate from one end to the other. No longer did masses of their friends and parents come to make Christmas Cakes for the school fair. No longer did we make the scenery together for the school plays at home on the lawn. They were on their own journey now so I needed a place more for my own creativity to blossom. Looking back, all our homes allowed an internal process to develop. Woodley, Hook End, Monksbridge and Maida Avenue brought forth our children, held our marriage and the birth of my own innate creativity. Brockhurst helped me to realize and find that there was life after David. There was a future.

A new step was approaching. An inner call ushered forth from within my being to find a place where creativity could happen. Initially, I was looking around where Matthew was going to school near Eastbourne on the coast, but it was not to be. As it had been with Brockhurst, a single black and white paper in an envelope mysteriously appeared in the post. It was of a house in West Sussex called Old Bilsham Farmhouse. It had previously been a piggery, which had long since deteriorated with the change of owners. The principal house built in the 15th Century had two attached cottages on the backwater of the main farm, which later we merged into one. It needed lots of work. It found me. The answer to my call.

Old Bilsham Farmhouse was to help me further to know "Who I AM" and "What I Truly was Born to BE!" I was guided by life to know how to create a "House of Light, a Sanctuary for the Spirit" where people could come. First, to be found within me and then for it to manifest visibly in many ways. I had already had a cycle of experiences, which guided me to be healthier on the physical level. This built a foundation ready to serve the plan of my soul. At the time, I had no idea.

I had a phase whereby I was confronted to develop on the emotional level. I had to become the conductor of my heart since I was on the way to serve humanity more. My creativity had to take flight for it would open the doorway further. The vision was coming closer. Cecil often referred to it as the opening of "The Eye of the Heart," encouraging us to remember a world once known and nearly forgotten.

I worked together with one of my best mates, Alan Lee, best known as Dreamy, and his team, to convert what was falling down to become a home of "Sacred Heart and Beauty." I was further inspired to create *living walls of sculpture*. I experimented with the technique I had learned through the Steiner methods for sculpture, but on a larger scale upon the walls and ceilings.

What was a tiny corridor entrance, became etherically larger. The straight lines, barely meeting each other, changing into a flow of feminine softness, and then disappearing into space worked! How, you might ask? The work is completed by you because the lines do not meet. Subconsciously, you have to go into your creative realms to do this. So often, the mind wants to have a completed form in order to understand. In doing so you see from the eyes of the soul, which is infinite. The corridor became limitless, as limitless as who you truly are!

Another wonderful aspect of this process is that it is one with nature, by the simple fact that it is not a definite work of art. It was *Living*, the shadows of its minimal definition moved with the movement of the light. Slowly, slowly, changing as the sun became the night and the night became the day. This could be achieved by creating artwork that reflected the highest triad of life on earth. A vision reflected the harmony between the masculine (the defined lines, the practical), the feminine (the flow, the bridge) and God in us (the space, union and Love). This technique opened the doorway.

My images further assisted and inspired others to be touched by the sacred qualities of God's gift to Humanity: Beauty, Goodness, Kindness, Truth, Gratitude, Love, and Friendship. Each of us has that Divine spark within. It is my quest to take the viewer on a journey of Return. To awaken and then ignite that Divine spark once again because mankind has nearly forgotten, the Way to Remember.

There was not a day during my time at Old Bilsham that the shadows in my mind and heart stayed for long, as I walked amongst its corridors. Within each moment, the rays of light fell upon my face, as did the stars at night as I sat to read or to create. My divine experiment was working. It would even work in the city because the cycle of light is everywhere. My *Living Walls* of sculpture could be anywhere.

Spring was one of my favorite times there. The Mallard ducks came each season and had their ducklings who played in the pond with the Koi swimming below. Each season we had to build little stairs for them to get out and follow their Mum until their wings matured. We often had drake parties on the decking at sunset. They would fly in over where I sat in the garden like jets, chat away and then leave. There was one season, when one mum and dad duck stayed and would follow Steve Gent, my project manager, into the woodworking room, leaving their footprints in the sawdust, quacking, seemingly giving their opinions. So tender. So sweet. A blessed moment with nature.

The conversion took nearly two years with "walk in angels" for sure and another team called Creative Construction. Dreamy had to have an operation on his knee and could no longer work for us. He completed the little house and finally our temporary kitchen moved from the outbuilding away from our nighttime visitors-rats.

Our workmen use to tell stories about sitting there after the pub and a pint, having a cigarette, while overhead the rats would scurry along the wooden beams waiting for them to leave a morsel or two. The bedrooms were ready too. No more sleeping on mattresses on the floor. The kids felt more at home except for one thing. There was no internet yet. Broadband hadn't reached down our lane.

There was so much more to finish when our new team took over. Creating a Sanctuary where they will come was massive. Major work became necessary to convert the barns and piggery. The makeshift office in the stables had sheets of paper pinned on the wall of the schedule: the electrics, plumbing, sewerage, rainwater drainage, plus, a Conservatory, Koi fish pond, three creative studios, two workrooms, mini gym, meditation room, my private quarters, gallery and lecture room.

All the floorboards were up. No room for roller-skating. Our washer and dryer balanced between the support beams upstairs. The entire inner garden was a mud hole with mini diggers that look like large toys. And, last but not least, there was to be a six foot winged angel up in the apex near the gallery. When finally finished my Mom exclaimed, "*You have an Angel in your house...That big?*" Old Bilsham's soul was being raised beyond being a deserted piggery into being a Sanctuary for all who came there; a place where the "ART of Living" through creating Beauty, could be explored.

Many mornings I could be found behind an angle-grinder or a sanding machine dressed in a white paper overall and a hooded face mask looking like I had just landed on the moon. One day when I was working on the narrow miniature entrance hallway, the postman arrived with our mail. The door stood open, but a cloud of dust prevented his entry. He beckoned through the dust, "Is there a Mrs. Gilmour Home?" As I walked from out of the cloud, removing the hooded face mask, I said, *"Yes, I am Mrs. Gilmour."* The look of astonishment on his face told a thousand stories. I smiled, putting down the sander then removing my gloves in order to sign for the package.

One of my most influential thoughts, which carried me through this part of my journey, was when Nico asked if I had realized that I had the *"soul of an artist."* He had observed me over the last ten years and no matter what I put my hands to it was a piece of artwork. We often spoke about what we identify with as "who we are" influences every moment. Joel Osteen says it so well, *"God has planted a divine spark in our DNA. You can believe what someone else says you are or even who you think you are not. Or you can believe how divine you are. You can believe what God says you are and live a higher purpose."* I was beginning to see my divine purpose and its treasure. My mother was right; I was born to be an artist. She led the way while my path followed its course in sometimes-strange directions. During this phase, my foundations were further laid ready to take off.

What was most wonderful, was how Nico helped me Not to poison the love I had experienced most of my life especially with David. It is often tempting to burn down the forest of the heart when difficult times of change appear. He inspired me to accept that there is always a silk lining to be found, which aids your next step. I could build on what went before that was Beauty and Love. I did not have to lock it away or destroy it, in order to move forward. He always said to me, "*Accept life as it is and then make it special.*"

There was something special in the "making" within the walls of Old Bilsham. For me it was time to feel free to awaken the gift God had given me to use and that was to be the *soul of an artist*. I had a purpose that filled my heart, which lit the days to come thereafter. Eventually even my workmen saw the virtue of my fairy glass that put rainbows everywhere. My neighbors said that the clouds and the sky on my garden walls always brought the sunshine. They asked me one day, "*Ginger, what do you do when it is overcast?*" I answered, "*Well, I don't look up! I look at the Bright Side.*"

One night I had a guiding vision. I had built the environment, a place where "It" could happen. Now I needed to create artwork that could go out to the world. I started a series called the "Art of Sacred Relationship." It began with *Mother and Child*. I found it most endearing and all the love I had in my mother's heart for my children went into its creation. *Lovers* came next.

Just to give you an idea if you have not seen my work yet, it is beyond the normal human proportions. It seems to grow in its manifesting process to be rather elongated. Often, if it is a bit squat energetically during the creative process, something will happen making sure, I did not think it was finished. Either it would fall over on its own accord or a cat would knock it over with a brush of its tail. I grew to see the hints from God that it needed to reach for heaven more. "*Taller, Taller!*" went through my mind. "*Ok, I got it!*" I agreed and continued.

I called it my artistic lobotomy as I reached into the chicken wire support inside the wet clay. With a pair of miniature pliers, I would set about pulling and cutting. Then with one hand, I would raise the form higher while adding extra clay with the other. It grew and grew reaching for the heavens.

As it began to manifest, The *Lovers* was extremely special to me. I wanted to capture the sacred heights that a Man and a Woman could potentially share. I wanted to create the Divine Love with God formed in their union. What's interesting is that it was finished on the eve of Valentine's Day without my conscious intention.

That summer Daniela Lavender, wife of Ben Kingsley, stayed with me as she was performing in a *Midsummers Night Dream* at Arundel Castle. She had to leave early one morning and when I awoke, she had left a trail of little pink Post-it hearts leading up to the *Lovers* saying she wanted to buy it in bronze for Ben's Christmas present. *"Call me, to discuss it soon."*

Next was *Sacred Vow,* which sought to capture the sacred commitment between a man and a woman through marriage and God. Their hands bound together with a white cloth of purity. At one of my exhibitions in Arundel, a woman came up to me and asked about the intention of this sculpture. I asked *"Why?"* she shared with me that her own impression was of Love but her sister felt differently. In fact, she insisted that they had to leave NOW for it really disturbed her.

I further asked, *"May I ask if she has had a recent emotional upset in a relationship?"* I waited, giving her space to respond. *"You do not have to answer, if you do not feel it appropriate."* She said with a lump in her throat, *"Yes, she is in the middle of a divorce."* I told her the deepest intention of *Sacred Vow*. I felt that if she had spent more time with the sculpture it might have touched her heart with the Love she so desired. I explained further that my artwork is "living art" and seeks to uplift and heal mankind. Sometimes that means facing the veils, which prevent healing.

One of my most favorite in this series is *Angelic Whisper.* It is an angel whispering closely to a woman dressed in simple robes like the Madonna. She whispers words from God *"I love you."* The birth of this sculpture was rather challenging for her wings kept falling off. It was a fine balance between the wet clay and its drying process, as I built the extended wings that reached high beyond the angel's body.

Many have asked me if it is based upon the moment that the Angel Gabriel speaks to Mary, *the Annunciation*. I have pondered this over the years. "*Thank you, but not consciously*," I would respond but many hear her whisper. Over the years, *Angelic Whisper* has found her way into many homes, including a special one I created for my Mom. I made her one in clear pink that glowed from the light in her front window. When visitors, even repairmen, came to the house in her last years, she would proudly show them. She told me that many would shed tears when being in front of her. Even the photos brought this emotion to others. Now she has a new home with my brother Marcus and his wife, Jana.

I loved this phase of my life, discovering the *soul of the artist*. Each time I went to my studio to create, even today, I am inspired by words from Cecil Collins classes. He's quoted as saying:

> "The Art of the future, will be to feed the interior life of the individual and will not be dominated by theory political, philosophical or spiritual. There must be in the world a revolution of human consciousness from the idea of fear and desire, victory and defeat, courage and cowardice, ownership and sharing. We need to return to the eternal values which are being human and divine."[1]

That is the well of spring water, of inspiration, from which I seek to create for mankind.—It is my quest.

'WORLD GOODWILL'

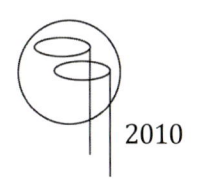

2010

'Hope'
"Save the World"
Artwork by Ginger Gilmour

CHAPTER 85

HOPE

I was on my way to California again and was part of a co-exhibition at the Institute of Noetic Sciences based in Petaluma, California. It was the brainchild of Apollo 14 astronaut, Edgar Mitchell. He said that his experience of observing the Earth from outer space changed his entire viewpoint as a scientist and as a fellow human being about the creation of the world. No answers came except to know of the incredible wonder of Life. This epiphany initiated another kind of exploration into the nature of things. Thus IONS, the Noetic Institute of Sciences, was born. Noetic referring to mental activity or the intellectual quality of the mystical experience to grasp the sense of revelation.

So it was Three Women—Three Artists who came together to launch a new artistic movement—*Art on Purpose*. Referring to work that is deliberate in its intention to uplift humanity. Californian based artists Dana Lynne Andersen and Annie Harrison and I collaborated in an exhibition called "Zeitgist-The Spirit of the Times." I first met Dana at the Inspirational Arts Festival in London and later met Annie when I got to Petaluma. Our friendship grew ever since as we shared a similar vision. We were passionate about the power of art to change consciousness and touch God realization.

Just one of Dana's contributions to this vision, apart from her wonderful paintings, was to found the Awakening Arts Network. It is a global resource nexus connecting hundreds of artists throughout the world who are engaged in creating art that is Evolutionary and Transformative. Annie in her way seeks to use the ancient science of sacred geometry to create stone and glass sculptures that feature flowing water as their central element. Successful artists individually—we were quite a team working together to galvanize a renaissance of art with conscience and consciousness.

During the flight, as I snuggled under my flight blanket, I chose to watch the movie *Bobby*, which was based on the life of Robert Kennedy. So many memories came forward of that time. Most of all how much the nation's heart was hurt again since the assassination of JFK, and Martin Luther King Jr. Hope seemed to vanish with a third assassination that of Robert Kennedy. His genuine vision of heart for the people had developed, healing us and giving Hope. He held the Nation like his brother. His actions spoke for the Heart of the Nation. Then he too was gone. I cried as the memories returned.

***

I was home from school that day when I heard the broadcast over the radio. I nearly fainted climbing the stairs from the den to the kitchen grasping the handrail in dis-belief...."*How? Really? NO!*" Voices were heard, weeping with the reality. Now their leader was gone. America was already a nation of discord at the time. The violence that rose focused around Vietnam, Poverty and Racial issues. I was just a young teenager impressionable searching for Peace, for a way forward, as the call went out across the nation and the world.

I was reminded of how the Kennedys stood for the true values amongst men. Challenged within the dramas of their century. Their words resound and sadly still apply today. I quote part of Bobby's speech after the assassination of Martin Luther King Jr.

> "This is a time of shame and sorrow. It is not a day for politics. I have saved this one opportunity to speak briefly to you about this mindless menace of violence in America which again stains our land and every one of our lives.
>
> It is not the concern of any one race. The victims of the violence are black and white, rich and poor, young and old, famous and unknown. They are, most important of all, human beings whom other human beings loved and needed. No one - no matter where he lives or what he does - can be certain who will suffer from some senseless act of bloodshed. And yet it goes on.
>
> Why? What has violence ever accomplished? What has it ever created? No martyr's cause has ever been stilled by his assassin's bullet. No wrongs have ever been righted by riots and civil disorders. A sniper is only a coward, not a hero; and an uncontrolled, uncontrollable mob is only the voice of madness, not the voice of the people.
>
> Whenever any American's (or person's) life is taken by another American (or individual anywhere in the world) unnecessarily - whether it is done in the name of the law or in the defiance of law, by one man or a gang, in cold blood or in passion, in an attack of violence or in response to violence - whenever we tear at the fabric of life which another man has painfully and clumsily woven for himself and his children, the whole nation is degraded.[1]

These words so spoken from the truth and wisdom of his heart. To all who listened, encouraging us to remember that we are here on Earth to do God's work. Each time, both he and his brother, and Martin Luther King Jr called upon us to ask for God's blessing and help to stand up for an ideal to improve the lot of another. For they knew that each time one stands up for this ideal it sends forth a tiny ripple of "Hope." And then they were no longer. Gone were the three men that stood for injustice in their time inspiring us to dare to make God's work truly our own. Believe it or not, one day we will realize the benefit from what hope we pass on does for one another and society. As JFK said,

"Ask not what your country can do for you. Ask what you can do for your country."[2]

***

Years passed when we were now living in Old Bilsham Farmhouse. It was the weekend and Matthew was home from boarding school. During the night, I awoke to the sound of Matthew screaming. I ran into his room and in the darkness he was crying out, *"Help! Help! Mom! Mom!"* I held my sobbing child in my arms wrapping us in a blanket stroking his hair, *"What's wrong Matt?* He cried, whimpering as he told me the story of his nightmare, "It was terrible! A plane crashed into two buildings and people were falling out of the buildings from high up!" "Now. Now. It was only a bad dream, I am here." Gosh, Thank Goodness it was only a bad dream. I stayed with him until he was calm, gently rocking him back to sleep.

Matthew returned to boarding school on Sunday and on that next Tuesday morning I turned on the telly. What I witnessed, filled me with shock. The twin towers in NYC were attacked. A plane flew into one of the buildings, there was an explosion. People were falling from the buildings. Had Matthew seen the foretelling of the future? I couldn't get it out of my mind as we all shared the shock for days and days as the story unfolded. September 11, 2001 was a day that brought the world to their knees. As we stood in the rubble, America had a choice to inspire or to fight as the dust settled and healing began.

The city called out to artists and architects to submit artwork for Ground Zero. Doreen called to tell me, and asked, "Ginger, we need artwork that uplifts our hearts and holds the Divine Light. Can you make something?" I set about the task and created a maquette of a fireman holding the Earth, sitting on a bench in the arms of an angel. I called it "Hope." It was an installation proposal that included several other benches. The second and third would have life-size Angels, waiting to hold you within its wings. The fourth would be a place for contemplation and perhaps there would be more throughout the site and the world.

Recently, someone on Facebook commented on "Hope." "*The angel isn't above him—But with him—It's the feeling.*" Hope awaits us. Within the voice of madness still lies Hope. It beckons us to live our lives for truth, for goodness, and justice for we have the power to do so!

As Martin Luther King Jr. said in his final words to us, along with many others throughout history, "I just want to do God's will."

And there in, lies Hope.

'Visions of Beauty'
Co-Exhibition
Checquer Mead, East Grinstead
West Sussex, UK

CHAPTER 86

VISIONS OF BEAUTY

My first moment to acknowledge the *Bright Side of the Moon* was in a Press Release written about me, by Doreen Key, my BFF, in Los Angeles. The press release described an art exhibition, *Esotera-Visions of Beauty*, which Ioannis Antoniadis and I were to display. She wrote, "Exhibition takes Visionary Art to the Bright Side of the Moon." She so further captured our flavor writing, "Combining the effortless beauty of Ginger's Sculptures with the vibrant wonder of Ioannis' ethereal paintings, the curtain raising event marks a timeless moment in the power of artistic expression to enlighten the spirit and move the soul."

For years, I have been working to manifest an exhibition, which incorporated large metaphysical paintings of an ethereal quality. Along with sculptures that explored the same world of light, color and form, which together, encourages feelings of contemplation and serenity. This vision had come to me in a dream, so powerfully directive that afterwards I spent long hours creating first the sculptures. During this time, I met Ioannis. His paintings and creative philosophy touched me. I felt we were kindred spirits on the path, as artists, to re-awaken and stir the soul.

Ioannis described his passion for painting in this statement: "As I look deeper into a frame of a blank canvas, I feel like I am looking into a luminous white world. The more I look, the more I feel that a transformation takes place. My mind becomes a visual prism translating white light into an infinite number of possibilities, colors, ideas, feelings and forms." He added, "We call this exhibition *Esotera-Visions of Beauty* because Esotera means 'inner world' from the Greek word 'Eso' (he is Greek) and the Latin word 'terra'.

Cecil Collins inspired me more by saying that the art gallery could also be a place where the Holy Spirit could visit, as it does in the church and in our hearts. Ioannis was also inspired by this possibility, so we came together to try. We rented the Chequer Mead Art Gallery in East Grinstead, West Sussex, UK and began to prepare for the event. Our intention, hopefully, was for our collaboration to uplift, heal and nurture the viewer in a way that expressed the archetypal power of art to touch the heart with beauty. Suspended from the exposed support beams in the ceiling was my 7-foot angelic sculpture *Heaven*, watching over the exhibition.

At first, we set up the gallery in the traditional manner, with sculptures placed either in the corners or in the middle of the room and the paintings on the walls. I proposed to Ioannis to experiment with the arrangement differently, that is, create a story of relationship between the sculpture and the paintings. I tried to show him, but he very quickly objected. This idea would have fulfilled what my dream had inspired. I attempted but had to put it aside, especially out of respect for him. A few days later though, the tide had changed. One morning I found him moving one of my sculptures in front of his painting. Not too close to block the view but close enough to try my idea. I smiled silently. He put his arm around my shoulder and said, "*Ok, let's try.*" The result was beautiful. At least I thought so.

For me, exhibitions are not so much about the artwork, but more of an interactive experience through the stimulation of the creative imagination. Creative imagination becomes active primarily in three ways: One, through the vibratory colors, glazing and symbolic imagery, which catches the archetypal relationship between the natural, and the supernatural of life. Secondly, the intention of the artist plays a major role in opening the doorway. Thirdly, by creating a new relationship between the second dimension (painting) and the third dimension (form) challenges the imagination of the viewer.

With my artwork, I've sought to capture and perhaps reflect the multi-dimensional and energetic levels of what we are as human beings. I attempt to create this with a question to myself. How much physical form is required to allow the viewer to recognize "who they are," and show a representational doorway to the *invisible* aspects of "who we are?" I feel there is more to us than the material physical aspects of life that we have become so familiar with.

My quest is to capture the wholeness—given to us by our creator. We have forgotten our invisible beauty, including the divine spark given to us to BE. My path walks hand in hand getting closer to this vision. Recently, I have taken this further. I have integrated my *Living Walls* with my paintings onto canvas. Another experiment born to capture one's imagination. I am always on the quest to live and manifest our highest potential both in daily life and in my artwork. My inspiration, which has stayed with me is a quote from Aristotle.

> *"The aim of Art is to represent not the outward appearance of things, but their inward significance."* [1]

The days passed and Ioannis and I began to understand the virtue of placing artwork with the intention of telling a story. Our artwork individually encouraged the viewer to enter the invisible realms of their soul and their imagination. Ioannis in his imagery and colors, and my artwork in its relationship of the line, curve and space. Together in this new story, something else happened; an invisible energy wave called out in the spaces between. Creating another story, which invoked the viewer's inner being. The viewer was not accustomed to this subconsciously because it broke the normal pattern of relating to artwork in a gallery. It took them further by the gentleness of what they perceived into their creative world.

Our vision was successful if the comments in our guestbook were anything to go by. Many said that we had created a place where the angels came. Many found it a sanctuary of peace and sacredness. Then there was the best comment that touched our hearts. Someone referred to our exhibition as a *Church of the Almighty in a Gallery*. She felt she could pray there and be heard.

It was an awesome experience, where two individuals came together and surrendered to create something more. Ioannis and I came with a similar vision, a pathway to God though separate cultures. I often wonder, what would happen if we attempted to create this environment with many individuals of different philosophies and cultures through art in this way. Could we achieve a sanctuary of peace together? What story would emerge? Would we even take the challenge or just return to our separate corners? I wonder.

There is another part of the story, I feel important to share with you. Something occurred inwardly during our exhibition. I heard guidance from within during the night. It stated that I must let go of Old Bilsham Farmhouse, (my sanctuary). I was starting to identify with it being ME, instead of a place that revealed, *Who I was born to BE.* It had served its purpose. I struggled a while, in fact, months before I accepted its wisdom. Eventually, I dared to go deeper to know me and put it on the market. It took nearly three years before it was to sell. However, before that many adventures would happen.

SONG THAT IS ME

Across the valley of my heart

I wonder…

Where will you take me?

The distant hills of my soul

Calling…

To continue upon the journey.

My Heart burns with the longing

To go…

But fear often grips my surrender.

My body aches with the pain

Each morning…

What shall it be? Beauty or the Beast?

Then as the sun filters into the room

I know…

How to awaken to the Song that is ME.

© Ginger Gilmour

Phil & Electra May & David & I
Grand Canal, Venice

CHAPTER 87

VENICE
A NIGHT OF WONDER

Venice, a night of Wonder?...I wonder. As I sat finishing my illustrations for the book of dreams *Under the Mango Tree*, by Miriam Freedman, the news came to me. Pink Floyd is to do a concert in Venice, on a Barge in the Grand Canal, off St Mark's Square. I could not believe what I was hearing. Would this really be a night of Wonder?

For years David, Alice and I had gone to Venice in November, to celebrate the mutual birthdays of Phil May, (singer and friend from the Pretty Things), and his daughter, Sorrel, who was Alice's Best friend at the time. His wife, Electra, came when she could. She and I were very close friends as well. Many Italian friends from Lindos often met us there. Patrizia and Enzo Molinari from Rome showed us the sights. They are still special friends with whom we share a common interest-ART. Patrizia is a painter and Enzo is a rather tall man with a gracious and generous heart who supports her talent and their family with Love.

One November, we took our small plane to Venice. We were to meet with Mary Moore, daughter of Henry Moore, the sculptor, and her husband. St Mark's Square was flooded as it usually is at that time of year. There were slatted walkways allowing the tourists to get across. We had coffee in one of the side cafés watching the pigeons flying over, waiting for a morsel to fall their way. The lapping of the water softened the edges, which we brought with us from England. We felt nurtured by the wind underneath our warm jumpers and scarves sitting there while St Mark's Square was being surrounded by the encroaching sea. The lagoon was taking over. A strange sight to observe, it felt like something out of the movie *Planet of the Apes*. Buildings desolate and History being left behind.

We loved Venice, especially being on the water and walking instead of driving to get about. It was so romantic especially taking a gondola in the night. The pink antique glass streetlights poetically lined the canal creating reflections of the Piazzi, which rippled in moving colors as we passed. Deeper and deeper we went into the heart of the city through little hideaway passages and canals exploring, riding in a gondola.

I leant back into the velvet chair, with my hand drifting in the water listening to the songs of Venice taking me into ancient memories when it was a Republic. Free from religious fanaticism, free from tourism visiting their city, free from pollution, artistic and caring. It was night, our favorite time, for Venice was ours as a stillness cloaked the earlier presence of the tourists. The teenagers no longer were climbing on the bronze sculptures eating their McDonalds. Its beauty tiptoed out from behind the illusion of consumerism to nurture us instead.

As years passed, we all became aware of something hidden behind the mask. There is another side unbeknownst to many, knowledge of which even attempted to shatter our magical dreams about Venice. Or maybe perhaps raise further concern. At first, it was hard for me to swallow as I strolled over the footbridges. The canals may shimmer enigmatically in the sunshine, or twinkle in the moonlight, but there is a sad mystery about them trying to hide.

It is becoming a challenge to live there or to visit. A challenge because the canals stink from rotting garbage and sewage that seeps out of the old Palazzi. The smell is hard to transcend within the Beauty of the buildings and the Gondolas. It is plain to see why the Venetians by the year are leaving and selling their homes, surrendering to the inevitable decay. Tourism may be lucrative and Pink Floyd in Venice may go down in history as the gig of the century, but at what cost?

There's more at play than what's visible to the eye, our noses and our fantasy. Not only is it hard to be healthy there anymore but it is hard to acquire even the basics to live between the Murano glass, trinkets and masks. Tankers are eroding the seabed with their traffic. Venice is slowly sinking into the mud, which we are aware. It's also slowly being over taken by virulent nasty's including dioxin and heavy metals. Tens of thousands sewer rats scurry in the night from house to house. They are more resilient and larger than Rome and Naples.[1] Then there are the giant mosquitos plaguing you in the night. Thus, making you a regular customer at the pharmacy from the bites and allergic reactions. (Sorry to share this with you but if we truly care we must know.)

Despite the decay, Venice's artistic and historical qualities of Beauty still calls beckoning us to her shores...Calling for help. But really how deep is our notion to "Save Venice?" I wonder. Its decay along with Death has been glamorized throughout the centuries. The paradox between the idolization of its Beauty and yet its Poetic loss continues to be romantic. Do we really know how valuable the role Beauty plays in our lives? Will we realize and awaken when it is gone? Will it be too late?

The attraction to this aspect of romantic decay does not make the city fathers' job any easier as caretakers. As the late Italian senator and native Venetian Bruno Visentini once said, "The management of decadence is a delicate task." OMG. The Italian government has made repeated attempts ever since the great flood in 1966 to preserve the city and protect it from flooding, sinking or rotting to death; but there seems to be constant bickering while

Venice sinks waiting for decisions to be made and money to be raised and spent.[1]

I have joined the many with the notion of "Saving Venice." Its beauty alone has not been enough to protect it from the ravages of time or industrial pollution or politics or even Rock 'n' Roll concerts, it seems. In a small way, I have been eating "Veneziana" pizza at Pizza Express ever since they joined the Venice in Peril Fund. They contribute ten pence with each order. In a larger way, I cherish Beauty and dedicate my life to it. However, it is not enough because the essence of this problem is bigger than Venice. It lies in our values.

I am amazed the Floyd even got permission to begin with or even wanted to do it. It usually requires 37 signatures from 24 offices, from local to national levels to get anything done. *"If we decide to plant a new mooring pole,"* says Giancarlo Galan, president of the Venice region, *"do you know how much time it takes before the crane arrives to put it in place? Six years."*[1] So how did the Floyd get permission? I wonder?

Story goes that Italy's disco-dancing former foreign minister, Gianni De Michelis, under his direction, acting as the unanointed city supremo, got Venice to give the go-ahead for the concert to happen, despite public disapproval. Some called it a disaster. Some called it a *Night of Wonder*. Sadly, it turned St Mark's Square into a giant latrine and damaged the surrounding buildings through amp vibration. Apparently, the concert was almost cancelled a few days before, as the Superintendent of Monuments objected because of the potential risk of damaging the buildings from the vibration. However, a compromise was agreed.

The Floyd turned down the volume, but unfortunately, the damage still occurred to the marble cladding and streetlights from fans climbing on them to see. It is recorded that 250,000 people sat before them with an additional 100,000 watching in 20 countries.

For whatever reason, the city authorities failed to provide facilities for the visiting fans, many of whom slept in St. Mark's Square. They left behind 300 tons of litter, which the army had to clear away. Apologies were handed out to the local residents with promises that it will never happen again. Many of the committee chose to stand down and the concert is referred to as an UNIQUE happening-a once in a lifetime happening.[1]

While I watched the TV coverage of the performance, it was beyond unique. It was a once in a lifetime happening certainly. I just wonder if there is not a deeper responsibility for artists, who are given the unique ability to bring Beauty and Wonder to the world. How much do we have to think beyond the box to serve? Cecil used to say, "Look at the ripples and then decide if it is real Beauty or Illusion…One leaves a divine fragrance while the other destroys."

Ultimately, each of us are responsible for the space we stand in. We do have a choice about what we create or leave behind. I ask the questions, "Why was there 300 tons of rubbish in Venice after the concert? Why is there an island of plastic floating in the South Pacific? Why are we *Fracking* and potentially destroying our planet? Finally, what will it take—for us to care for the planet where we live?"

"We do have a choice.
We can create or we can destroy
So what do You choose Today?"

Doorway to Inner Beauty

CHAPTER 88

DOORWAY TO INNER BEAUTY

I thought it important to share with you what has developed into the essence of my work, through all the experiences you have read about so far. It is the quality of Beauty. Have you ever wondered what is Beauty? I have and do. Throughout my life, I have often asked myself... What is Beauty? Why throughout the ages has mankind asked the same question? In my time, it often seems like an entrapment forced upon us, so we can be good consumers, even better lovers, maybe even rich if we drive a certain car. In fact, in our culture, especially in the current art world, Real Beauty has bad press!

As a child in the United States, I fell right into the Hollywood and Disney thing. I dreamt of being a star, discovered at the local soda fountain by some director. I dreamt of being on the front page of Vogue. I dreamt of my "Prince Charming." In fact, I did become a model and owned a fashion boutique. I got a lead role in a film, three days before signing the contract...my prince charming appeared, and I left it all...for England. All of this I have shared with you already, but I had no idea at the time what all of this would lead me to discover.

As you know, time passed and I was challenged with a very deep personal Crisis—David leaving. It seemed that I was walking on a tightrope across a chasm of fire. I sought counsel from Lily with whom I had trained and worked beside. I cried and said, "*Lily, I can't stand it. What should I do? How can I cope?*" To many, Lily was like the ultimate Fairy Godmother. On that day, she wrapped me in her arms and said, "*Child, what you must first do is to place a flower every day by your bedside, so that each morning when you awake the first thing you will see is Beauty.*" And so I did. It took me years to understand fully the wisdom of her words, which is what I want to share with you now.

I have come to realize that Beauty is not a lead role in a film or being on the front page of Vogue. In fact, Beauty is the essence of Life itself. It is the Invisible Key within each of us; there is a spark of Beauty—innate, waiting to be awakened. It often comes on the breath of the wind as it moves the petals of the poppies. You may suddenly turn and catch the rainbow in the sky as the rain falls from the clouds lit by the sun.

Beauty will come silently, hold you for a moment and warm your heart. You will try to capture it with a picture, but it is elusive. God made it that way to spark each of us on our journey of return. Stimulating our interest to go deeper into our hearts and then discover the Divine Spirit hidden there. One of my art teachers once said, "*Beauty is a gift from God and our Gift is to use it, to BE it and Beautify Everything! It leads us to Truth.*"

As my life journey continued, Beauty became more and more a driving force and influence. I worked more and more with the knowledge that I was born with the *soul of an artist*. This was my way to Beautify. In my studio, I was safe to dare to touch the depth of all my dreams. It became a place where All Dreams Come True. I created my *Knight in Shining Armor*—I created the *Love in my Heart* for my children—I created the *Angels from Heaven*—Most of All, I created *Song of Woman*, which was ME. Old Bilsham was becoming my sanctuary for the spirit. It gave me shelter, a haven to give birth to my rising vision. There I could reveal God's gift within me and manifest it within my artwork.

NO longer did it matter if people said that I was in The Land of the Fairies or that I was Old-Fashioned.—*WHAT?*—*God?*—*Angels?*—*Beauty?*—*Healing?*—*Vegetarian?*—*Poor David!*—They exclaimed, "*Most of all, she seeks the sacred and the divine.*" Really? Admittedly, most of my Life I was identified with all kinds of fears, judgments and desires. I wanted to be accepted. I created many limitations for myself. I allowed images on the NEWS to be my only reality and the longing for the World of Light and Love was kept hidden deep within the Darkness. I put it away as Fantasy, as Make Believe. It was a painful time. My inner core felt torn apart. Through all of my deception, my soul beckoned.

Then little by little, like the early morning mist, Beauty crept into my Heart. Through creating my secret dream world, Beauty began to heal my hurts and sorrows. It began to give me energy, hope and purpose. My Inner Sun emerged from behind the clouds and gave warmth to everyday. Inner Happiness and Joy was no longer a fantasy or something read in a book. It was real and I was not going to go back. Another chapter was unfolding for I had chosen to discover *Who I was Born to BE!*

You know there is a moment just when you open your eyes in the morning, if you really pay attention. It is just before all the mind chatter begins to speak to you, when you can create your day or at least influence it. A moment when you can choose whether the sun will shine inside and touch all the challenges with its wisdom, or, you can choose if you will be immersed in the Clouds all day.

With that realization, I was filled with Joy to know that I could create the day I wanted to have. I had a choice! That is when I began to play again. Joy returned and laughter. Nothing would steal it away again. I found the more I aspired towards Beauty; the more

I did think Beauty; the more I felt Beauty; slowly, slowly my inner nature was transforming. Inner Beauty became my outer reality.

Rest assured, it does take practice. Sometimes the littlest things captured the twinkle of heaven, twinkles of grace. One day my daughter called me, to say she was on her way to Chichester to see her accountant, which worried her. She had decided to write many Post-it notes with affirmations. Like *Have a Joyful Day, Love and Sunshine, You are GREAT*! She said that she then placed them throughout the town to uplift her day and others. "*Ah*, Little acts of kindness," I said, with a smile. We did little things often.

Our culture is at an end of a cycle. We are on the edge of a great opportunity to create a more sustainable future to be reborn. AS I see it.

We are not just experiencing a Global Financial Crisis.

We are not just experiencing a Potential Ecological Disaster.

We are actually experiencing a Crisis of Beauty.

We have actually forgotten to create a world, which is

Sacred and Divine.

Many feel we are at a decisive moment in the Evolution of Mankind. There is a new and finer experience awaiting us of such Beauty and Goodness. We are actually facing a re-birth, an awakening of consciousness. But to make this possible—We need to change the destructive images, which speak loudly within our Minds and Heart. We need to change the images our eyes witness in the "Spin" all around us, which we have accepted as the Truth. Most of all, we need to choose to create Beauty on all levels, both visible and invisible. Ultimately, Heaven must return to Earth. God is there wanting us to do it.

Cecil Collins felt deeply that art should be the incarnating and releasing that of which a society considers to be "beautiful" and worthy of attention. All art brings a message into the world. We are guided by what is considered as the "norm," established by the intelligentsia as being worthy of contemplation as a reflection of life. But modern society, in its fractured and traumatized state, has come to accept art in an infinitely broader sense.

Artists have been given total freedom to create anything. Therefore, an icon has a very definite message, and apparently so does a pile of bricks. Modern society accepts both as "art." Therefore, our work is cut out for us because the art of an epoch is its spiritual thermometer. So what do we want to create? Images that feed our soul, or images, which result in the trivialization of society?

I say for this to happen, the Arts will play a great part in the future, but Only if it is creative and not destructive. By that, I mean the artists will create from a response to one's True Soul Nature, ideally from serving the Divine intention. They will create images and forms that reflect the deep essence of Life. Most of All, the artists will create such Beauty, that it will awaken us from our slumber and remind us that We are BEAUTIFUL and OUR HEARTS ARE PURE! So that, once again, *We shall Live the Art of Beauty!* We shall walk towards the Bright Side.

'Angel of Might'

Sculpture by Ginger Gilmour

CHAPTER 89

ANGEL OF MIGHT

After our exhibition, Ioannis told me of an initiative "Art for Humanity" to raise funds for the Red Cross in the UK. They were asking artists for submissions to donate art towards their International Fund Raising efforts. My work was just becoming visible, but I took the step to offer my sculpture *Angel of Might*. I made an appointment to meet their committee. I was nervous when I approached the door, but I could see them through the little window smiling, chatting. Their warm greeting calmed my shaky disposition as they guided me to my chair. Kindness and commitment filled the evening as I listened and waited my turn.

A great philosopher once said, "*We are what we contemplate.*" In these modern times, mankind is constantly confronted with images of conflict and world disasters, it seems VERY important to contemplate the Beautiful. As you know, it has become my personal crusade as an artist. Ever since I can remember, my innermost nature has always been to do acts of kindness and to create; from saving lost animals, to organizing charitable events; from mothering our four children to now giving birth to the *Art of Beauty*. This is my passion. This is my life.

Over the years, I have found writing poetry is a great way to communicate what my artwork seeks to say, as well as what my visionary quest is leading me to BE. So I wrote this poem for them, hopefully to bridge the gap:

Angel of Might

Throughout History, in most cases, the symbol of an Angel
Represented upliftment, love, care and beauty.

To me, in an earthly sense, The Red Cross is
Humanity's Guardian Angels.

Therefore, I felt the *Angel of Might* is most appropriate
As a donation for the
'Art of Humanity'

For it not only takes Great Heart, But it also takes Great Might
To Be an Universal Caretaker.

© Ginger Gilmour

Through donating my sculpture, *Angel of Might,* to the Red Cross I took another step in my quest to serve humanity as a World Server. We are all co-creators in the one work, to be as God created us, to Be in his likeness. For me, this is the power of art. It reaches beyond all cultural barriers, all philosophies and unites. The Red Cross "Art for Humanity" Initiative has that as its core vision. In doing so, they are forerunners in initiating the next step towards inspiring global peace and unification in a diverse world.

This event was just the beginning of my relationship with the Red Cross for they eventually invited me to join the committee. I served for three years until I left the UK on a sabbatical. The last event I worked on was the annual British Red Cross Gala Ball that raised over £250,000 for the charity from its 500 guests. The Ball's theme was "East Meets West," which brought together influential people from across the world and reflected the Red Cross' principles of neutrality and universality. Guests attended a reception and dinner at one of a selection of Ambassadors' residences before going to Old Billingsgate for entertainment, auction and dancing. Jazz musician Jamie Cullum, headlined the variety show, presented by Angela Rippon and Maria Shammas, president of the IFC for the Red Cross.

I had successfully arranged for more than 25 donations to be auctioned including the creation of a 6-ft panel called the *Cross for Humanity*. They also gave me one large area in the venue to showcase it, along with other artwork. I created an installation called "Coming Together." One of my sculptured angels, *Heaven*, suspended from above, floating amongst the voile fabric trailing from the ceiling. Three life-size sculptures, *Contemplation-Visualize World Peace*, majestically sat upon tall triangular plinths along the wall guarding the silent intent for the evening.

I was sitting at a table with my good friends Hayley Mills, Miriam and Lennie Freedman and David and Gill Graham during the evening entertainment. At one point in the evening, Angela Rippon presented Awards for "Service to Humanity." My heart nearly stopped when I heard my name called to come to the stage. Unexpectedly, I was being awarded. It was a beautiful certificate placed within an elegant mirrored frame. Tears of honor ran down my face as I returned to my table. Everyone was clapping and smiling as I sat down. Alice was up in the rafters proudly saying to others there, "That's my Mom!" she was there to help me as one of my crew. Later, when we met to dis-mantle the artwork, she greeted me with such a smile; like the Cheshire cat from Alice in Wonderland. And a huge hug! What a special moment.

'Contemplation'
"Make Poverty History"

Artwork by Ginger Gilmour

CHAPTER 90

LIVE 8
THE LONG WALK TO JUSTICE

2 JULY 2005

It was the Twentieth Anniversary of Live Aid and the vision once planted to eliminate World poverty still existed. Live 8 was to be louder; our voices would be heard in unison across the world. Three billion people joined in, reunited, stronger. The Global Call for Action Against Poverty went forth. More than 1,000 musicians performed carrying the message, purposely planned just before the gathering of the G8 leaders. Ten simultaneous concerts were held on 2 July and one on 6 July. All of them broadcast on 182 television stations and 2,000 radio networks. The result was favorable, in that the G8 leaders pledged to double 2004 levels of aid to poor nations from US $25 billion to US $50 billion by the year 2010. Half of the money was to go to Africa.[1]

The world waited in anticipation for the day to arrive because Sir Bob achieved something that not many could have done. He inspired, (coerced? LOL) the Pink Floyd to all play together after years of separation clothed in anger and hurt. Sir Bob, once again, was fearless taking on the tiger for the world. He rang Roger. Roger was up for it as he was already doing a lot for the plight of humanity. David wasn't so easy. He was angry and held on to it with great resistance even for the world.

Bob shares the story of how it happened in his later interview. He went to visit David in the country home to discuss the idea. David said very affirmably, "NO!" As Bob left the house to go to the station he insisted, "Think about it before you say NO. Promise?" but David kept saying, "NO." Bob kept saying repeatedly, "David don't say NO until you think about it," until the car door closed.

A few days later Roger called asking how it went. Bob related the conversation to him. "It didn't go well. I don't think he will do it." Roger asked for David's phone number and said he would speak to him. Just when Bob thought no chance, two weeks later, he got a very short and abrupt phone call from David saying he would do the concert! Bob did wind him up trying to get clarity while loving the friendly banter, being the jester. They seem to have that sort of relationship. Bob laughed commenting that David had made an old man happy.[2] Needless to say—the world as well.

During the week prior, the band met for rehearsal. One of the kids said, "Dad is finding the rehearsals one of the most difficult experiences of his life." I nodded in acknowledgement, "I am not surprised. They would be transforming a lot of stuff." The day arrived and all the children went. I took up my station in the kitchen of Old Bilsham, snacking throughout the day sitting on my blue chair before the telly. I had a running commentary of the show, and backstage from their hourly text messages. One after another, the kids thought of Mom.

The warm afternoon sun had gone and night came upon us. Bob came on stage and introduced the band that they had been waiting for years to hear again. The band who had not played together since 1981 at Earls Court and now after twenty-four years they would stand together once again. The lights dimmed and through the darkness, the Floyd entered the stage. The sound of a heartbeat pulsated through the air. The audience rose with excitement as the unbelievable moment was about to happen. Swirling sounds and white searchlights joined the shouts of glee. The music resounded, piercing the night air as images of pigs floated behind on stage. The audience cheering with jubilation, "NO MORE EXCUSES" lit high above them, as David on slide began the journey once again. Perhaps for the last time?

Memories, memories returned as my heart was touched. Alice in her polka dot dress below the stage in Cleveland and Chicago, the unions and the rain, just the beginning of what seemed the end. Yet after years of criticism trying to figure out who is Pink, the world is united in a single voice. As David began to sing "Breathe," history was being made for humanity. The power of music to unite was evident. Roger was jubilant like I have never witnessed before. Far from the microphone, he sang all the words with passion. He was happy!

The first song was over when "Ching, Ching" resounded in the air. The audience stood as the searchlights swayed covering them in red. "MONEY!" David's voice so familiar had them cheering. Memories of the number of times I danced at the mixer returned as I stood in my kitchen. A song that took them into large arenas to fill and in the end created alienation. Tonight it brought joy and unity as the images of records rotated round and round on the screen. Dick Perry, bearing gray hair, elegant in his white shirt and trousers swayed as his saxophone had us leaping, preparing the way for when David's guitar would soar.

A statement from the past so appropriate of who was right, filled the spaces. David's body messages were still holding on. I knew the wall was still there. I shouted at the screen, pleading for him to let go. "Let go, David. Let go. Trust the music as when you were young." Then Roger spoke to us from his heart. A tear burst the bubble in mine as I felt the truth that held me. He said, "*It is quite emotional after all these years to be standing on stage with these guys. Standing to be counted with the rest of you. Anyway, we're doing this for everybody who's not here, particularly, of course, for Sid."*[3] Many others had passed too from the Floyd family, Steve O'Rourke and Michael Kamen. Roger's alienation with the audience seemed to melt away as he spoke. I cried further as the pain released within the freedom of knowing the bricks were falling. But how far and for how long?

More memories returned as "Wish you were here" began. The day we got married and Sid at Abbey Rd. I wept and wept with the mixture of Joy and sadness. I love this song. The audience too. *And could we tell?* Everyone singing the lyrics founded on heart singing together. David smiled at Nick and over to Roger and Rick. The wall was dissolving. Did they know that there was more being transformed as David and Roger joined the waving hands below, smiling? Joy was becoming infectious. Warm hearts were united, standing together.

Then the evening soared with "Comfortably Numb," David's guitar captivated us and took us to a place where unity existed, beyond the struggle. The memories of him silhouetted in the light upon the Wall played before me inside. Each time penetrating beyond the veils, as it has always done since its creation. Freedom stretched across the sky. *Make Poverty History*, etched in red across the Wall, appeared as a reminder of what the event was for—The Long Walk to Justice. The audience faces were all aglow, as we were touched by what had been achieved. Perhaps just for a moment that could last forever. Perhaps there was more?

For me the Floyd gave more than what was visible. They gave so much more to the world by letting go of the anger, the war that divided them. A true step forward, for humanity to witness. It can be done! It spoke deep within our hearts and our heart is where *Make Poverty History* begins. First, with ourselves and then with our neighbor. It brings to mind a prayer I said every evening before bed as a child.

Our Father

Our Father who art in heaven,
hallowed be thy name.
Thy kingdom come.
Thy will be done
on earth as it is in heaven.
Give us this day our daily bread,
and forgive us our trespasses,
as we forgive those who trespass against us,
and lead us not into temptation,
but deliver us from evil.
For thine is the kingdom,
the power, and the glory,
for ever and ever.
Amen.

For me, *To forgive those who trespass against us*, happened that evening. The Global Call for Action Against Poverty went further than raising money. We were all united in the forgiveness the Floyd had found with each other and the Beauty of Creativity. A living example of the power of Forgiveness. Being the fundamental condition of the reconciliation of us all. We were united in our Heart's desire for Peace and Love amongst men.

Live 8 was a prayer whether we knew it or not beckoning a doorway to open with Heaven. Hoping for a miracle. It closed with a moment of connection with each other and our Divine Creator. A kingdom united forever and forever, if we chose. But there is so much more work for us to do. The *Our Father* is a hint, if we listen.

We were lost in the music and yet found,

The Bright Side of the Moon.

I have found,

as one door closes

another door opens,

rich in possibilities.

In Beauty,

Ginger Gilmour

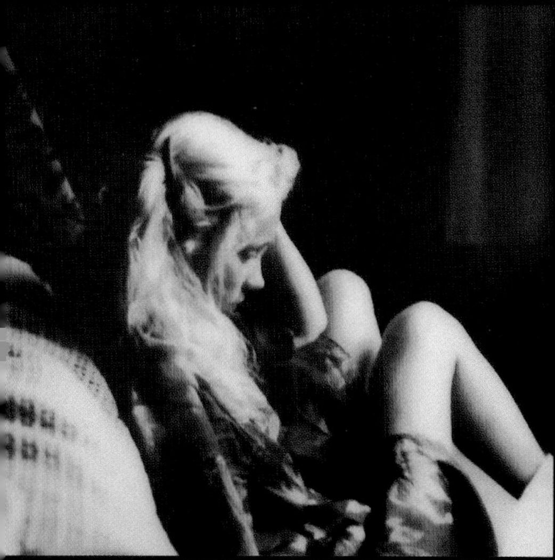
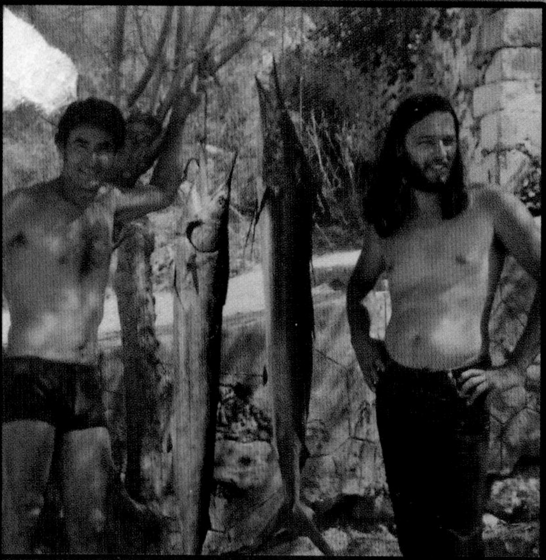
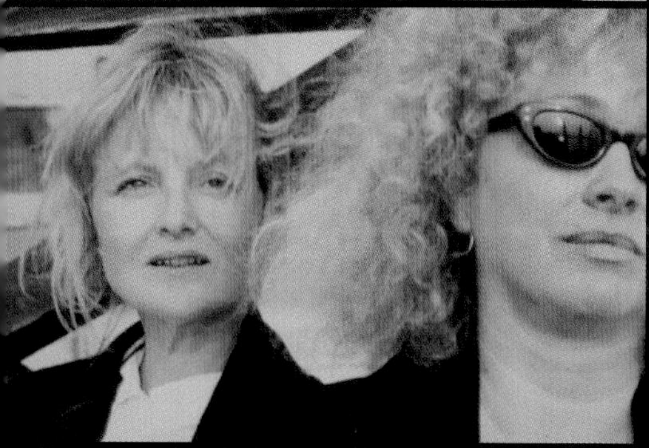
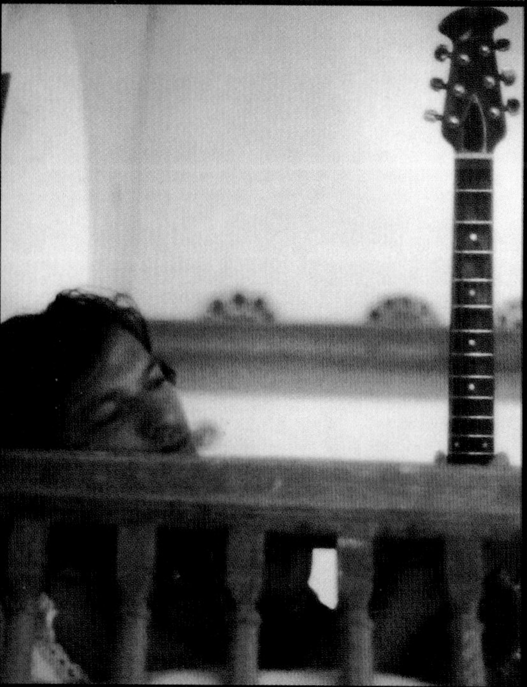
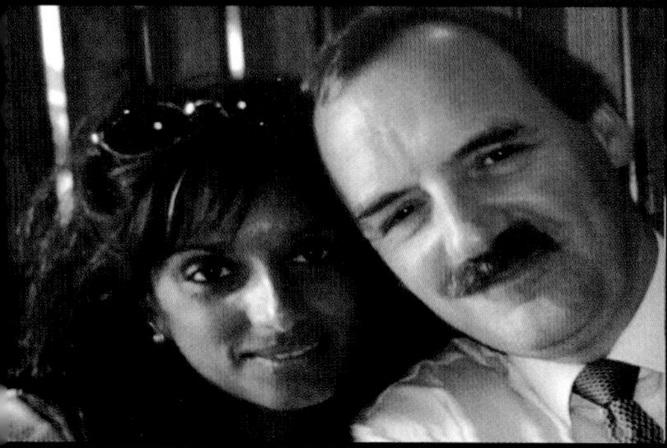
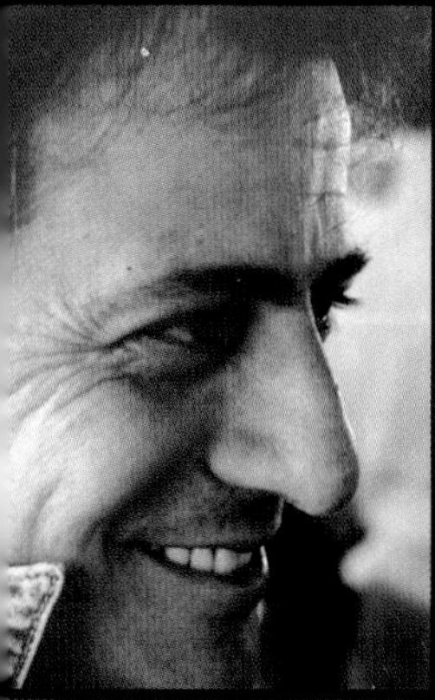
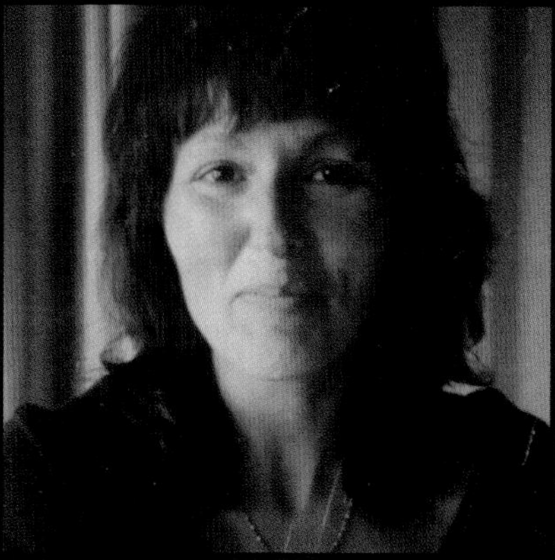
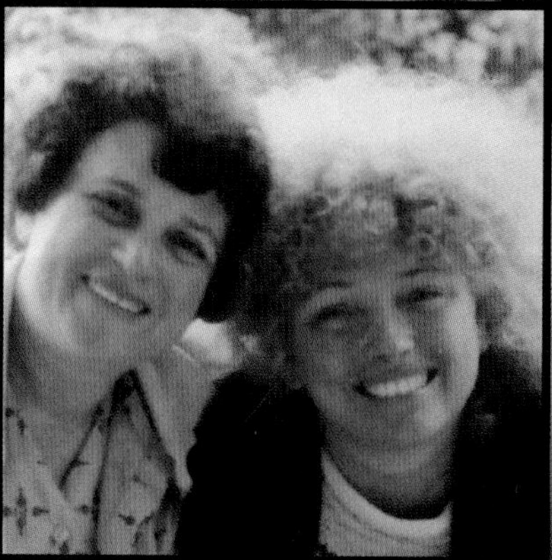

AFTERWORD

As I wrote my memoirs, I was astonished how much I had remembered. How much I still could feel all the stories of my life's challenges and adventures. My journey sent me spiritual teachers, psychologists, therapists, friends AND adversaries to guide me to Let go, to Forgive, to be Grateful. Yet still, I could remember, I could feel. I wondered why was this so. Why did it linger?

I discovered while writing that there had always been a video running 24/7 simultaneous to another path, which was in the foreground taking me into my future. A parallel story of service to Humanity through my art and through my life of helping others. A story important for the future so that we would Remember Beauty and the Sacred.

But why was this video still running so clearly after so much internal work and willingness to Let-go, to go forward? Today, my question was answered. As I handed over my manuscript to a friend to review, I realized its purpose. It was in God's plan all along.

Years ago a voice came to me in my meditation, so clear, so directed. "Ginger you must write your story of Love." I waited. I contemplated for nearly two years. I trusted the voice but who was it? Little did I know what that would entail to write my story of love until I started. I had said, "Yes."

Now it is clearer. It has become a story of how it is possible to return to God and to realize he has been there always through Life's experiences guiding the way. I know why he wanted me to write it, for it is a story of Love, of Forgiveness, of Realization, of

Courage, despite extreme challenges. A story mankind needed to hear.

God wanted this story written, which is why I had to remember everything. I had to carry the pain, the blessings, and make it visible so that it could be resolved in this way before you. It was in the Divine Plan so that you the reader would know the truth of my journey of Return, to the Joy of Living and God's Majesty when death was so close.

I was given the opportunity to carry this for so long to then go through my transformation within each word. Not only am I sharing my journey, my quest but also my catharsis. With each memory, I was getting closer to my freedom to be *What I was born to Be*. I awakened to what had always been my destiny, my soul purpose.

I see it clearly now. It was a journey of Return to God and to serve. Each step, each road was about bringing Heaven to Earth. Each day I now speak to Him, my closest friend. I do not divert around the corners doubting, wondering, fearing. I am creating a direct line to His Love, to pure Love. I know he is Alive and there watching over us all. My heart is lighter and I know so much more Joy is waiting for me, for my children and for you.

May Peace Be with YOU,

SPECIAL THANKS

My Children & Family;
Donna & Scott Shepherd & Children
Stephen & Mona Hasenbein & Children
Toni & Vincent Messura-Caronia
Marcus and Jana Messura
David Gilmour
Polly & Family

WITH ALL MY APPRECIATION

Isaac Ian Otwell, Cathy Holmes, Mike Holmes, Dr Rajendra Sharma, Val Brady, David & Gill Graham, Steve Gent, Sturt Williamson, Miv Watts, Richard & Sue Clarke, Nigel & Jenny Gordon, Kathryn Peat, Johnny & Versha Rae, Miriam Freedman, Annette, Christian, Joachim, Maria Louise & Alexander Skovbo, Emo-Ion Moore, Matthew Scurfield, Bob Ezrin, James Guthrie, Tim Hain, Claire Johnson, Andrew Johnson & children, Tim Wheater, Olivia Harrison, Jo Parker, Daisa Morgan, Lucinda Drayton, Doreen Key & Michael Benner, Marguerite Gaffney & Family, Patrick & Nicholas Keegan, Christine Koetsier & Family, Julia Hauserman, Molly Harvey, Christian Mouzon, Nancy Roof, Dorothy Maver, Nico Thelman, Lief & Michele De Prins, Key Minnebo, Dana Lynn Andersen, Melissa, Tchaik, Dixie, Clancey, Mary Clow, Roy & Shirley Faichney, Dreamy & Mel Lee, Danny & Cathy Johnson, Cynthia Campbell, Aaron Campbell, Winsome & Pete Mount, Barry Knight, Rita Bold, Scarlett Raven, Charles Littledale, Trina Williamson, Gita Saraydarian, Vicki & Jon Lord, Jackie Paice, Astrid & Ken Rush, Michalis Melenos, Demetri & Michaelis Mavrikos, Andoni & Phaedra Mingos, Jose Alebian (Spain), Bruno Dubois (France), Linda Hewitt, Christine and Mike Box, Nicki Claird-Lowe, Nick Mason, Duncan Carmichael-Jack, Paul Nixon, Cassie & Jonti White, Leslie MacDonald, Father Ian, Frank Inscore, Peter Long, Randy & Rita Smith, Matt & Jacob Smith, Edward Galante, Mike Carparelli, Dave Daley, Pat Comiskey, Steve Anderson, Scot Garland, Helen Beaufont, Maryann Ehmann, Georgina Norfolk, Tony Molina, Ann Aldridge, Moyra Mulholland, Karina Wiles, Kitty Grigsby and Worzalla.

Plus, everyone who has helped to make this possible in so many ways not mentioned.

GREAT CLOUD OF WITNESSES

Mom & Ron, Daddy & Agnes, Nannan & Poppop, Doug & Sylvia Gilmour, Catha Gilmour, Cecil & Elizabeth Collins, Torkom Saraydarian, Dr Sharma, Sir John Tavener, Lily Cornford, Irina Tweedie, Raff Ravenscroft, George Harrison, Warwick McCreddie, Lennie Freedman, Dr Werner Engel, Dr Gerhard Adler

I would like to take this moment
to express how grateful I am
for God's grace and loving guidance on a
most extraordinary journey and task He
has set before me.
In Jesus' name.
Amen.

Ginger

PHOTO CREDITS

All photographs are courtesy of Ginger Gilmour's personal collection except for a few photographs listed below.
All sculptures, paintings and poems equally belong to Ginger Gilmour's Gallery of creative expressions as an artist.

Every effort has been made to trace copyright holders but should there be any omissions or errors we would be happy to correct them in future editions of the book. Please contact the publisher.

We would like to thank our friends below for allowing the use of their photos.

© 1972 Liechner, "Ginger Model Cover"	36
© Mary Clow, "Ginger Lindos"	56
© 1972 Paris Match, "Gini Tour, Marrakech"	78
©Terry Doran, "Just met a girl"	94
© Essential Detail-Marketing UK, "Young Island"	106
© John Davies, "Ponji"	264
© Claremont Resort, "Claremont San Francisco"	312
© Sim Canetty-Clark, "Sir John Tavener" 2001,	458
© Unknown, "Sanctuary Bay, Dolphins"	546

David Graham Photography-Photographs and Layout Design of Artwork,
www.davidgraham.net
Chris Holmes Photography-Cover Photograph,
www.holmesphoto.net

SCRIPTURE
Scripture taken from the New King James Version © copyright 1982 by Thomas Nelson, Inc. Used by permission, All rights reserved. pg, IV

© 2015 Ginger Gilmour-Photos, All rights Reserved

"Ginger 1970"	XVI
"David & Ginger 1972"	16
"Doug & Sylvia Gilmour"	22
"Ginger Modeling 1971"	28
"David"	42

PHOTO CREDITS

"Ted & David Japan"	46
"David, Alice & baby Clare"	90
"David and Ginger Married, 1975"	98
"David & baby Alice, 1986"	114
"Stepdad-Ron, Mom, Toni, Marcus"	124
"Donna and Ginger"	128
"David, Woodley, Roydon"	138
"Ginger Hotel Frankfurt"	142
"David, Ginger, Alice-Athens"	146
"David, Ginger, Alice on Tour"	150
"Rick Wright"	154
"Ginger & Sister Donna, 1970"	160
"David, Ginger-Kuaui"	164
"Nick Mason on Tour"	170
"Hasenbein Family"	176
"Ginger, Juliette, & Jamie-NYC"	180
"Dr. Sharma & Companion"	188
"David, Ginger & Alice-Turkey"	198
"Christian-Turkey"	202
"Kaunos-Turkey"	210
"Ginger & baby Alice-Greece"	214
"David, Alice, Dixie"	226
"Clare & David-Greece"	230
"Ginger-L.A."	240
"Concert USA"	246
"Hook End"	252
"On Film Set for the Wall"	258
"Ginger, Clare, Christian-Lindos"	270
"Ginger & baby Sara-Lindos"	274
"Ginger-Sri Lanka"	280
"Ginger-NYC"	294
"David, Joe, Lisa-Epping Forest"	300
"Mrs. Tweedie"	304
"Steve O'Rourke"	318
"Elizabeth Collins & Ginger"	326
"Cecil Collins"	332
"Guy Fawkes Party"	336
"About Face Band"	342
"About Face Tour"	350
"David & baby Matthew"	366
"David & Ginger-Greece"	374
"Ginger & Children-Toronto"	380
"Gig"	388
"Kalu Rinpoche & Bella"	394

PHOTO CREDITS

"Ginger & Genevieve Zermat"	400
"Ginger & Lily Cornford"	408
"Momentary Lapse of Reason Gig"	412
"Ginger & Matthew-Japan"	416
"Emo & Pip"	424
"Ginger, Michael Benner, Doreen Key"	434
"Ginger & Children"	440
"Jill Robson"	446
"Ginger"	454
"Samantha & Stan Khury"	464
"Ginger & Dolphin"	472
"House-Kuaui"	480
"Ginger"	486
"Ginger, Susan & Graham Nash"	494
"Gig"	500
"Merry Elves"	504
"Ginger-Greece"	514
"Ginger"	536
"Miriam, Lennie Freedman & Hank"	540
"Ginger Exhibition"	576
"Ginger, David, Electra & Phil May"	582
"Pefkas, Greece"	588
"Ginger-Red Cross, German Embassy"	594

© 2015 Ginger Gilmour-Ginger Art, All Rights Reserved

"Angel of Might" 2003	15
"Lovers" 2002	21
"Awakening" 2002	41
"Brotherhood" 2006	55
"Contemplation-Spirit of Peace"	72
"Dove of Peace" 2009	77
"Rose in the Desert" 2013	89
"Breath" 1998	93
"Wings of Joy" 2004	105
"Sacred Vow" 2003	113
"Mother & Child 2" 2006	127
"Ball of Wonder" 2000	137
"Humanitarian Heroes" 2008	159
"Angelic Whisper" 2005	163
"Heart 2 Heart" 2008	175
"Aeriel Miniature's" 2006	187
"Angelic Blessing" 2005	197
"Abstract Mother and Child" 1998	239
"Spiritual Sun" 2010	251

PHOTO CREDITS

"Beauty" 1990   273
"Moment" 2001   299
"Grace" 1999   317
"My Icarus" 1983   322
"Embrace" 1991   325
"Contemplation" 2005   341
"Kwan Yin" 2007   357
"Drawing-We Can Save the World"   358
"Torch of Light" 2010   365
"Garden of Beauty" 2009   379
"Golden Messenger" 2010   393
"Sisters" 2008   399
"Serenity" 2009   433
"Earth-Song of Woman" 1988   445
"Aeriel" 1999   453
"Angel on the Threshold" 1991   479
"Collage"   493
"God's Warrior" 2005   499
"Angel of Compassion"   522
"Seated Angel" 1998   529
"Reflection"   530
"Woman and 2 Angels" 2006   535
"Golden Dawn" 2006   545
"Box of Illusions"   554
"Doorway to Beauty" 2008   559
"Heavenly Angel" Ginger   560
"World Goodwill" 2010   569
"Hope"   570
"Contemplation"   598

© 2015 Ginger Gilmour-Poems

"Breath of Life"   206
"Our Last Smile"   526
"Final Words"   527
"New Beginning"   558
"Song That is Me"   581
"Angel of Might"   696
"A Love Poem"   636

© 2015 Angelscript

"Angels Protect Us"   VIII
"Sea of Glass"   XII
"Doorway"   640

613

COLLAGE DIRECTORY

All collage photos are property of Ginger's personal Collection.

PAGE 45

1. *(Top left) Ginger*
2. *(Top right) David and Ginger*
3. *(Center) David, baby Alice, Ginger*
4. *(Left bottom) Wedding Day-Cyndy and Jerry Shirley with their son Aaron, Ginger and David, Willie Wilson, Lynnie and Rickie Wills with baby Nickie.*
5. *(Bottom right) David*

PAGE 123

1. *(Top left) David and Venetta Fields*
2. *(Top right) Lorelie and Durga McBroom, Rachel Fury*
3. *(Center left) David*
4. *(Center right) Ginger*
5. *(Bottom left) David and Christian-Turkey*
6. *(Bottom right) Annette Skovbo and Ginger-Lindos*

PAGE 225

1. *(Top left) David and Ginger-Pefkas*
2. *(Top right) David and Ginger-Lindos, Greecec*
3. *(Center left) Barrie Knight-roadie*
4. *(Center right)David, Ginger and baby Alice*
5. *(Bottom left) Versha, Ginger, Emo, Suzanne Mendes, My Birthday*
6. *(Bottom right) Ginger and Clare*

PAGE 263

1. *Hammersmith Odeon*
2. *(Center left) David*
3. *(Center right) David and Nick Mason*
4. *(Bottom left) Ginger and Doreen Key*
5. *(Bottom right) Sister-Donna and Scot Shepard, Ginger*

COLLAGE DIRECTORY

PAGE 335

1. *(Top left) David-Lindos*
2. *(Top right) Ginger Modeling*
3. *(Center left) David and Ginger-Mavrikos Lindos*
4. *(Bottom left) Storm Thorgerson, David*
5. *(Bottom right) Ginger-Lindos*

PAGE 407

1. *(Guy Fawkes Celebration at Monksbridge) David and Mick Ralphs*
2. *(Center left) Ginger-Lindos 1974*
3. *(Center right) Matthew Gilmour and Sara Gilmour*
4. *(Bottom left) David and Alice-Big Sur*
5. *(Bottom right) Ginger, NYC, About Face Tour*

PAGE 493

1. *(Top) Sara, Alice, Ginger, Clare, Clancey, Melissa, Dixie*
2. *(Center left) David and baby Clare*
3. *(Bottom left) Riggatta Lindos-Hobie Cat Team*
4. *(Bottom Right) Ginger*

PAGE 605

1. *(Top left) Ginger*
2, *(Top right) Willard Manus and David*
3. *(Center left) Miv Watts and Ginger*
4. *(Center left) Versha and Johnny Rae*
5. *(Center right) David in Sala*
6. *(Bottom left) Bob Ezrin*
7. *(Bottom center) Val Brady*
8. *(Bottom right) Miriam Freedman and Ginger*

NOTES

Chapter 9 Today-Spirit of Peace
1. Roof, Nancy, "Spirit of Peace," Participant, September 18, 2013, *Kosmos Journal* founder and editor.
http://www.kosmosjournal.org/contributor/nancy-b-roof/
2. Wikipedia contributors, "Four Freedoms," *Wikipedia, The Free Encyclopedia*, http://en.wikipedia.org/w/index.php?title=Four_Freedoms&oldid=644519936
3. Wikipedia contributors, "Nicholas Roerich," *Wikipedia, The Free Encyclopedia*, http://en.wikipedia.org/w/index.php?title=Nicholas_Roerich&oldid=653124504

Chapter 12 Knebworth Concert
1. Waters, Roger, *Pink Floyd Lyric Book, Blandford,* 1982 (a 1975 interview with Nick Sedgwick)

Chapter 14 Paradise on Young Island
1. Wikipedia contributors, "HMS Bounty," *Wikipedia, The Free Encyclopedia*, http://en.wikipedia.org/w/index.php?title=HMS_Bounty&oldid=650577161

Chapter 31 Lost in Time at Kaunos
1. Wikipedia contributors, "Kaunos," *Wikipedia, The Free Encyclopedia,*http://en.wikipedia.org/w/index.php?title=Kaunos&oldid=644945551

Chapter 32 Tax Exile
1. Wikipedia contributors, "Karlheinz Stockhausen," *Wikipedia, The Free Encyclopedia*, http://en.wikipedia.org/w/index.php?title=Karlheinz_Stockhausen&oldid=645566924
2. Gilmour, David, "*David Pays Tribute to Richard Wright*," September 15, 2008, http://davidgilmour.com/news_2008.htm

Chapter 34 Another Child is Born-Clare
1. Buddhapadipa Temple, "Buddhist Followers"
http://www.buddhapadipa.org/dhamma-corner/buddhist-followers/

Chapter 38 Clash of the Titans
1. Martin Luther King, Jr., "The Global Freedom Struggle, "*Beyond Vietnam*," New York, N.Y., 4 April 1967,
http://mlkkpp01.stanford.edu/index.php/encyclopedia/documentsentry/doc_beyond_vietnam/
2. Miller, David. "Eartha Kitt, CIA Target." Huffington Post, March 25, 2011,
http://www.huffingtonpost.com/danny-miller/eartha-kitt-cia-target_b_153684.html

Chapter 43 "What Was That?"
1. Scarfe, Gerald. *The Making of Pink Floyd: The Wall*. Da Capo Press. pg.216
Wikipedia contributors, "Pink Floyd–The Wall," *Wikipedia, The Free Encyclopedia,*
http://en.wikipedia.org/w/index.php?title=Pink_Floyd_%E2%80%93_The_Wall&oldid=645307226

Chapter 45 Meeting Mrs. Tweedie
1. F.M. Alexander, "NYC Alexander Technique."
http://www.nycalexandertechnique.com/alexander-technique-information/founder-fm-alexander/
2. Freedman, Miriam. *Under the Mango Tree*, Gilmour, Ginger Illustrator, Astoria London, 1989 "A Lion and a Rabbit"

Chapter 47 Flying Again-About Face
1. Kendall, Charles, David Gilmour, *About Face,* Interview with the "Source," 1984.

Chapter 51 Guy Fawkes
1. Wikipedia contributors, "Guy Fawkes," *Wikipedia, The Free Encyclopedia,*
http://en.wikipedia.org/w/index.php?title=Guy_Fawkes&oldid=643626305

Chapter 63 Daddy Too Loud-Japan
1. Wikipedia contributors, "Saihō-ji (Kyoto)," *Wikipedia, The Free Encyclopedia,*
http://en.wikipedia.org/w/index.php?title=Saih%C5%8D-ji_(Kyoto)&oldid=596941553
2. Wikipedia contributors, "Japanese garden," *Wikipedia, The Free Encyclopedia,*
http://en.wikipedia.org/w/index.php?title=Japanese_garden&oldid=642865483

Chapter 69 Sir John Tavener Passes Over
1. Ranklin, Ben. "Sir John Tavener Dead: Princess Diana funeral composer dies peacefully at home aged 69." UK Mirror, 12 November 2013
http://www.mirror.co.uk/news/uk-news/john-tavener-dead-princess-diana-2785091#ixzz36JmMXGg4
2. Princess Diana 97, "Princess Diana's Funeral Part 20: Song of Athene by Sir John Tavener."
https://www.youtube.com/watch?v=II_QgNkG5jg

Chapter 74 Together We Save the World
1. Wikipedia contributors, "1968 Democratic National Convention," *Wikipedia, The Free Encyclopedia,* Dan Rather's "A Reporter Remembers", "David Farber Chicago 1968"
http://en.wikipedia.org/w/index.php?title=1968_Democratic_National_Convention&oldid=645059808
2. Wikipedia contributors, "1968 Chicago riots," *Wikipedia, The Free Encyclopedia,* Coates, James (19 December 2007). "Riots Following the Killing of Martin Luther King Jr.". *Chicago Tribune*. Retrieved May 25, 2011
Report of the Chicago Riot Study Committee to the Hon. Richard J. Daley. Chicago, IL. 1968. p. 72.
http://en.wikipedia.org/w/index.php?title=1968_Chicago_riots&oldid=642940053
3. Tremulant444, "Chicago," Crosby, Stills, Nash & Young

May 1, 2007.
https://www.youtube.com/watch?v=fEFsBF1X1ow

Chapter 78 Life after David
1. E.G. Monk,1861 "Angel Voices," Published by the Authority of the General Assembly of the Presbyterian Church, U.S.A. 1895.
http://www.hymnary.org/text/angel_voices_ever_singing

Chapter 84 Sanctuary of the Spirit
1. Allitt, John Stewart, "The Magic Mirror: Thoughts and Reflections on Cecil Collins," 2010,

Chapter 85 Hope
1. Speeches, Robert F. Kennedy Speeches, Remarks to the Cleveland City Club, April 5, 1968, Robert F Kennedy Senate Papers, JFKL.
http://www.jfklibrary.org/Research/Research-Aids/Ready-Reference/RFK-Speeches/Remarks-of-Senator-Robert-F-Kennedy-to-the-Cleveland-City-Club-Cleveland-Ohio-April-5-1968.aspx
2. Series: Great Speeches of the 20th Century, "*JFK Inaugural Address.*" The Guardian, 22 April 2007
http://www.theguardian.com/theguardian/2007/apr/22/greatspeeches

Chapter 86 Visions of Beauty
1 Aristotle, "The aim of Art is to represent not the outward appearance of things, but their inward significance." 384 BC–322 BC

Chapter 87 Venice-A Night of Wonder
1. Gumbel, Andrew, "Bickering While Venice Sinks," The Independent, February 1996.
http://www.independent.co.uk/life-style/bickering-while-venice-sinks-1316639.html

Chapter 90 Live 8-The Long Walk to Justice
1. Wikipedia contributors, "Live 8," *Wikipedia, The Free Encyclopedia,*
http://en.wikipedia.org/w/index.php?title=Live_8&oldid=637616478
2. Artisan News Service, "Pink Floyd Reunion As Told by Bob Geldof," May 2, 2007,
http://www.artisannews.com/2007/05/page/60/
3. Waters, Roger, During the Hyde Park performance of Live-8, July 2005.

Any internet references contained here are current at time of publication, but the publisher can't guarantee that a specific resource or location will continue to be maintained.

CURRICULUM VITAE

I am a contemporary artist with a vision to create forms and environments that touch the heart of the community with beauty and tranquillity—qualities which throughout time have served to uplift our spirits and restore peace of mind.

WORK HISTORY:

November 2014: STARS ON CANVAS: Charity Auction raising funds for Willow Charity to give special days for the terminally ill

November 8-11 2014: WAR CHILD AUCTION: Ginger painted an acoustic guitar donated by Carparelli Guitars to raise funds for War Child at Bonhams, NYC, USA

May 23-Oct 2014: ART PARKS INTERNATIONAL: Annual Exhibition: Sausmarex Manor Art Park, Sausmarex Rd, St Martin, Guernsey, UK

May 2013: BRIGHTON OPEN HOUSE: 'Step into the Light': co-Exhibition: The Holistic Art House: Ginger exhibited with four other female artists and they were nominated out of 250 houses to be in the top three for the Best Art House in the 2013 Brighton Art Festival

.**May 23-Oct 2013: ART PARKS INTERNATIONAL:** Annual Exhibition: Sausmarex Manor Art Park, Sausmarex Rd, St Martin, Guernsey, UK

November 2012: Mind, Body, Spirit Event: with Lorna Byrne: Ginger exhibited three angels on stage; 'Angel of Might' & 2 'Angel of Compassion'; Regents House, London, UK

November 2012: Apnea Evolution Event: Venice, Italy, Ginger gave a presentation 'WE ARE the SEA' to 400 school children, teachers & government officials to aid a 'Charter for the Sea'.

Sept 2012: UN International Day of Peace Conference: A Celebration of sustainable Peace for a sustainable Future: What Can We Do? Rights & Humanity Conference venue the "Light', Royal Liver Bldg., Liverpool, UK: Ginger spoke on the 'Beauty of Peace'.

July 16 2012: Arundel Castle Olympic Torch Relay Event: Ginger was invited to showcase her Olympic Artwork and was part of the Steering Group organising the event. She inspired the singing of the song "Aspire to Insprie' written and composed by Colin Martin by the local Arun schools. Arundel, West Sussex, UK

February 16, 2012: EXPO GALLERY: 'Flame of Spirit' is moved to the gallery from airside, Heathrow Airport, T5, UK

October 2010-July 2012: EXPO GALLERY: Ginger's Olympic Artwork on Exhibit & for sale; portion of sales donated to Paralympic Assoc. & young athletes. Heathrow Airport, Terminal 5,

February 4-May 2012: Arts Alive Exhibition: Co-exhibition: 'Global Angelic Blessings'. Artists have painted banners which are hung along Hwy 101, California USA for three months then auctioned.

October 2, 2011: Presentation of 'Dolphina': Sculpture donated to the Odyssey Cancer Center, Westfield Lakes, Humber, UK

June- August 2011: Summer Exhibtion-Art Parks International: Co- exhibition, Guernsey, UK. Art Parks is open year round and sells on-Line.

June 2011: Brighton Stadium Commission: Glass sculpture created as a symbolic gesture of appreciation to Tony Bloom for his generous contribution towards the creation of the new Brighton & Hove Stadium, UK

February-Olympics 2012: EXPO GALLERY: Co-exhibition: 'Art of Olympic and Paralympic Sports', Fund-raising for British Olympic Assoc. and British Paralympic Assoc., Heathrow Airport, Terminal 5, UK

February 12-15 2011-Mindfulness Retreat Maui: 'Heart of Beauty through Creativity', co-facilitated, Nihiku, Maui, Hawaii, USA

February 1-28 2011-Art People Gallery: Solo-exhibition, 'Messengers of Beauty', Crocker Galleria, San Francisco, Calif, USA

July 16-19 2010-Art in Action: Annual Creative, Educational & Fund-raising Event; Co-Exhibition with Cliff Wright, illustrator for Harry Potter: Waterperry, Oxfordshire, UK

June 30-5 July 2010-Henley Regatta-Leander Club: Co-Exhibition, Olympic Artwork exhibited.

March 2010-October 2010-BAA: Expo Programme, 'Flame of the Spirit' exhibited on Main Departure Concourse, Heathrow Airport, Terminal 5

February 11, 2010: Canada House: Opening of Vancouver 2010: Co-exhibition from Lloyds TSB Private Banking Art of Sport Collection, Canada House, Trafalgar Square, London, UK

December 2009-March 2010-BAA & Lloyd's TSB: Co-Exhibition, "Art of Sport", fund raising for young athletes for 2012, Heathrow Airport, Terminal 5, UK

December 2009-August 2010: Co-Exhibition: Yoga Ananda Holistic Center, 46 Albert Rd. North, Reigate Surrey, RH12 NY, UK

November 2009-Lloyd's TSB"Art of Sport": Co-Exhibition: Christmas Exhibition, Fund-rainsings for young athletes for 2012, Grosvenor House, London, UK

July 2009-Lloyd's TSB"For the Journey to London 2012": Co-Exhibition: 'Art of Olympic and Paralympic Sports', Fund-raising for British Olympic Assoc. and British Paralympic Assoc., Guildford & Worthing, UK

July 2009-Lloyd's TSB"For the Journey to London 2012": Co-Exhibition: 'Art of Olympic and Paralympic Sports', Fund-raising for British Olympic Assoc. and British Paralympic Assoc., Cardiff & Swansea, UK

June 2009-Lloyd's TSB"For the Journey to London 2012": Co-Exhibition: 'Art of Olympic and Paralympic Sports', Fund-raising for British Olympic Assoc. and British Paralympic Assoc., Cheltenham, UK

June 2009-Lloyd's TSB"For the Journey to London 2012": Co-Exhibition: 'Art of Olympic and Paralympic Sports', Fund-raising for British Olympic Assoc. and British Paralympic Assoc., Plymouth & Abingdon, UK

April 2009-Lloyd's TSB"For the Journey to London 2012": Co-Exhibition: 'Art of Olympic and Paralympic Sports', Fund-raising for British Olympic Assoc. and British Paralympic Assoc., Nottingham, UK

March 2009-Lloyd's TSB "For the Journey to London 2012": Co-Exhibition: 'Art of Olympic and Paralympic Sports', Fund-raising for British Olympic Assoc. and British Paralympic Assoc., Bristol, UK

May 2008 Summer Exhibition-'The Angel and the Absence of Time' Co-Exhibition: Cassiel Art Gallery, Rye, W Sussex, England

April 2008-Lloyd's TSB-"For the Journey to London 2012": Co-Exhibition: 'Art of Olympic and Paralympic Sports', Fund-raising for British Olympic Assoc. and British Paralympic Assoc., Grosvenor House, London

October 2007-Exhibition-Sacred Relationships: Co-Exhibition: Art People: Gallery, San Francisco, Calif., USA

August 2007-Exhibition-Lloyd's Private Banking: Fund-raising for Barnardos Charity, Edinburgh Festival, Scotland

July-October 2007-Exhibition-Arundel Castle Grounds: Eight large sculptures exhibited, plus, Humanity Series part of Arundel Gallery Trail

June 2007-Exhibition-UBS Evening at Wallace Collection: Fund-raising exhibition for *'Looking for Change'*, a school-based art programme which UBS is running in partnership with Tate

June 2007-Two Installations 'Coming Together'-Red Cross Gala Fund-raising Ball 'East Meets West': Main Installation-two stories high including suspended angel; Third year on committee; Received British Red Cross Award for 'Services to Humanity', Old Billingsgate, London, England

June 2007-Exhibition: Society of Women Artists: Two sculptures submitted and accepted: Mall Galleries, The Mall, London-www.society-women-artists.org.uk

February 2007-Exhibition-Lloyd's/Bentley Evening: Fund-raising exhibition for Barnardos Charity: Pulborough, West Sussex, England

September 2006-2007 Exhibition: Co-exhibition 'Three Women, Three Artists': Institute of Noetic Sciences founded by Edgar Mitchell, Apollo 14 astronaut; Petaluma, Calif, USA

June 2006-Exhibition: Society of Women Artists: three sculptures accepted; 'Song of Woman' received Talisman award for sculpture; Mall Galleries, The Mall, London-www.society-women-artists.org.uk

June 2006-Red Cross Fund Raising Gala Ball Committee: Second year on committee; London, England

May 2006-RHS Chelsea Flower Show-Stall; Sculptural Terrace Design: Received Certificate of Commendation for outstanding presentation, London, England

April 2006-Exhibition: Inspirational Arts Festival; Premier of new seven-foot glass winged sculpture 'In Unity', plus, four other sculptures, 20th Century Theatre, London

March 2006-Spiritual Tides Festival-Environmental and Holistic Living Event: Exhibition of 'Dolphina', 'Angel of Might', 'Lovers', Mother & Child', Kent Showground, Maidstone, Kent

January 2006-Red Cross Committee Membership 'A Celebration of Humanity' Gala Ball in June 2006:

June 2005-Exhibition: Society of Women Artists: three sculptures accepted; Mall Galleries, The Mall, London-www.society-women-artists.org.uk

December 2005-Exhibition and Set Design: Ballet 'In the Tracks of Hercules'; Created 13 six foot sculptural paintings and masks for Ballet, plus exhibited other sculptures 'Heaven', 'Imagine-Disciples on the Path', Wathan Hall, Barnes, London
November 2005-Art for Humanity: Red Cross Auction Donation, 'Angel of Might', Embassy of Federal Republic of Germany, London.
October 2004-Installation: Mind Body & Spirit Festival; 'Contemplation: Visualize World Peace', Amex Center, Manchester-www.mindbodyspirit.co.uk
August 2004- Exhibition: Arundel Arts Festival; 'Aeriel', a eight foot bronze sculpture placed in the grounds of the Cathedral: separate exhibition of other sculptures depicting our 'Divine Relationships' and furniture in the Parish Rooms, Arundel, West Sussex-www.arundelgallerytrail.co.uk
June 2004-Exhibition: Society of Women Artists; four sculptures accepted; received an associate membership to society; Mall Galleries, The Mall, London-www.society-women-artists.org.uk
May 2004-Installation: **Mind Body & Spirit Festival;** 'Contemplation: Visualize World Peace' and 'Guardian of Humanity'; Royal Horitcultural Hall, London-www.mindbodyspirit.co.
April-May 2004-Exhibition; Brighton Arts Festival; 20 sculptures; **Installation:** 'Guardian of Humanity'; Christopher Gull, Ship Street, Brighton
December 2003- Installation; International Dolphin Watch Convention: 'Dolphina', a eight-foot sculpture; **Exhibition**: sculptures-'Guardian of Humanity'; **Installation** in Chapel 'Aeriel'; Open University, Milton Keynes-www.idw.org
June-July2003-Exhibition:'Aeriel', Oxmarket Center of Arts, Chichester, West Sussex-www.oxmarket.com.
May 2003-Commission:'The Mighty Oak Award' created for Soroptimist International of the Verdugos -presented to Hayley Mills as a Woman of Distinction 2003-www.caminorealregion.org.
March 2000-2002-House & Garden design project: 'Old Bilsham Farmhouse and six studios'-complete renovation and additional, sculptural environments-self-executed; ie interior design, wall reliefs, wood-panel sculpture, lamps, 7 foot angel placed on the apex of gallery-hallway and other installations, including garden and pond design-www.gingerart.net
May 1999-Exhibition:'Song of Woman' exhibited within group exhibition, Chequer Meade, East Grinstead, West Sussex
March 1999-Illustration: 'Staying Awake Forever', Phil Murray, Perfect Words and Music Ltd.-cover design; painting 'Solar Eclipse', fifteen illustrations.
December 1998-Event conception, design & project manager: 'Christmas Fair', Michael Hall School, Forest Row, W Sussex-organizing coordinator, graphics designer for merchandizing and marketing, individual set designs, window artwork and life-size angel for storytelling room.
May 1996-Illustration: 'Before the Beginning is a Thought', Phil Murray, Perfect Words and Music Ltd.-cover design; painting 'Box of Illusions'; Russian edition,
April 1994-Illustration: 'Before the beginning is a thought', Phil Murray,Perfect Words and Music Ltd.-cover design; painting 'The Moment of Creation', 'pac' of cards and 5 additional illustrations

December 1992-Exhibition: Wholelife Exposition, Los Angeles, California, USA- exhibition of paintings

July 1989-Illustration: 'Under the Mango Tree', Miriam Freedman, Astoria Publications-cover and 16 additional illustrations

December 1989-Event conception & project manager: 'Christmas Carol Fantasy', charitable event, Westminster Central Hall, London, England-concept designer, producer, graphic designer for merchandizing.

August 1988-Illustration: 'Reflections on the Quest', R. M. Wildego and J. G. Miller, Vantage Press, Inc., NY, NY-cover and 8 additional illustrations

March-April 1987-Exhibition: one woman exhibition-'An Affair of the Heart', Themes and Variations Gallery, London, England

EDUCATION:

September-June 1998-2002- Rudolf Steiner Sculpture studies, West Hoathley, West Sussex, England

September-June 1983-1990- Life drawing with Cecil Collins, City Lit, London, England

January 1989- 1991- Jungian analyst with Mrs Dr Adler, London

September-December 1988-1989- Jungian analysis with Dr Gerhard Adler, London

December- July 1988- Jungian analysis with Dr Werner Engel, NYC

September-June 1988-1995- Mental Colour Therapy with Lily Cornford; further teacher's training; taught and practiced in center in Kilburn, Switzerland, Italy, Houston (USA) and in my home until present. Trustee of the Mental Colour School of Healing.

Michigan State University 1967-69 foundational course in Chemical Engineering and Art

High School Education 1962-1966 Wayne High School, Wayne, Michigan, USA-graduated Cum Laude

Primary Education 1954-1961- various elementary schools, U.S.A.

MATTHEW GILMOUR

Releases his first album

The Grey

Available
at
www.matthewgilmour.com

Further Interest

Ginger Gilmour

The Art of Relationship-Published by Ali Meamar (Art People) 10/21/2012
www.magcloud.com/browse/issue/452432
GingerArt, Ginger's website providing a space to view her inspirational art work.
www.gingerart.net

Lucinda Drayton

Keep it True. Keep it Simple and watch your Joy grow. Lucinda is a musician, songwriter, producer & spiritual inspiration for many. Her voice brings forth the angels into our lives. Together with Andrew Blisset they run a 10 piece band (Bliss), lead workshops in meditation and self growth, plus, take art programs into prisons.

www.blissfulmusic.com   https://youtu.be/fY4Z76JTVwI

Sara Gilmour

A London based stylist, consultant and creative director. Currently, she is freelance and has been Fashion Editor for Tank Magazine and Because Magazine. Her work has led her to work with many top fashion photographers. Sara's images capture the timeless Beauty of the moment suspended in each photograph within the colors.

www.saragilmour.com   saragilmour@btinternet.com

Clare Gilmour

Freelance Photographer specializing in all things wonderful from Nature to Children. She has the ability to capture Life's Beauty in a glance.

www.claregilmour.com

Daisa Morgan

Author and Creator of the Magical World of Fingley®. A storybook world that's brought to life with authentic children's books, gifts and Dodl Bear that are Fun, Magical, Educational and Inspirational.

www.fingley.com

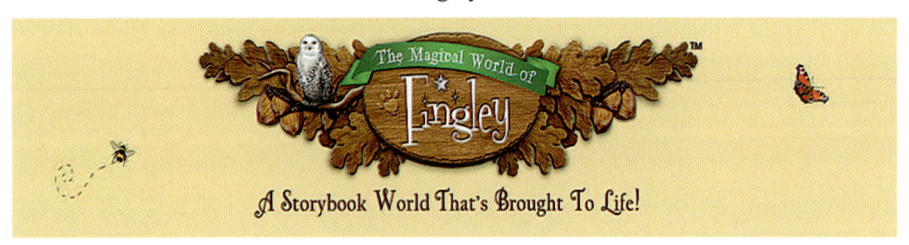

Horace Dobbs

Author of numerous children's books, Horace is now recognized worldwide as an authority on dolphins and especially on their part in healing humans.

www.horacedobbs.com   www.dolphinfriend.com

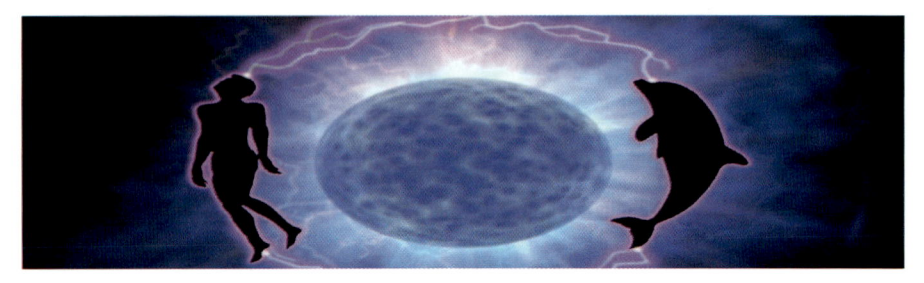

Maryann Ehmann

Transformational leader-Create Your Magnificent Life Now. Maryann Ehmann empowers people to transform their lives from mundane to magnificent. With a diverse background in law, finance and ministry, Maryann, in partnership with God, produces powerful mindset shifts, clarity of purpose, and strategic action. She is the author of 'Have I Ever Told You, You're My Favorite!"

www.maryannehmann.com   www.haveievertoldyou.com

Lizard Gardens by Richard McAlpine and Laura Foster

Smart ideas for people who want to educate themselves on how to make the most out of simple household items for their basic needs. We cover a range of methods related to raisin organic food and vegetables with a variety of other useful tips.

www.lizardgardens.com

Mark D Pendergrass

Author/Composter/Graphic Artist, has won awards in all three categories. His novel 'The Green Man' and a children's book series featuring Waylon & Stogic are among his most recent works.

http://www.amazon.com/B00G3MU5V1   www.amazon.com/0692389309

David Graham Photography

Making Art out of Life. David has been photographing my artwork, GingerART, for over 12 years.

www.davidgraham.net   post@davidgraham.net

Miriam Freedman

Author of 'Love is Always the Answer', the story of how Miriam survived through the holocaust and her spiritual journey with Irina Tweedie which awakened her heart, survivor of a very similar story to Anne Frank. Silently she and her family were hidden in a room during the Nazi occupation. She could barely walk once given freedom to be saved through training to be a Yoga Teacher. Her life led her from trauma to love. This is her story.

http://www.amazon.co.uk/Love-Always-Answer-Holocaust-Spiritual/dp/1577332865

MWD interiors

Organically designed homes, with passion not fashion. Homes that reflect the history of a family life and the beauty of nature. Miv Watts will guide and inspire you all the way.

www.wattswishedfor.com   miv.watts@gmail.com

Inner Id Designs

Post Production is an intensely personal medium. We specialize in creating digital visual effects, no matter if you are entertaining one or thousands.

www.innerid.com

Rights and Humanity: (Not for Profit)

Founded in 1986 by Julia Hausermann MBE, Rights and Humanity has been a pioneer in bringing together people of many faiths, cultures and walks of life in common commitment to prevent and relieve human suffering.

www.rightsandhumanity.org

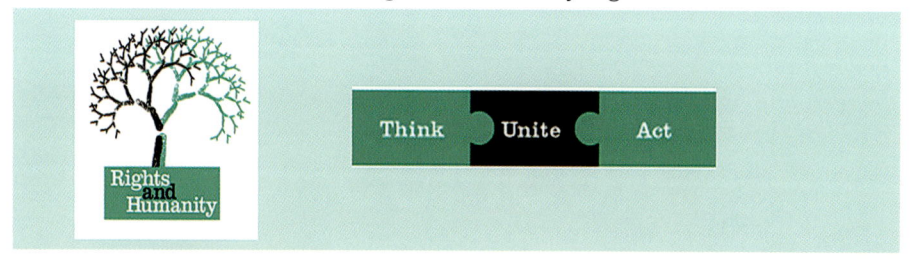

Apnea Evolution

Apnea Evolution is founded by Alexander Vergendo and Rosarita Gagliard. Their founding vision is based upon the "Deep Inside" methodology that combines a water & self awareness of the person in harmony. They work with companies, Olympic sports champions and schools with the project "Rights of the Sea".

www.apneaevolution.it   www.rightsofthesea.org   www.alessandrovergendo.com

John Michael Talbot

Was a guitarist for Mason Proffit when he embarked on a spiritual journey that led him through Native American religion and Buddhism to Christianity. This book 'The Master Musician' uses the metaphors of music to draw us into closer union with Jesus and each other by opening our hearts and minds to God's grace.

www.johnmichaeltalbot.com

Kosmos Journal

Our mission at Kosmos Journal is to inform, inspire and engage individual and collective participation for global transformation in harmony with all Life. We do this by sharing transformational thinking and policy initiatives, aesthetic beauty and collective wisdom.

www.kosmosjournal.org/about/mission

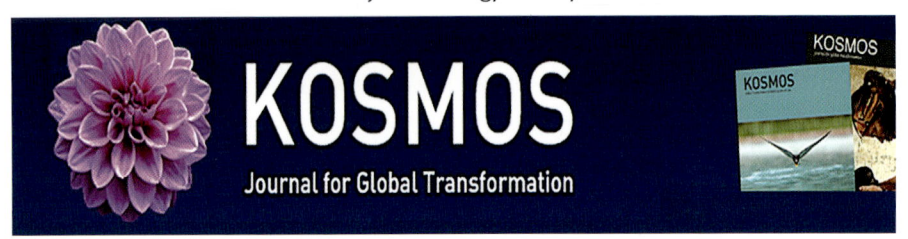

Joel Osteen Ministries

Developing a Habit of Happiness
https://youtu.be/RQ3FDeyYcX8
http://www.joelosteen.com/Pages/WhatWeBelieve.aspx

http://www.joelosteen.com

Melenos Hotel and Restaurant, Lindos

From the rubble Michalis Melenos has created an unique hotel capturing the ancient beauty of the architectural wonder of Lindos and influences from his travels to Turkey and the Middle East. His exquisite taste and eclectic design is breathtakingly poised just below the Knight's Castle and overlooking the bay.

www.melenoslindos.com info@melenoslindos.com

Cosmos Jewelry, Lindos

Cosmos Jewelry is the inspiration of Nikos Kaplanis. It is like a goldmine hidden in the back streeets of Lindos, with the most incredible ethnic pieces from around the world from ancient to contemporary jewelry and antiques.

www.cosmos-lindos.gr   E: mariapikoula@yahoo.gr

Mavrikos Restaurant, Lindos

In the main square of Lindos is the traditional restaurant where our family and many before us have dined regularly almost every night since 1972 when on holiday. The owners, Demetris and Michalis Mavrikos, are family to us and so we grow old together watching our children care for the village as we do.

www.facebook.com/MavrikosRestaurantLindos

Ambrosia Restaurant, Lindos

Ambrosia is the vision of George, Litsa & Dimitris to create "food of the gods" full of color and flavor from the specialities of Greece and the neighboring countries. They are dear friends of heart with us all.

http://www.lindostreasures.com/ambrosia/photos.html

GELoBLU, Lindos

As you enter the doorway of Geloblu Ice Cream Parlour your senses are filled with the sights and aromas of spectacular home made cakes, ice creams, fruit sorbets and the best fresh coffee. We visit there in the morning and then last thing at night with the children...yummy!

http://www.exclusivelylindos.com/channels/cafe-bars-in-lindos/gelo-blu.aspx#VaeTDLJpH3bJahvI.99

Mare Mare, Lindos

Papa George's restaurant has been on the small beach for years serving us breakfast after a morning swim across the bay, Greek lunch for the kids while they played on the sand, and a Papa George Special - Ice Coffee Frappe with Ice cream. His smile beckons us to the beach where he has watched our children grow into adults.

https://www.facebook.com/maremare.lindos?fref=ts

angelscript.com

ghostmedia.org

www.JupiterTelling.com

On one side is the palm,

on the other are the knuckles...

which ever side is showing

is the side you see...

Isaacian

Bright Side of the Moon
Reviews

"A very moving and uplifting book, it took me on the journey of Ginger's life. Times spent with Pink Floyd and her own honest inner search to find love and happiness. It has left me inspired for the beauty of Life."

GEORGINA NORFOLK

"Once you pick up Ginger Gilmour's *Memoirs of the Bright Side of the Moon*, you will not be able to put it down. In this absorbing narrative, Ginger takes us on a fascinating journey through her years as former wife to David Gilmour of Pink Floyd fame. Not your typical tell-all, Ginger displays remarkable respect, dignity, and appreciation for what this band has achieved in history. As intriguing as that is, however, Ginger's *Memoirs* are so much more. Asking eternal questions and discovering the answers. Ginger speaks to our hearts, as she transparently lets us in on the intimate details of her quest for truth, beauty, and utter fulfillment. I loved this book."

MARYANN EHMANN,
Transformational Leader

"Reading Ginger Gilmour's story led me across continents and customs around the world. It brought me into the feelings and visions of a true artist. It took me on a fascinating journey through the lifestyle of celebrated artists and her own personal story of marrying a world-renowned musician of Rock n Roll. It took me to the tenderness of a loving Mother, the struggles of finding soul and spirit while being a force for healing and beauty in the world. I couldn't put the book down."

NANCY B. ROOF,
Kosmos Journal, Founder

"With her riveting and inspiring book, Ginger Gilmour courageously shares her journey in search of a fulfillment to be found beyond the confines of traditional pathways. Her story speaks to the seeker in all of us and her truth resonates for any reader who has sought out the way to live with an open heart."

MOYRA MULHOLLAND,
Makeup Artist, Entertainment-Film

"This book is the extraordinary story of Ginger Gilmour, a person who has always followed her heart. She had the courage (or naivety) to leave behind her American small-town life and jump feet first into a new land, a new life, a new culture, and find her true self, her "soul of an artist." Through her fairy-tale romance with David Gilmour of Pink Floyd, her life with the band on some of their major tours in the 70s and 80s, she retained her integrity and her innate belief that Beauty was always the goal through the chaos. The difficulties facing the band members whilst creating ground-breaking music and shows, are related as the background to Ginger's own creative life. The births of her and David's four children are described in loving detail. Her vision to encourage creativity and Beauty in their home and their life, and her own awakening to her soul's purpose through her study under the renowned artist, Cecil Collins, is a fascinating read. Interspersed with some incredible coincidental meetings in her life are beautiful images of her artwork—paintings and sculptures, which are uplifting and inspiring and her recognition as an important artist of our time is well-deserved. I so enjoyed reading this book and the inspiration of "Beauty" will remain with me long after the book is finished. It is a book to keep close by and to savor daily the images Ginger has created to bring Beauty into our own live."

GILL GRAHAM

"*Be careful of what you wish for*, has been a true phrase that Ginger Gilmour lives, endures, and inspires with. Her story reflects of a journey that happens only once. A choice she took to experience the beautiful, and luck from the unexplained in the years of a time that sought to unearth the beauty of perception. With no route to go by, only with the truth in her heart, she took this course set before her, which only needed strong will to endure the distance. Yet, ambition turned into challenge for her to stay on the path, for it became terrain testing between heart and mind. Her route became an odyssey with lifetimes lived, illusions realized, heartbreak climbs, the flash of magic, and discovery in strength of her inner self. Her transit reveals a consciousness that grand designs are the curves within the lines. And maybe it's healthier that "perfect," is not for real because her life's reward is experience, whatever the result; beauty of the unknown to learn. Ginger's trajectory, blessed and cursed, gifted her with humility and realization that life's real destiny is wisdom gained to be returned to the ones who stand at the beginning of life's road, wondering how to take the first step. Ginger's simple wisdom is, live the journey to the fullest with just a first step. Challenge and the unexpected is beautiful. Embrace experience and live to find yourself. Just choose a path."

TONY MOLINA,
Filmworks
Director of Photography
Cinematographer

A LOVE POEM

I thought I knew what Love IS

Then one day, I saw crystal colours everywhere

Brighter and Brighter the air surrounded me with the Light of Heaven

My spirit was bathed in a waterfall of Joy

Nurtured, Uplifted, and Restored within its Wonder

I heard the song of the Great Father

My Heart rejoiced within his fragrance

Now I dance in a meadow of Gold

For I know more of what Love IS!

© Ginger Gilmour

*I would like to say
THANK YOU
for purchasing my book.*

*Please, feel free
to drop me a line at
www.angelscript.com*

*I would love
To hear from You.*

Ginger

DOORWAY

There is a doorway
that provides refuge from the storm.
On cloudy days you can dream with the clouds.
On rainy days you can paint.
On winter days you can sit by the fire.
On days like these you can play
or maybe even fly.
Said the whisper in the sky

© 2015 Angelscript